Shelf Life Evaluation of Foods

Edited by

C.M.D. Man
Senior Lecturer
Food Science Division
School of Applied Science
South Bank University
London

and

A.A. Jones
Group Technical Manager
Rayner & Co. Limited
London

BLACKIE ACADEMIC & PROFESSIONAL
An Imprint of Chapman & Hall

London · Weinheim · New York · Tokyo · Melbourne · Madras

Published by
Blackie Academic and Professional, an imprint of Chapman & Hall

Chapman & Hall, 2–6 Boundary Row, London SE1 8HN, UK

Chapman & Hall GmbH, Pappelallee 3, 69469 Weinheim, Germany

Chapman & Hall Inc., One Penn Plaza, 41st Floor, New York NY 10119, USA

Chapman & Hall Japan, Thomson Publishing Japan, Hirakawacho Nemoto Building, 6F, 1-7-11 Hirakawa-cho, Chiyoda-ku, Tokyo 102, Japan

DA Book (Aust.) Pty Ltd, 648 Whitehorse Road, Mitcham 3132, Victoria, Australia

Chapman & Hall India, R. Seshadri, 32 Second Main Road, CIT East, Madras 600 035, India

First edition 1994

Reprinted 1996

© 1994 Chapman & Hall

Typeset in 10/12 Times by Acorn Bookwork, Salisbury, Wiltshire
Printed in Great Britain by St Edmundsbury Press Ltd, Bury St Edmunds, Suffolk

ISBN 0 7514 0033 5

A catalogue record for this book is available from the British Library
Library of Congress Catalog Card Number: 94-70985

JOIN US ON THE INTERNET VIA WWW, GOPHER, FTP OR EMAIL:

WWW: http://www.thomson.com
GOPHER: gopher.thomson.com
FTP: ftp.thomson.com
EMAIL: findit@kiosk.thomson.com

A service of **I(T)P**

∞ Printed on acid-free text paper, manufactured in accordance with ANSI/NISO Z39.48-1992 (Permanence of Paper)

Preface

The subject of shelf life of foods is not a new one. Increasing consumer interest in food safety, quality and date marking, competitive pressures from retailers and extensive legislative changes, however, have combined to give the subject a new significance. The proper and correct determination of shelf life is of course fundamental to Good Manufacturing Practice (GMP) for the food and drink industry. Manufacturers who aim to produce safe, wholesome and attractive food products 'right the first time' and 'right every time' will already know the importance of proper shelf life evaluation. Incorrect shelf lives can potentially bring about dire legal, safety or financial consequences. This is not to belittle the difficulty of failing to meet consumer expectations consistently as a result of shelf lives that have been arrived at unreliably.

A proper evaluation of shelf life must be grounded on sound scientific principles, supported by up-to-date techniques in food science and technology. This book, therefore, begins with five chapters reviewing the principles of shelf life evaluation. These are followed by ten chapters on a number of selected food products. All the authors either have first hand experience on the practice of shelf life evaluation or are involved in research of the subject. Because of the diversity and complexity of food products now available, no attempt has been made to cover every product group, let alone every product conceivable. It is our belief that sufficient practical information has been included for the beginner as well as for those who are more experienced in shelf life evaluation. It has been our intention to include the most up-to-date practice. Readers will have to decide for themselves whether or not it is the best practice. Constructive criticism is very much welcome. Either through quiet reflection or active discussion and exchange of views, it is very much hoped that new ideas for refinement and improvement in existing techniques will emerge, as will ideas for future research and development in this important area of food technology.

We dedicate this volume to those working in the food industry worldwide, for whom the evaluation of shelf life, directly or indirectly, is a major part of their livelihood, and whose care and diligence have helped to ensure the supply of safe, wholesome and quality food products. We dedicate it too, to our authors who, despite heavy workloads, have contributed to make this book a reality. We would like to thank the publishers for their understanding, patience, enthusiasm and support, particularly at times when it looked as if the project was never going to finish. Last but not least, we would dearly love to thank our families for their forbearance in their bewilderment at the fuss the subject of shelf life of foods has caused.

C.M.D.M
A.A.J

Contributors

T.F. Brocklehurst   Senior Scientific Officer, Biocolloids Group, Food Biophysics Department, AFRC Institute of Food Research, Norwich Research Park, Colney, Norwich, NR4 7UA, UK.

R.H. Dale   Technical Executive, Eden Vale, Dale Farm Dairy Group, Northern Foods plc, Warrington Road, Cuddington, Nr. Northwich, Cheshire, CW8 2SN, UK.

R.C. Eburne   Technical Manager, NewMarket Foods Limited, Little Wratting, Haverhill, Suffolk, CB9 7TD, UK.

M.J. Ellis   Area Manager (Shelf Life), Quality Assurance and Scientific Services, H J Heinz Co Ltd., Kitt Green, Wigan, Lancashire, WN5 0JL, UK.

D.M. Gibson   Head of Microbiology Department, Torry Research Station, Ministry of Agriculture, Fisheries and Food, PO Box 31, 135 Abbey Road, Aberdeen, AB9 8DG, UK.

M.R. Goddard   Core Area Manager, Natural Products Department, Unilever Research Colworth Laboratory, Colworth House, Sharnbrook, Bedford, MK44 1LQ, UK.

J.A.K. Howarth   Quality Services Manager, Kellogg Company of Great Britain Ltd., Park Road, Stretford, Manchester, M32 8RA, UK.

F. Johansson   Packaging Scientist, SIK, The Swedish Institute for Food Research, PO Box 5401, S-402 29, Göteborg, Sweden.

A.A. Jones   Group Technical Manager, Rayner & Co Ltd., 4 Bull Lane, Edmonton, London N18 1TQ, UK.

H.P. Jones   Development Manager, Lyons Bakeries (UK) Ltd., Fish Dam Lane, Carlton, Barnsley, South Yorkshire, S71 3HQ, UK.

A. Leufvén   Packaging Scientist, SIK, The Swedish Institute for
                          Food Research, PO Box 5401, S-402 29, Göteborg,
                          Sweden.

M. Lewis   Product Development Manager, Eden Vale, Dale
                          Farm Dairy Group, Northern Foods plc, Warrington
                          Road, Cuddington, Nr. Northwich, Cheshire, CW8
                          2SN, UK.

C.M.D. Man   Senior Lecturer, Food Science Division, School of
                          Applied Science, South Bank University, Borough
                          Road, London SE1 0AA, UK.

A.V. Martin   Senior Packaging Scientist, Yorkreco, Nestec (York)
                          Ltd., PO Box 204, York YO1 1XY, UK.

G. Prentice   Quality Services Manager, NewMarket Foods
                          Limited, Little Wratting, Haverhill, Suffolk, CB9
                          7TD, UK.

A. Reilly   Food Technologist, Gateway Foodmarkets Limited,
                          Gateway House, Hawkfield Business Park, Whit-
                          church Lane, Bristol BS14, 0TJ, UK.

R.P. Singh   Professor of Food Engineering, Department of Biolo-
                          gical and Agricultural Engineering, University of
                          California, Davis, CA 95616, USA.

U. Stöllman   Head of Flavour Analysis Section, SIK, The Swedish
                          Institute for Food Research, PO Box 5401, S-402 29,
                          Göteborg, Sweden.

H. Symons   Former Senior Vice President, Research and Tech-
                          nical Services, American Frozen Food Institute, 1764
                          Old Meadow Lane, Suite 350, Mclean, VA 22102,
                          USA.

S.J. Walker   Principal Research Officer, Microbiology Depart-
                          ment, Campden Food & Drink Research Association,
                          Chipping Campden, Gloucestershire, GL55 6LD,
                          UK.

Contents

Part 1 – The principles

4 Packaging and food quality
U. STÖLLMAN, F. JOHANSSON and A. LEUFVÉN

52

5 Preservation technology and shelf life of fish and fish products
D.M. GIBSON

72

Part 2 – The practice

15 Frozen foods   296
H. SYMONS

Part 1 – The principles

1 Scientific principles of shelf life evaluation

R.P. SINGH

1.1 Introduction

Foods are perishable by nature. Numerous changes take place in foods during processing and storage. It is well known that conditions used to process and store foods may adversely influence the quality attributes in foods. Upon storage for a certain period, one or more quality attributes of a food may reach an undesirable state. At that instant, the food is considered unsuitable for consumption and it is said to have reached the end of its shelf life. In this chapter, certain major modes of food deterioration will be examined. These modes of deterioration will be expressed mathematically as rate equations. Reaction kinetics and various models that are used in practice to express quality changes in foods will be discussed. At the end of the chapter, a brief discussion of sensors that indicate time and temperature exposures of foods and their use in monitoring shelf life of foods will be presented.

1.2 Major modes of food deterioration

During storage and distribution, foods are exposed to a wide range of environmental conditions. Environmental factors such as temperature, humidity, oxygen and light can trigger several reaction mechanisms that may lead to food degradation. As a consequence of these mechanisms, foods may be altered to such an extent that they are either rejected by the consumer, or they may become harmful to the person consuming them. It is therefore imperative that a good understanding of different reactions that cause food deterioration is gained prior to developing specific procedures for the evaluation of the shelf life of foods. Chemical, physical and microbiological changes are the leading causes of food deterioration. A brief discussion of these changes is presented in this section. For more extended coverage of these topics, the reader is referred to books by Coultate (1989), Fennema (1985) and Labuza (1982) as well as later chapters of this book.

1.2.1 Physical changes

Physical changes are caused by mishandling of foods during harvesting, processing and distribution; these changes lead to a reduced shelf life of foods. Bruising of fruits and vegetables during harvesting and post-harvest handling leads to the development of rot. Crushing of dried snack foods during distribution seriously affects their quality. Tuberous and leafy vegetables lose water when kept in atmospheres with low humidity and they subsequently wilt. Dried foods when kept in high humidity may pick up moisture and become soggy. In the case of frozen foods, fluctuating temperatures are often destructive, for example, fluctuating temperatures cause recrystalization of ice cream leading to an undesirable sandy texture. Freezer burn is a major quality defect in frozen foods that is induced from the exposure of frozen foods to fluctuating temperatures. If the fluctuations are large and the food undergoes a phase change then there are more prominent undesirable changes, for example changes caused by thawing and refreezing of foods. Similarly, phase changes involving melting and solidifying of fats are detrimental to the quality of candies and other lipid containing confectionery items.

1.2.2 Chemical changes

During the processing and storage of foods, several chemical changes occur that involve the internal food components and the external environmental factors. These changes may cause food deterioration and reduce the shelf life. The most important chemical changes are associated with enzymic action, oxidative reactions, particularly lipid oxidation that alters the flavour of many lipid containing foods, and non-enzymic browning that causes changes in appearance.

At favorable temperatures, such as room temperature, many enzymic reactions proceed at rapid rates altering the quality attributes of foods. For example, fruits upon cutting tend to brown rapidly at room temperature due to the reaction of phenolase with the cell constituents that are released upon cutting of the tissue in the presence of oxygen. Enzymes such as lipoxygenase, if not denatured during the blanching process, can influence food quality even at sub-freezing temperatures. In addition to temperature, other environmental factors such as oxygen, water and pH induce deleterious changes in foods that are catalyzed by enzymes.

The presence of unsaturated fatty acids in foods is a prime reason for the development of rancidity during storage as long as oxygen is available. While development of off-flavors is markedly noticeable in rancid foods, the generation of free radicals during the autocatalytic process leads to other undesirable reactions, for example, loss of vitamins, alteration of color, and degradation of proteins.

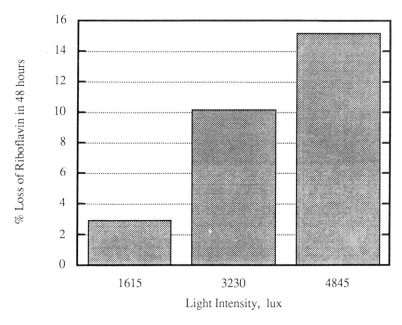

Figure 1.1 Loss of riboflavin in whole milk stored in blow molded high density polyethylene bottles under light at 4.4°C.

The rates of lipid oxidation are influenced by several factors. As indicated previously in this chapter, the environmental temperature is an important variable. The presence of oxygen in the immediate vicinity of the food leads to increased rates of oxidation. Similarly, water plays an important role; lipid oxidation occurs at high rates at very low water activities. In determining the shelf life of foods that contain lipids, the important reaction mechanisms and their rates of reactions must be known. In addition to lipid oxidation, there are other chemical reactions that are induced by light such as loss of vitamins, and browning of meats. The influence of light on riboflavin loss in milk stored in high density polyethylene bottles is shown in Figure 1.1 (Singh *et al.*, 1976).

Non-enzymic browning is a major cause of quality change and degradation of nutritional content in many foods. This type of browning reaction occurs due to the interaction between reducing sugars and amino acids. These reactions result in the loss of protein solubility, darkening of lightly colored dried products and the development of bitter flavors. Environmental factors such as temperature, water activity and pH have an influence on non-enzymic browning.

1.2.3 Microbiological changes

In determining the influence of microorganisms on the shelf life of foods, the rates of microbial growth as a function of various environmental factors must be known. Microbes have the ability to multiply at high rates when favorable conditions are present. Prior to harvest, fruits and vegetables have generally good defense mechanisms against microbial attacks, however after separation from the plant, they can easily succumb to microbial proliferation. Similarly, meat upon slaughter is unable to resist rapidly growing microbes. Microbial proliferation in cottage cheese stored at three temperatures is shown in Figure 1.2 (Shellhammer and Singh, 1991). Microbial growth in foods results in food spoilage with the development of undesirable sensory characteristics and in certain cases the food may become unsafe for consumption.

The pathogenicity of certain microorganisms is a major safety concern in processing and handling of foods. Upon ingestion, microorganisms such as *Salmonella* species and *Escherichia coli* strains cause infection while others such as *Aspergillus flavus*, *Clostridium botulinum* and *Staphylococcus aureus* produce chemicals in foods that are toxic to humans. Botulism is a well known food poisoning because of the high potency of the toxin and the high rates of fatality associated with it. Food poisoning

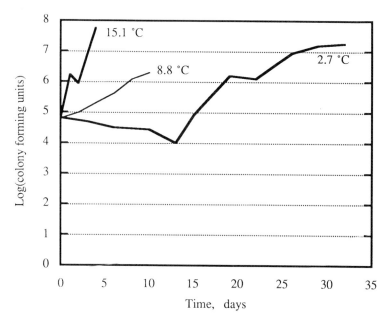

Figure 1.2 Standard plate count for cottage cheese stored at three constant temperatures.

due to *Staphylococcus* is more frequent although it is not as severe as botulism. The presence of molds and their growth on a food product may result in undesirable appearance and off-flavors. Under certain favorable conditions mold spores may also produce chemicals that are toxic to humans. During food processing and storage, special procedures are employed to minimize or prevent the occurrence of pathogenic and spoilage microorganisms.

Various measures commonly used to minimize or prevent microbial growth in foods include altering the environmental temperature, such as either lowering the temperature to slow the growth processes, or raising temperature to destroy the microbes; removing water such that it is unavailable to the growing microbes; controlling the environmental gases such as lowering oxygen or increasing carbon dioxide concentration; reducing or stopping the microbial growth by adding acid; and promoting fermentation thus lowering the pH.

1.3 Evaluation of food quality

A common practice employed to evaluate the shelf life of a given food product is to determine changes in selected quality characteristics over a period of time. One may consider quality of a food as a gross measure of the food deterioration occurring in a food item. However, it should be recognized that the term quality is meant to encompass several quality attributes or characteristics. From a consumer's standpoint, the sensory expectations derived from the presence (or absence) of desirable (or undesirable) characteristics of a given food determine the quality of a product. Therefore a food product noted for its high quality has more of the desirable characteristics.

Empirical or analytical techniques may be used to quantify the quality attributes of food. For example, enumeration of microbes or determination of chemical components of a product are analytical techniques, whereas the use of human subjects to monitor changes in the magnitudes of quality characteristics constitute empirical techniques. Considerable research has been conducted on quality evaluation of foods with an aim to determine their shelf life (Jul, 1984; Van Arsdel *et al.*, 1969; Singh *et al.*, 1986; Labuza, 1982).

In the case of frozen foods, shelf life has been described by the use of various terms. For example, practical storage life (PSL) is defined as 'the period of frozen storage after freezing of an initially high quality product during which the organoleptic quality remains suitable for consumption or the process intended' (IIR, 1986). This definition requires the use of a number of sensory evaluation procedures and statistical analysis techniques. Most of these procedures rely on the use of sensory difference tests (discrimination methods), and the shelf life failure is determined with strict statistical criteria. Shelf life failure is often identified by 'Just Noticeable Difference' (JND). JND is the 'earliest time when a difference between the quality of test and control samples can be detected by trained sensory panels' (Van Arsdel et al., 1969). The use of this criterion is not restricted to one specific quality attribute or characteristic, rather it represents the overall quality of a product.

Using statistical analysis, the degree of difference between the test product and the control may be assessed at any predetermined confidence level. It may even be related to the noticeable difference between the test and the control sample that may be of commercial significance. The use of a difference test, such as JND, provides information on how long a product may be stored, for example, the PSL of a product. Readers are referred to Table 15.1 (Chapter 15) for PSL values of some common foods. While this is useful information on shelf life of different foods, it fails to provide a measure of the rate at which the quality attribute is changing.

There is considerable evidence in the literature that temperature plays a major role in causing changes in food quality during storage. Higher storage temperatures generally lead to increased quality deterioration. In the past, there have been several attempts to use mathematical techniques and models to describe changes in food quality as influenced by storage temperature. Some of the earlier interest in this area was stimulated by observations that fluctuating storage temperatures caused more detrimental change in frozen foods than storage at constant temperature. Hicks (1944) modeled the changes in food quality by assuming an exponential relationship between the rate of quality change and temperature. He used an *effective mean temperature* to represent a diurnal temperature fluctuation. The *effective mean temperature* was a constant value that produced the same change in quality as a regular sinusoidal temperature change. Other temperature functions, such as square and sawtooth functions, were modeled by Schwimmer et al. (1955). Using mixed linear and exponential relationships between temperature and rate of quality change, Schubert (1977) also developed an effective mean temperature for the periodic temperature fluctuations. He used an empirical function containing three experimentally derived parameters to describe the effect of temperature on the rate of quality change. Employing chemical kinetic theory, Labuza (1979) used random variable temperature conditions to obtain effective temperature. These approaches have simplified the incorporation of fluctuating temperatures in calculating quality changes in foods.

Use of the chemical kinetic approach to model changes in food quality was suggested by Kwolek and Bookwalter (1971). The kinetic approach and the Arrhenius relationship that describes the influence of temperature on the reaction rate constants was also promoted by Saguy and Karel (1980). Lai and Heldman (1982) developed methods to determine the value of the activation energy of food quality losses from shelf life data at known temperatures. A computer-aided method to simulate changes in food quality during storage of frozen foods was used by Singh (1976). Wells *et al.* (1987) provided a graphical representation of the temperature history and food quality relationships.

1.3.1 Reaction kinetics

Chemical kinetics involves the study of the rates and mechanisms by which one chemical species converts to another. The rate of a chemical reaction is determined by the mass of a product produced or the reactant consumed per unit time. In general, the rates of reactions may be determined by monitoring the concentration of either the reactants or the products of the reactions. The mechanism of a reaction, on the other hand, is more difficult to determine since it involves the sequence of steps that produce the overall result. Mechanisms of reactions are determined only in simple systems.

A general form of kinetic model may be obtained by considering the following chemical reaction

$$a\text{A} + b\text{B} \underset{k_\text{b}}{\overset{k_\text{f}}{\leftrightarrow}} c\text{C} + d\text{D} \tag{1.1}$$

where A and B are reactants, C and D are the products, and a, b, c and d are stoichiometric coefficients for the reactants and products, and k_f and k_b are forward and backward reaction rate constants. The rate at which a reactant, for example reactant A, changes would be given by

$$-\frac{d[\text{A}]}{dt} = k_\text{f}[\text{A}]^\alpha[\text{B}]^\beta - k_\text{b}[\text{C}]^\gamma[\text{D}]^\delta \tag{1.2}$$

where [A], [B], [C] and [D] are the concentrations of reactants (mass per unit volume); α, β, γ and δ are the reaction orders with respect to each product or reactant; and t is time. Equations (1.1) and (1.2) are for a general case, since these equations are unsolvable because of too many unknowns, therefore simplifying procedures are used. For example, the reaction conditions may be chosen such that either the forward or the backward reaction is predominant. If the concentration of reactant B in equation (1.1) is kept very high then the change in concentration of B is negligible. As a consequence, the backward rate constant will be considerably smaller than the forward reaction rate constant. For this case, the rate of reaction can be represented by

$$-\frac{d[A]}{dt} = k'_f[A]^n \qquad (1.3)$$

where k'_f is the pseudo forward rate constant, and n is the reaction order. The rate of reaction is described mainly by the concentration of a species. Due to the complex nature of foods, it is difficult to determine the actual mechanisms of the intermediate reactions that lead to a particular change in quality. The following approach is commonly used to analyze general quality changes in foods.

A general rate expression may be written as follows for a quality attribute Q

$$\pm \frac{dQ}{dt} = kQ^n \qquad (1.4)$$

where $\pm$ refers to either decreasing or increasing value of the attribute Q, k is the pseudo forward rate constant, n is the observed order of reaction. It is assumed that the environmental factors such as temperature, humidity and light and concentrations of other components are kept constant.

Equation (1.4) may be rewritten more specifically for a quality attribute that is decreasing with time and following an 'nth' order of reaction,

$$-\frac{dQ}{dt} = kQ^n \qquad (1.5)$$

1.3.1.1 Zero order reaction. Consider a quality attribute Q, that decreases during the storage period as shown in Figure 1.3. A closer examination of the linear plot implies that the rate of loss of a quality attribute is constant throughout the storage period and it does not depend on the concentration of Q. This assumption has been widely used in the food science literature. This linear plot represents a zero order reaction, therefore substituting $n = 0$ in equation (1.5) we get,

$$-\frac{dQ}{dt} = k \qquad (1.6)$$

Equation (1.6) may be integrated to obtain

$$Q = Q_o - kt \qquad (1.7)$$

where Q_o represents some initial value of a quality attribute and Q is the amount of that attribute left after time t.

If the end of shelf life, t_s, is noted by the quality attribute reaching a certain level, say Q_e, then

$$Q_e = Q_o - kt_s \qquad (1.8)$$

Therefore, the shelf life, t_s, may be calculated as

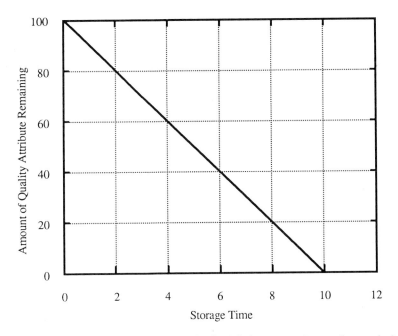

Figure 1.3 Decrease in a quality attribute of a food during storage (zero order reaction).

$$t_s = \frac{Q_o - Q_e}{k} \qquad (1.9)$$

The use of zero order rate equation (1.6) is useful in describing such reactions as enzymic degradation, non-enzymic browning and lipid oxidation that leads to development of rancid flavors.

1.3.1.2 First order reaction. Consider Figure 1.4 where a quality attribute, Q, decreases in an exponential manner with storage time. The rate of loss of a quality attribute is dependent on the amount of quality attribute remaining; this implies that as time proceeds and the quality attribute decreases so does the rate of reaction. This exponential plot between quality attribute and time represents a first order reaction, $n = 1$, and equation (1.5) is modified as follows,

$$-\frac{dQ}{dt} = kQ \qquad (1.10)$$

By integration, we get

$$\ln \frac{Q}{Q_o} = -kt \qquad (1.11)$$

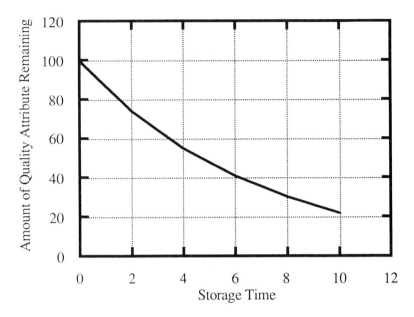

Figure 1.4 Decrease in a quality attribute of a food during storage (first order reaction).

where Q is the amount of quality attribute left at time t.

At the end of shelf life, t_s, for a certain final level of quality attribute, Q_e, we can also write equation (1.11) as

$$\ln \frac{Q_e}{Q_o} = -kt_s \tag{1.12}$$

or

$$t_s = \frac{\ln \dfrac{Q_o}{Q_e}}{k} \tag{1.13}$$

Sometimes, it is desirable to know the time for half-life of a reaction. To obtain the half-life time, equation (1.13) may be modified by substituting $Q_e = 0.5\, Q_o$,

$$t_{1/2} = \frac{0.693}{k} \tag{1.14}$$

The types of food deterioration reactions that show first order losses include vitamin and protein losses and microbial growth.

In analyzing experimental data on rate of change of a given quality attribute, the following two issues are important. First, the analytical pre-

Table 1.1 An estimate of percentage error in reaction rate constant, k, as a function of analytical precision and change in reactant species monitored

Analytical precision (%)	Change in reactant species monitored						
	1%	5%	10%	20%	30%	40%	50%
± 0.1	14	2.8	1.4	0.7	0.5	0.4	0.3
± 0.5	70	14	7	3.5	2.5	2	1.5
± 1.0	>100	28	14	7	5	4	3
± 2.0	>100	56	28	14	10	8	6
± 5.0	>100	>100	70	35	25	20	15
±10.0	>100	>100	>100	70	50	40	30

Source: Benson, 1960.

cision of measuring attribute level affects the value obtained for rate constant. In Table 1.1 an estimate of percentage error in reaction rate constant, k, is given for different levels of analytical precision (Benson, 1960). As seen in this table, as analytical precision decreases, when the change in reactant species monitored is small, there is a greater percentage error in the calculated value of the reaction rate constant.

The second important issue in kinetic analysis is the change in reactant species monitored. In Figure 1.5, two plots are shown, one for zero order

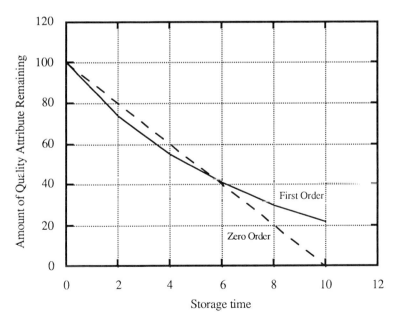

Figure 1.5 Decrease in a quality attribute of a food following two different orders of reactions.

reaction and the other for a first order reaction. In this case, the overlap between zero order and first order plots, for up to about 55% reduction of the quality attribute, indicates that either zero or first order model can be used to describe the change in the attribute. However, beyond 55% reduction, there is a considerable difference in the level of quality attribute predicted by the zero order and first order models. Therefore, if the experimental data on the rate of change of a quality attribute are available only for less than 55% reduction in the quality of an attribute, then a simple zero order reaction model would be sufficient. However, use of that model to extrapolate more than 55% change can lead to serious errors if the correct reaction order was first order. Thus, caution must be exercised in determining the reaction order. Labuza (1984) has illustrated some of the common pitfalls that should be avoided in using statistical evaluation of rate of loss of quality.

Most reactions showing losses in food quality may be described by zero or first order; there are some studies in the literature that indicate use of other orders. A second order reaction was used by Singh and Heldman (1976) to describe vitamin C degradation in canned infant foods. In studying oxygen uptake in lipid oxidation kinetics, Labuza (1971) found a half order reaction with respect to oxygen for relatively pure lipids. The order of reaction increased to first order when antioxidants were added.

1.3.1.3 Temperature effects. The influence of temperature on the reaction rate may be described by using the Arrhenius relationship, as follows

$$k = k_o \exp\left[-\frac{E_A}{RT}\right] \qquad (1.15)$$

where k_o is the pre-exponential factor, E_A is the activation energy, R is the ideal gas constant, and T is the temperature (absolute scale).

The temperature dependence of the reaction rate can be shown graphically as in Figure 1.6. On a semilogarithmic axis, a linear plot is obtained between rate constant and the inverse of absolute temperature. The slope of the straight line gives the activation energy. A steeper slope implies that the reaction rate constant is influenced to a larger extent by a change in temperature.

Another parameter that is often used in the literature to describe the relationship between temperature and reaction rate constant is the Q_{10} value. Q_{10} is defined as follows

$$Q_{10} = \frac{\text{reaction rate at temperature } (T + 10)°C}{\text{reaction rate at temperature } T°C} \qquad (1.16)$$

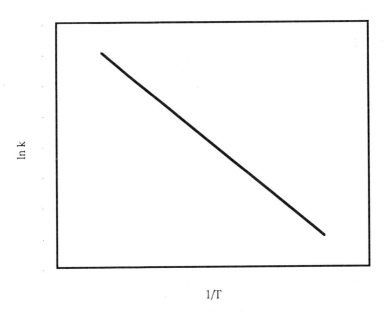

Figure 1.6 Influence of temperature on the reaction rate constant. Slope $= E_A/R$.

It can be shown that Q_{10} and activation energy E_A are related by the following expression (Singh and Heldman, 1993)

$$\log Q_{10} = \frac{E_A}{2.303R}\left[\frac{10}{T_A(T_A + 10)}\right] \tag{1.17}$$

1.3.2 Determination of kinetic parameters

In order to describe the influence of temperature on the reaction rates, such as by use of the Arrhenius expression, it is necessary to know the values of kinetic parameters such as rate constant and activation energy. Two procedures are most commonly employed to determine these kinetic parameters.

(a) The linear regression method involves plotting the log of rate constant against the reciprocal of temperature (absolute). It is necessary to obtain rate constants for at least three different temperatures. Since this plot should be a straight line, linear regression procedures are used to determine the slope and intercept, thus obtaining values for the pre-exponential factor and the activation energy in equation (1.15).

(b) A non-linear regression method suggested by Arabshahi and Lund (1985), Cohen and Saguy (1985) and Haralampu et al. (1985) is used to determine the activation energy directly from the concentration or level of a quality attribute. This method precludes the determination of rate constants. The advantage of this method is the use of original data points related to the variation of quality attribute in calculating the desired kinetic parameters. Standard computer routines such as SAS NONLIN (SAS Institute Inc, 1982) and BMDP 3R (University of California, 1983) are available for non-linear regression.

The expression describing change in quality attribute in a non-linear form for a zero order reaction is as follows:

$$Q_{ij} = Q_o - k_o t_{ij} \exp\left(-\frac{E_A}{RT_j}\right) \tag{1.18}$$

and for a first order reaction, the expression is,

$$Q_{ij} = Q_o \exp\left[-k_o t_{ij} \exp\left(-\frac{E_A}{RT_j}\right)\right] \tag{1.19}$$

where the subscripts i and j indicate the time and temperature of the corresponding quality attribute measurement.

1.3.3 Shelf life plots

Labuza (1982) presented a simple approach to determine the effect of temperature on food quality. His method is particularly suited for situations when the available data are meager, for example in cases where the experimental data are available only as time needed to reach a certain value of a quality attribute. This is true for many published studies on shelf life in the literature. A brief introduction to developing shelf life plots is as follows.

For a given reaction order the following can be written,

$$k = \frac{\text{amount lost at time } t_s}{t_s} \tag{1.20}$$

where the numerator, the amount of quality lost at a time t_s, for a first order reaction $= \ln Q_o/Q_e$, and for a zero order reaction $= Q_o - Q_e$

Taking logarithm of both sides of equation (1.20), we get

$$\ln k = \ln (\text{amount lost at time } t_s) - \ln t_s \tag{1.21}$$

The Arrhenius expression, equation (1.15), may be rewritten as

$$\ln k = \ln k_o - E_A/RT \tag{1.22}$$

Equating right hand sides of equations (1.21) and (1.22), and rearranging we obtain

$$-\ln t_s = -\ln (\text{amount lost at time } t_s) + \ln k_o - E_A/RT \tag{1.23}$$

According to the preceding equation, a plot of t_s with respect to $1/T$ on a semilog paper should give a straight line (Figure 1.7); the activation energy can then be obtained from the slope of the line, $+E_A/2.303R$. For a small temperature range, less than $\pm 20°C$, t_s may be plotted directly against T without significant error (Labuza, 1982) as shown in Figure 1.8. Then the equation for the straight line shown in Figure 1.8 may be written as

$$t_s = t_o e^{-aT} \tag{1.24}$$

where t_o is the shelf life at a reference temperature, a is the slope of the line, and T is the temperature difference between the temperature at which the shelf life, t_s, is desired and the reference temperature.

For a zero order reaction, shelf life and rate constant are inversely proportional. Equation (1.16) may be rewritten as

$$Q_{10} = \frac{\text{Shelf life at } T°C}{\text{Shelf life at } (T + 10)°C} \tag{1.25}$$

Then from equations (1.24) and (1.25)

$$Q_{10} = e^{10a} \tag{1.26}$$

or,

$$a = \frac{\ln Q_{10}}{10} \tag{1.27}$$

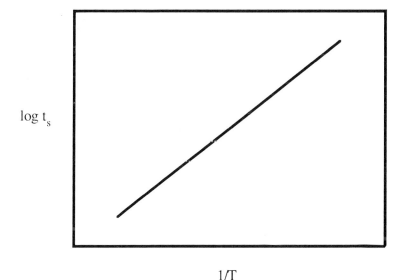

log t_s

1/T

Figure 1.7 A shelf life plot using inverse of absolute temperature for x-axis.

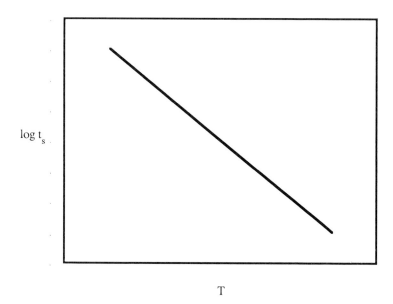

Figure 1.8 A shelf life plot. Slope $= a = \ln Q_{10}/10$.

The preceding equation is useful in designing accelerated shelf life tests. An example is shown in Figure 1.9. If the shelf life at 25°C is 20 months, a series of lines may be drawn through the point representing 25°C and 20 months for different Q_{10} values as shown in Figure 1.9. If the accelerated tests are to be conducted at 40°C, then the accelerated shelf life times for different Q_{10} values may be obtained from this plot. Thus, if $Q_{10} = 4$, the shelf life at 40°C is 2.5 months, if $Q_{10} = 8$, the shelf life at 40°C is 0.88 months. The same procedure can be easily implemented on a computer with a spreadsheet programme. In Figure 1.10, a spreadsheet program and results for the preceding example are shown.

1.4   Use of sensors to monitor shelf life of foods

Recently there has been an increased interest in sensors that can be used to monitor quality of stored foods. Many developmental efforts have focused on the time–temperature indicators. As the name suggests, these sensors provide information related to the temperature history. Since temperature is one of the most important environmental factors that influence a number of quality attributes in foods, there is a recognized merit in knowing the temperature exposure of a food consignment during storage

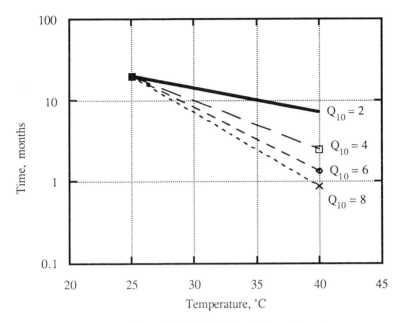

Figure 1.9 Accelerated shelf life plots for different Q_{10} values.

and distribution. For the indicators to be most useful for this purpose, they must be irreversible. Preferably, they should provide an integrated response of both time and temperature. During the last few decades, a number of patents have been issued related to devices that can indicate the integrated effect of time and temperature (Schoen and Byrne, 1972; Taoukis *et al.*, 1991; Kramer and Farquhar, 1976; Farquhar, 1977; Byrne, 1976; Olley, 1976; and Wells and Singh, 1992). These devices provide an indication of temperature history using a variety of different principles, such as mechanical, enzymic, or chemical change, development of color or movement of color along a scale.

The time–temperature indicators may be classified as either critical temperature indicators, partial history indicators or full history indicators (Taoukis *et al.*, 1991; Singh *et al.*, 1984).

1.4.1 Critical temperature indicators

Critical temperature indicators give a response only when the temperature either goes above or below a certain pre-selected temperature. These indicators do not integrate time with temperature therefore they fail to provide the temperature history effect. These types of indicators are useful to indicate if a certain temperature was reached during the exposure

	A	B	C	D	E	F
1	Ti	25	C		Enter reference	
2	T	40	C		temperature Ti in cell	
3	Q10	2			B1, temperature T at	
4	a	.069	←=LN(B3)/10		which shelf life is desired	
5	shelf life at Ti	20			in cell B2, Q10 in cell	
6	shelf life at T	7.071	←=B5*EXP(-B4*(B2-B1))		B3, and shelf life at	
7					temperature Ti in cell	
8					B5. Enter formulas as	
9					shown in cells B4 and	
10					B6. The results will be	
11					shown in cell B6.	
12						
13						

Figure 1.10 A spreadsheet to calculate accelerated shelf life at a higher temperature.

period, e.g. whether a freeze sensitive product was exposed to freezing temperature. This type of information is useful if quality attributes of the product are sensitive to some critical temperatures. The MonitorMark™ Thaw Indicator and MonitorMark™ Freeze Indicator (manufactured by Packaging Division/3M, St Paul, Minnesota) are examples of critical temperature indicators.

1.4.2 Partial history indicators

The partial history indicators provide a response only when the temperature exceeds (or is below) a certain predetermined value. An example is the MonitorMark™ Extended Response Indicator (manufactured by Packaging Division/3M, St Paul, Minnesota). This type of indicator described in detail by Manske (1976, 1983) contains a pad saturated with a chemical mixture. The chemical diffuses along a porous wick after the pad is brought into contact with the wick and only when the temperature exceeds the melting point of the chemical. Since the diffusion process is temperature dependent, then for temperatures greater than the melting point of the selected chemical, one obtains a time–temperature integrated response from this type of indicator. Different chemicals with their corresponding melting points are used for needed applications. The performance of these indicators and their applications have been reported by Taoukis and Labuza (1989a, 1989b), Taoukis *et al.* (1990), and Fu *et al.* (1992). These types of indicators have been used in the shipment of pharmaceutical products to tropical regions by World Health Organization.

1.4.3 Full history indicators

Full history indicators provide a continuous response based on changes in the temperature; the response of these indicators is at a rapid rate at higher temperature and at slow rate at lower temperature. Examples of full history time–temperature indicators include LifeLines Freshness Monitor (manufactured by LifeLines Technologies, Morristown, New Jersey) and IPOINT Time/Temperature Monitor (manufactured by I-POINT Biotechnologies A.B., Malmo, Sweden). The principle of IPOINT Time/Temperature Monitor is described by Blixt and Tiru (1977), Blixt (1983) and Blixt et al. (1977). This indicator involves two pouches, one containing a lipolytic enzyme and the other containing a lipid substrate. The indicator is activated by breaking the seal between the two pouches and mixing their contents. An enzymic hydrolysis of a lipid substrate results in a decrease of pH with a consequent change in color. Different indicator response times can be obtained by changing the concentration of the enzyme-substrates. The activation energies of these indicators can be made to vary from 15 to 35 kcal/mole, which covers a broad range suitable for many quality degradation reactions during storage and distribution. This indicator has been extensively studied by Taoukis and Labuza (1989a) and Wells and Singh (1988c).

The Lifelines[TM] Fresh-Scan indicator (manufactured by LifeLines Technologies, Morristown, New Jersey) uses a temperature dependent polymerization reaction (Patel and Yang, 1983; Patel et al., 1976; Patel and Yee, 1980; Fields and Prusik, 1986). In this type of indicator di-substituted diacetylene crystals are allowed to polymerize. As the polymer is formed there is a distinct change in color. A specially designed optical reader is used to measure the reflectance of the polymer. The indicator is in active state upon manufacturing therefore it requires special care during shipment prior to its attachment to a food package. The range of activation energy is 20–24 kcal/mole, useful for many food storage applications. The application of this indicator has been explored for a number of foods (Wells and Singh, 1988b, 1988c; Taoukis, 1989; Taoukis and Labuza, 1989a).

The usefulness of these sensors in monitoring quality depends on how well they can mimic changes in quality. Studies conducted to date show that these indicators are suitable to follow changes in selected quality attributes due to temperature. In a comprehensive study conducted with 12 different foods (Wells and Singh, 1988b), selected quality attributes were monitored both sensorily and analytically. It was found that a number of these changes were due to temperature exposure. This study also showed that the indicator response of several models could be used to monitor changes in the selected quality attributes. For example, in the case of frozen strawberries, a decrease in firmness (an attribute measured

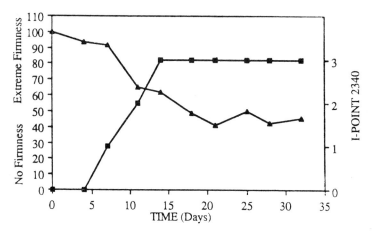

Figure 1.11 A comparison of mean response of I-POINT model 2340 (■) and mean sensory score of tomato firmness (▲) at 15°C (Wells and Singh, 1988b).

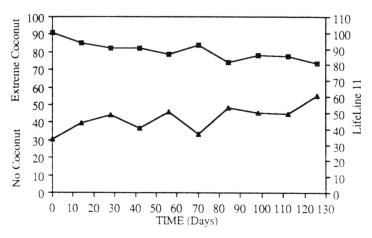

Figure 1.12 A comparison of mean response of LifeLine model 11 (■) and mean sensory score of coconut flavor (▲) in UHT sterilized milk stored at 5°C (Wells and Singh, 1988b).

using sensory panels) and a decrease in measured amount of ascorbic acid were well correlated with the response of IPOINT model 2340 indicator as shown in Figure 1.11. Similarly the development of coconut flavor in UHT sterilized milk was strongly correlated with the response of LifeLines Freshness indicator as seen in Figure 1.12. Published studies on correlation of time–temperature indicator response with quality attributes in various foods include hamburgers (Singh and Wells, 1985; Chen et al., 1989); frozen strawberries (Singh and Wells, 1987); tomatoes, lettuce, UHT milk, fruitcake (Wells and Singh, 1988b); pasteurized whole milk (Mistry and Kosikowski, 1983; Cherng and Zall, 1989; Grisius et al., 1987); ice cream (Dolan et al., 1985); refrigerated ready-to-eat salads (Campbell, 1986); refrigerated orange juice (Chen and Zall, 1987a); pasteurized cream (Chen and Zall, 1987b) and cottage cheese (Shellhammer and Singh, 1991; Chen and Zall, 1987b).

The mathematical basis of how the full history indicators mimic a given quality attribute is amply presented in the literature (Wells and Singh, 1992, 1988a). Kinetic models are useful to describe changes in food quality along with the response of time–temperature indicators (Wells and Singh, 1992; Fu et al., 1991). Briefly, their approach involved using (a) indicator response at a constant reference temperature and (b) the activation energy of the indicator, to predict a constant temperature equivalent of indicator response change for any interval between successive indicator inspections. The constant temperature equivalent was then used to predict the amount of a food quality attribute expected during the same interval. The mathematical derivations that describe this approach for a first-order reaction model were presented by Wells and Singh (1988a) and for a zero-order reaction by Wells and Singh (1992). The equivalent temperature used by these authors is different from the *effective mean temperature* used by Hicks (1944) and Schwimmer et al. (1955). The equivalent temperature is calculated on the basis of time–temperature indicator and the elapsed time between indicator inspections. If the time intervals between the successive inspections is small or the temperature of storage is constant then the equivalent temperature predicted by the time–temperature indicator will be approximately equal to the effective mean temperature calculated from the change in food quality. The advantage of using the equivalent temperature approach is that it does not require the food quality to be observed experimentally or predicted theoretically based on temperature history recorded by a data acquisition system.

The time–temperature indicators have proven to be useful aids in monitoring the quality of foods during storage and distribution. The information provided by the indicators can be implemented in computer-aided quality based inventory management systems (Singh and Wells, 1989; Singh, 1989; Wells and Singh, 1989). It is important to note that a time–temperature indicator provides a history of temperature changes in the immediate vicinity of the indicator. Mathematical models have been proposed to extend this local temperature history to that of the entire unit package used for a food with known thermal properties (Malcata, 1990); these models need to be verified for industrial conditions.

1.5 Conclusions

In studying shelf life of foods, it is important to measure the rate of change of a given quality attribute. As shown in this chapter, these rates can be modeled using simple zero-order or first-order kinetics. The shelf life plots are useful in incorporating the effect of temperature on changes in food quality. The principles of shelf life evaluation discussed in this chapter should assist a reader in the development of predictive capabilities. This quantitative treatment is necessary to improve and maintain the storage and distribution segment of the food chain.

References

Arabshahi, A. and Lund, D.B. (1985) Considerations in calculating kinetic parameters from experimental data. *J. Food Process Engineering*, **7**, 239–51.

Benson, S.W. (1960) *Foundation of Chemical Kinetics*, McGraw-Hill, New York.

Blixt, K.G. (1983) The I-point, TTM – a versatile biochemical time-temperature integrator. IIR Commission C2 Preprints, *Proc. 16th Int. Cong. Refrig.*, Intl. Inst. Refrig., Paris, p. 629.

Blixt, K.G. and Tiru, M. (1977) An enzymatic time/temperature device for monitoring the handling of perishable commodities. *Dev. Biol. Std.*, **36**, 237.

Blixt, K.G., Tornmarck, S.I.A., Juhlin, R., Salenstedt, K.R. and Tiru, M. (1977) Enzymatic substrate composition absorbed on a carrier. US Patent 4,043,871.

Byrne, C.H. (1976) Temperature indicators – the state of the art. *Food Technol.*, **30**(6), 66.

Campbell, L.A. (1986) Use of a time-temperature indicator in monitoring quality of refrigerated salads. *M.S. Thesis*, Michigan State University, E. Lansing.

Chen, J.H. and Zall, R.R. (1987b) Packaged milk, cream and cottage cheese can be monitored for freshness using polymer indicator labels. *Dairy Food Sanit.*, **7**, 402.

Chen, J.H. and Zall, R.R. (1987a) Refrigerated orange juice can be monitored for freshness using a polymer indicator label. *Dairy Food Sanit.*, **7**, 280.

Chen, H.C., Singh, R.P. and Reid, D.R. (1989) Quality changes in hamburger meat during frozen storage. *Int. J. Refrigeration*, **12**, 88–94.

Cherng, Y.S. and Zall, R.R. (1989) Use of time temperature indicators to monitor fluid milk movement in commercial practice. *Dairy Food Environ. Sanit.*, **9**, 439.

Cohen, E. and Saguy, I. (1985) Statistical evaluation of Arrhenius model and its applicability in prediction of food quality losses. *J. Food Proc. Preserv.*, **9**, 273–90.

Coultate, T.P. (1989) *Food, the Chemistry of its Components*, Royal Society of Chemistry, London.

Dolan, K.D., Singh, R.P. and Wells, J.H. (1985) Evaluation of time-temperature related quality changes in ice cream during storage. *J. Food Proc. Preserv*, **9**, 253.

Farquhar, J.W. (1977) Time-temperature indicators in monitoring the distribution of frozen foods. *J. Food Qual.*, **1**(2), 119.

Fennema, O.R. (1985) *Food Chemistry*, Marcel Dekker, New York.

Fields, S.C. and Prusik, T. (1986) Shelf life estimation of beverage and food products using bar coded time-temperature indicator labels, in *The Shelf Life of Foods and Beverages* (ed. G. Charalambous), Elsevier Science, Amsterdam, p. 23.

Fu, B., Taoukis, P.S. and Labuza, T.P. (1991) Predictive microbiology for monitoring spoilage of dairy products with time temperature indicators. *J. Food Sci.*, **56** (5), 1209–15.

Fu, B., Taoukis, P.S. and Labuza, T.P. (1992) Theoretical design of a variable activation energy time-temperature integrator for prediction of food or drug shelf life. *Drug. Dev. Ind. Pharm.*, **18**(8), 829–50.

Grissius, R., Wells, J.H., Barrett, E. and Singh, R.P. (1987) Correlation of time-temperature indicator response with microbial growth in pasteurized milk. *J. Food Proc. Preserv.*, **11**, 309–24.

Haralampu, S.G., Saguy, I. and Karel, M. (1985) Estimation of Arrhenius parameters using three least squares methods. *J. Food Proc. Preserv.*, **9**, 129–43.

Hicks, E.W. (1944) Note on the estimation of the effect of diurnal temperature fluctuations on reaction rates in stored foodstuffs and other materials. *J. CSIRO, Australia*, **17**, 111–14.

International Institute of Refrigeration (1986) *Recommendations for the Processing and Handling of Frozen Foods*, 3rd edn, IIR, Paris.

Jul, M. (1984) *The Quality of Frozen Foods*, Academic Press, New York.

Kramer, A. and Farquhar, J. (1976) Testing of time-temperature indicating and defrost devices. *Food Technol.*, **30**(2), 50.

Kwolek, W.F. and Bookwalter, G.N. (1971) Predicting storage stability from time-temperature data. *Food Technology*, **25**(10), 1025, 1026, 1028, 1029, 1031, 1037.

Labuza, T.P. (1971) Nutrient losses during drying and storage of dehydrated foods. *Crit. Rev. Food Technol.*, **3**, 355.

Labuza, T.P. (1979) A theoretical comparison of losses in food under fluctuating temperature sequences. *J. food Science*, **44**(4), 1162–8.

Labuza, T.P. (1982) *Shelf-Life Dating of Foods*, Food and Nutrition Press, Westport, Connecticut.

Labuza, T.P. (1984) Application of chemical kinetics to deterioration of foods. *J. Chem. Educ.*, **61**, 348.

Lai, D. and Heldman, D.R. (1982) Analysis of kinetics of quality changes in frozen foods. *J. Food Process Engineering*, **6**, 179–200.

Malcata, F.X. (1990) The effect of internal thermal gradients on the reliability of surface mounted full-history time-temperature indicators. *J. Food Proc. Preserv.*, **14**, 481.

Manske, W.J. (1976) Selected time interval indicating device. US Patent 3,954,011.

Manske, W.J. (1983) The application of controlled fluid migration to temperature limit and time temperature integrators. *C2 Preprints 16 Intl. Cong. Refrig.*, Intl. Inst. of Refrig., Paris, p. 797.

Mistry, V.V. and Kosikowski, F.F. (1983) Use of time-temperature indicators as quality control devices for market milk. *J. food Protect.*, **46**(1), 52.

Olley, J. (1976) Temperature indicators, temperature integrators, temperature function integrators and the food spoilage chain. *Aust. Natl. Comm. Joint Mtg. Comms.* C2, D1, D2, D3 and E1, *Intl. Inst. Refrig.*, Paris, p. 1.

Patel, G.N. and Yang, N. (1983) Polydiacetylenes: an ideal system for teaching polymer science. *J. Chem. Educ.*, **60**(3), 181.

Patel, G.N. and Yee, K.C. (1980) Diacetylene time-temperature indicators. US Patent 4,228,126.

Patel, G.N., Preziosi, A.F. and Baughman, R.H. (1977) Time-temperature history indicators. US Patent 3,999,946.

Saguy, I. and Karel, M. (1980) Modeling of quality deterioration during food processing and storage. *Food Technol.*, **34**(2), 78–85.

SAS Institute Inc. (1982) *SAS User's Guide: Statistics, 1982 Edition*, SAS Institute, Cary, North Carolina.

Schoen, H.M. and Byrne, C.H. (1972) Defrost indicators: many designs have been patented yet there is no ideal indicator. *Food Technol.*, **26**(10), 46–50.

Schubert, H. (1977) Criteria for application of T–T indicators to quality control of deep frozen products. *Science et Technique du Froid IIF-IIR*, **1**, 407–23.

Schwimmer, S., Ingraham, L.L. and Hughes, H.M. (1955) Temperature tolerance in frozen food processing: Effective temperatures in thermal fluctuating systems. *Ind. Eng. Chem.*, **47**(6), 1149–51.

Shellhammer, T.H. and Singh, R.P. (1991) Monitoring chemical and microbial changes of cottage cheese using a full-history time-temperature indicator. *J. Food Sci.*, **56**(2) 402–5, 410.

Singh, R.P. (1976) Computer simulation of food quality during frozen food storage. *Int. Inst. Refrig. Bull. Supp.*, **1**, 197–204.

Singh, R.P. (1989) Computer-aided inventory management using time-temperature indicators, *in Food Properties and Computer-Aided Engineering of Food Processing Systems* (eds. R.P. Singh and A.G. Medina), Kluwer Academic, The Netherlands.

Singh, R.P., and Heldman, D.R. (1976) Simulation of liquid food quality during storage. *Trans. Am. Soc. Agric. Eng.*, **19**(1), 178–84.

Singh, R.P. and Heldman, D.R. (1993) *Introduction to Food Engineering*, Academic Press, San Diego.

Singh, R.P. and Wells, J.H. (1985) Use of time-temperature indicators to monitor quality of frozen hamburger. *Food Technol.*, **39**(12), 42–50.

Singh, R.P. and Wells, J.H. (1987) Monitoring quality changes in stored frozen strawberries with time-temperature indicators. *Int. J. Refrig.*, **10**, 296–300.

Singh, R.P. and Wells, J.H. (1989) Time-temperature indicators in food inventory management, in *1989 Food & Beverage Technology International USA*, pp. 195–8.

Singh, R.P., Heldman, D.R. and Kirk, J.R. (1975) Kinetic analysis of light-induced riboflavin loss in whole milk. *J. Food Sci.*, **40**, 164–7.

Singh, R.P., Heldman, D.R. and Kirk, J.R. (1976) Kinetics of quality degradation: ascorbic acid oxidation in infant formula during storage. *J. Food Sci.*, **41**, 304–8.

Singh, R.P., Wells, J.H., Dolan, K.D., Gonnet, E.J. and Munoz, A.M. (1984) Critical evaluation of time-temperature indicators for monitoring quality changes in stored subsistence. Report prepared for US Army Natick Research Development Center, Natick, Massachusetts. (Contact No. DAAK60-83-C-0100).

Singh, R.P., Barrett, E.L. Wells, J.H., Grisius, R.C. and Marum, W. (1986) Critical evaluation of time-temperature indicators for monitoring quality changes in perishable and semi-perishable foods. Report prepared for U.S. Army Natick Research and Development Center, Natick, MA. January (Contract No. DAAK60-84-C-0076).

Taoukis, P.S. (1989) Time-temperature indicators as shelf life monitors of food products. *Ph.D. thesis*. University of Minnesota, St. Paul.

Taoukis, P.S. and Labuza, T.P. (1989a) Applicability of time-temperature indicators as food quality monitors under non-isothermal conditions. *J. Food Sci.*, **54**, 783.

Taoukis, P.S. and Labuza, T.P. (1989b) Reliability of time-temperature indicators as food quality monitors under non-isothermal conditions. *J. Food Sci.*, **54**, 789.

Taoukis, P.S., Reineccius, G.A. and Labuza, T.P. (1990) Application of time-temperature indicators to monitor quality of flavored products, in *Flavors and Off-Flavors '89* (ed. G. Charalambous), Elsevier Applied Science, London and New York, p. 385.

Taoukis, P.S., Labuza, T.P. and Francis, R.C. (1991) Time temperature indicators as food quality monitors. *Food Packaging Technology*, ASTM STP 1113, ASTM, Philadelphia, p. 51.

Taoukis, P.S., Fu, B. and Labuza, T.P. (1991) Time temperature indicators. *Food Technology*, **45**(10), 70–82.

University of California (1983) *BMDP Statistical Software*. (ed. W.J. Dixon) University of California Press, Berkeley.

Van Arsdel, W.B., Coply, M.J. and Olson, R.L. (1969) *Quality and Stability of Frozen Foods*, Wiley-Interscience, New York.

Wells, J.H. and Singh, R.P. (1988a) A kinetic approach to food quality prediction using full-history time-temperature indicators. *J. Food Sci.*, **53**(6), 1866–71, 1893.

Wells, J.H. and Singh, R.P. (1988b) Application of time-temperature indicators in monitoring changes in quality attributes of perishable and semiperishable foods. *J. Food Sci.*, **53**(1), 148–56.

Wells, J.H. and Singh, R.P. (1988c) Response characteristics of full-history time-temperature indicators for perishable food handling. *J. Food Proc. Preserv.*, **12**, 207–18.

Wells, J.H. and Singh, R.P. (1989) A quality based inventory issue for perishable foods. *J. Food Proc. Preserv.*, **12**, 271–92.

Wells, J.H. and Singh, R.P. (1992) The application of time-temperature indicator technology to food quality monitoring and perishable inventory management, in *Mathematical Modelling of Food Processing Operations* (ed. S. Thorne), Elsevier Applied Science, London.

Wells, J.H., Singh, R.P. and Noble, A.C. (1987) A graphical interpretation of time-temperature related quality changes in frozen foods. *J. Food Sci.*, **52**(2), 435–44.

2 The methodology of shelf life determination
M.J. ELLIS

2.1 Integration of shelf life procedures into a total quality system

Shelf life is an important feature of all foods (Table 2.1). All those involved in the handling of foods should be aware of it. These may include growers, ingredient suppliers, manufacturers, wholesalers, retailers and the consumers. Shelf life of a food product may be defined as the time between the production and packaging of the product and the point at which it becomes unacceptable under defined environmental conditions. Storage and distribution are necessary links in the food chain. Quality (and safety) considerations dictate the conditions and maximum duration of these links in the chain although most food deteriorations take place gradually.

A total quality approach (Figure 2.1) must embrace all aspects of a food from its conception, through development and production to its consumption, and for a manufactured food product this will include:

- product design (including hazard analysis and risk assessment to ensure safety)
- specification and testing of ingredients and packaging materials
- manufacturing processes
- transport, storage and retail display
- storage at home and consumption

Since the food must be safe and have an acceptable quality when consumed, the time for which this is maintained – the shelf life – is therefore an essential aspect of product design the control of which is a requirement of Good Manufacturing Practice (GMP) (IFST, 1991) as well as a requirement of the international standard for quality systems, ISO 9001 (ISO, 1987).

Shelf life determination of a new product often requires storage for significant periods, and includes samples from early development stages as well as initial production runs. Through the evaluation of stored samples, potential storage problems can be identified and, either eliminated or controlled before the food goes into production. When in production, an ongoing quality assurance system is equally important, and involves assessment of freshly made products, typically before the production has been released into distribution. Samples stored for up to the assigned shelf life

Table 2.1 Examples of food products and their typical shelf lives

Food Product	Typical shelf life	Main limiting factors
Bread	up to 1 week at ambient	Stale flavour, texture change
Sauces, dressings	1–2 years at ambient	Stale/rancid flavour, colour change
Pickles	2–3 years at ambient	Stale flavour, texture change
Chilled foods	up to 4 months at 0–8°C	Microbiological spoilage, flavour change
Frozen foods	1–1½ years in freezer cabinets	Colour/texture change
Canned foods (e.g. unlacquered cans)	1–1½ years at ambient	Tin pick-up
Canned foods (e.g. lacquered cans)	2–4 years at ambient	Texture/flavour change

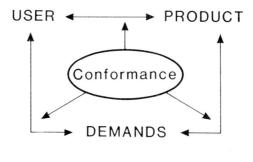

User

(safety, quality, satisfaction and loyalty)

Product

(safety, quality, consistency and perceived value)

Demands

(legality, standards, specifications and cost)

Figure 2.1 A total quality approach – the relationship between user, product and demands.

should also be evaluated, so that any change in the storage performance can be noted, and appropriate actions taken if necessary. Furthermore, an efficient customer complaint management system will provide early warning signals concerning potential shelf life problems. Finally, an up-to-date, operable and effective product recall system is the last resort should the need to recall an unsafe or defective product arise. Thus an adequate shelf life system will require appreciable resources, and these should be allowed for when planning the overall quality budget.

Since most aspects of shelf life evaluation for new products and monitoring of standard production involve similar sample handling and analysis procedures to the rest of the quality system (perhaps with the added requirement of suitable storage facility), it is logical and normally most convenient to integrate shelf life procedures into the total quality regime. As the manufacturer is likely to be responsible for most if not all product development activities, he will normally be responsible for both the shelf life determination during product development and on-going monitoring once regular production has begun. Even if development work has been sub-contracted out, it is essential for the manufacturer's 'due diligence' system to be able to demonstrate the validity and reliability of any shelf life quoted.

2.2 Food legislation and shelf life

Food legislation in many developed countries requires most prepacked foods to carry a date of 'minimum durability'. The inference is that procedures have been established (in the main by the manufacturers) for shelf lives to be evaluated. In the UK, for instance, 'best before' date is the usual date mark required by current legislation to appear on the labelling of prepacked foods. The 'best before' date however must be replaced by the 'use by' date when the food is microbiologically highly perishable and therefore likely after a short period to contribute an immediate danger to human health. It is an offence to sell any food after its 'use by' date.

The 'best before' date is the date up to and including which the food 'can reasonably be expected to retain its specific properties', providing it has been stored properly. Food may still be edible after that date, but its appearance and quality could suffer; for example crisp biscuits might become soggy (MAFF, 1991). Naturally, meaningful storage instructions are required alongside the 'best before' date if the food is to be enjoyed at its best. While the term 'specific properties' may not be well defined for many foods, the regulations, e.g. The Food Labelling Regulations (HMSO, 1984), require that product names and descriptions are correct and it can be expected that these will be considered misleading if the shelf life which is set allows marked changes in the properties of the food between being freshly made and the 'best before' date. Examples of such changes may include the watery or oily separation which occurs during the shelf life of salad cream and mayonnaise. Foods in unlacquered cans may dissolve enough tin to infringe the UK Tin in Food Regulations

Table 2.2 Examples of some shelf life aspects and their legislative control in the UK[a]

Shelf life aspects	Examples of relevant legislation
Hygiene	*Food Hygiene (General) Regulations* (1970)
	Food Hygiene Directive (93/43/EEC)
Temperature control	*Food Hygiene (Amendment) Regulations* (1990)
	Food Hygiene (Amendment) Regulations (1991)
Packaging migration	*'Plastics' Directive* (90/128/EEC)
	Plastics Materials and Articles in Contact with Food Regulations (1992)
Processing	*Food (Control of Irradiation) Regulations* (1990)
Use of preservatives	*Preservatives in Food Regulations* (1989)
Strict product liability	
(design, manufacture, etc.)	*Consumer Protection Act* (1987) Part 1

[a]Source: Jukes, 1993.

(HMSO, 1992). Such food may be confiscated as unfit for human consumption. Vitamin claims may become invalid if loss occurs during storage. Cakes may not rise sufficiently during baking as a result of failure of the baking powder in the cake mix to effect the desired chemical aeration. Sensory property of a beverage may be impaired due to either simple flavour loss or deteriorative chemical changes.

The seller is generally legally responsible for compliance when the food is sold to the consumer. However, in the case of manufactured foods a retailer would normally demand goods with sufficient remaining shelf life to sell and for the consumer to store for a reasonable period of time before use. An inappropriate shelf life set by a manufacturer could conceivably lead to prosecution since a retailer would be able to demonstrate due diligence in accepting the manufacturer's data.

It should also be recognised that if foods reach the marketplace in substandard condition the legal sanction imposed by the regulatory authority is likely to be trivial compared with the adverse publicity such action would attract, especially for a large or well known firm. Publicity generated by product recalls, for example, due to yeast contaminated fat free Thousand Island Dressing (*The Daily Telegraph*, 1991) and off-flavour Smarties (*The Globe and Mail*, 1993) respectively is something that every manufacturer would do its best to avoid.

Examples of other shelf life aspects that may need to be considered and are subject to legislative control in the UK are given in Table 2.2.

2.3 Forms of quality deterioration during storage

Most foods change progressively during storage, and the changes in most cases render the food less attractive and palatable and eventually unfit for

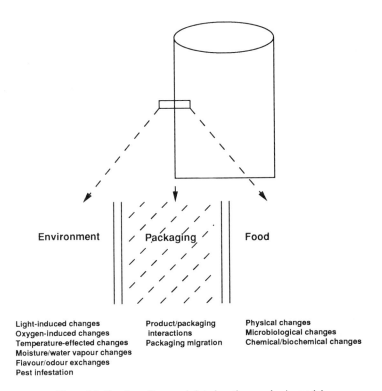

Figure 2.2 Food spoilage and deterioration – a basic model.

consumption. Figure 2.2. (IFST, 1993) summarises the main deteriorative changes commonly encountered in foods.

Watery separation and 'setting up' can occur in thickened foods in cans and jars while suspended particles tend to settle in thinner products. Oil can separate from emulsion products such as salad cream giving a similarly unattractive appearance. Many food components change in the presence of oxygen. Thus the oil in emulsion products can develop 'rancid' flavours. Many foods acquire a stale, sometimes 'cardboard' like taste as they age. Natural pigments e.g. lycopene, change colour and in the case of tomatoes from red to brown. Filling tomato products in unlacquered tinplate cans mitigates this colour effect as the exposed tin scavenges the headspace oxygen during sterilisation and storage giving the food considerable protection from colour and indeed flavour changes but tin dissolves in the process. This can also give a metallic taste and contravene the UK *Tin in Food Regulations* if the uptake of tin in the food exceeds 200 mg per kg within the assigned shelf life unless the latter is reduced to allow for this. Tin dissolution however can be uneven with some foods; localised attack can expose the steel base plate which then reacts with the steel to generate hydrogen creating internal pressure (swell) which would normally be interpreted as a sign of microbial growth. Continued attack can eventually perforate the can in extreme cases and allow contamination. Tin dissolution is increased by the presence of dissolved headspace oxygen, nitrate from water or ingredients, or residual sulphur dioxide (FAO, 1986). Tin dissolution can be avoided if the cans are fully lacquered internally, but oxygen-induced changes are then potentially greater.

Glass is inert to all foods so offers no oxygen scavenging effect, and colour and flavour changes can occur in the surface layer of bottled foods due to reaction with oxygen present in the headspace or leaking in the event that the cap seal is not perfect. Sealed plastic packages (bottles and bowls) used for long life foods can give more rapid oxidative changes as all plastics have some oxygen permeability.

During storage of frozen foods, 'freezer burn' may appear as white surface areas caused by sublimation of water vapour from exposed portions. These areas are usually also toughened due to the dehydration. Some components such as vegetables can change colour during frozen storage. Growth of ice crystals and other physical changes in sauces and dessert type frozen foods can give an icy and granular mouthfeel, rather than the desired smooth texture. Ice cream can lose volume during frozen storage due to loss of the air incorporated during manufacture. Since ice cream is normally sold by volume, this loss may cause infringement of the relevant Weights and Measures Regulations.

In dried foods, oxygen sensitive components may be more exposed than in the same foods when fresh, giving rapid development of rancidity in oil containing foods such as formation of 'musty' or 'hay' flavours in dried herbs. Loss of crispness can occur quickly if the food is hygroscopic unless protein is offered by the use of suitable packaging.

Deterioration in many fresh foods is largely due to growth of microorganisms but wilting of vegetables is a result of water loss while staling of baked goods can be partly explained by changes in the structure of their starch component.

2.4   Procedures for direct determination and monitoring of shelf life

Direct shelf life determination requires batches of samples to be taken at significant stages in the development or modification of a product. These samples should be examined during storage, usually under controlled environmental conditions, until their quality becomes unacceptable. The time when this occurs is the maximum product shelf life, and therefore the determination necessarily requires at least this time to complete.

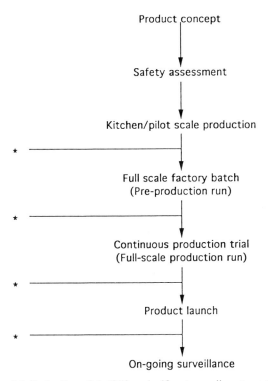

Figure 2.3 Evaluation of shelf life – significant sampling stages (★).

Section 2.5 outlines methods for shortening the process for long life foods to avoid delays to product launches due to shelf life testing.

Significant sampling stages within the programme of shelf life evaluation include (Figure 2.3):

1. The successful experimental kitchen or pilot plant batch. While scale-up to production will normally highlight some differences, this stage may precede lengthy development activities such as market research or plant construction, allowing longer storage experience to be gained. At this stage it is possible to investigate formulation, process or packaging changes to improve the shelf life without the costs of factory time and material quantities.
2. The successful full scale factory batch. This is the most important sampling stage as the food should be substantially the same as subsequent production and examination of samples of the product will provide data for the setting of shelf life and specification standards.
3. The first continuous production trial. Examination of products should confirm the data from earlier samplings.

4. Early runs of standard production not supervised by development personnel. This constitutes the transition between the development and production stages. Examination of samples from these runs forms a major part of the development review, allowing a first opportunity to adjust the shelf life should the need arise.

As part of an on-going surveillance system, samples should be taken at suitable intervals for storage trial. The sampling interval should typically be 20% of the shelf life which will provide samples of 6 different ages from fresh to the full shelf life, for examination at any time. For long life products more frequent intervals may be useful to detect any changes in storage performance (e.g. every two months for a two year shelf life) while for shorter life products a frequency greater than monthly is usually unnecessary.

Shelf life samples should be subjected to conditions effectively simulating the normal storage and distribution conditions the food is likely to encounter. For ambient stable foods this usually means normal room temperature and relative humidity, but as laboratory and experimental kitchen temperatures are likely to be higher than in the warehouse, a store cooled to and maintained at the mean warehouse temperature may be required.

For foods packed in impermeable packaging, relative humidity of the storage environment is unlikely to be important in influencing shelf life. However if shelf life is limited by moisture gain/loss (for instance biscuits and cakes respectively) or if the food is packed in moisture sensitive oxygen barrier plastics such as ethylene vinyl alcohol copolymer (EVOH), control of the relative humidity becomes a major consideration in the shelf life study.

If performance in tropical or sub-tropical conditions is required, similar storage conditions should be used as many chemical changes will be accelerated under these conditions. Similarly, if temperatures near or below freezing are envisaged, they should be used in testing as the conditions may destabilise thickeners such as modified starches.

Frozen foods are normally stored at between $-25°C$ and $-30°C$ for long periods by manufacturers and $-18°C$ during distribution, retail display and in the home freezer. A realistic storage trial regime incorporating these temperatures should be employed, and, since frozen foods are frequently taken home after purchase in ambient or insulated containers only, a suitable period at an appropriate temperature should also be included. If storage instructions on the pack are to provide permissible periods in 'star' (*) marked freezers or frozen compartments of refrigerators, storage periods at $-12°C$ (**) and $-6°C$ (*) should also be included (UKAFFP, 1978).

Some foods such as jams, pickles, sauces, meat pastes, margarines and low fat spreads are normally used over a varying period of time (from days to weeks) after the pack has been opened; an 'open' shelf life storage test should be included for these products involving removal of portions for tasting or other examination at pre-determined intervals and re-closing the pack over a suitable time span. Storage of the package between successive openings should be under recommended conditions (or likely conditions if mis-use/abuse is expected). The latter usually means either room temperature or that of a domestic refrigerator.

The basis of shelf life examination of foods is often subjective with appearance, smell, texture and flavour being the main attributes to assess. Such assessments are frequently inexact as there may not be a suitable control sample with which to compare the stored samples, this being particularly so for new products. Freezing can often be a useful means of preserving reference/standard samples but there is no universal method for keeping them. In many cases remaking of reference samples every time a comparison with stored samples is made may be the only option. It follows then that the importance of proper handling, storage and identification of reference samples cannot be overemphasised.

Quantitative measurements, for example of colour, texture, viscosity and amount of water or oil separation should be included if they either closely relate to subjective quality or can be used as reliable indicators of quality deterioration.

Expert or consumer panels producing statistically analysed results may give the best measure of storage changes and acceptability but can be very expensive for regular use. An individual shelf life assessor with proper training and experience of normal storage changes may be employed to carry out most assessments and other resources such as analytical services or expert taste panels used where necessary.

In addition to subjective assessments, other tests may be necessary. These may include tin content of products in unlacquered cans, vitamin content where a claim is made or microbiological examination of fresh or chilled foods.

As previously mentioned, as a general rule, samples of product retained for shelf life determination should be evaluated about 6 times during the assigned shelf life of the product. Thus short life 'fresh' or chilled foods may require daily examination until they become unacceptable, while long life products, for example canned foods, may need to be evaluated once every six months.

As a shelf life scheme generates a substantial body of information, control and documentation of this information is important, especially if a large number of different products are involved and there is a continuing programme of innovation and development. A convenient basis of control is the allocation of a number to each different product and a serial number for each batch of samples tested during development and the commercial life of the product. For instance, a particular canned soup could be given the number 123 and thus 123/5 might be the fifth batch to be tested. Even if the product name is changed during or after development the same 'shelf life' number can be retained for easy identification. Each batch of experimental or production samples can then be assigned an evaluation record identified by this number and kept as a file indexed by product shelf life number, making the shelf life history of a product readily accessible. Where a substantial number of different products are under development and being monitored on an on-going basis, data control and, in particular, 'cross indexing' to identify similar product or packaging changes over a period of time can still be cumbersome and in this case the use of a computer spreadsheet or database will probably be feasible and worthwhile even if the total record system is not computerised.

2.5 Methodology for accelerated estimation of shelf life

The system described in the previous section necessarily requires the full shelf life, possibly several years, to produce results. Development of long life foods will normally require results in a much shorter time to meet product launch schedules. More rapid alternative techniques are available but they should always be supplemented by normal condition testings ('direct determination') for confirmation since it is hardly possible to predict the storage performance of a product under normal conditions with certainty from its behaviour when 'abused'.

A number of accelerated techniques are in use. When using these it is a general rule that the more rapid the degradation induced, and thus the further from normal storage conditions, the less reliable the shelf life estimate is likely to be. The potential problems and possible errors that can arise in the use of accelerated techniques have been described elsewhere (IFST, 1991; Robertson, 1993). There is no advantage in destabilising a product which is perfectly stable during normal storage. The results obtained from accelerated techniques must be interpreted with caution as they are not applicable to all products. Using experience of similar products, the likely shelf life of a new or modified product can often be estimated before any storage tests are done. A conservative shelf life with a generous margin of safety should be given in this case so that the shelf life can be confirmed or modified as soon as accelerated and normal storage data have become available.

Raising the storage temperature will accelerate many ageing processes and this is the basis of many of the accelerated methods. Storage at 30 to 33°C can give a 2 to 3 fold increase for many, in particular, flavour changes. Storage at 35 to 40°C can bring about a 4 fold speed up of oil or water separation and facilitate tin dissolution in unlacquered cans. Storage at 55°C for a period of 4 to 6 weeks can show up instability in pickle and sauce products. Products that remain stable after this storage will probably be stable for a long time at ambient temperature; however such high temperature has been shown to cause acid hydrolysis of starches in normally stable foods.

Cycling the product between 0°C and room temperature will accelerate watery separation in starch-thickened foods. Absence of any separation after 30 cycles over 2 months normally suggests that the product will be stable for up to 2 years or more at ambient temperature.

Where oxygen causes flavour or colour changes in permeable (e.g. plastics) packaging, high oxygen atmospheres will speed up changes, as will a high relative humidity if EVOH is used as the oxygen barrier layer. Storage of the products in a nitrogen atmosphere should also be considered alongside air or enhanced oxygen conditions so that the effects of oxygen can be isolated from those due to other changes.

Controlled shaking (at 250–300 strokes per minute) to provide moderate product agitation for several hours will cause separation in unstable emulsion products. Shaking rates and package geometry must be closely controlled (or preferably standards should always be shaken alongside experimental samples) as these parameters greatly influence product movement and shearing.

Storage defects in frozen products can be accelerated by storage at higher than normal temperatures. Thus more rapid changes will occur at −18°C compared with the normal long term storage temperature of below −25°C, and still faster changes will occur at −10°C. Certain forms of deterioration, such as ice crystal growth and freezer burn will also be accelerated if the storage temperature is made to fluctuate while the food still remains frozen.

2.6 The importance of shelf life to quality and distribution

Production of foods of consistently acceptable quality with shelf lives adequate for their intended uses together with the correct communication to the consumer of their durability are important to the manufacturer, retailer and consumer. The consideration which is most important is that the food must reach the consumer in good condition and retain its quality for the period expected, including a period after the package has been opened if normal use implies this. All other factors are subordinate. Consumers will not continue to buy unsatisfactory products.

Modern manufacturing processes are often more efficient if long production runs are made. This will impose a constraint on shelf life if a number of different products are made on the same plant as inventory must be accumulated to cover the period between production runs. The quality of the food made before and after the required storage period must be similar, and both must be acceptable.

While consumer demand and rate of production will normally be matched to minimise storage and thus inventory costs, unforeseen fluctuations in demand can necessitate storage of products for longer than intended. For certain food products such as some bakery goods, frozen storage may be used successfully to extend the shelf life as a means of stockpiling prior to an expected period of increased sale. In addition, many foods are distributed nationally or internationally, so time is required for transport, handling and transit storage at various stages. Careful considerations must also be given to the different environmental conditions prevalent in the different export markets in respect of adequate packaging protection to maintain shelf life. Today's larger retailers will normally turn stock over rapidly; small retailers will frequently be slower in selling and may well operate less controlled stock rotation systems.

Finally, the retailer will require time to sell the food to the consumer. Large retailers will usually have rapid stock turnover and thus an actual need for relatively short storage, while smaller shops with lower volumes may need a longer time to sell the food. Also, commercial considerations may dictate that a shorter shelf life will suffice so as to give the product a 'fresher' image. All will require a 'best before' (or 'use by') date sufficiently long after delivery for their needs. With their very large purchasing influence, major retailers may well be in a position to demand in their contracts a long residual shelf life on foods delivered to them.

Frequently there may be a conflict between quality and the logistic requirements of manufacture and delivery, so some compromise may have to be made. Quality (and of course safety) should always be given the greatest weight and statutory quality standards must never be compromised. It may well be better in the long term not to produce and market a food product if quality and an adequate shelf life cannot be simultaneously realised.

2.7   Conclusions

For most foods, adequate shelf life can be achieved. Knowledge of the factors affecting shelf life and use of valid and appropriate methodology are vital to the delivery of an acceptable product to the consumer. Sufficient care and adequate resources should be devoted to shelf life evaluation. A safe, high quality product that consistently pleases its customer has its origin in good product design which includes properly conducted and documented shelf life procedures and on-going surveillance, evidence that can be used to prove that the manufacturer has considered his products and problems and that he does care about what he produces.

References

FAO (1986) Guidelines for can manufacturers and food canners: prevention of metal contamination of canned foods. *FAO Food and Nutrition Paper 36*, Food and Agriculture Organisation, Rome.

HMSO (1984) *The Food Labelling Regulations*, SI 1984 No. 1305.

HMSO (1992) *The Tin in Food Regulations*, SI 1992 No. 496.

IFST (1991) *Food and Drink – Good Manufacturing Practice: A Guide to its Responsible Management*. 3rd edn, Institute of Food Science and Technology, London.

IFST (1993) *Shelf Life of Foods – Guidelines for its Determination and Prediction*. Institute of Food Science and Technology, London.

ISO (1987) *Quality Systems – Model for Quality Assurance in Design/Development, Production, Installation and Servicing*. ISO 9001 – 1987. International Organization for Standardization.

Jukes, D.J. (1993) *Food Legislation of the UK – A Concise Guide*. 3rd edn, Butterworth Heinemann, Oxford.

MAFF (1991) *Best Before and Use By – A Guide to the changes*. Food Sense, London.

Robertson, G.L. (1993) *Food Packaging*. Marcel Dekker, New York.

The Daily Telegraph (1991) Recall of Kraft Fat Free Thousand Island Dressing. 9th September, London.

The Globe and Mail (1993) Smarties recall announced. 21st August, Toronto.

UKAFFP (1978) *Code of Recommended Practice for the Handling of Quick Frozen Foods*, 2nd edn, United Kingdom Association of Frozen Food Producers, London.

3 The principles and practice of shelf life prediction for microorganisms

S.J. WALKER

3.1 Introduction

Prior to determining the shelf life of a food, it is essential to determine which factor(s) limit the shelf life. Such factors may cause chemical, physical and biological changes which result in a sensory change in the food. If the limiting factor is not correctly identified, then subsequent studies will be flawed. Unfortunately, in many cases, the factors studied are those most easily measured rather than those which limit the shelf life. For the remainder of this chapter, only microbial changes will be considered. With microbial growth, it is often useful to consider safety and spoilage separately although the controlling factors for both may be identical. Issues relating to safety must take precedence over those relating to spoilage.

Traditionally, food microbiologists have determined the microbial shelf life of foods using 'expert judgement', storage trials or challenge tests. Unfortunately, 'expert judgement' tends to be very subjective and with the greater onus on food manufacturers to demonstrate due diligence, this option has become less desirable. Both shelf life trials and challenge tests, if done correctly, are very powerful weapons in the food microbiologist's armoury and have served the food industry well (Brown, 1992). A challenge test is the laboratory simulation of what may happen to a food during its life and may involve inoculation with specific microorganisms and/or storage at abuse temperatures. Useful guidance on challenge testing is available (Anon, 1987). Whilst the results from these are extremely valuable, challenge tests tend to be costly and time-consuming. Furthermore, the results of a challenge test apply specifically to those conditions tested and any change in a product's formulation or storage temperature may invalidate the results previously obtained. Consequently, there has been a great deal of interest in other ways to determine the shelf life of foods. Perhaps the most promising method is the use of predictive models for microbiology. These models allow the user to predict the fate of microorganisms when a food is stored under specific conditions of temperature, pH, gaseous atmosphere and so on.

The use of predictive models for foods is not new and the safe thermal

processing of many canned goods is based on models for microbial inactivation developed over 70 years ago (Esty and Meyer, 1922). More
recently however, there has been much interest in the development of
models for microbial growth and non-thermal inactivation. Predictive
models for microbial growth can be divided into two main types: those
which predict the probability of an event occurring (probability models)
and those which predict the change in microbial numbers (kinetic
models). In some circumstances, probabilistic models are very powerful
and have been used to predict the likelihood of *Clostridium botulinum*
growing in cured meat products (Roberts and Jarvis, 1983). Kinetic
models are often more useful as they not only indicate the ability to grow
but also provide information about the rate and extent of growth that
occurs in a given time period. The major advantage of predictive models
is that they may be used to predict the fate of microorganisms in conditions not specifically tested during the construction of the model.

3.2 Development of predictive models

The development of predictive microbiological models for use in foods is
neither simple nor inexpensive. A number of stages must be successfully
completed if a model is to be of widespread use and applicable to foods.

3.2.1 Experimental design

As with all scientific research, the experimental design is crucial. An
inappropriate design may result in the collection of vast amounts of
unnecessary data or in data that cannot be successfully modelled. Furthermore, the factors modelled (e.g. temperature, pH, salt content, atmosphere) and their ranges must be appropriate to the intended use of the
model. For example, there is little merit in a model for a psychotrophic
pathogen which applies only to high storage temperatures (25–35°C) if
the major concern is with its growth at refrigeration temperatures.

3.2.2 Data collection

The accumulation of data on the growth or inactivation of microorganisms is undoubtedly the most costly stage of model development. Most
work is done using microbiological media as they are of consistent composition and can be easily and reproducibly adjusted to the conditions
required for study. The inherent variability of foods coupled with the
microbial response tend to result in few studies directly in foods (Maxcy
and Wallen, 1983), although simple models have been developed in largely
homogeneous foods such as milk (Griffiths and Phillips, 1988). Most data

have been developed from studies using plate count techniques, although automated techniques such as optical density and conductimetry (Gibson, 1985) have been used. As workers develop models containing four or more factors, the requirement for automated data collection techniques will increase.

Guidelines on data collection and recording have been developed (Walker and Jones, 1993) and a greater standardisation of data collection and recording will certainly aid the future of predictive microbiology throughout the world.

3.2.3 Modelling

To date, a number of techniques have been used to model the data and include Gompertz-polynomial (Gibson *et al.*, 1988; Buchanan and Phillips, 1990) and Bêlehrádek-type (Ratkowsky or square root) models (McMeekin *et al.*, 1993). These models are applicable to growth of the microorganisms. More recently, newer modelling techniques have been developed to predict both the growth, survival, and non-thermal inactivation of microorganisms (Figure 3.1) (Jones and Walker, 1994). Such techniques permit the use of data with greater ranges than models based solely on growth, and so may have greater applicability. At present, it is

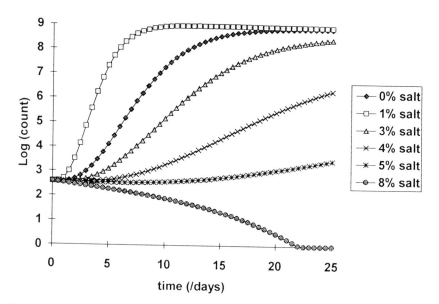

Figure 3.1 Use of a new modelling technique to predict growth, survival and inactivation of *Yersinia enterocolitica* as affected by salt.

inappropriate to recommend any single modelling technique. Rather, the technique should be suitable for the data used and should be economical. The modelling techniques currently employed are largely descriptive in nature. The development of mechanistic models which are based on an understanding of how a microorganism behaves will be one of the major advances in the future of modelling.

3.2.4 Model validation

Perhaps the most important stage associated with the development of models in microbiological media is their validation. One approach to model validation has been described by McClure *et al.* (1994). The validation should ensure that not only does the model describe accurately the data used to produce it, but it should also demonstrate the applicability of the model to foods. This latter stage is crucial if the users of models are to have confidence in the models' predictions. Food validation may be done using data from the published literature, industry generated data or specific inoculated food studies (Figure 3.2). Any deficiencies in a model to predict well for some, or all, foods should be evident to the model user.

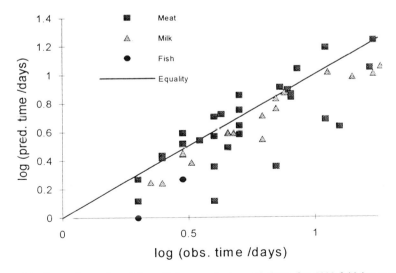

Figure 3.2 Comparison of model predictions and observed times for 1000-fold increase in microbial numbers from foods inoculated with *Yersinia enterocolitica*.

3.2.5   Obtaining predictions

The final stage of model development is to ensure that the user can obtain predictions. Developments in computer hardware and software have permitted the output of models to be presented in a variety of ways. Some systems available have been described by Buchanan (1991), Zwietering *et al.* (1992) and Jones (1993). The trend is for systems to use personal computers and to offer a lot of flexibility in their use. The vast majority of models available are for pathogenic bacteria, although models have been developed for the spoilage of milk (Griffiths and Phillips, 1988), meat (Zamara and Zaritzky, 1985) and soft drinks (Cole and Keenen, 1987). Part of the reason for this focus on pathogens is the high cost of developing models and major initiatives in the UK and USA are funded by Government with a view to improving food safety. Within the UK, the Ministry of Agriculture, Fisheries and Foods has funded a large research programme (1989–1994) to predict the growth, survival and inactivation of foodborne pathogens and is available as a commercial service, the 'Food Micromodel'. Models have been produced for *Aeromonas hydrophila*, *Bacillus cereus*, *B. subtilis*, *Campylobacter*, psychrotrophic *Clostridium botulinum*, *Clostridium perfringens*, *Escherichia coli* 0157:H7, *Listeria monocytogenes*, *Salmonella*, *Staphylococcus aureus* and *Yersinia enterocolitica*. Further details on this programme have already been described by Gould (1991) and Walker and Jones (1994b).

3.3   Uses of models

Once developed, models can be used in a variety of ways to help ensure the safety and quality of foods. Although the majority of applications has been developed for pathogenic bacteria, they may also be used for spoilage microorganisms provided appropriate, validated models are available.

3.3.1   Product formulation and reformulation

The design of a product formulation or reformulation is fundamental to the safety and quality of the food. Relatively small changes in the formulation may have a profound effect on microbial growth and may result in an unsafe product or a product of poor quality. Increasingly, food manufacturers are under pressure to change the formulation of foods (e.g. reduction in salt levels or removal of preservatives), many of which have had a long and safe history. Such changes may potentially permit microbial growth in food previously considered stable. Unfortunately, the microbial safety or quality of a product formulation or reformulation is

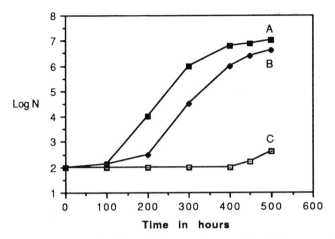

Figure 3.3 The effect of product formulation on the growth of *Aeromonas hydrophila*. A, *Aeromonas hydrophila*, salt (% w/v) 2.3, pH 6.1, 7.0°C; B, *Aeromonas hydrophila*, salt (% w/v) 4.3, pH 6.1, 7.0°C; C, *Aeromonas hydrophila*, salt (% w/v) 2.3, pH 5.6, 7.0°C.

often one of the last parameters to be considered. If a product is subsequently shown to be microbiologically unstable, then the development costs to this point have been wasted. By using predictive models, the microbial stability of a product formulation can be rapidly assessed. Formulations that are intrinsically unsafe or unstable can be readily eliminated, so that subsequent development work is effectively targeted. Although this could be done using challenge tests, predictive models provide answers rapidly and cost-effectively. The effect of various product formulations on growth of a pathogen is shown in Figure 3.3.

Until predictive models have been widely accepted and have proven their applicability for food products, many food manufacturers may consider it prudent to do a microbiological challenge test on the final product to validate the model predictions. The nature and scope of this challenge test however, will be considerably less than that required if predictive models had not been used.

3.3.2 Process design

The shelf life of many foods is dependent, not only on formulation, but also on processes applied during manufacture (e.g. pasteurisation). Often the product formulation cannot be such to prevent microbial growth and so processing is necessary. With the development of models for inactivation, the process can be designed to ensure that the target microorganism(s) are effectively eliminated.

Although the traditionally used D and z values have been widely used to determine safe processes, as with other types of predictive modelling, alternative approaches to modelling thermal inactivation have been identified (Cole *et al.*, 1994).

3.3.3 HACCP

Hazard Analysis, Critical Control Points (HACCP) is a philosophy that has been applied to the production of food. This concept may be applied to both food safety and food quality. As a technique it has gained wide approval as a proactive way to assure food safety and quality. Seven principles have been identified in the application of a HACCP plan (Anon, 1992):

1. Conduct a hazard analysis. Identify and list the hazards and specify control measures.
2. Identify the critical control points.
3. Establish target level(s) and tolerances which must be met to ensure each CCP is under control.
4. Establish a monitoring system to ensure control of the CCP.
5. Establish the corrective action to be taken when monitoring indicates that a CCP is moving out of control.
6. Establish documentation.
7. Establish verification procedures.

When considering microbial hazards, specific knowledge of factors affecting the growth, survival and inactivation of microorganisms is required. Predictive models can be used to indicate if a hazard exists at a particular process step (principle 1). To determine if a process step is critical (principle 2), use of a decision tree is often recommended (Figure 3.4). Again valuable information to progress through the decision tree can be obtained from models. Once a process step has been identified as a critical control point (CCP), its control is essential. Predictive models can be used to identify the optimal target value for correct operation of this step and the tolerances that may be permitted (principle 3).

The application of models can therefore aid the application of HACCP to food manufacture by ensuring that good quality, systematic and objective information is used in the decision making process.

3.3.4 Time–temperature profiles

With many foods, particularly those stored chilled, the control of temperature during storage of a food is important in ensuring the safety and quality. During storage, the food will be subject to a fluctuating temperature profile. If this profile is known, predictive models can be used to

Answer each question in sequence at each step for each identified hazard

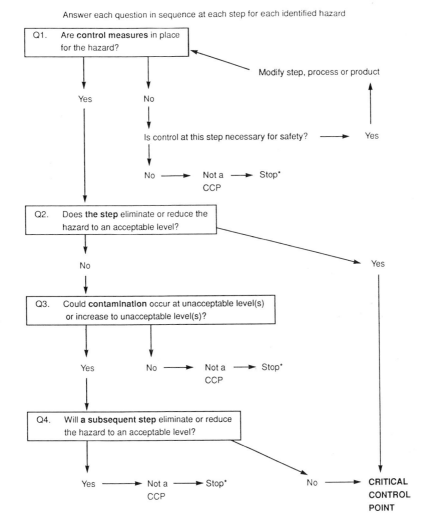

Figure 3.4 CCP Decision Tree for HACCP Analysis (Anon, 1992).

determine the cumulative effects of this storage (Gould, 1991). Obviously the quality of the prediction is dependent on the quality of the time–temperature profile collected. For example, if only the air temperature is monitored, the prediction of microbial growth in the food, which may not mimic the air temperature profile, may be erroneous.

3.3.5   Training and education

The development of predictive models in a user-friendly PC format can provide a useful training and educational tool. It provides a rapid and cost-effective mechanism whereby the benefits of doing a job correctly, or conversely the consequences of failing to do a job correctly, can be readily demonstrated. For example, the results of inadequate cooking, failure to use the correct product formulation or improper storage of a food can be demonstrated and quantified.

As an educational tool, the use of predictive models in the basic training of food scientists and food technologists will allow them to appreciate more fully how factors (e.g. temperature, pH) act independently and together to affect the growth, survival and inactivation of microorganisms.

3.4   Limitations of models

Whilst predictive models for microbiology are very powerful, care is needed to ensure their correct use. Misuse of models may give the user a false sense of security about the microbial safety or quality of a food.

Firstly, it is important that the user understands which microorganism(s) is of concern. If this is incorrect then all subsequent predictions may be inappropriate. Whilst most systems currently available are based on foodborne pathogens, the growth of food spoilage microorganisms often limits the product shelf life. Therefore, both must be considered when determining the shelf life.

Secondly, the factors (temperature, pH etc.) used for the predictions must be carefully identified and measured. If there is a natural variation in these factors (e.g. batch-to-batch variation) this must be considered. Normally, the levels of the factors that are least inhibitory to microorganisms would be selected otherwise the use of the prediction may result in some batches which may be of poor quality or even hazardous.

The majority of models available are based on foodborne pathogens. As discussed previously, the microbiological shelf life of many foods is based on both the microbial safety and quality of those foods. In the absence of generally accepted and validated models for microbial quality, the estimation of a product life will require storage trials and/or challenge tests. Some work in predicting spoilage has started (McClure et al., 1993).

There has been concern with the errors associated with predictions from microbial models. With validated models based on good quality data, experience has shown that the errors obtained are generally less than those associated with repeating microbiological challenge tests.

Finally, most models available indicate the likelihood or the extent of microbial growth or inactivation that will occur. They do not indicate that a food will be safe or do not indicate the microbial shelf life of a food. Both these activities require judgement from an experienced microbiologist. In the absence of definitive data about the minimum infectious doses to cause disease for many pathogens and a poor understanding about the relationship between microbial numbers and food spoilage, the ability of predictive models to indicate the shelf life of a food will be limited.

3.5 The future

The shelf life of a food is dependent on the raw material quality, the formulation of that food, the processes applied, the hygiene of production and storage and the temperature of storage, distribution and sale. This will be aided by the use of quality systems which incorporate well trained staff. It is obvious that predictive models can be applied to many of the stages involved in the manufacture and sale of foods which minimises the risks posed by microorganisms. Models therefore, do not replace the food microbiologist, but should result in the food microbiologist having better information, on which to base judgements.

In addition to a very active and co-ordinated programme of research in the UK, much research in predictive microbiology has also been carried out in the USA, continental Europe and Australia. One of the next major hurdles to be overcome is that of international collaboration. The collection and storage of data in a common format will allow data sets from around the world to be combined. The resultant models will have greater useful ranges of applicability and may be more robust. With collaboration, unnecessary duplication of data collection, which tends to be extremely costly, can be managed and perhaps additional factors may be studied. Furthermore the development and acceptance of an agreed system internationally, will enable models to be used to facilitate international trade and perhaps legislation.

The development of validated predictive models for the microbial spoilage of foods, will be very important from a commercial perspective. Essential to this, however, is an understanding not only of microbial growth but also an understanding of microbial activity and how this relates to sensory changes in foods. When such understandings are available it will then be possible to develop expert systems for the application of predictive models. Some developments in this area have started (Zweitering et al., 1992).

Predictive food microbiology has emerged from within food microbiology to become a discipline in its own right with an undoubted future. To date, the development of models has been progressed largely by food microbiologists. In the future, inclusion of other scientific disciplines, particularly microbial physiology, mathematics, statistics, computer programming and knowledge engineering, will aid the next stages in the development of predictive models (some of which may become truly mechanistic), application software and expert systems. Consequently, the power, flexibility and application of predictive models will ensure their greater use by the food industry to provide good quality information in a rapid and cost-effective manner. This will in turn permit better decisions on microbial safety and quality to be reached.

References

Anon (1987) Microbiological Challenge Testing. *Campden Food and Drink Research Association Technical Manual No. 20.*

Anon (1992) HACCP: A Practical Guide. *Campden Food and Drink Research Association Technical Memorandum No. 38.*

Brown, H.M. (1992) Shelf-life determination and challenge testing, in *Chilled Foods: a Comprehensive Guide* (eds C. Dennis and M. Stringer), Ellis Horwood, Chichester, pp. 289–307.

Buchanan, R.L. (1991) Using spreadsheet software for predictive microbiology applications. *J. Food Safety*, **11**, 123–34.

Buchanan, R.L. and Phillips, J.G. (1990) Response surface model for predicting the effects of temperature, pH, sodium chloride content, sodium nitrite concentration and atmosphere on the growth of *Listeria monocytogenes*. *J. Food Protection*, **53**, 370–6, 381.

Cole, M.B. and Keenen, M.H.J. (1987) A quantitative method for predicting shelf-life of soft drinks using a model system. *J. Industrial Microbiol.*, **2**, 59–62.

Cole, M.B., Davies, K.W., Munro, G., Holyoak, C.D. and Kilsby, D.C. (1994) The effect of pH, NaCl concentration and temperature on the thermal inactivation of *Listeria monocytogenes*, in *Predictive Microbiology and Computer Modeling for the Food Industry* (eds R.L. Buchanan, S.A. Palumbo and R.C. Whiting), Macmillan, New York (in press).

Esty, J.R. and Meyer, K.F. (1922) The heat resistance of spores of *Cl. botulinum* and allied anaerobes. *J. Infectious Diseases*, **31**, 650–63.

Gibson, D.M. (1985) Predicting the shelf-life of packaged fish from conductance measurements. *J. Applied Bacteriol.*, **58**, 465–70.

Gibson, A.M., Bratchell, N. and Roberts, T.A. (1988) Predicting microbial growth: growth responses of salmonellae in a laboratory medium as affected by pH, sodium chloride and storage temperature. *Int. J. Food Microbiol.*, **6**, 155–78.

Gould, G. (1991) Predictive mathematical modelling of microbial growth and survival in foods. *Food Sci. Technol. Today*, **3**, 89–92.

Griffiths, M.W. and Phillips, J.D. (1988) Modelling the relation between bacterial growth and storage temperature in pasteurized milks of varying hygienic quality. *J. Soc. Dairy Technol.*, **41**, 96–102.

Jones, J.E. (1993) A real-time database/models base/expert system in predictive microbiology. *J. Industrial Microbiol.*, **12**, 268–272.

Jones, J.E. and Walker, S.J. (1993) Advances in modelling microbial growth. *J. Industrial Microbiol.*, **12**, 200–205.

Maxcy, R.B. and Wallen, S.E. (1983) Heterogeneity of samples as a problem in shelf-life prediction. *J. Food Protection.*, **46**, 542–4.

McClure, P.J., Baranyi, J. Boogard, E., Kelly, T.M. and Roberts, T.A. (1993) A predictive model for the combined effect of pH, sodium chloride, and storage temperature on the growth of *Brochothrix thermosphacta*. *Int. J. Food Microbiol.*, **19**, 161–78.

McClure, P.J., Blackburn, C. de W., Cole, M.B., Curtis, P.S., Jones, J.E., Legan, J.D., Ogden, I.D., Peck, M.W., Roberts, T.A., Sutherland, J.P. and Walker, S.J. (1994) Modelling the growth, survival and death of microorganisms in foods. *Int. J. Food Microbiol.*, in press.

McMeekin, T.A., Olley, J.N., Ross, T. and Ratkowsky, D.A. (1993) *Predictive Microbiology: Theory and Application*, Research Studies Press, Somerset.

Roberts, T.A. and Jarvis, B. (1983) Predictive modelling of food safety with particular reference to *Clostridium botulinum* in model cured meat systems, in *Food Microbiology: Advances and Prospects* (eds T.A. Roberts and F.A. Skinner), Academic Press, London, pp. 85–95.

Walker, S.J. and Jones, J.E. (1993) Protocols for data generation for predictive models. *J. Industrial Microbiol.*, **12**, 273–276.

Walker, S.J. and Jones, J.E. (1994) Microbiology modelling and safety assessment. *Food Technology International Europe 94* (ed. A. Turner), pp. 25–29.

Zamara, M.C. and Zaritzky, N.E. (1985) Modelling of microbial growth in refrigerated packaged beef. *J. Food Sci.*, **50**, 1003–6, 1013.

Zwietering, M.H., Wijtzes, T., de Wit, J.C. and Van't Riet, K. (1992) A decision support system for prediction of the microbial spoilage in foods. *J. Food Protection*, **55**, 973–9.

4 Packaging and food quality

U. STÖLLMAN, F. JOHANSSON and A. LEUFVÉN

4.1 Introduction

In the developed world, the purchase of fresh farm produce is not a viable option. The time available for family shopping is too limited to allow the frequent visits to numerous retail outlets that such a system would require. The supply of exotic foodstuffs that consumers have learned to take for granted would also be impossible to maintain without some means of preservation and packaging. However, different products have different demands. Some products are sensitive to oxygen or moisture, others to microbial growth or light. Thus there is no general packaging solution and the type of packaging to be used must be determined individually for each product.

Packaging systems should not only ensure that the food is microbiologically sound, make it easy to handle and convey pack information to the consumer, but also retain the desired sensory characteristics of the food. Such retention of sensory characteristics requires the package to act as an oxygen barrier, moisture barrier, aroma barrier or light barrier depending on the sensitivity of the particular food and the prevailing environment. Thus packaging plays a vital role in the maintenance of the shelf life of foods and it is this aspect of packaging and that of plastics packaging in particular, which will be dealt with in this chapter.

Primary packaging may be flexible, made from plastics film, paper or thin laminate; semi-rigid, like thermoformed plastics, aluminium foil, laminate and paperboard; or rigid, such as thick plastics, metal and glass (Miltz, 1992). In many of today's food products, plastics are used in the primary packaging. These plastics may be used together with aluminium or paper in laminates. The main advantages of plastics are their great diversity and range of properties. Most plastics polymers have a density of around 1000 kg/m^3, making them lightweight materials. They are also relatively cheap, easily processed and shaped. The major technical drawback is that they do not provide an absolute barrier to gases and vapours and that they may interact with the packed food.

Environmental awareness has caused a great deal of attention to be focused on what is regarded as overpackaging. A long maximum storage time is not always perceived as a positive attribute. Nevertheless, an abundant supply of high quality food is demanded by the consuming public. To ensure this high quality in an environmentally friendly way is one of today's most challenging tasks for the packaging and food manufacturers.

In the following sections, the most commonly used plastics as well as some packaging systems including some recent developments will be reviewed. Finally, two examples (sections 4.4 and 4.5) are given to illustrate that packaging can have major influence on the storage quality and shelf life of foods.

4.2 Plastics packaging materials for food

4.2.1 Polyolefins

The most widely used polymers for food packaging applications are the polyolefins. Because of their characteristic heat sealing properties, polyolefins are often used as internal linings in flexible pouches or box-type containers for beverages (Shorten, 1982). The main properties of two polyethylenes (PEs), polypropylene (PP) and ionomers are outlined below.

4.2.1.1 Polyethylene (PE). The molecular formula of PE is $(CH_2)n$ and the presence of branches prevents close packing of the polymer chains so that the density of the finished product is low. The presence of many branched chains also lowers the overall degree of crystallinity which has a major effect on some of the properties of the polymer (Brydson, 1982). There are four main types of polyethylene available, which differ in structure and properties as well as with respect to the manufacturing processes that produce them. They are:

- high density polyethylene (HDPE)
- low density polyethylene (LDPE)
- medium density polyethylene (MDPE)
- linear low density polyethylene (LLDPE).

(a) LDPE. This variety accounts for the largest proportion of plastics for packaging. It is relatively inert chemically, moderately permeable to water vapour but highly permeable to oxygen. In general, the permeabilities to gases are high, with poor odour barrier characteristics. LDPE can be laminated, extrusion-coated, or in some cases, coextruded. The main attractive features of PE, in addition to its low price, are good processability, toughness, flexibility, containing relatively few additives and, in thin films of certain grades, transparency. LDPE has good heat sealability and is easily coated onto other materials such as paper and aluminium.

(b) HDPE. Compared with LDPE, HDPE is stiffer, harder, less transparent, and has a less waxy feel. It is more resistant to oils and greases, and has a higher softening point but lower impact strength and permeability to water vapour.

4.2.1.2 Polypropylene (PP). PP is the next member in the series of polyolefins. It is possible to prepare PP in which the methyl (CH_3) groups are largely arranged on the same side of the polymer chain. The regular arrangement of the CH_3 groups produces a polymer with a higher crystallinity. This polymer is harder, has a higher softening point than HDPE and greater resilience. Its permeability to water vapour and gases lies between those of LDPE and HDPE. Further uses of this polymer are in biaxially oriented films and bottles. The material is stretched in two directions at right angles, under suitable temperature conditions. The resulting material has improved clarity, impact strength and barrier properties to water vapour and oxygen. Commercially available PPs have a density of 900–910 kg/m^3, one of the lowest among polymers.

4.2.1.3 Ionomers. Ionomers are defined as polyolefins copolymerised with a minor portion of an acid such as methacrylic acid, with some of the acid groups present in the form of a metal or quaternary ammonium salt. Ionomers are flexible, tough, transparent, and have excellent heat sealability. One of the trade names for ionomers is 'Surlyn'.

4.2.2 Polyvinyl chloride (PVC)

A number of plastics are available in which a hydrogen atom of ethylene has been substituted by a halogen or other group. These constitute the vinyl plastics. PVC is hard, stiff and clear, with excellent resistance to moisture, low gas permeability and high impact strength. Incorporation of plasticisers makes the resulting film softer and more flexible but lowers its tensile strength. PVC offers good resistance to oils and fats.

4.2.3 Polyvinylidene chloride (PVdC)

The monomer contains an additional chloride atom substituted into the ethylene molecule. The polymer is hard with a high degree of crystallinity. It produces a clear film with good strength properties and very low permeability to gases and water vapour. 'Saran' is a common trade name for PVdC.

4.2.4 Ethylene vinyl alcohol (EVOH)

Ethylene vinyl alcohol (EVOH) is commonly used in packaging because of its good gas barrier properties. EVOH, trade name 'EVAL', is an excellent gas barrier and commercially available in several grades with different ratios of ethylene/vinyl alcohol in the chain. The major limitation of EVOH is that its effectiveness as an oxygen barrier is severely reduced at high levels of humidity, due to disruption of the polymer–polymer hydrogen bonds. Also, because of the hydroxyl groups in the polymer backbone, EVOH tends to be extremely soluble in water.

4.2.5 Polystyrene (PS)

Styrene consists of an ethylene molecule in which one of the hydrogens has been replaced by a phenyl group. The bulky nature of the phenyl group prevents close packing of the macromolecular chains. Hence, PS is amorphous. The polymer is transparent and a good barrier to gases, except water vapour. It is brittle, but this may be overcome by copolymerisation with butadiene and/or acrylonitrile (ABS and SAN respectively). Another way of modifying PS is by making a blend of polystyrene and rubbery materials, i.e. a polystyrene SBR blend. This high impact polystyrene (HIPS) has greater impact strength than ordinary polystyrene but lower tensile strength as well as hardness, and a lower softening point.

4.2.6 Polyamides (nylons)

These comprise a series of polymers prepared by condensation of di-acids with di-amines or through self-condensation of certain amino acids. The amide group (CO–NH) is strongly polar and promotes strong hydrogen bonding between the CO and NH groups on adjacent polymer chains. Hence, nylons are strong, highly crystalline materials with high melting and softening points and low gas permeability. They absorb moisture depending on the relative proportions of hydrocarbons and amide groups in the polymer chain and may lose up to 50% of their strength when wet.

4.2.7 Polyesters

Polyester resins exist in many forms. The most widely used polyester is polyethylene terephthalate (PET). PET has good mechanical properties, excellent transparency and relatively low permeability to gases. Biaxially oriented PET is often used in the production of bottles for carbonated beverages. Laminates with PET as one of the components are also very common in sterilisable pouches and 'boil-in-bag' applications.

4.2.8 Polycarbonates (PC)

Polycarbonates are linear polyesters of carbonic acid with aromatic or aliphatic dihydroxy compounds. Most commercial polycarbonates are tough, stiff, hard and transparent. Their disadvantages are high cost and the fact that they absorb moisture, with resulting deterioration of their mechanical properties and processability. An additional disadvantage, for packaging, is their poor gas barrier properties.

4.2.9   Lamination and coextrusion

Many new packaging materials or combinations of materials have been used in food packaging in recent years. The main driving force has been to increase the barrier properties of the package and thereby the protection of food products with more complex material structures. A single polymer is often unable to provide all the properties necessary to create suitable barrier characteristics. This has generated a need for multilayer structures and techniques such as lamination and coextrusion. Coextrusion is not simply a competitive alternative to lamination. There are laminate properties that coextrusion is unable to meet, and non-thermoplastic materials such as paper and aluminium foil, which are often used in the lamination process, obviously cannot be coextruded. In addition, printing ink which can be protected if enclosed in a laminate, can only be applied on the surface of a coextruded film. There are also applications where the two technologies are combined, i.e. when a coextruded film is used in a laminate. For example, ionomers have excellent sealing characteristics, but are relatively expensive. PE/ionomer coextrusion can give the sealing properties needed in a more cost-effective way than an ionomer monofilm (Meadows, 1991). Such a structure may be produced by adhesive lamination of the materials or by coextrusion coating of the other material. The principal advantage of coextrusion over lamination is that the materials are extruded simultaneously, without a separate lamination process (Meadows, 1991).

In flexible packaging, laminates and metallised films have replaced single material structures. This has greatly improved the light and oxygen barrier properties of the materials, and extended the product shelf life. A drawback of the metallised laminates is the environmental load, even though only tiny amounts of metal are used. The long established trend towards using more laminates may be hit by recycling legislation when the industry will be controlled by requirements to make packaging products recyclable. Even though laminates exhibit many advantages such as flexibility in terms of stiffness, strength, barrier and sealing properties, many structures may have to be simplified, and there may have to be an increased use of compatible base films so that the whole structure can be recycled via the same path (Meadows, 1991). However, the need for high-performance barrier packaging to give shelf stability under a wide range of storage conditions continues to grow. Table 4.1 lists typical oxygen (OTR) and moisture vapour transmission rates (WVTR) for various plastics films for food uses (Turtle, 1987).

Table 4.1 Oxygen and moisture vapour transmission rates for various plastics films

Film (25 μ)	OTR ($cm^3/m^2/24h/atm$ at 25°C and 50% RH)	WVTR ($g/m^2/24h$ at 25°C and 75% RH)
PVdC	2	1
EVOH	0.5–10*	40
Nylon 6	50–150*	40
Polyester	80	8
PVC (unplasticised)	200	20
HDPE	1400	2
OPP	1600	1.5
LDPE	8000	5

*Humidity dependent.
Source: Turtle, 1987.

4.3 Some packaging systems and recent developments

4.3.1 Trends in food packaging

The rate of development of new packaging materials and packaging techniques in recent years has been remarkable. Many of the new packaging materials have been developed to complement developments in new preservation techniques such as modified atmosphere packaging (MAP), or to meet increased demands for recyclability or other environmental considerations (Yokoyama, 1992).

4.3.2 Silica-coated films

To achieve extra barrier properties, films have been coated with silica (SiO_2). Silica-coated plastics, also referred to as glass-coated, have several benefits: being clear barrier materials, they are microwaveable, retortable and recyclable without any step to separate components being required. So far, the SiO_2 coating has been deposited on PET containers, polyester, LDPE, and PP films. The film requires no pretreatment in order to obtain good adhesion of the SIO_2 coating to the film (Rice, 1992b). A 30 nm (300 Å) SiO_2-coated LDPE film has a 10 $cm^3/m^2/day/$ atm. oxygen transmission rate. The oxygen transmission rates for coated OPP (biaxially oriented polypropylene) are said to be comparable to those of metallised OPP. Silica-coated PET films have a 1 $cm^3/m^2/day/$ atm. oxygen transmission rate. Consequently, these coated films could offer barrier properties approaching those provided by multilayer plastics structures, foil laminates or metallised films. Silica-coated plastics enable the use of a monolayer plastics film with an extremely thin SiO_2 layer.

Early problems reported in the development of these products were yellowing and fragility of the glass coatings. However, these problems seem to have been overcome (Rice, 1992a). There have also been reports of micro-cracks in the SiO_2 coatings. These cracks make tunnels through which oxygen may diffuse into the container (Yoshii, 1992). At this point, there seem to be three factors slowing down the commercial application of glass-coated packaging materials (Rice, 1992a):

– economy;
– technical difficulties in ensuring good silica adhesion to certain substrates;
– lack of converter and packer's experience of these new packaging materials.

In 1988 a multilayer microwaveable pouch with a glass-coated polyester barrier layer was introduced in Japan. Today, several other applications are available. These are discussed by Rice (1992a).

4.3.3   Active packaging technologies

Active packaging systems involve an interaction between the packaging material itself, the internal atmosphere and the food. The intention is to extend the shelf life of foods. New technologies which combine active packaging with modified atmosphere packaging (MAP) are being developed (Sneller, 1986; Wolpert, 1987).

4.3.3.1   Packaging materials with preferential permeability. Selected permeable packaging materials can be regarded as highly functional barrier packaging materials. In general, the gas transmission rates of gas barrier resins such as PVdC and EVOH increase in the order of nitrogen, oxygen and carbon dioxide, and their transmission ratios (e.g. CO_2/O_2) are constant for each barrier resin. Some foods require not only permeation of unfavourable gas generated from the inside but also maintenance of the oxygen barrier. Demands for packaging materials to meet these contradictory requirements have risen recently. An example of this is a packaging material which allows compounds from the smoking process to penetrate into the surface of, for instance, sausages under high temperature. After processing this material affords high barrier characteristics below ambient temperature, thus maintaining the quality of the product (Yoshii, 1990). Another example, this time from the dairy industry, is a packaging material with preferential permeability during the ageing of cheese. This material allows permeation of the carbon dioxide formed during the ageing process of Cheddar and Gouda cheese, yet prevents oxygen ingress from the outside.

4.3.3.2 Oxygen scavenging. Another new trend in barrier packaging materials concerns chemical barriers or oxygen-absorbing materials. These materials can be effectively used together with modified atmosphere packaging techniques. These chemical barriers are used together with the so-called physical barriers, such as PVdC or EVOH. One example is the 'OXBAR' system, with PET as the main component (96%), poly-metaxylylene adipamide (MXD-6) as the oxidisable component (4%) and an organic cobalt salt added as the oxidising catalyst at a 50–200 ppm level. This composition can be extruded to make blown bottles, which are said to be able to maintain the oxygen level inside the container at as low as 0% for two years (Yoshii, 1992). Barrier life time is a function of two main variables: scavenging capacity and rate of consumption. The former depends on the composition of the blend (MXD-6 and cobalt salt content) and the latter, the wall thickness of the container and the environmental conditions. Another example is an oxygen-absorbing plastic called 'Long Life', which can extend the shelf life of oxygen-sensitive drinks. This material is said to be insoluble in water and of a structure similar to that of haemoglobin (Yoshii, 1992). The hydroxyl groups of the base polymer react with silica, which also combines with a metal to form a complex.

Another method for actively controlling the oxygen level in a food package is to use an enzyme reactor surface, which will react with certain substrates to scavenge incoming oxygen. A new active packaging system developed by PharmaCal Co. (USA) utilises glucose oxidase and catalase enzymes for the removal of oxygen from liquid products (Yoshii, 1992).

There is one commercial application that uses a mixed iron powder–calcium hydroxide sachet in which both oxygen and carbon dioxide are scavenged (Labuza and Breene, 1989). It is being used to pack fresh ground coffee in flexible bags. This packaging system is said to more than triple the shelf life of the product. Other chemical scavenger systems include reactive dyes, ascorbic acid and cathecol-based reducers.

4.3.3.3 Temperature-compensating films. A newly developed film called 'Intelimer' has a temperature 'switch' point at which the permeation of the film changes abruptly. The switching mechanism is accomplished by the long-chain fatty alcohol-based polymeric side chains patented by the Landec Corporation (Figure 4.1). Below a preset temperature, these side chains are crystalline and provide a relatively effective gas barrier. However, above this preset temperature, these side chains convert reversibly to an amorphous structure, which is up to 1000 times more permeable to gas and may be tailored to the very large increase in respiration rates of fresh produce at temperatures above 5°C (Day, 1993). Because the change is physical and not chemical, this process is continuously

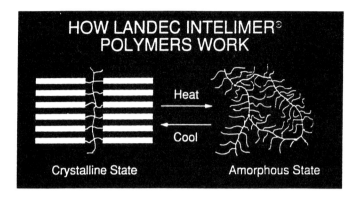

Figure 4.1 At a specified temperature the side chains of the Intelimer® film melt and convert to an amorphous structure that renders the film gas permeable (Anon, 1992).

reversible. The transition point can be moved by increasing or reducing the average number of carbon atoms in a chain. The switch point may be set anywhere between 0 and 45.5°C, and controlled within 2°C. The switch also changes the adhesiveness and stiffness of the film. Intelimer films are intended to be used for packaging highly respiring produce, but commercialisation is still several years away (Anon, 1992).

Another temperature-compensating film for produce has recently been patented and relies on the same principle as a bimetallic strip, but uses two different plastics films instead of two metals. Temperature sensitive apertures are cut into laminated plastics film in the form of small strips or 'petals'. At a selected temperature, the laminated film is flat and has minimum opening area. However, at higher temperatures the free area for gas exchange increases as the petals curl, and the permeability of the film can be engineered to increase proportionally to the rise in the respiration rate of the produce. The rate of curl is a function of the coefficient of expansion of the two separate films, and the extent of opening is controlled by the length and shape of the petals surrounding the aperture.

4.3.3.4 Moisture absorbers. Humidity will build up in the headspace of a food package either due to respiring produce or due to water vapour from moist foods. This in time will allow the growth and development of microorganisms. A desiccant film or sachet can be used to overcome this problem (Geeson *et al.*, 1985). A Japanese company has developed a film which is made into a pillow with entrapped propylene glycol (Labuza and Breene, 1989). When placed in contact with the surface of meat or fish, it absorbs water and slows the growth of spoilage bacteria.

4.3.4 Modified atmosphere packaging (MAP)

MAP is defined as the enclosing of food products in an atmosphere inside gas-barrier materials, in which the gaseous environment has been modified to slow down respiration rate, microbial growth and reduce enzymic degradation, all with the intention of extending the shelf life (Parry, 1993). Such modifications usually result in a reduced oxygen content in the head-space atmosphere, but increased carbon dioxide and nitrogen levels.

Carbon dioxide is the most important constituent in the gas mixture. Several factors influence the antimicrobial effect of carbon dioxide, specifically the microbial load, gas concentration, temperature and pack-aging film permeability. To be effective against aerobic spoilage micro-organisms, a concentration of 20–60% carbon dioxide is required in the package headspace (Greengrass, 1993). One of the most important factors influencing the antimicrobial effect of carbon dioxide is the permeability of the packaging film (Gill, 1990). The success or failure of MAP for foods depends on the impermeability of the packaging materials to both oxygen and carbon dioxide, in order that the correct gas mixture in the package headspace can be maintained. In addition, films used in MAP packaging should have low water vapour transmission rates (WVTRs), so as to minimise changes in moisture content inside the pack.

Plastics commonly used for gas packaging of foods include polyester, PP, PVdC, EVOH, and PE. Since all of the desired characteristics of a packaging film, i.e. strength, impermeability, and heat sealability, are seldom found in one single material, separate materials are laminated to one another to produce films with the desired characteristics for gas packaging of foods. Examples of such laminated structures include nylon/PE, nylon/PVdC/PE and nylon/EVOH/PE. Such composite structures have the desired characteristics for the gas packaging of food products: strength is provided by the outermost layer of nylon; gas and moisture vapour barrier is provided by EVOH and PVdC; and heat sealability by PE (Brody, 1989).

Development of optimum gas packaging materials is even more challenging for fruits and vegetables as these products respire. The ideal packaging material for gas packaging of these products must be able to keep low oxygen concentrations within the package headspace while preventing the build-up of high carbon dioxide concentrations. Packaging films commonly used to achieve such a balance include LDPE and PVC (Zagory and Kader, 1988). Packaging films with the correct permeability must be chosen to avoid depletion of oxygen and accumulation of carbon dioxide caused by respiring products. Recently developed highly permeable microperforated films such as P-Plus and Crop appear to be most suitable at present (Gill, 1990; Geeson et al., 1988). These films allow the product to breathe as it ripens inside the package.

A key feature of the MAP described below is the controlled permeation of O_2 and CO_2, as well as the scavenging of ethylene or controlled release of other compounds which could have a preservative effect on the food (Labuza and Breene, 1989). One way of controlling the oxygen level directly in a package is to use an oxygen scavenger system (Takahashi *et al.*, 1984). The simplest scavenger is reduced iron. The amount of iron needed depends on the initial oxygen level in the headspace, the amount dissolved in the food and the oxygen transmission rate of the film (Labuza and Breene, 1989). One gram of iron will react with 300 cm³ of oxygen. The iron is separated from the food by being kept in a small highly oxygen-permeable pouch.

4.3.5   Aseptic/ultra-high temperature (UHT) packaging

Packaging materials for aseptic processing/packaging must be sterilisable, suitable for aseptic filling and permit the maintenance of sterility of the product during storage and handling (Smith *et al.*, 1990a). Glass containers offer similar advantages as metal containers, but have the additional disadvantages of fragility and high density. Plastics materials offer versatility, but cannot be used alone as they do not possess all of the required properties. Consequently, they must be laminated to other materials to give packages with the appropriate requirements.

At present, the Tetra Pak concept, using a paperboard-foil-plastics laminate, is widely used for aseptic packaging. This laminated structure consists of as many as six layers of materials: PP, Surlyn, foil, PE, paperboard, and PE as the inner food contact layer. Other combinations that can be used include laminations of EVOH, PE and PS; or a metallised polyester. Aluminium foil is the most commonly used barrier material. PP or PE, i.e. polyolefins, are the most common heat sealing and food contact materials used. Foils need to be protected from mechanical damage, and protection is usually provided by paperboard which also gives rigidity. All of the composite materials described act as barriers to moisture, oxygen, light and microbes, and have the strength and heat sealability needed for aseptic packaging.

A review of aseptic processing has been made by Lopez (1987). Historical perspectives on aseptic packaging technology and the use of plastics packaging materials are further described in other recent publications (Downes, 1989; Eidman, 1989; Fox, 1989; Kern, 1989).

4.3.6   Sous vide (vacuum cooking/packaging) technology

There has been a tremendous increase in recent years in the use of 'sous vide' processing technology to extend shelf life and maintain the quality of fresh food (Smith *et al.*, 1990b). This technology has been developed in response to consumer demands for ready-to-eat, microwaveable, convenience foods with extended shelf life, that retain 'closer-to-fresh' characteristics. The term sous vide means 'under vacuum'. In sous vide processing, foods are cooked in sealed, evacuated, heat-stable pouches or thermoformed trays in such a way that much of the natural flavour, aroma and nutritional quality is retained by the product. This technique requires highly controlled packaging/cooking conditions. Packaging materials used in sous vide processing must withstand pasteurisation and chill temperatures as well as protecting and maintaining product quality.

4.3.7 *Edible films*

Recently, an edible film of polysaccharides has been used in certain packaging applications (LaBell, 1991). The polysaccharide film looks like a plastics film. The edible polysaccharide beads are seamless spheres of polysaccharide measuring 1–8 mm in diameter, which are dissolved by heat and moisture. Dry ingredients, such as spices and seasoning mixes, can be portion-packed in edible film pouches. The entire pouch can be added, for instance, to a soup, and it will dissolve quickly. However, the polysaccharide films are more permeable to gases than plastics films. In addition, their tensile strength is not as high as that of plastics films. This will create problems in automatic form/fill/seal machines.

In Japan, edible polysaccharide films are already widely used in the meat industry for packing of processed meats, such as ham and poultry products (Labell, 1991). Processors can wrap the meat in edible film before smoking and steaming. The smoke flavour permeates the film during the smoking process and the film dissolves during steaming. The surface structure and texture of the finished ham are improved. Also, yields are better, as less moisture is lost during processing.

The shelf life of fresh fruit and vegetables can be extended by using an edible film. Plastics films can be used to provide a gas barrier to protect the products, but moisture from the packed material will collect inside the film. An edible packaging film will gradually absorb the moisture given off from the product, preventing it from accumulating inside the package. This would lead to reduced risk of mould growth. Eventually, the moisture absorbed may cause the film to dissolve.

4.4 The influence of 'scalping' on food

As plastics packaging is becoming more widely used for direct contact with foods, compatibility with the food must be considered. The sorption of flavour compounds, or scalping, is one of the most important compatibility problems. The problem of aroma absorption by plastics packages has been recognised for many years. The tendency towards absorption varies with the type of plastics. For example, polyolefins can absorb certain flavour constituents selectively from products (Foster, 1987).

The quality of juices packed in aseptic cartons has been the subject of intensive research in recent years. Early work focused on volatile absorption from sources external to the package (Gilbert and Pegaz, 1969). Haydanek *et al.* (1970) and Gilbert *et al.* (1982) examined the volatile uptake by various packaging materials. PE and PP have been used widely in contact with food in packages due to their low costs, heat sealability and relative lack of additives, but they are particular susceptible to pervasion by organic vapours. The use of PE and PP in plastics packages has raised questions concerning sorption of intrinsic food flavours (Durr *et al.*, 1981).

4.4.1 The limonene controversy

Most juices that are filled aseptically are packed into laminated carton packages such as the Tetra Pak or Combibloc, in which the food contact material is PE (Mannheim *et al.*, 1987). Mannheim found that the product shelf life of orange and grapefruit juices was significantly shorter in laminated cartons than in glass jars. Moshonas and Shaw (1989), Mannheim *et al.* (1988) and Sizer *et al.* (1988) have investigated how aseptic packaging can affect the quality of citrus products, with the emphasis on flavour loss. Hirose *et al.* (1988), Shimoda *et al.* (1984) and Durr and Schobinger (1981) have studied the sorption of citrus flavour components by packaging materials. Baner *et al.* (1991) found that the food contact layer, usually polyethylene, largely controlled the sorption behaviour. This means that any improvements of flexible materials regarding aroma sorption must come from new food contact layers and not from new barrier layers.

Citrus flavour has often been used in model systems for flavour absorption studies (Durr and Schobinger, 1981; Marshall *et al.*, 1985; Hirose *et al.*, 1988; Kwapong and Hotchkiss, 1987). (+)-Limonene, the predominant volatile in citrus oils and essences, is often used as a probe compound in such studies. Compositionally, limonene is a non-polar, unsaturated terpene hydrocarbon. Many flavour compounds contain an ester, alcohol, and other polar functional groups. Essential oils from citrus fruit consist of terpenes, sesquiterpenes, oxygenated terpenoids, and non-volatile components. The oxygenated compounds are important contributors to the citrus flavour (Moshonas and Lund, 1969). Many research groups have reported that polar compounds are absorbed to a much lower extent in PE than limonene and other hydrocarbon volatiles. An understanding of the differences between various plastics materials as regards the sorption of essential oil constituents could help the processor reduce the flavour absorption problems.

4.4.2 The influence of pulp content on scalping

Shimoda *et al.* (1984) showed that in juice from satsuma mandarins, the limonene sorption by plastics is lower in the presence of juice pulp. Maeda *et al.* (1984) and Osajima (1983) reported that a low pulp content in orange juice resulted in higher absorption of aroma compounds. This is in agreement with the results of Gherardi (1982) and Granzer (1982). Fruit juice volatiles remain stable in the juice while they are absorbed by or suspended in the pulp (Yamada *et al.*, 1992). However, the amount of pulp, such as cellulose powder, which must be added if it is to be used to control the sorption of volatiles by LDPE is large.

4.4.3 Comparison of instrumental and sensory analysis

Mannheim *et al.* (1985) documented changes in aseptically packed citrus juices by sensory as well as chemical analysis. They related loss of orange juice flavour to the absorption of (+)-limonene into the polyolefin packaging material. However, in a comparison of the sensory quality of orange juice stored in polyethylene-lined paperboard cartons at different temperatures, Durr *et al.* (1981) reported the temperature to be the main variable affecting the flavour, even though orange oil expressed in terms of limonene was absorbed by the polyolefin food contact layer. They suggested that limonene absorption was an advantage, since limonene was known to be a precursor of off-flavour compounds. They also reported that desirable aroma volatiles were practically unabsorbed.

Although it is well documented that certain constituents of orange juice are absorbed by polymeric materials and that the absorption of flavour compounds changes the aroma profile (Mannheim *et al.*, 1985), it has not been established unequivocally that these changes are caused by absorption of odour-active constituents of orange juice (Marin *et al.*, 1992).

Most reported studies on flavour scalping in orange juice were performed with model solutions, not actual orange juice, or with orange juice which had not been commercially produced and packaged (Pieper *et al.*, 1992). Many of the investigations too, were performed without sensory evaluation. Pieper *et al.* (1992) showed that a sensory panel could not distinguish between orange juice stored in glass bottles and juice stored in laminated paperboard packages with LDPE as the food contact plastic, even though absorption of up to 50% of the (+)-limonene and small amounts of aldehydes and alcohols by the packaging materials was observed.

Marin *et al.* (1992) exposed plastics packaging materials, i.e. PE and Surlyn, to orange juice and measured the changes in the limonene content of the juice using a gas chromatograph equipped with a flame ionisation detector (GC–FID). They determined the components which were most important to the aroma using gas chromatography–olfactometry (GCO). More than 70% of the limonene content was absorbed by the plastics in 24 hours at 25°C. However, results from the GCO analysis indicated that the limonene had only trace odour activity. Furthermore, the plastics did not substantially alter the odour-active components detected in orange juice. These reports emphasise the importance of using real food systems whenever possible, and supplementing the instrumental analysis with organoleptic evaluation.

4.4.4 Influence of scalping on barrier and mechanical properties

As has been shown in the reports outlined above, the scalping process may not alter the sensory quality of packed juices. However, absorption of flavour components by the package may alter the mechanical properties of the plastics, causing delamination, or modifying the barrier properties of the packaging materials. Miltz *et al.* (1990) showed that the absorption of (+)-limonene increased the oxygen permeability of the three plastics films used. If the efficiency by which a packaging material reduces the entry of oxygen into the package is impaired, foods sensitive to oxygen will deteriorate quickly. The result will be a shortened shelf life of the product.

4.4.5 Methods of suppressing scalping

Yamada *et al.* (1992) suggested methods of suppressing the sorption of volatiles by the food contact layer.

1. Sorption of volatiles could be reduced considerably by reducing the thickness of the heat seal layer. This could, however, cause the sorbed compounds to permeate the polyolefin layer and change the structure and properties of the barrier layer, or result in delamination of the laminate.
2. Sorption of volatiles could also be reduced by using a food contact layer that has already absorbed some fruit juice essence (i.e. presorption).

Treatments of the plastics surface and judicious selection of materials, such as use of plastics with crystalline polymers (Shimoda *et al.*, 1988), use of polymer blends (Subramanian, 1990), fluorination of plastics surfaces (Hobbs *et al.*, 1990), and inert coatings, e.g. silica, on the plastics surfaces (Charara, 1987) have also been proposed in the literature to circumvent the scalping of flavour compounds from food products.

4.5 Flavour transfer problems in refillable PET bottles

The debate about the environmental impact of packages and the demands for reuse and recycling of packages have led to the development of the refillable PET bottle system for soft drinks. All refillable systems involve certain problems with regard to product safety. Legislation and hygiene are essential aspects in this context. The washing procedure is a particularly critical step in the refilling of PET bottles, due to the limited heat resistance of the packaging material. To avoid shrinkage of the bottle the temperature must not exceed 58–59°C. It is crucial to the sensory quality of the packed product that aroma compounds from one product are not absorbed by the material and then transferred to the next product filled in the bottle. Numerous chemical substances can be absorbed in the PET material (Figure 4.2), and some of these compounds may impart off-flavours to subsequent fillings.

In order to assess the risk of flavour transfer between products when a returnable PET bottle is refilled with a different soft drink, sensory

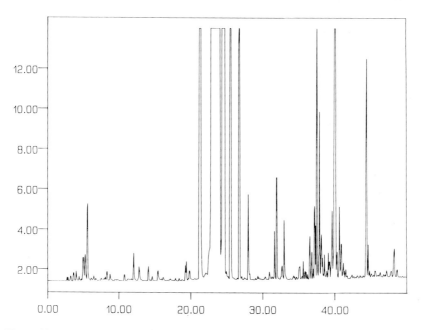

Figure 4.2 Gas chromatogram of a headspace sample of a PET bottle that has been filled with a citrus drink.

analyses are performed. First the bottle is filled with the test product. After storage the bottle is emptied, washed and refilled with the second product on which the assessment of possible flavour transfer will be made. Different kinds of soft drinks such as citrus drink, cola and mineral water have been used as the second fillings. For each of these products the intensity of any flavour transfer is evaluated separately. The test product will be approved for filling in returnable PET bottles only if it is approved in all the tests using the different soft drinks. Results so far showed that some products are unsuitable for the refilling system, especially those which have a very intense and strong flavour. For this reason some ciders and citrus fruit drinks have been rejected because some of their flavour has been detected in the second product filled in the bottle. Highly delicate products such as mineral water are to date only filled in new bottles.

To supplement the sensory evaluation of the soft drinks, chemical analyses are needed to determine which flavour/aroma compounds are absorbed by the PET material and eventually migrate into the product filled subsequently. If this could be done, the next step would be to investigate their role as flavour components in the soft drinks and, if possible, replace or reduce them. In a production situation, it will be important to have equipment set up to identify foreign odours prior to refilling in order to avoid customer-introduced contamination.

4.6 Conclusions

The sensory quality of a packaged food is the result of a complex interaction between the food, the pack and the environment. Substances from both the food and the environment can be absorbed/adsorbed in the packaging material. Such sorption from the food and the environment may not only change the taste of the food *per se* but also change the barrier and other physical characteristics of the packaging material. Changed barrier characteristics may result in a higher diffusion of oxygen into the package, resulting in the development of off-flavour due to oxidation of the food. The oxidation products may also, for better or worse, be absorbed into the packaging material. These interactions between aroma compounds, oxygen and the pack can result in a dynamic and time-dependent change of the food quality.

A number of sophisticated technical solutions to preserve food for a long time are available today. Whether or not these solutions are economically and environmentally acceptable or even marketable have to be considered for each specific application. It is pointless to make a completely impermeable package if the consumer refuses to buy the product because it is considered to be artificial (it will 'keep too long') or over-packaged (environmentally unsound) compared with other similar products on the market. In the future, it will be of increasing importance to a food manufacturer to use environmentally friendly packaging materials if he plans to stay in business. On the other hand, packaging in an environmentally friendly way cannot be allowed to comprise the fundamental requirement of having always to ensure the safety and quality of the food.

In addition to such obvious considerations as keeping the food microbiologically safe, a food manufacturer has to decide what his product should taste like, and the length of time it should remain acceptable. Once these decisions have been made, an economically and environmentally suitable packaging solution can be sought. To stay in business, food manufacturers and packaging suppliers must co-operate in order to face up to the demands of the product, the demands of the environment and the expectation of the consumer.

Finally, it should always be remembered that the ultimate decision is made by the consumer in terms of whether to buy or not to buy.

References

Anon (1992) Temperature compensating films for produce. *Prepared Foods*, **95**, 82.

Baner, A.L., Kalyankar, V. and Shoun, L.H. (1991) Aroma sorption evaluation of aseptic packaging. *J. Food Sci.*, **56** (4), 1051.

Brody, A.L. (1989) Flavor interacts with packaging. *Prepared Foods*, pp. 128, 158.

Brydson, J.A. (1982) *Plastics Materials*, 4th edn, Butterworth Scientific, Oxford.

Charara, Z.N. (1987) Evaluation of orange flavor absorption into polymeric packaging materials, *MS Thesis*, University of Florida, Gainesville.

Day, D.P.F. (1993) *Modified atmosphere packaging–state of the art*. SIK MAP Seminar, April 27th, Gothenburg, Sweden.

Downes, T.W. (1989) Food Packaging in the IFT Era: Five decades of unprecedented growth and change. *Food Technol.*, **43**(9), 228.

Durr, P. and Schobinger, U. (1981) The contribution of some volatiles to the sensory quality of apple and orange juice odor, in *Flavour '81*, (ed. J. Schreier), Walter de Gruyter and Co., Berlin, p. 179.

Durr, P., Schobinger, U. and Waldvogel, R. (1981) Aroma quality of orange juice after filling and storage in soft packages and glass bottles. *Alimenta*, **20**, 91.

Eidman, A.L. (1989) Advance in barrier plastics. *Food Technol.*, **43**(12), 91.

Foster, R.H. (1987) Ethylene vinyl alcohol copolymer resins for better solvent, aroma and flavor barrier. *Future-Pack '87, 5th International conference on packaging innovations*, Ryder Associates, Atlanta, Georgia.

Fox, R.A. (1989) Plastics packaging – The consumer preference of tomorrow. *Food Technol.*, **43**(12), 34.

Geeson, J., Everson, H. and Browne, M. (1988) Microperforated films for fresh produce. *Grower*, **109**(14), 31.

Geeson, J.D., Browne, K., Maddison, J., Sheppard, H. and Guraldi, F. (1985) Modified atmospheric packaging to extend shelf life of tomatoes. *J. Food Tech.*, **20**, 339.

Gherardi, D.S. (1982) Packaging and quality. *Proceedings of the International Congress of Fruit Juice Producers*, Munich, Germany.

Gilbert, S.G. and Pegaz, D. (1969) Find new way to measure gas permeability. *Package Engineering*, Jan., 66.

Gilbert, S.G., Harzidimitriu, E., Lai, C. and Passy, N. (1982) Study of barrier properties of polymeric films to various organic aromatic vapors, in *Instrumental Analyses of Food* (eds G. Charalambous and G. Inglett), Vol. 1, 405.

Gill, M. (1990) High permeability films for MAP of fresh produce. *International Conference on MAP*. Campden Food and Drink Research Association, Chipping Campden, Gloucestershire.

Granzer, R. (1982) *Proceedings of the International Congress of Fruit Juice Producers*, Munich.

Greengrass, J. (1993) Films for MAP of foods, in *Principles and Applications of Modified Atmosphere Packaging of Foods* (ed. R.T. Parry), Blackie Academic & Professional, Glasgow, 63–100.

Haydanek, M.G., Woolford, G. and Baugh, L.B. (1970) Premiums and coupons as potential sources of objectionable flavor in cereal products. *J. Food Sci.*, **44**(3), 850.

Hirose, K., Harte, B., Giacin, J., Miltz, J. and Stine, C. (1988) Sorption of d-limonene by sealant films and effect on mechanical properties, in *Food and Packaging Interactions* (ed. J. Hotchkiss), ACS Symposium Series 365, Washington DC.

Hobbs, J.P., Anand, M. and Campion, B.A. (1990) Fluorinated high-density polyethylene barrier containers, in *Barrier Polymers and Structures* (ed. W.J. Koros), ACS Symposium Series 423, Washington DC.

Kern, C.L. Jr. (1989) High-performance polyester for food and beverage packaging. *Food Technol.*, **43**(12), 93.

Kwapong, O.Y. and Hotchkiss, J.H. (1987) Comparative sorption of aroma compounds by polyethylene and ionomer food contact plastics. *J. Food Sci.*, **52**(3), 761.

LaBell, F. (1991) Edible packaging. *Food Proc.*, **52**(12), 24.

Labuza, T.P. and Breene, W.M. (1989) Applications of 'active packaging' for improvement of shelf-life and nutritional quality of fresh and extended shelf-life food. *J. Food Proc. Preserv.*, **13**(1), 31.

Lopez, A.A. (1987) *A Complete Course in Canning and Related Processing*, 12th edn; The Canning Trade Inc., Baltimore, Maryland.

Maeda, H., Takahashi, Y. and Ifuku, Y. (1984) Adsorption of citrus nastsudaidai Hayata juice with polyvinyl pyrrolidone, Nylon 66 and high porous polymer. *Nippon Shokuhin Kogyo Gakkaishi*, **26**, 1.

Mannheim, C.H., Miltz, J., Ben-Aryie, G. and Lavie, R. (1985) *Interaction Between Carton Packages and Aseptically Packed Citrus Juice*. Presented at the 45th Annual IFT National Meeting, Atlanta, Abstract 131.

Mannheim, C.H., Miltz, J. and Letzer, A. (1987) Interaction between polyethylene laminated cartons and aseptically packed citrus juices. *J. Food Sci.*, **52**(3), 737.

Mannheim, C.H., Miltz, J. and Passy, N. (1988) Interaction between aseptically filled citrus products and laminated structures, in *Food and Packaging Interactions* (ed. J. Hotchkiss), ACS Symposium Series 365, Washington DC.

Marin, A.B., Acree, T.E., Hotchkiss, J.H. and Nagy, S. (1992) Gas chromatography-olfactometry of orange juice to assess the effects of plastic polymers on aroma character. *J. Agric. Food Chem.*, **40**, 650.

Marshall, M.R., Adams, J.P. and Williams, J.W. (1985) Flavor absorption by aseptic packaging material. *Proceedings ASEPTIPAK 85*, Princeton, New Jersey.

Meadows, P. (1991) Building barriers. *Packaging Today*, **October**, 59.

Miltz, J. (1992) Food packaging, in *Handbook of Food Engineering* (eds D.R. Heldman and D.B. Lund), Marcel Dekker, New York.

Miltz, J., Mannheim, C.H. and Harte, B.R. (1990) Packaging of juices using polymeric barrier containers, in *Barrier Polymers and Structures* (ed. W.J. Koros), ACS Symposium Series 423, Washington DC.

Moshonas, M.G. and Lund, E.D. (1969) Aldehydes, ketones and esters in Valencia orange peel. *J. Food Sci.*, **34**(2), 502.

Moshonas, M.G. and Shaw, P.E. (1989) Flavor evaluation and volatile flavor constituents of stored aseptically packaged orange juice. *J. Food Sci.*, **54**.

Osajima, Y. (1983) *Study on the Influence of Plastic Films Against the Food Aroma*, Japan Food Industry Bulletin.

Parry, R.T. (ed.) (1993) *Principles and Applications of Modified Atmosphere Packaging of Foods*, Blackie Academic & Professional, Glasgow.

Pieper, G., Borgudd, L., Ackermann, P. and Fellers, P. (1992) Absorption of aroma volatiles of orange juice into laminated carton packages did not affect sensory quality. *J. Food Sci.*, **57**(6), 1408.

Rice, J. (1992a) Silica-coated plastic packaging. *Food Proc. (Am.)*, **53**(6), 78.

Rice, J. (1992b) Silica-coated films to go commercial in '93. *Food Proc. (Am.)*, **53**(10), 82.

Shimoda, M., Ikegami, T. and Osajima, Y. (1988) Sorption of flavor compounds in aqueous solution into polyethylene film. *J. Food Sci. Agric.*, **42**, 157.

Shimoda, M., Nintanda, T., Kadota, N., Otha, H., Suetsuna, K. and Osajima, Y. (1984) Adsorption of satsuma mandarin juice aroma on plastic films. *J. Jpn. Soc. Food Sci. Technol.*, **31**, 67.

Shorten, D.W. (1982) Polyolefins for food packaging. *Food Chem.*, **8**, 109.

Sizer, C.E., Waugh, P.L., Edstam, S. and Ackermann, P. (1988) Maintaining flavor and nutrient quality of aseptic orange juice. *Food Technol.*, **42**, 429.

Smith, J.P., Ramaswamy, H.S. and Simpson, B.K. (1990a) Development in food packaging technology. Part 1: processing/cooking considerations. *Trends Food Sci. Technol.*, **Nov**, 107.

Smith, J.P., Ramaswamy, H.S. and Simpson, B.K. (1990b) Developments in food packaging technology. Part 2: storage aspects. *Trends Food Sci. Technol.*, **Nov.**, 111.

Sneller, J.A. (1986) Smart films give a big lift to controlled atmospheric packaging. *Modern Plastics*, **August**, 58.

Subramanian, P.M. (1990) Polymer blends – Morphology and solvent barriers, in *Barrier Polymers and Structures* (ed. W.J. Koros), ACS Symposium Series 423, Washington DC.

Takahashi, J., Yuda, S. and Yanagslawa, H. (1984) Oxygen scavenger systems. *Japan Food Packaging*, **28**, 40.

Turtle, I. (1987) The use of flexible plastics for food packaging. *Food Technology International Europe*, Sterling Publications, London, pp. 289–96.

Wolpert, V.M. (1987) Oxygen scavenging for extended shelf life. *Paper, Film and Converter*, **12**.

Yamada, K., Mita, K., Yoshida, K. and Ishitani, T. (1992) A study of the absorption of fruit juice volatiles by the sealant layer in flexible packaging containers (The effect of package on quality of fruit juice, part 4). *Packaging Technol. Sci.*, **5**, 41.

Yokoyama, T. (1992) Food packaging overview. *Packag. Japan*, **13** (68), 25.

Yoshii, J. (1990) Smokable casing Krehalon, 'SMO Casing'. *Packag. Japan*, **11**(55), 35.

Yoshii, J. (1992) Recent trends in food packaging development in consideration of environment. *Packag. Japan*, **13**(67), 74.

Zagory, D. and Kader, A.A. (1988) Modified atmosphere packaging of fresh produce. *Food Technol.*, **42**(9), 70.

5 Preservation technology and shelf life of fish and fish products

D.M. GIBSON

5.1 Introduction

The food matrix has a positive rather than simply a passive role in preservation methods because it interacts with the microbial flora responsible for its deterioration and can moderate by compartmentalisation within its structure the chemical, biochemical and physical changes which take place during storage.

Fish and fish products will be used here as examples of past, current and proposed technologies for food preservation and for methods to assess their effectiveness. Most technologies have been applied to try to reduce the perishability of fish and hence increase the short shelf life. It is a worldwide resource with a current yield of about 100 million tonnes per annum. Utilising this resource tests food technologies to their limit. Harvesting is unpredictable; catches may yield gluts or there may be shortages. The species mix, the size mix, the intrinsic condition of fish are all uncontrollable, yet the products have to compete in sophisticated international markets, as well as meet local needs. Farmed fish is an increasing resource; husbandry techniques are still evolving and there are considerable problems of losses caused by diseases to the stock, by escape to the environment, and by predators such as birds and sea mammals. As many farms are located in regions remote from the processing factories and markets, the logistics of supply are not simple. Fish is sold as whole fish or fillets, fresh or frozen, smoked, dried, salted, fermented, marinaded, as added value products, and in recipe dishes mixed with other ingredients. These products may only have been available in restaurants a few years ago, that is, prepared for immediate consumption, but now are sold in supermarkets and given substantial shelf lives.

Food poisoning consequent to the consumption of fish is relatively rare, except in countries where much fish is consumed raw. Thus, fish is implicated in 2% of food linked diseases in the UK, but in 11% of outbreaks in the USA, 20% of those in Australia, and 70% in Japan. Illness is attributed to bacteria, their toxins, viruses, algal toxins, parasites, and to heavy metal ions. Shelf life can be limited by spoilage or by safety considerations. Fisheries can be closed either temporarily as in the case of algal blooms or permanently where pollution, for example, by mercuric or cadmium ions, has been detected.

This chapter describes, in an illustrative manner, the technologies which are or could be applied to fish and fish products and their effects on the shelf life of the products. Despite the diversity of the resource there is a remarkable uniformity in the effects of applied technologies. Indeed, the same principles and considerations can easily be applied to other foods.

5.2 Properties and spoilage of fish

Fish are cold blooded aquatic vertebrates broadly classified as bony such as cod, salmon, and herring or cartilaginous such as the skates, rays and sharks. Their sizes range from a few centimeters to meters, and their shapes from round to flat. The edible tissue is about 50% of the live weight. Some of the remainder is used, for example oils are extracted from the livers, but most is discarded. It can be converted to animal feed or fertiliser in the form of fish meal or silage. The edible portion is mainly muscle which is arranged in conical structures. During life, this flesh is sterile, protected by the skin through which antimicrobial compounds, such as lysozyme, are secreted, and by antibodies in the blood.

Regarding composition, fish are classified as lean, being 20% protein, <5% lipid, with little carbohydrate, or fatty with 10–30% lipid. Their lipid content varies with season or availability of food. When the lipid content is high, the water content is low, as the sum of lipid plus water is usually 80%. The low molecular weight pool represents 1–3% by weight and is significant for shelf life, being the readily available nutrients for bacteria. The pH of the flesh is near neutral. It is highly buffered, due to the protein content, phosphates, and creatine, a muscle constituent. The oxidation–reduction potential during life is relatively low due to the environment.

The intrinsic condition of fish, that is the biological condition on harvesting or capture, varies with season depending on spawning and migratory cycles, and with method of fishing, as exhausted fish may be in poor condition or damaged. Also, large catches cannot be handled sufficiently quickly.

As with all forms of life, harvesting causes death which is characterised by a cessation of the supply of energy to the organism. During life, food is consumed, digested to small molecules, some of which are used as carbon and nitrogen sources for the biosynthesis of macromolecules and tissues, and others to provide energy for this. Tissue turnover also occurs. On death of the animal, food supply ceases as does the supply of energy, but turnover of molecules can continue. Energy reserves are used up and so the natural integrity and defences of the animal deteriorate. For example, cell membranes are no longer energised and molecules and ions can freely diffuse; antimicrobials are no longer produced nor distributed. Bacteria which have been kept on the outside surfaces (skin, intestines, gills) by secretions, can penetrate the skin and flesh. The purely biochemical and chemical changes in the tissue cannot be arrested by the application of preservation technologies, only slowed by temperature effects on their kinetics, except by drastically altering the material, as for example by cooking. Technologies can have effects on the activities of bacteria. It has been shown for many foods that biochemical changes which may reduce their desirability as foods do not cause sufficient changes such that they are regarded as spoiled. It is the effects of bacteria found on the raw materials or in the environment in which they are processed, that cause the sensory changes resulting in spoilage. Within the microflora, it is recognised that only a proportion of the bacterial types present is responsible for producing the off-odours, flavours, appearance and textural changes which constitute spoiled fish.

How can spoilage be characterised and measured? Systematic studies by technologists have resulted in quality assessment schemes which are used by industry and by regulators. The changing sensory features have been described in detail for many species and an example is given in Table 5.1. For non-destructive testing, the odour of the gills has been considered the

Table 5.1 Score sheet for sensory changes of white fish

Raw Quality	Score	Gill odour	General appearance
Fresh	10	Seaweed, sharp metallic	Convex eyes, shiny red blood, flesh translucent
Spoiling	7	Bland, loss of tanginess	Eyes flat, dull skin, no translucence
Stale	5	Milky, mousy, yeasty	Sunken eyes, browning of gills, opaque mucus, waxy flesh
Putrid	3	Acetic acid, 'old boots', sour sink	Eyes very sunken, yellowing flesh, brown blood, yellow bacterial slime

Cooked Quality	Score	Odour/flavour	Texture
Fresh	10	Slight sweet/meaty	Dry
Spoiling	7	Bland/neutral	Firm/succulent
Stale	5	Some amines, 'off'	Softening
Putrid	3	Bitter, sulphides	Mushy

most reliable and reproducible. The cooked flavour of fish portions, steamed or microwaved without added condiments, is the most precise. Tasting requires a group or panel of people to reduce individual bias. Scoring systems have been devised. Flavour, odour and appearance descriptions are agreed by the panel, the actual words having little true meaning, being memory aids, and scores given such that there is a linear relationship between the change in score with storage time at a constant temperature. It is evident from Table 5.1 that sensory characteristics such as flavour have more distinct stages than others such as appearance and texture.

The organoleptic changes are caused by bacteria. In fish taken from temperate marine waters, the active bacteria are psychrotrophic or cold loving, well adapted to growth under chill conditions. They have one particular property which results in the high perishability or short shelf life of fish products. Marine fish contain trimethylamine oxide (TMAO), as an osmoregulator. Some bacteria can reduce this to trimethylamine which has the odour of stale fish. The bacteria can obtain energy from this reaction and use it as electron acceptor in the absence of oxygen. The system is similar to nitrate reduction and shares some components. Fresh water fish contain little TMAO and generally have a longer shelf life. The technologies for marine fish preservation are essentially those which reduce or eliminate the activities of the TMAO-reducing bacteria. There is little fermentation activity in the microflora, a well recognised source of energy in other foods. This is because of the low carbohydrate content of most fish. The concentration of TMA has been used as an index of spoilage either alone or as a component of 'total volatile bases', which includes ammonia and other amines. These have proved useful in research in comparative trials but less so in commerce due in part to batch to batch variability. In addition, because bacterial numbers show a lag (Figure 5.1) before increasing, chemical indices of bacterial activity are insensitive to changes in very fresh fish. Setting limits or standards for the permitted concentrations of such volatiles can be a problem with packaged fish where they accumulate to higher levels than in unpackaged fish for the same organoleptic quality because they can no longer vaporise and escape. An alternative chemical index is hypoxanthine, derived from the breakdown of adenosine triphosphate (ATP). This accumulates from the death of the fish and is applicable to marine and fresh water species. It shows some species variation to the differing concentrations of ATP during life. A more complex measurement is the 'K' value, based on ATP, adenosine diphosphate (ADP), adenosine monophosphate (AMP) and hypoxanthine. 'Total volatile bases' concentration and nucleotide metabolites are used as indices for other proteinaceous foods. Lipid oxidation can be measured by standard techniques such as malonaldehyde content or by HPLC methods but these are not generally used outside the research laboratory.

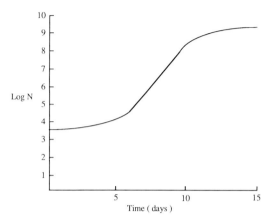

Figure 5.1 Changes in the number (N) of bacteria on fish stored at 0°C.

Storage trials and tests are usually done on products stored under the temperature conditions anticipated in industry. Accelerated tests done at higher temperatures are of little value for shelf life determination of fish as the developing microflora may differ and the pattern of spoilage may alter. Challenge testing for pathogen growth and survival, however, can be done in that way.

Spoilage results in changes in the electrical properties of the skin and tissue, due in part to membranes no longer being energised. Changes in the dielectric properties of whole fish and of skin-on portions can be made in an instant non-destructive manner using a handheld device such as a Torry Fish Freshness Meter (Figure 5.2). The measurements obtained relate more to an estimation of the remaining shelf life than to the lapsed shelf life. These instruments are used in some countries for sorting fish.

5.3   Conventionally preserved fish and fish products

Except for artisanal fisheries for purely local markets, most fish are chilled soon after capture with ice. They may be gutted, that is, have their intestines removed. For some species this is essential as otherwise the digestive enzymes and the bacteria in the gut would soon attack the flesh, although in others this may not be necessary due to the anatomical location of the gut cavity relative to the edible parts. In some fisheries, it is customary to wash the fish, to remove blood, remnants of guts and so on. However, washing can remove some of the natural antimicrobial secretions and may not be advantageous to the storage life. The importance of rapid chilling cannot be overstressed. Chilling reduces the rates of chemical and biochemical reactions. Microbial growth is slowed or even stopped. However,

Figure 5.2 Torry Fish Freshness Meter in operation on cod boxed in ice.

because the temperature at which the fish live is, in many parts of the world, relatively low, chilling of fish does not have such a large effect as the chilling of meat from warm blooded animals. Ice is a very good coolant. It is also cheap; it must be made from pure, unpolluted and bacteria free water. It has a large heat absorbing capacity due to the latent heat of ice–water transition, and the melt water provides excellent contact with the fish. It is essential that this water can drain as fish spoil rapidly in stagnant water. Chilling reduces the temperature of fish to 0°C. If the temperature is reduced further, the effect on bacterial growth is greater. Marine fish do not freeze until −3°C. 'Superchilling' is being developed for other foods. Its usefulness depends on avoiding slow freezing or freeze–thaw cycles as this has a deleterious effect on the appearance and texture of the products. Chilled environments become colonised with a microflora well adapted for the conditions. Good hygienic practices are needed to reduce the possibility of contamination of products. This is achievable on land but is more difficult on board fishing vessels. Fish may spend 2 weeks stored at sea.

Freezing of fish, at sea or on land, is a well established technology. When frozen, bacterial growth ceases, however, chemical and biochemical reactions, including those carried out by microbial enzymes, can continue. During freezing, the formation of ice crystals results in a concentrated solution of substrates and enzymes. Rapid freezing is essential so that this 'soup' is inactivated as soon as possible. Not all the water is frozen even at $-20°C$. The main deteriorative effects on eating quality are toughening due to protein denaturation, more prominent at high ($-10°C$) and fluctuating temperatures, and rancidity due to lipid oxidation. Exclusion of oxygen, by suitable packaging or glazing, reduces this. Due to their high proportion of unsaturated fatty acid residues, fish lipids are particularly susceptible to oxidation. These non-microbial changes can reduce the future processability of the products and their consumer desirability. The temperature of storage for lean fish should be better than $-20°C$, for small fatty fish $-30°C$, and for large fatty fish such as tuna, $-70°C$. Freezing does not have a significant effect on killing bacteria on and in foods. Frozen and then thawed foods have similar bacterial numbers to the starting material. There may be an increase in the lag period before growth due to the thermal injury, but the damage to the food matrix probably allows easier access of the bacteria to their potential nutrients.

Smoking fish is a traditional method of preservation, done nowadays more for flavour than for long term preservation. The process consists in lightly salting the fish, smoking in a kiln at either low or high temperature, with simultaneous drying. The salting, done either by sprinkling dry salt on the surface or by immersion in strong salt solutions (brining) serves to inhibit the spoilage flora. The smoke vapours impart flavours to the product but are also inhibitory to bacteria due to their content of aldehydes, organic acids, and phenols. Some drying also occurs. Cold smoking, at temperatures of $25°C$, yields products with perhaps twice the shelf life of the raw material. The normal spoilage flora is partially inhibited and spoilage is initiated by yeast and moulds which are found in the wood shavings and sawdust used to generate the smoke. Final spoilage may be caused by bacteria which are no longer inhibited as the smoke components vaporise. These products generally require cooking before consumption. In hot smoking, temperatures $>60°C$ are reached and so the product is well pasteurised and cooked. Significant drying especially of the surface occurs. Spoilage, as characterised by amines or other off-odours, may take months to be noticeable.

Traditionally, fish have been heavily salted (salt content $>25\%$), and/or dried to a water content of $<25\%$. The microflora is inhibited by low water activity. Strictly speaking, the water activity is a concept which requires equilibrium conditions to be established. These high salt–low water conditions inhibit the normal flora. Spoilage can occur due to the activities of halophilic pink bacteria or some brown xerophilic moulds ('dun'), both originating in the salt. These products have a shelf life of years provided that they are protected from taking up moisture. They can only be produced in areas of low humidity; otherwise mechanical drying systems are needed.

Lowering the pH by fermentation or by the addition of organic acids

such as vinegar (acetic acid) is another traditional method of fish preservation. The spoilage flora is active in the pH range 5.5–8.5, and
TMAO reduction in the pH range 6.0–8.0. For safety reasons (see section
5.5), the pH of acidified products should be < pH 4.5. Because of the high
buffering capacity of fish tissue and low carbohydrate content of fish
flesh, fermentative microbes require the addition of sugars, to be effective.
Many fermented fish sauces are produced in the Orient. Marinaded
products are popular in some countries. Many additives such as herbs and
spices are added to enhance flavours. In Finland, a fish product, gefilde
fish, is made by raising the pH with alkali. This is an acquired taste, the
soapy flavour being unique.

Adequate thermal processing is another example of preservation used
with fish. This kills microbes and yields a stable product. A well established method of thermal processing is canning. Salmon, tuna, sardines
and pilchards are well known examples of canned fish. Because of the risk
of botulism (section 5.5), a full heat treatment (121°C, 15 min.) is
required. Thus only strongly flavoured species such as those listed are
canned. Others such as cod and sole develop undesirable characteristic
flavours. Breakup of structure and texture also limit the applicability of
canning.

Waste fish and excessive supplies of fish can be reduced to fish meal.
The raw material is cooked and then dried. High quality fish meals or
flours extracted from them have been used directly for human consumption. Lesser heat treatments are described in the following section.

5.4 Modern technologies

Probably the greatest change in the marketing of fish in recent years has
been the use of flexible packaging materials for chilled products. Prepackaged fish dominates sales in some countries, especially where traditional
fishmongers have lost out due to city centre redevelopments. Packaging
does not improve the quality of fish, only its presentation. The rate of
spoilage and therefore the shelf life of packaged and unwrapped fish is
generally similar. Extensions to shelf life claimed for certain types of
packaging depend on the definition of the quality level at the end of shelf
life. The end of shelf life is generally expressed in terms of taste panel
score. Public health authorities use a low score, equivalent to gill odour
or cooked flavour of 4.5 (see Table 5.1). At this stage, fish products have
a strong stale or putrid odour. Supermarket technologists reject fish at a
higher score, equivalent to 5.5 or 6.0. At this stage the product is stale.
Much of the claimed extension to shelf life due to packaging systems
occurs in this last region, spoilage being the same until staleness is evident
but at a slower rate in the stale to putrid stage. For some products and

for some markets this may well be acceptable, but in many instances, the quality is poorer than the retailer would wish. The main determinants of quality for packaged fish are the storage temperature and time. Vacuum packaging and modified atmosphere packaging have a role in the presentation of fish products, and in arresting rancidity changes, but not in maintaining high quality shelf life. On the other hand, if there is accidental temperature abuse, then the product would be less offensive for longer.

Pasteurisation of fish products can be done with heat or irradiation. There is a growing market for 'sous vide' products. These are partially cooked and require only reheating before consumption. The raw materials are vacuum packed and then heat treated. Fish cooks so quickly that the thermal process may be completed in a few minutes at 65–70°C. The normal spoilage flora is destroyed so that such products do not develop characteristic odours during storage. As the heat treatment is insufficient to destroy the spores of *C. botulinum* (section 5.5), limits must be set on the maximum time and temperature of storage.

Irradiation from cobalt-60 or other electron sources has been fully investigated. The process is bactericidal but the limiting factor is the development of off-odours and flavours caused by the process. These are described as being like burnt hair or feathers and are due to reactions of thiol groups. Sterilisation is therefore not practical. Pasteurisation, equivalent to a 3D process, that is reduction of the microbial load by a factor of 1000, is feasible and done in some countries yielding products with no appreciable irradiation odours. To be effective for shelf life extension, only fresh fish should be used. The spoilage flora is reduced, especially the bacteria able to reduce TMAO, and shelf lives similar to those obtainable with meat are possible. To prevent recontamination, products are packed. There is an effect on the appearance, in that juice or drip is released from the fish. There are no unequivocal tests for detecting irradiated fish. There is no improvement in the quality of the product due to the process so there is no possibility of poor quality spoiled fish being converted to good quality. However, there are said to be instances of poor quality fish having unexpectedly low bacterial counts.

There has been a huge increase in the amount of farmed fish being marketed worldwide. In temperate zones, the main species have been salmon and trout for which markets have had to be created. These species are sold in various retail forms, usually packed, as steaks, fillets, and especially smoked. Cold smoked salmon and hot smoked trout are sold vacuum packaged. Compared with wild caught fish, they have a comparatively long shelf life because the time between harvesting and processing is short, harvesting can be done according to demand, and much processing is done under contract. The shelf life limits are safety rather than quality related. Internationally, there are plans to transport farmed fish under

Table 5.2 Approximate shelf lives of various products

Product	Temperature (°C)	Shelf life (days)
Cod (raw)	0	16
	5	7
	10	4
	16	1
Herring (raw)	0	10
	5	4
Salmon (raw)	0	20
	10	5
Plaice (raw)	0	18
	10	8
Cod (smoked)	5	14
Kipper (smoked herring)	5	10
Salmon (smoked)	5	20
Cod (sous vide)	0	28
Cod (irradiated)	0	20
Cod (salted)	0	500
Herring (marinated)	5	100
Beef	0	40
Chicken	0	14
Bacon	5	21

controlled atmospheres. Probably, the close control of temperature in such systems will be more important than the gas mixture used, except perhaps for colour retention. Table 5.2. gives a summary of approximate shelf lives of various products achievable by different preservation technologies.

5.5 Sensory quality and safety

Sensory assessment schemes for fish have been referred to in section 5.2. Such scoring systems have been derived in research laboratories for research purposes, for example, to compare the technological quality of two treatments of fish. Consumer based quality testing, though not so well developed, is becoming more widely used. In extensive trials with cooked fish samples it was apparent that, in controlled triangular tests, many assessors had difficulty identifying the type of fish being presented let alone commenting on the quality. Preferences were found for all qualities of fish, and a significant proportion of assessors did not like fresh, technologically best quality, fish products. However, consumers do not generally like to meet strong ammoniacal or sulphydryl odours on opening packs.

Accordingly, with fresh fish, the comments on shelf life extensions based on the selection of cut off organoleptic scores (section 5.2) are technologically rather than consumer based, but represent the strategy adopted by many major retailers.

Fish and fish products generally have a good record with regard to safety to the consumer; shellfish, some of which are eaten raw, cause many cases of food poisoning. The main safety considerations relate to botulism, vibriosis, histamine intoxication, algal toxins, and to a lesser extent, parasites and heavy metal ions. Presence of *Listeria monocytogenes* causes problems in commerce.

All aquatic environments can harbour spores of *Clostridium botulinum* which can contaminate fish, both in marine and fresh water environments. Numbers of cases per annum worldwide are low, but because of the seriousness of the effects of the toxins, technologies are implemented such that there is no increase in the risk of botulism. The organisms can be classified into two groups: the proteolytic strains which develop foul odours, and the non-proteolytic types which are covert in their action. The former do not grow below 10°C, but the latter can grow and produce toxin at temperatures above 3.3°C. Their toxins are heat labile, being easily destroyed during normal cooking. There is no way that the raw material – newly harvested fish – can be made free of the risk of botulism. With fish stored raw, spoilage precedes toxicity such that the products would not be consumed. Although the organism can grow at chill temperatures, the spoilage flora can grow faster. With semiprocessed products, where spoilage flora is removed or inhibited, the risk of botulism is higher, but it should be stressed that most of the recorded cases of human botulism related to fish consumption have been traced to products prepared domestically rather than in industry. Smoked products should be made with a salt content (in the water phase) of >3.5% NaCl, which is inhibitory to botulinum strains below 10°C. Marinated products should have a pH <4.5. Hot smoked products which are consumed without cooking should have reached an internal temperature >70°C, or according to a recent UK government report, >90°C. If not one of these conditions of salt content, pH, or temperature treatment is met, the report recommends that the maximum shelf life be 10 days, assuming a storage temperature <10°C. Clearly, these conditions mean that the shelf life is based on safety, and the shelf life extensions given by various technologies are lost. The recommendations apply to packaged (vacuum, modified atmosphere), and to 'sous vide' products.

Vibrio parahaemolyticus is the leading cause of food poisoning in Japan where much fish is eaten raw. The organism is present on fish when landed but, as the infectious dose is high, there has to be some temperature abuse to allow for growth. It does not grow below 10°C, dies out at chill temperatures, and is heat labile. As it is halophilic, it survives salting and thus smoking. Control is therefore by proper chill storage.

Histamine poisoning or scombrotoxicity is associated with the consumption of scombroids such as tuna and mackerel. It is a mild illness of short duration but the symptoms can be alarming to the victim. The histamine arises from histidine which is found in high concentration in the fish muscle. The decarboxylation is carried out by enteric bacteria, which do not grow below 10°C. As histamine is heat stable, it survives all smoking procedures which may kill the producing bacteria. Control is carried out by specifying the absence of histamine in raw materials followed by chill temperature control.

There is a global increase in the presence of algal toxins in shellfish, for unknown reasons. More toxins are being identified. There are now over 20 saxotoxin derivatives, which cause paralytic shellfish poisoning, ten diarrhetic poisons, some neurotoxins, and some which cause loss of memory. Shellfisheries are regulated by monitoring schemes to reduce any risk to the consumer so that toxic products should not enter the food supply. There is some evidence, however, that some toxins may move up the food chain, by for example fish eating shellfish, and there are reports that some outbreaks of scombrotoxicity, where little histamine has been found in the food consumed, may be due to algal toxins. There is no production of such toxins during storage of fish or shellfish.

The major concern in recent years to the fish processing industry has been with *Listeria monocytogenes*. There have been few authenticated cases of human listeriosis associated with the consumption of fish or fish products, but there are some due to shellfish. In many surveys, *Listeria* has been detected in 20% of samples, normally at < 1 cell per gram. As many specifications for food include the virtual absence of *L. monocytogenes*, this can cause problems for food manufacturers. In addition, the organism can grow at chill temperatures and is not inhibited by the levels of salt in smoked products. Shelf life can thus be limited by the shelf life predicted by modelling given the storage temperature profile. Smoked salmon is the product most affected in trade as it is cold smoked and eaten without further cooking, but it must be stressed that no outbreaks of the disease have been traced to this product.

5.6 Conclusions

As fish products have moved from specialist processors and independent retailers into the mainline food industry and supermarkets, and as supplies have become global rather than just local, it would be unusual if there were no problems relating to quality or safety. Technologists have assessed the effects of each innovation and have produced codes of practice which have been apparently successful in providing the consumer with desirable and safe products for which the demand grows. With the knowledge and data base already acquired, there is no reason to believe that the industry will not continue to grow and thrive, provided that adequate respect is shown to the technology and to realistic shelf lives.

Bibliography

Anon (1991) A workshop – Behaviour of gram-negative pathogens on refrigerated foods. *Int. J. Food Microbiol.*, **13**, 183–238.

Baker, D.A. and Genigeorgis, C. (1990) Predicting the safe storage of fresh fish under modified atmospheres with respect to *Clostridium botulinum* toxigenesis by modeling length of the lag phase of growth. *J. Food Protection*, **53**, 131–40.

Bligh, E.G. (1992) *Seafood Science and Technology*, Fishing News, Oxford.

Conner, D.E., Scott, V.N., Bernard, D.T. and Kautter, D.A. (1990) Potential *Clostridium botulinum* hazards associated with extended shelf-life refrigerated foods: a review. *J. Food Safety*, **10**, 131–53.

Eyles, M.J. (1986) Microbiological hazards associated with fish products. *CSIRO Food Res. Q.*, **46**, 8–16.

Farber, J.M. (1991) Microbiological aspects of modified-atmosphere packaging technology – a review. *J. Food Protection*, **54**, 58–70.

Farber, J.M. (1993) Current research on *Listeria monocytogenes* in foods: an overview. *J. Food Protection*, **56**, 640–3.

Gould, G.W. (ed.) (1989) *Mechanisms of Action of Food Preservation Procedures.* Elsevier Applied Science, London.

Harrigan, W.F. and Park, R.W.A. (1991) *Making Safe Food*, Academic Press, London.

Huss, H.H., Jakobsen, M. and Liston, J. (eds) (1992) *Quality Assurance in the Fish Industry. Developments in Food Science*, **30**, Elsevier, Amsterdam.

Kramer, D.E. and Liston, J. (eds) (1987) *Seafood Quality Determination. Developments in Food Science*, **15**, Elsevier, Amsterdam.

Lambert, A.D., Smith, J.P. and Dodds, K.L. (1991) Shelf life extension and microbiological safety of fresh meat – a review. *Food Microbiol.*, **8**, 267–97.

Parry, R.T. (1992) *Principles and Applications of Modified Atmosphere Packaging of Foods*, Blackie Academic & Professional, Glasgow.

Part 2 – The practice

6 Delicatessen salads and chilled prepared fruit and vegetable products

T.F. BROCKLEHURST

6.1 Introduction

Delicatessen salads and prepared fruit and vegetables represent groups of short shelf life products that have shown considerable and steady market growth over the past decade (Young, 1984; Hilliam, 1986; Horne, 1989).

Delicatessen salads can be defined here as products that contain chopped, shredded, or entire cooked or raw vegetable or fruit tissue with or without inclusions of animal origin and contained in a dressing, which is most frequently either mayonnaise or vinaigrette. Mayonnaise is an oil-in-water emulsion, whereas a vinaigrette is a dressing also made from oil and an aqueous phase, but it is usually not emulsified. The pH of products in mayonnaise dressing is normally within the range of 3.2–5.1, in vinaigrette dressing 3.7–4.0, and in other dressings 4.0–5.7 (Rose, 1984), although the pH of some products can be as high as 6.6 (Pace, 1975; Terry and Overcast 1976). Examples of such salads include potato salad, Florida salad, vegetable salad and coleslaw and its variants. On the supermarket shelf the products are usually packaged in plastics tubs, and large buckets of salad are sold by some manufacturers for institutional catering.

Prepared fruit and vegetables, on the other hand, do not have a dressing, and examples range from single commodity packs of ready-to-eat washed, sliced, chopped or shredded prepared vegetables or fruits, and 'dry' coleslaw mixes, to complex mixed salads and stir-fry products. Ready-to-use prepared fruit and vegetable products are a popular range in France where they are known as 'Légumes de 4ème Gamme'. The predominant market for these attractive and colourful products is the supermarket shelf and packing for this sector is usually on expanded polystyrene or PVC trays overwrapped with a stretch film of plasticised PVC (Figure 6.1), or in a vertical form-fill-seal 'pillow-pack' made from oriented polypropylene (Figure 6.2). Some prepared vegetables are available in catering packs, which are often made from laminates containing low density polyethylene and are sometimes vacuum packed.

All of the products discussed here are highly perishable and subject to deterioration caused by biochemical, physical and microbiological changes

Figure 6.1 Chilled prepared fruit and vegetable products packaged in trays overwrapped with a PVC cling film.

occurring within them during shelf life. Chilled storage is a major factor in the stability of all of this diverse range of products, and research workers and producers alike repeatedly state that storage at low temperatures can retard the deteriorative changes that limit shelf life. The Institute of Food Science and Technology recommend a storage temperature of 0–5°C for dressed salads of pH 5.0 or above and prepared salads without a dressing (IFST, 1990), and a storage temperature of either 5°C or 8°C (depending upon the composition of the food) was stipulated for chilled foods in the UK Food Hygiene (Amendment) Regulations 1990 (Anon, 1990). Even within this temperature range, however, the shelf life obtainable in the case of prepared un-dressed products is only a matter of a few days: delicatessen salads marketed in a dressing contain additional preservation factors and their shelf life tends to be longer. The temperature dependence of changes that determined shelf life in salads with and without dressings was shown by Williams (1990) to follow a square root relationship, which can be used for predictive purposes.

It is vital that only ingredients of the highest quality are used in the production of delicatessen salads and chilled prepared fruit and vegetables, and that suitable precautions are taken to ensure the absence of

Figure 6.2 Prepared salads in vertical form-fill-seal 'pillow packs' made from oriented polypropylene.

pathogenic microorganisms, which may be part of their naturally associated microflora (Roberts, 1990). Removal of damaged or dirty areas of vegetables or fruits should be the first step in their preparation, for this can decrease the numbers of microorganisms associated with them (Adams et al., 1989). Washing or dip procedures are adopted by manufacturers to decrease the numbers of microorganisms still further. These treatments are usually based on proprietary washing agents and the accumulated experience of the producer. Much research has been directed towards improving washing treatments, and in the choice of washing agents, but an effective decrease in the numbers of viable microorganisms associated with cut vegetable or fruit tissues, or inhibition of their growth during prolonged storage of the product is difficult to achieve (Shapiro and Holder, 1960; Priepke et al., 1976; Bolin et al., 1977; Nguyen-The and Prunier, 1989). Some washing agents have deleterious effects on flavour, texture or appearance (Huxsoll and Bolin, 1989).

Garg et al. (1990) investigated the use of chlorine dips in a processing factory. They found that the numbers of viable bacteria were not always decreased by the dip procedure and that their target concentration of free chlorine of 300 mg l^{-1} was not always attainable, probably a result of the reaction of the chlorine with the tissues being treated.

Adams *et al.* (1989) showed that washing cut lettuce tissue in chlorinated water removed 97.8% of the microorganisms, which was little better than the use of tap water, but acidification of the chlorinated water improved the decrease in the numbers of viable microorganisms.

Addition of a surfactant to washing water decreased the numbers of microorganisms to a greater extent than a treatment without surfactant. Although this can introduce taints into the cut tissues, it is an indication that many of the microorganisms on the surface of vegetable tissues may be protected in areas that are difficult to wet in normal washing processes (Adams *et al.*, 1989).

Additionally, dips to prevent organoleptic deterioration of cut vegetables or fruits either to be marketed 'dry' or as components of coleslaw have been suggested (Kaufman and Lutz, 1954; Chen and Peng, 1980). Some (such as ascorbic acid) have been used successfully for the retardation of discoloration (O'Bierne and Ballantyne, 1987; King and Bolin, 1989; Bolin and Huxsoll, 1991), while complex mixtures are also available (Dziezak, 1988), and others (such as sulphites) have associated toxicological hazards and have been banned in some countries. Calcium dips can maintain the firmness of tissues by reacting with the pectic substances in the middle lamella (King and Bolin, 1989). Many manufacturers, however, prefer not to compromise the 'fresh' image of their products with the use of such chemical treatments, while any 'further use' of products so treated must also be considered. For example, surface discoloration of chilled peeled potato strips was prevented by solutions of ascorbic acid, but when these strips were fried their colour was poor (O'Bierne and Ballantyne, 1987).

6.2 The products – their characteristics

All of the products within this grouping are complex processed foods. A high proportion of the product is usually shredded, chopped or diced. The characteristics of these processed vegetable or fruit tissues differ considerably from those of their entire counterparts. In addition, the dressings of delicatessen salads also undergo interactions with the solid ingredients of the products; such interactions may influence the composition of the dressing quite markedly and affect salad shelf life.

Although some of the ingredients in these products may have been cooked or canned prior to inclusion (Brocklehurst and Lund, 1984) most of the vegetable and fruit components are living tissues. Accordingly, they retain enzyme activity and may remain contaminated with microorganisms. Both of these characteristics can contribute to a reduction in quality or shelf life.

The number of products within the product range is enormous and increases almost daily. It is unnecessary, however, to consider each product as radically different from others within the range because certain fundamental characteristics can be identified as having considerable effect on their shelf life. All of the products may be considered as being composed of a number of different phases (i.e. solid, aqueous, lipid and gas phases) and the deteriorative changes that can occur during product shelf life are due to interactions between these phases.

In the case of delicatessen salads, the solid phase is the included tissue of vegetable or animal origin; the aqueous phase includes the liquid that exudes from the cut surface of the vegetable or animal tissue and this is continuous with, and effectively indistinguishable from, the aqueous phase of the dressing; the lipid phase is the oil component of the dressing; and the gas phase is the headspace above the salad within the packaging.

In mayonnaise-based delicatessen salads the solid ingredients may constitute between 50% and 75% (w/w) of the product. The oil in mayonnaise (typically between 29% and 76% (w/w), though the more recent 'diet' dressings contain much less oil than this) in present as dispersed droplets with a mean droplet diameter of about 5 μm (Tunaley et al., 1985; Ranken, 1988). Other ingredients in the mayonnaise usually include vinegar, sugars, sodium chloride, egg yolk solids (as emulsifier), stabilisers (such as guar, tragacanth or xanthan gums) and additional minor ingredients like mustard powder, lactic acid, colourings, or preservatives such as sorbic acid or benzoic acid (Brocklehurst and Lund, 1984).

In the case of prepared fruit and vegetables, the solid phase is the fruit or vegetable tissue; the aqueous phase is confined to the exudate that is released from the cut surface of the tissues; and the gas phase usually constitutes a large volume within the pack, is in contact with most of the surfaces of the vegetable or fruit components, and its composition may be modified deliberately at the time of packing.

Whereas most of the major changes that limit shelf life can be explained by reference to interactions between the phases described here, it is also true that certain minor components of delicatessen salads exhibit changes during shelf life that are unique to those ingredients (Geeson et al., 1987).

6.3 Specific factors affecting shelf life

The shelf life of delicatessen salads and prepared fruit and vegetable products is influenced very strongly by changes that occur during storage and that, if allowed to continue unabated, would lead to microbiological or organoleptic spoilage.

6.3.1 Delicatessen salads

The characteristics of the mayonnaise or vinaigrette dressing have considerable influence on the shelf life of these products. The object of the manufacturing process should be to produce a product in which the solid ingredients are intimately associated with the dressing, which should be specifically formulated in order to confer some organoleptic and microbiological stability on the solid ingredients. A knowledge of the interactions that occur between the phases of the dressings and the dressing and the solid ingredients of the food, therefore, is fundamental to an understanding of the factors that limit shelf life.

6.3.1.1 Interactions between phases

(a) Behaviour of organic acid preservatives in the aqueous phase. The aqueous phase of the dressing contains chemical components that confer organoleptic quality to the dressing, but that also increase the safe shelf life of the salads by killing, or retarding the growth of, microorganisms. These components may be in the form of traditional ingredients of the dressing, such as acetic acid, lactic acid, sodium chloride and sucrose, or preservatives (such as sorbic acid or benzoic acid) added deliberately to extend shelf life. The organic acids are the most potent antimicrobial agents in the dressings, but the concentration of sodium chloride and sugars can increase the microbiological stability (Tuynenburg Muys, 1971). Their influence is included in the CIMSCEE (1985) equations, but the concentration of these components in dressings is usually quite low (Brocklehurst and Lund, 1984) and alone is insufficient to prevent the growth of microorganisms (Lueck, 1980). In any case, the concentration of sodium chloride and sucrose decreases markedly by dilution when the dressing is mixed with the solid ingredients of the salad, as discussed later.

In the preservation of delicatessen salads, it is the concentration of organic acids, then, that is most important and a chemical characteristic that affects their efficacy as antimicrobial agents is that of dissociation. This is the property of a molecule to separate into specific component parts, and in the case of organic acid food preservatives this occurs by an ionisation reaction. The general reaction for dissociation is:

$$RH \rightleftharpoons R^- + H^+ \qquad (6.1)$$

and for acetic acid, for example, this would read:

$$CH_3COOH \overset{K_a}{\rightleftharpoons} CH_3COO^- + H^+ \qquad (6.2)$$

undissociated	dissociated
acetic acid	acetate ion and proton

Table 6.1 Published values for dissociation constants and pK_a values at 25°C for some common organic acids

Organic acid	Dissociation constant[a]	pK_a
Acetic	1.76×10^{-5}	4.76
Lactic	1.37×10^{-4}	3.86
Benzoic	6.46×10^{-5}	4.20
Sorbic	1.73×10^{-5}	4.76

[a]mol l^{-1}

In this case, the dissociation reaches an equilibrium. This is characteristic of a weak acid as it is only partially ionised in aqueous solutions at normal concentrations. The degree of dissociation of an acid is described by a constant, called the dissociation constant (K_a), which is the ratio of the product of the concentrations of the dissociated species to the concentration of the undissociated acid at equilibrium, at a standard temperature. The dissociation constant is characteristic of a particular acid, and in the case of weak acids is a somewhat cumbersome small number (Table 6.1). Its negative logarithm, however, is more easily manipulated, and this is known as the pK_a (Table 6.1). The value of K_a is affected slightly by temperature, and useful equations for determination of this are given by Robinson and Stokes (1959).

Dissociation is important in food preservation because the antimicrobial activity of the undissociated and dissociated species differs and it is the undissociated acid that is the predominantly antimicrobial agent (Baird-Parker, 1980; Eklund, 1983). The site of microbial growth in emulsion dressings is in the aqueous phase (Tuynenburg Muys, 1971) and hence it is the concentration of the undissociated acid in this phase of the dressing that is most pertinent to a shelf life that is microbiologically safe and stable. The concentration of undissociated acid is influenced by the acidity of the food as the following shows:

$$CH_3COOH \underset{\text{decreasing acidity}}{\overset{\text{increasing acidity}}{\rightleftharpoons}} CH_3COO^- + H^+ \qquad (6.3)$$

When the acidity of the food is increased (i.e. the pH is decreased) the concentration of H^+ in the food increases and this influences the above equilibrium (which is still governed by the pK_a), driving equation (6.3) to the left thereby increasing the concentration of the undissociated acid.

The concentration of the undissociated acid is a function, therefore, of the initial concentration of that acid in the food, its dissociation constant and the pH of the food. The concentration of the undissociated acid at a given pH can be calculated by using the Henderson-Hasselbalch equation:

Table 6.2 Calculated effect of pH on the proportion of acetic acid present as the undissociated
acid, assuming a pK_a of 4.76.

pH	% undissociated
3.0	98.29
4.0	85.19
4.2	78.41
4.4	69.61
4.5	64.54
4.6	59.11
4.76	50.00
4.8	47.71
5.0	36.52
5.2	26.64
5.4	18.64
5.5	15.40
5.6	12.63
6.0	5.44
7.0	0.57

$$pH = pK_a + \log_{10} \frac{\left(\substack{\text{concn. of dissociated species} \\ \text{i.e. the salt/conjugate base}}\right)}{(\text{concn. of undissociated acid})} \qquad (6.4)$$

It follows that when the pH of the food is equal to the pK_a of the acid,
the concentrations of the undissociated acid and its dissociated species are
the same. As the pH falls below the pK_a, the proportion of antimicrobial
undissociated acid increases (Table 6.2). Any interaction occurring within
these products that changes the pH will, therefore, have a direct influence
on the concentration of undissociated acid available as an antimicrobial
agent.

(b) *Aqueous phase/lipid phase interaction – organic acids.* The undissociated organic acids are lipophilic, and hence soluble in the lipid phase of
foods, but to varying extent. The relative solubility of these acids in the
lipid and aqueous phases is described by their partition coefficients (Table
6.3). The low partition coefficient of acetic acid explains its being used as
the predominant antimicrobial agent in these foods, but the high partition
coefficients of benzoic acid and sorbic acid, which are sometimes deliberately added as preservatives to multiphase foods, mean that a high proportion of these acids is unavailable as an antimicrobial agent in the
continuous aqueous phase.

Clearly, the redistribution of an organic acid preservative through partition affects its concentration in the aqueous phase of the dressing before
this is mixed with the salad ingredients as well as being relevant to its
final concentration in the same phase in the entire delicatessen salad. The

Table 6.3 Published values for partition coefficients of some common organic acids

Organic acid	Oil:water partition coefficient
Acetic	0.03–0.07
Benzoic	6–13
Sorbic	3.1

Source: Gordon and Reid, 1922; Bodansky, 1928; von Schelhorn, 1964; Leo *et al.*, 1971.

magnitude of the effect is influenced by any change in pH that occurs within the dressing before or after it is mixed with the solid ingredients of the product as this affects the concentration of the undissociated acid.

6.3.1.2 Interactions within the salad. The preparation of a delicatessen salad from its component solid parts and dressing is rapidly followed by many interactions within the product. These involve the redistribution of components between the phases, and, although they are complete within six hours after mixing the salad, these interactions have implications for the sensory and microbiological stability as well as shelf life of the product (Kirsop and Brocklehurst, 1982; Brocklehurst *et al.*, 1983; Brocklehurst, 1984; Brocklehurst and Lund, 1984; Tunaley *et al.*, 1985; Davies and Brocklehurst, 1986). Such interactions can readily be measured and used as the basis of a predictive scheme in order to anticipate the spoilage potential of products with a given compositional profile. Specific interactions follow, and the next sections deal with the ways in which the results of these interactions limit the shelf life of the products.

(a) Solid phase/aqueous phase interaction – moisture. Moisture passes from the vegetable components of the product into the aqueous phase of the dressing (Boyar *et al.*, 1985). The movement of free moisture is in response to the difference in osmotic potential between the vegetable or fruit tissues and the dressing, which is created by the relatively large concentration of solutes in the aqueous phase of dressings. This moisture can represent some 16% of the total moisture that is contained in the vegetable tissue in coleslaw (Davies and Brocklehurst, 1986). The change in volume fraction of the aqueous phase of the dressing caused by the ingress of moisture can be measured directly (Boyar *et al.*, 1985), or the change in oil content per unit volume of dressing can also be used as an indicator (Table 6.4).

The redistribution of water is completed within six hours after mixing the salad. It can result in a loss of turgidity of the vegetable tissue, and one effect of the dilution of the dressing is a marked loss in its viscosity (Table 6.4 and Figure 6.3).

Table 6.4 Oil content and viscosity of mayonnaise before making salads, and of mayonnaise separated from salads six hours after mixing

Salad	Before making salad		Six hours after mixing	
	Oil content (% w/v)	Viscosity (Pas)	Oil content (%w/v)	Viscosity (Pas)
Coleslaw	61	2.54	40	0.32
Florida salad	29	2.03	18	0.36
Potato salad	76	0.69	61	1.38
Vegetable salad	29	2.03	23	1.23
Spanish salad	29	2.03	22	0.80

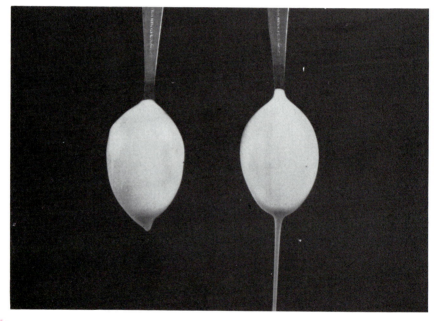

Figure 6.3 Mayonnaise used to make coleslaw is viscous and clings to a spoon (left). During the first six hours after mixing with the solid ingredients of the salad the viscosity of the mayonnaise decreases and it no longer clings (right).

(b) Solid phase/aqueous phase interaction – potato cells. Examination of Table 6.4 shows that although dilution of the mayonnaise caused by the movement of moisture from the vegetable tissue into the aqueous phase occurred in all of the salads studied it was not accompanied in all cases by the expected drop in viscosity. The observed increase in viscosity of the mayonnaise in the potato salad and the less than anticipated decrease in

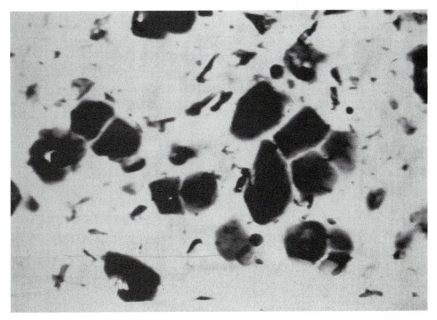

Figure 6.4 Potato cells in the mayonnaise of potato salad, which have sloughed off the cooked diced potato during the mixing of the salad. The cells contain gelatinised starch (stained here with iodine solution). (Micrograph prepared by Mary Parker, IFR Norwich.)

viscosity of the mayonnaise in the vegetable salad were probably due to the release of large numbers of free cells of potato tissue into the aqueous phase of the mayonnaise. These were cooked cells containing gelatinised starch (Figure 6.4), that had been sloughed from the outer surface of the pieces of parboiled diced potato in the salad during the mixing process. This interaction is an easily observed physical effect in that the potato cells confer a granular appearance on the mayonnaise. It is a mechanical effect that occurs immediately the potato tissue is mixed with the dressing. No further granularity occurs during shelf life and this interaction serves to decrease or reverse the somewhat deleterious effects of dilution with moisture on the viscosity of the dressing.

(c) Solid phase/aqueous phase interaction – organic acids. The concentration of undissociated organic acids in the aqueous phase of mayonnaise is fundamental to the microbiological stability of most dressed delicatessen salads, and it is usually the concentration of acetic acid that is the most important. As noted above, the effect of partition between the aqueous and lipid phases of dressings on the concentration of acetic acid is slight, and the pH and the concentration of undissociated acetic acid in the aqueous phase of dressings used in delicatessen salads are often quite suffi-

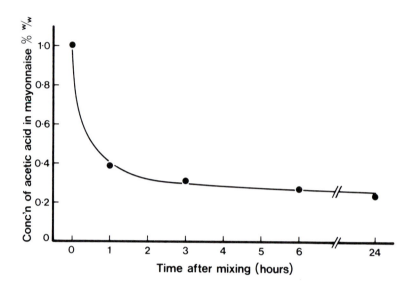

Figure 6.5 Migration of acetic acid from the mayonnaise of coleslaw into the vegetable tissue of the salad. The migration is completed within six hours of mixing the mayonnaise with the solid ingredients of the salad, and the concentration in the mayonnaise remains constant thereafter.

cient to render the dressings sterile. Nevertheless, it is this same aqueous phase in delicatessen salads that provides a hospitable environment for the growth of the microorganisms that can lead to the microbiological spoilage of the products. An appreciation of the interaction that occurs between the solid phase of these products and the undissociated organic acids in the aqueous phase is, therefore, essential if this change in the environment that eventually allows microbiological spoilage to occur is to be understood.

When the solid ingredients of the salad are mixed with the mayonnaise the undissociated acetic acid migrates into the vegetable tissue, from which it can be recovered quantitatively (Brocklehurst et al., 1983; Brocklehurst and Lund, 1984). The migration occurs rapidly and is completed within six hours (Figure 6.5).

The decrease in the concentration of acetic acid in the aqueous phase of the product causes a concomitant increase in pH (Kirsop and Brocklehurst, 1982; Brocklehurst et al., 1983; Brocklehurst and Lund, 1984; Boyar et al., 1985), and this, combined with the dilution of the aqueous phase by the movement of moisture noted earlier, results in a new concentration of undissociated acetic acid far lower than that originally present (Table 6.5). This new level of acetic acid in the product is no

Table 6.5 Calculated concentrations of undissociated acetic acid (%w/w) and pH in the aqueous phase of mayonnaise[a] before making salads, and of mayonnaise separated from salads six hours after mixing

	Before making salad		Six hours after mixing	
Salad	pH	Concentration of undissociated acetic acid	pH	Concentration of undissociated acetic acid
Coleslaw	3.4	4.6	4.1–4.3	0.6
Florida salad	2.7	3.5	3.4–3.5	0.8
Potato salad	3.4	2.1	4.3–4.4	0.2
Vegetable salad	2.7	3.5	3.9–4.1	0.8
Spanish salad	2.7	3.5	3.6–3.8	1.0

[a]the proportion of the mayonnaise occupied by the aqueous phase was calculated by exclusion of the oils and solids.

longer microbicidal, but can permit the growth of microorganisms in the product limiting shelf life by causing spoilage.

(d) Solid phase/lipid phase interaction – oil. A fairly minor effect in those delicatessen salads that contain chopped or shredded leaf tissue (such as cabbage leaf tissue) is the movement of dispersed oil from the dressing into the air spaces of the leaf tissue (Boyar *et al.*, 1985). It is probably a consequence of the affinity between the oil fraction of the dressing and the waxy hydrophobic cuticle lining the air spaces, and is again complete within six hours after mixing the vegetable tissue with the dressing. Loss of oil from the mayonnaise in coleslaw by this mechanism was calculated to be only 5.2% of the total oil in the mayonnaise (Davies and Brocklehurst, 1986), but the effect of this redistribution on the cabbage tissue was marked. The tissue became translucent (Brocklehurst, 1984), and this was perceived in sensory analysis as a deteriorative change (Tunaley and Brocklehurst, 1982; Tunaley *et al.*, 1985).

6.3.2 Prepared fruit and vegetables

If these products contained a dressing they would have the characteristics of delicatessen salads. If the products were composed solely of entire fruits or vegetables their characteristics would be those of stored commodities. The fact that the products are composed of chopped or shredded components gives them characteristics that fall between these two categories. The act of chopping or shredding the tissues results in a very large cut surface area of damaged cells. This leads to considerable instability in the products which may then have a shelf life of only a few days, and it is interactions occurring within the products that again limit

shelf life. The extent of damage by machines or operatives can influence
the rate at which deteriorative changes occur, both by the acceleration of
physiological deterioration as a result of cellular rupture as well as contributing to exuded liquid. For example, shredded lettuce cut with a sharp
knife using a slicing action had a shelf life about twice that of lettuce cut
using a chopping action, and the use of a blunt knife decreased shelf life
even further (Bolin et al., 1977). These authors also showed that small
shreds (1 mm thick) had a shorter shelf life than larger shreds (3 mm
thick), which was related to the exposed cut surface area, and they and
others (Bolin and Huxsoll, 1991) reduced damage and hence extended
shelf life by tearing, rather than cutting, the lettuce leaf tissue.

6.3.2.1 Solid phase/aqueous phase interaction – moisture. Vegetable or
fruit components used in the manufacture of these products are usually
immersed in water or chlorinated water as part of a cleaning regime, and
excess of water removed from the tissues, usually in a centrifuge, prior to
packing. It might appear curious, therefore, to talk of an aqueous phase
influencing the shelf life of these products, but, nevertheless, this is so. An
aqueous phase is present as the film of liquid that exudes from the
damaged surface of the tissue, and that contains moisture and nutrients.
It can be added to by any washing water, and the presence of free
moisture or cellular fluids on the surface of shredded lettuce decreased its
shelf life (Bolin et al., 1977; Bolin and Huxsoll, 1991). The cellular fluid
on the cut surface of the tissue contains many enzymes including phenolase, catalase and peroxidase (Bolin et al., 1977) and these can cause discoloration of the cut surfaces due to the oxidation of phenolic
compounds, which can limit shelf life (Goupy, 1989). The loss of moisture
can also lead to wilting or even desiccation of the tissues, and it is this
exudate that allows the microorganisms associated with these products to
multiply faster, and to greater numbers, than on intact tissues. Comparison of the relatively small numbers of bacteria on a leaf blade surface
(Figure 6.6) with the large numbers forming a microbial film or colony on
the cut surface (Figure 6.7) clearly demonstrates the importance of the cut
surface in its contribution to the growth of microorganisms.

6.3.2.2 Solid phase/gaseous phase interaction – respiration. Fruit or
vegetable tissue that has been damaged by cutting has a respiration rate
higher than that of undamaged tissue (Priepke et al., 1976; Brocklehurst
and van Bentem, 1990) (Figure 6.8), although the extent of damage
affecting the respiration rate is less if tissue is torn than if it is cut or
shredded (Bolin and Huxsoll, 1991). The rate of respiration also increases
as the temperature is raised.
    Measurements made on mixed salad products (Table 6.6) showed that
respiration rates could be as high as 82 mg CO_2/kg/hour during storage at

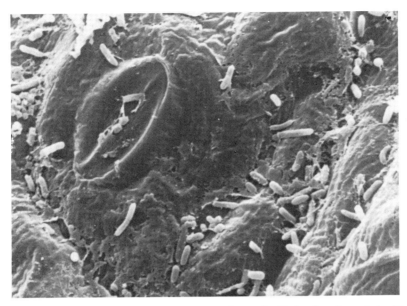

Figure 6.6 Scanning electron micrograph of bacteria on the blade of a piece of shredded lettuce leaf taken from a pack of prepared salad at the end of its shelf life. (Micrograph prepared by Mary Parker, IFR Norwich.)

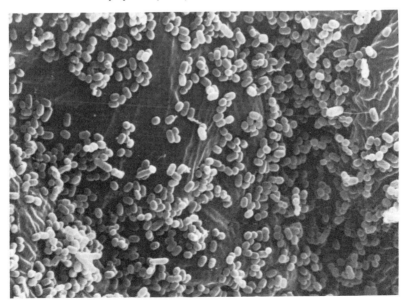

Figure 6.7 Scanning electron micrograph of bacteria on the cut surface of the piece of shredded lettuce leaf shown in Figure 6.6. (First published by Brocklehurst, T.F. and van Bentem, E. in *Food Science and Technology Today*, **4**(3), 156–8 (1990), and reproduced by courtesy of the publisher, the Institute of Food Science and Technology). (Micrograph prepared by Mary Parker, IFR Norwich.)

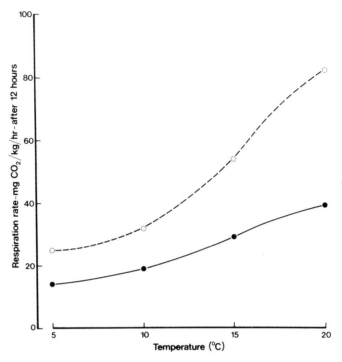

Figure 6.8 This graph shows that the respiration rate of shredded lettuce (○) is greater than that of whole lettuce (●) and that the respiration rates increase as the temperature increases. (First published by Brocklehurst, T.F. and van Bentem, E. in *Food Science and Technology Today*, **4**(3), 156–8 (1990), and reproduced by courtesy of the publisher, the Institute of Food Science and Technology.)

Table 6.6 Respiration rate[a] of chopped and shredded vegetable products during storage at 8°C

Pack contents	Respiration rate (mg CO_2/kg/hour)
Frise, radicchio, chicory, lambs lettuce	46
Chinese leaf, lettuce, frise, radicchio, red cabbage	38
Chinese leaf, white cabbage, cress, carrot, celery, red pepper, green pepper	82

[a]Unpublished reasurements made at the Institute of Food Research, Norwich

8°C, whereas similar commodities in their entire state had respiration rates of between 8 and 30 mg CO_2/kg/hour during storage at 10°C (Robinson *et al.*, 1975).

The result of such high rates of respiration can be to cause an over-modification of the pack atmosphere. This occurs when the packaging material is insufficiently permeable to allow the rapid escape of CO_2 and ingress of O_2. Atmospheres that contained no detectable O_2 and concentrations of CO_2 as high as 16% (v/v) have been found within commercially-produced retail packs of mixed salad originally packaged in air (Brocklehurst et al., 1987). Priepke et al. (1976) found concentrations of CO_2 as high as 20% (v/v) and O_2 as low as 1–2% (v/v) in packs of cut lettuce that again had been packed in air and stored at 4.4°C for 10 days. Concentrations of O_2 of less than 2% (v/v) induce anaerobic respiration of the vegetable and fruit tissues (Myers, 1989), and this can result in unacceptable organoleptic changes due to taints (McLachlan and Stark, 1985; Bolin and Huxsoll, 1991). Low concentrations of O_2 in these products may also present the hazard of the growth of anaerobic pathogenic bacteria such as Clostridium botulinum (Sugiyama and Yang, 1975; Tamminga et al., 1978). Where packaging films do not allow any escape of the accumulated CO_2, an obvious swelling of the pack can result.

Some tissues create an overmodified atmosphere more readily than others. For example, Priepke et al. (1976) found that the respiration rate of cut lettuce decreased as the concentration of O_2 in the pack became almost totally depleted, and the carbon dioxide produced by the tissues was equivalent to the oxygen available to support aerobic respiration. In packs of cut carrot, however, the concentration of CO_2 exceeded that possible by utilisation of the available oxygen in the air within the pack. This indicated that anaerobic respiration had occurred, although the authors were unable to determine whether this was the result of respiration of the carrot tissue alone or microorganisms within the pack had contributed to the overall CO_2 level.

The extent of the modification of the pack atmosphere can influence the amount of exudation from the damaged cells, which in turn can affect shelf life by supporting the growth of microorganisms. The leakage of K^+ ions from plant tissues is a useful indicator of exudation. Carlin et al. (1990) showed that the concentration of K^+ ions leaking from grated carrots decreased during storage in air and under some modified atmospheres, but not in an atmosphere composed of 40% (v/v) CO_2 and 10% (v/v) O_2, where exudation increased during storage at 10°C.

6.4   Determination of shelf life

6.4.1   Delicatessen salads

From previous discussion, it should be clear that delicatessen salads are highly dynamic multiphase foods in which many interactions occur that quite rapidly change the physical and chemical state of the food from that pertinent at the time of manufacture. It is very important to describe the chemical and physical state of these products as it exists after the redistributions have occurred, because it is these redistributions that dictate the eventual shelf life of the product. The interactions noted above serve to establish a chemical state in the entire product which, once established after the initial six hours after mixing, remains unchanged for the duration of the life of the product. These interactions, though, have destabilising effects on the products, which can lead to a wide range of deteriorative changes that undermine shelf life. Most published work concerns the shelf life of mayonnaise-based salads, and some examples of the factors that determine shelf life of these products follow.

6.4.1.1 Organoleptic changes in coleslaw during shelf life.

Whereas microbiological spoilage occurred during the storage of coleslaw, it was preceded by sensory changes (Tunaley and Brocklehurst, 1982; Tunaley et al., 1985). These are described here, and the microbiological studies, which parallel these sensory studies, are described in the next section.

The sensory changes occurred equally rapidly at 5°C and 10°C. The characteristics detected by a trained sensory panel as important in shelf life determination were 'creamy-oiliness', 'perceived acidity', and 'viscosity' which were assessed orally, and 'cabbage translucency' and 'mayonnaise consistency' which were assessed visually. For characteristics other than 'cabbage translucency' the panel assessed both the coleslaw and the mayonnaise which had been separated from the solid ingredients of the salad and found similar conclusions, suggesting that the sensory characteristics most important in the determination of shelf life of this product were those associated with the dressing.

The sensory analysis used a profile method (BSI, 1980), where characteristics were scored by placing a vertical mark along a 100 mm line at a position that the assessor felt best represented the perceived strength of each characteristic (Tunaley et al., 1985).

The 'creamy-oily' characteristic included mouthfeel and a flavour component. Its decline during storage was considered a good indicator of ageing (Figure 6.9), but it was subject to seasonal variation probably related to the variety of cabbage used in the coleslaw (Tunaley and Brocklehurst, 1982; Tunaley et al., 1985).

Perceived acidity, assessed orally, increased during storage (Figure 6.9), despite the absence of any change in the concentration of acetic acid in the mayonnaise after the initial redistribution, or any significant change in the pH. It has been suggested that changes in the physical properties of the mayonnaise that are related more to redistributions of oil and water may account for the apparent increase in perceived acidity during storage (Tunaley et al., 1985).

Viscosity of the mayonnaise declined during storage as did the consistency which declined from 'coating' to 'very runny' (Figure 6.10).

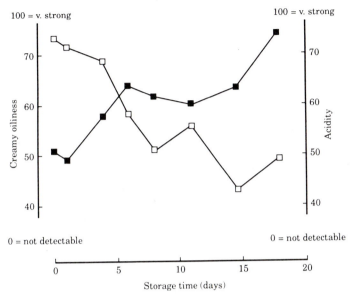

Figure 6.9 Changes in perceived creamy-oiliness (□) and perceived acidity (■) in mayonnaise separated from coleslaw stored at 5°C. (First published by Tunaley *et al.*, in *Food Science and Technology: Lebensmittel-Wissenschaft & Technologie*, **18**, 220–4 (1985), and reproduced by permission of the publisher, Academic Press, London.)

Overall this resulted in the progressive failure of the mayonnaise to coat the solid ingredients of the salad. The effect became more and more visible to the assessors, which was reflected in a perceived increase in translucency of the cabbage tissue with time (Figure 6.11) and this was described as 'aged', 'translucent' or 'grey'.

The flavour characteristic was affected by temperature and deterioration was greater at 10°C than at 5°C (Figure 6.12). This may have been evidence that the flavour change was the result of the activity of enzymes in the vegetable tissue (King *et al.*, 1976), some of which could also cause oxidative discoloration (Chen and Peng, 1980). After storage at 10°C for 18 days the assessors' descriptions included the terms 'mouldy', 'cheesy', 'sulphury', 'alcoholic', 'very acidic' and 'rancid' (Tunaley and Brocklehurst, 1982). Deterioration of the odour of coleslaw, faster at a higher (8°C) than lower (4°C) storage temperature, was also noted by Corry *et al.* (1980).

Whereas sensory analysis by a trained panel can give important insights into those quality attributes perceived as changing during shelf life, it is possible to equate some of them with instrumentally analysed parameters. Viscosity and consistency of mayonnaise were measured instrumentally by Tunaley *et al.* (1985) who found that the sensorily assessed attributes of

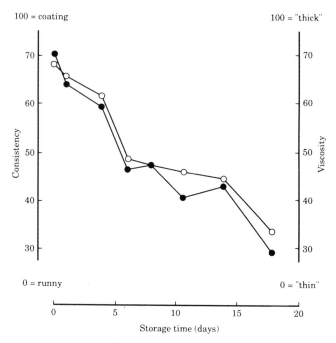

Figure 6.10 Changes in perceived viscosity (○) and perceived consistency (●) in mayonnaise separated from coleslaw stored at 5°C. (First published by Tunaley *et al.*, in *Food Science and Technology: Lebensmittel-Wissenschaft & Technologie*, **18**, 220–4 (1985), and reproduced by permission of the publisher, Academic Press, London.)

perceived consistency, perceived creamy-oiliness and perceived viscosity correlated well with the instrumental measurement of viscosity and that the perceived creamy-oiliness correlated well with instrumentally measured consistency.

6.4.1.2 Microbiological changes in mayonnaise-based salads during shelf life. Just as changes in the sensory attributes of these products have their origins in the interactions that occur during the first few hours after a salad is made, so the change in concentration of the undissociated acetic acid during this time is critical to the survival and growth of certain microorganisms in the product. Delicatessen salads are subject to spoilage due mainly to the growth of bacteria and yeasts. These may appear as colonies on the surface of the product (Figures 6.13 and 6.14) or they may cause spoilage due to the production of carbon dioxide within the dressing (Norberg and Åkerstrand, 1980; Wiberg *et al.*, 1983; Brocklehurst, 1984; Geeson *et al.*, 1987) (Figure 6.15). Although microbiological spoilage usually manifests itself after the sensory changes in the product

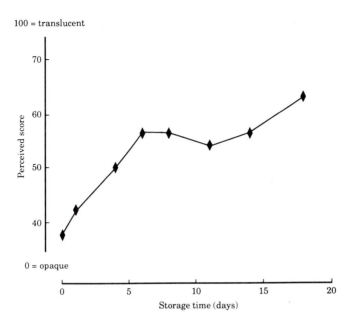

100 = translucent

Figure 6.11 Changes in perceived translucency of cabbage separated from coleslaw stored at 5°C. (First published by Tunaley *et al.*, in *Food Science and Technology: Lebensmittel-Wissenschaft & Technologie*, **18**, 220–4 (1985), and reproduced by permission of the publisher, Academic Press, London.)

have become evident, it is, nevertheless, a form of spoilage very obvious to the consumer.

Delicatessen salads can contain very many different types of bacteria and yeasts at the time of manufacture (Hankin and Ullman, 1969; Christianson and King, 1971; Fowler and Clark, 1975; Harris *et al.*, 1975; Pace, 1975; Terry and Overcast, 1976; Rose, 1984; Greenwood *et al.*, 1975), these being derived from the solid ingredients of the products and from the processing plant (Collins, 1982). By virtue of its organic acid content and its pH, the dressing is usually fully preserved. Typically, only a few species of bacteria and yeasts multiply in these products. The yeasts are predominantly *Saccharomyces exiguus* and *Pichia membranaefaciens* and the bacteria are predominantly *Lactobacillus* spp. (Holtzapffel and Mossel, 1968; Baumgart and Hauschild, 1980; Baumgart *et al.*, 1983). In a study of 24 different mayonnaise-based delicatessen salads, Geeson *et al.* (1987) found that *Saccharomyces exiguus* was present at greater than 10^5 g^{-1} of salad at the end of shelf life in 17 of the salads and that *Pichia membranaefaciens* was present at greater than 10^5 g^{-1} of salad at the end of shelf life in four of them. *Saccharomyces exiguus* is a fermentative yeast and causes spoilage due to production of carbon dioxide in the mayon-

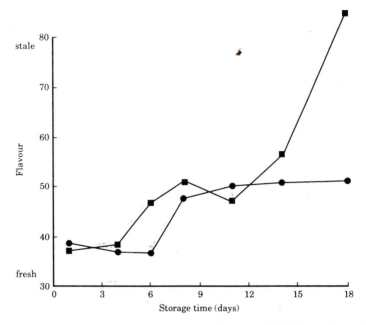

Figure 6.12 Changes in flavour of coleslaw stored at 5°C (●) and 10°C (■). (First published by Tunaley, A. and Brocklehurst, T.F. in *Chilled Foods*, Nov/Dec, 12–13 (1982), and reproduced by permission of the publisher, FMJ International Publications Ltd.)

naise (Figure 6.15). *Saccharomyces dairensis* has also occasionally been implicated in spoilage of mayonnaise-based salads (Dennis and Buhagiar, 1980; Brocklehurst *et al.*, 1983). Although this yeast is less tolerant to acetic acid than *Saccharomyces exiguus*, it is also fermentative, and was found to reach numbers likely to cause spoilage in a product that had been stored at 10°C for about 20 days (Brocklehurst *et al.*, 1983). *Pichia membranaefaciens* is an aerobic yeast and causes spoilage due to the formation of surface colonies (Figures 6.13 and 6.14).

The complexity and rate of growth of the associative microflora of mayonnaise-based salads were found to relate to the residual concentration of acetic acid in the dressing and its pH after the migration of acetic acid had occurred, and the storage temperature.

The following examples of the microbiology of delicatessen salads are from the work of Brocklehurst and Lund (1984):

1. In a potato salad where the residual concentration of undissociated acetic acid in the aqueous phase of the dressing was 0.2% (w/w) at pH 4.3–4.4 (Figure 6.16), the microorganisms able to grow in the product during storage at 10°C were mainly lactobacilli and the yeasts *Saccharomyces exiguus*, *Candida sake*, *Candida lambica* and *Yarrowia lipolytica*

Figure 6.13 At first glance the colonies of the spoilage yeast *Pichia membranaefaciens* (arrowed) seen here growing on the surface of vegetable salad during storage at 10°C, could be confused with vegetable ingredients. (First published by Brocklehurst, T.F. in *Food Manufacture*, April, 65 and 67 (1984) and reproduced by permission of the publisher, Morgan-Grampian (Process Press) Ltd.)

and *Geotrichum candidum*. Spoilage occurred after storage for 10 days and was due to gas production probably by both *Saccharomyces exiguus* and the lactobacilli.

2. In a coleslaw, however, where the residual concentration of undissociated acetic acid in the aqueous phase of the dressing was 0.6% (w/w) at pH 4.1–4.3, lactobacilli and other bacteria declined in numbers. Only *Saccharomyces exiguus* was able to multiply during storage at 10°C (Figure 6.17), subsequently causing spoilage due to gas production after 21 days.

3. *Saccharomyces exiguus* also predominated in a Florida salad, where the concentration of undissociated acetic acid was 0.8% (w/w) and the pH was 3.4–3.5, where it caused spoilage after storage at 10°C for 13 days (Figure 6.18).

4. In a vegetable salad where the concentration of undissociated acetic acid was 0.8% (w/w) and the pH was 3.9–4.1, spoilage due to gas production caused by the growth of *Saccharomyces exiguus* occurred after storage at 10°C for 8 days, but colonies of *Pichia membranaefaciens* appeared on the surface of the salad after 14 days (Figure 6.19).

Figure 6.14 Potato salad (right) and the product after very obvious spoilage due to the growth of colonies of the yeast *Pichia membranaefaciens* on the surface.

5. In a Spanish salad, on the other hand, the residual concentration of undissociated acetic acid in the aqueous phase of the dressing remained high at 1% (w/w) and the pH was at 3.6–3.8. During storage at 10°C, this product was found to support only slight growth of spoilage organisms (Figure 6.20).

It is evident, therefore, that the residual concentration of acetic acid in the aqueous phase of the dressing and the pH at equilibrium determined the survival of the naturally occurring microflora and their rate of growth, and hence influenced the microbiological spoilage of these products.

Temperature of storage is, of course, also important. During storage of these salads at 5°C neither the Florida salad, coleslaw nor Spanish salad supported the growth of microorganisms. The vegetable salad supported the growth of *Pichia membranaefaciens* and small numbers of lactobacilli, whereas the potato salad supported growth of *Candida zeylanoides*, *Candida lambica*, *Yarrowia lipolytica*, *Geotrichum candidum*, and lactobacilli and was the only salad to show microbiological spoilage at this temperature, but only after storage for 28 days (Brocklehurst and Lund, 1984).

Figure 6.15 Spoilage of coleslaw due to gas production caused by growth of the spoilage yeast *Saccharomyces exiguus*. (First published by Geeson *et al.*, in *Food*, February, 49–53 (1987) and reproduced by permission of the publisher, Turret Group.)

6.4.1.3 Changes in minor ingredients. The sensory and microbiological changes described above are the most important determinants of the shelf life of mayonnaise-based delicatessen salads. They are related to the various interactions that occur in the products and such changes could therefore be used to predict shelf life. Changes in the quality of many of the minor ingredients of delicatessen salads have been monitored by Geeson *et al.* (1987) (Table 6.7) and, although these changes may be encountered in any delicatessen product, they are unlikely to be regarded as significant enough to limit shelf life.

6.4.2 Prepared fruit and vegetables

The interactions occurring within prepared fruit and vegetable products are fewer than those identified in delicatessen salads, but they nevertheless combine to limit shelf life.

6.4.2.1 Changes in microflora. Visual assessment of product quality judged that products with a high initial number of bacteria (5.1×10^6 g^{-1} of salad) declined in quality faster than products with a lower number

Table 6.7 Changes in quality of some ingredients of mayonnaise-based salads during storage at 5° or 10°C[a]

Ingredient	Quality change
Apple	Brown discoloration of cut surface
Cabbage	Discoloration and translucency
Carrot (cooked)	Fragmentation and discoloration
Celeriac	Discoloration
Celery	Discoloration
Cheese	Development of odours described as 'butyric', 'plastic', 'fermented'
Mandarin orange	Fragmentation
Peas	Yellow discoloration
Red and green peppers	Discoloration
Potato (cooked)	Appearance described as 'grey' or 'glassy', fragmentation, development of strong 'earthy' odours
Prawns	Development of strong 'off' fishy odours
Walnuts	Leaching of colour into mayonnaise, development of strong 'mealy' odours

[a]First published by Geeson et al. (1987) and used by kind permission of the publisher, Turret Group plc.

$(5.8 \times 10^3 \text{ g}^{-1}$ of salad) (Bolin et al., 1977). Nguyen-The and Prunier (1989) found that the numbers of pectolytic pseudomonads in fruit and vegetable products were directly related to their deterioration.

At the time of packing the number of microorganisms associated with these products is often large. Bacteria, yeasts and moulds are included (Manvell and Ackland, 1986; Nguyen-The and Prunier, 1989; Brocklehurst and van Bentem, 1990; Garg et al., 1990) and many of these multiply during storage. For example, numbers of *Pseudomonas* spp. and lactic acid bacteria in excess of 10^8 g^{-1} have been isolated from retail packs of salad after storage at 7°C or 10°C, at the end of their shelf life (Brocklehurst et al., 1987; Nguyen-The and Prunier, 1989).

Some of the bacteria associated with the natural flora of prepared vegetables (such as *Bacillus* spp., *Cytophaga* spp., *Erwinia* spp., *Pseudomonas* spp.) (Nguyen-The and Prunier, 1989; Brocklehurst et al., 1987) can cause deterioration due to the production of pectic enzymes. These degrade the pectic substances inside the middle lamella between individual cells which cement together the cell walls of plant tissues. This degradation can lead to loss of turgor of the cells and can proceed to give soft-rotted areas of the tissue resulting in a translucent or watersoaked appearance.

Published studies of the microbiological changes that occur in these products during storage are confined largely to prepared vegetable products, and the comments that follow refer to these.

The predominant microorganisms present in packs of prepared vegetable salad products at packing include a wide range of Gram-positive and Gram-negative bacteria, such as members of the Enterobacteriaceae

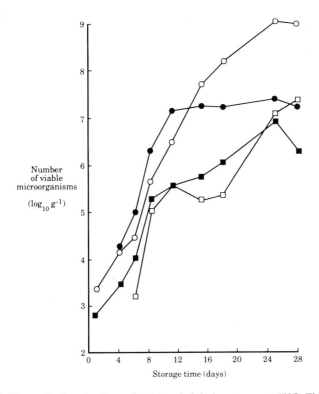

Figure 6.16 Changes in the microflora of potato salad during storage at 10°C. The salad had a pH of 4.3–4.4 and a residual concentration of undissociated acetic acid in the aqueous phase of the mayonnaise of 0.2% (w/w). ○, Lactobacilli; ●, *Saccharomyces exiguus*; □, *Geotrichum candidum*; ■, *Candida* species. (First published by Brocklehurst, T.F. and Lund, B.M. in *Food Microbiology*, **1**, 5–12 (1984) and reproduced by permission of the publisher, Academic Press, London.)

and Streptococcaceae, *Pseudomonas* spp., *Flavobacterium* spp., lactic acid bacteria and yeasts (Shapiro and Holder, 1960; Manvell and Ackland, 1986; Brocklehurst *et al.*, 1987). These are derived mainly from the naturally associated microflora of the plant tissues, but some sites within processing factories (particularly shredders and slicers) can be accumulation points for microorganisms, and could give rise to subsequent contamination of processed materials (Garg *et al.*, 1990).

Storage of these products at 8°C resulted in the multiplication of bile tolerant bacteria, *Pseudomonas* spp., lactic acid bacteria, yeasts and moulds (Manvell and Ackland, 1986; Brocklehurst *et al.*, 1987). This microbial growth was accompanied by a decrease in the concentration of oxygen and an increase in the concentration of carbon dioxide in the pack (Brocklehurst and van Bentem, 1990) (Figures 6.21 and 6.22), although this change in the gaseous composition could have been the result of the

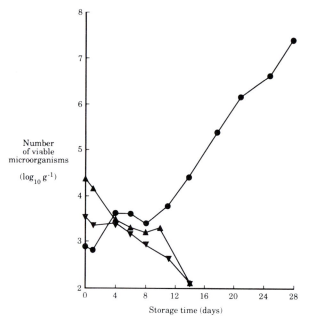

Figure 6.17 Changes in the microflora of coleslaw during storage at 10°C. The salad had a pH of 4.1–4.3 and a residual concentration of undissociated acetic acid in the aqueous phase of the mayonnaise of 0.6% (w/w). ●, *Saccharomyces exiguus*; ▲, Lactobacilli; ▼, other bacteria. (First published by Brocklehurst, T.F. and Lund, B.M. in *Food Microbiology*, **1**, 5–12 (1984) and reproduced by permission of the publisher, Academic Press, London.)

respiration of the plant tissue and the microorganisms. Such increases in the concentration of CO_2 within the pack favoured the multiplication of yeasts and lactic acid bacteria in packs of grated carrot (Carlin *et al.*, 1990). Babic *et al.* (1992) considered, though, that neither the number of yeasts nor the composition of the yeast flora were directly related to product shelf life. Manvell and Ackland (1986) suggested that the number of Gram-negative bacteria in these products was an important determinant of shelf life and used the *Limulus* lysate test as an indicator of shelf life. They also found that when products were stored at 30°C, lactic acid bacteria predominated, and these authors suggested, therefore, that an assay of the concentration of lactic acid produced as a by-product of the growth of lactic acid bacteria could be used as an indicator of temperature abuse. Other bacteria of significance isolated from retail packs have included *Escherichia coli* type 1, *Listeria monocytogenes*, *Yersinia intermedia*, and *Yersinia enterocolitica* (Brocklehurst *et al.*, 1987; Sizmur and Walker, 1988), although Brackett (1987) also lists a range of potential hazards derived from viruses and parasites in these kinds of products.

Products that contain prepared fruits or pieces of fruit are becoming

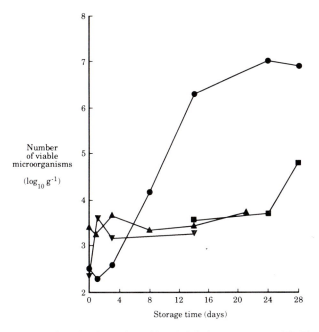

Figure 6.18 Changes in the microflora of Florida salad during storage at 10°C. The salad had a pH of 3.4–3.5 and a residual concentration of undissociated acetic acid in the aqueous phase of the mayonnaise of 0.8% (w/w). ●, *Saccharomyces exiguus*; ■, *Pichia membranaefaciens*; ▲, Lactobacilli; ▼, other bacteria. (First published by Brocklehurst, T.F. and Lund, B.M. in *Food Microbiology*, **1**, 5–12 (1984) and reproduced by permission of the publisher, Academic Press, London.)

more popular. The shelf life of these products will be constrained by the same types of interactions that influence the shelf life of vegetable products, except that the microflora will differ. The pH of the exudate from vegetable tissues is usually between pH 5.8 and 7.3, and hence it readily supports growth of bacteria. Fruit exudate, however, is more acidic and has a pH between 2.4 and 5.2 (von Schelhorn, 1951), and it tends to select for the growth of yeasts, moulds and lactic acid bacteria as the predominant microflora (Goepfert, 1980).

6.4.2.2 Organoleptic changes. The products may contain very large numbers of bacteria and yeasts that do not have an obvious influence on the quality of the product. In these cases the shelf life has been shown often to be determined by the rate of deterioration in colour, texture or flavour of the vegetable tissue components (King and Bolin, 1989), and oxidative discoloration, and pectinolytic and flavour changes of fruit slices (Heaton *et al.*, 1969; Ponting *et al.*, 1972). Many of these changes result from physiological processes that are inevitable in living tissues, but that are accelerated by tissue damage (Rolle and Chism, 1987). Loss of texture

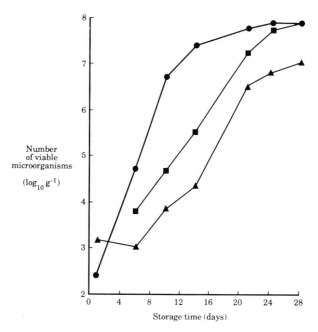

Figure 6.19 Changes in the microflora of vegetable salad during storage at 10°C. The salad had a pH of 3.9–4.1 and a residual concentration of undissociated acetic acid in the aqueous phase of the mayonnaise of 0.8% (w/w). ●, *Saccharomyces exiguus*; ■, *Pichia membranaefaciens*; ▲, Lactobacilli. (First published by Brocklehurst, T.F. and Lund, B.M. in *Food Microbiology*, **1**, 5–12 (1984) and reproduced by permission of the publisher, Academic Press, London.)

is related to a weakening of the polymeric structures of the plant cell wall and may be accompanied by a loss of turgor (King and Bolin, 1989), which is a result of exudation (Carlin *et al.*, 1990). Bolin *et al.* (1977) and Bolin and Huxsoll (1991) found that shredded lettuce darkened during storage, and that this change was accompanied by a loss in visual green pigmentation, which was greater at 10°C than at 5°C and greater at 5°C than at 2°C. This decrease in colour is usually accompanied by an increase in the discoloration of cut surfaces due to the action of the enzyme phenolase (King and Bolin, 1989). Flavour and appearance were judged on a hedonic scale by Priepke *et al.* (1976), who found that during storage of cut vegetables (lettuce, carrot, endive, celery, and radish), these attributes deteriorated faster than in intact tissue. Williams (1990) also found discoloration, odor development and drying of tissues to be determinants of shelf life in prepared mixed salads, and showed that the temperature dependence of these changes followed a square root relationship.

Constituents that might contribute to taste or flavour were studied by

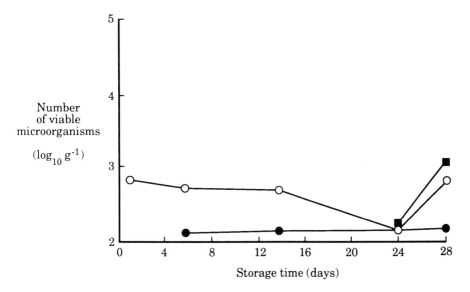

Figure 6.20 Changes in the microflora of Spanish salad during storage at 10°C. The salad had a pH of 3.6–3.8 and a residual concentration of undissociated acetic acid in the aqueous phase of the mayonnaise of 1.0% (w/w). ○, Lactobacilli; ●, *Saccharomyces exiguus*; ■, *Pichia membranaefaciens*. (First published by Brocklehurst, T.F. and Lund, B.M. in *Food Microbiology*, **1**, 5–12 (1984) and reproduced by permission of the publisher, Academic Press, London.)

Bolin and Huxsoll (1991). They found that the concentration of sugars and the titratable acidity of cut lettuce did not change during storage at 2°C, but the content of soluble solids, which would have included storage polysaccharide, declined and this was possibly due to the utilisation of carbohydrate by respiration.

Carlin *et al.* (1990) found that the concentrations of sucrose (which has considerable influence on carrot taste, Rumpf and Hansen, 1973), glucose, fructose and malic acid in grated carrots decreased dramatically during storage in air at 10°C, although the rates of disappearance of these constituents from this tissue could be slowed down by modification of the gaseous atmosphere.

Flavour taints caused by anaerobiosis of the plant tissue are related to the oxygen concentration within the pack and the threshold concentration at which the tissue becomes anaerobic (McLachlan and Stark, 1985). The end products of anaerobic metabolism are usually lactic and acetic acids and ethanol (Carlin *et al.*, 1989) although these authors suggested that the concentrations of these in the pack could be derived from the contaminating lactic acid bacteria as well as from the vegetable tissues.

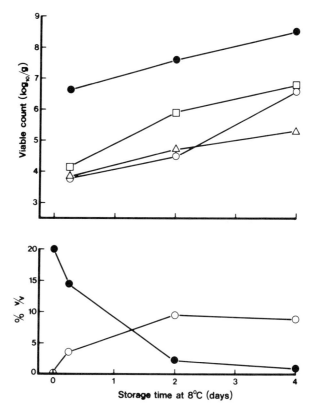

Figure 6.21 Changes in the microflora, and in the composition of gaseous atmosphere, of a pack of prepared mixed salad packaged in a tray and overwrapped with PVC cling film (15 μ in thickness) during storage at 8°C. The pack contained shredded Chinese leaf, shredded white cabbage, shredded carrot, chopped celery, chopped red pepper, chopped green pepper, cress and sweetcorn. Upper graph: ●, Pseudomonads; ○, lactic acid bacteria; △, yeasts and moulds; □, bile tolerant lactose fermenting organisms. Lower graph: ●, O_2; ○, CO_2. (First published by Brocklehurst, T.F. and van Bentem, E. in *Food Science and Technology Today*, **4**(3), 156–8 (1990), and reproduced by courtesy of the publisher, the Institute of Food Science and Technology (UK).)

6.5 Current developments and the future

6.5.1 Delicatessen salads

A logical development for the mayonnaise-based salads industry is the production of entire mini-meals based on the salads concept. Such products are in keeping with the image of a healthy diet, and they offer the manufacturer an opportunity for added value. What has limited this progression, however, has been the inherent difficulty in making a product that is both bland and safe. The product must be bland in order to allow

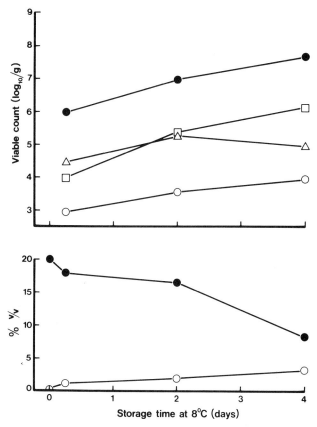

Figure 6.22 Changes in the microflora, and in the composition of gaseous atmosphere, of a pack of prepared mixed salad packaged in a tray and overwrapped with PVC cling film (19 μ in thickness) during storage at 8°C. The pack contained shredded frise, shredded radicchio, shredded chicory and lambs lettuce. Upper graph: ●, Pseudomonads; ○, lactic acid bacteria; △, yeasts and moulds; □, bile tolerant lactose fermenting organisms. Lower graph: ●, O_2; ○, CO_2.

consumption of the quantity needed to constitute a mini-meal, and yet a mild product would not have sufficient concentration of antimicrobial acids to ensure either microbiological safety or a sufficiently long shelf life.

This kind of development necessitates a thorough understanding and analysis of the chemical and physical interactions occurring within the products. Predictions that relate the concentration of undissociated acetic acid remaining in the aqueous phase of the mayonnaise after interactions have occurred within the product to that concentration required to inhibit the growth of microorganisms of interest could be described as follows:

target		function of		effect of		effect of		effect
concentration	=	the total	×	migration	×	pK_a and pH	×	of
of organic		concentration				of food on		partition
acid required		of organic acid				dissociation		

Information about the inhibitory concentrations of organic acids can be derived from the literature or from databases that are actively under construction in the UK and elsewhere, such as the newly introduced Food Micromodel by the UK Ministry of Agriculture, Fisheries and Food (MAFF, 1992).

The use of buffering systems within dressed salads has been adopted occasionally (Debevere, 1987). Buffer systems operate by creating a high concentration of weak acid and its salt (for example citric acid and trisodium citrate or acetic acid and sodium acetate) in the aqueous phase of the mayonnaise. The buffering system in the case of an acetate/acetic acid buffer operates as follows:

$$\underset{\substack{\text{undissociated} \\ \text{acetic acid}}}{CH_3COOH} \quad \overset{\text{acidity decreases}}{\underset{\text{acidity increases}}{\rightleftharpoons}} \quad \underset{\substack{\text{dissociated} \\ \text{acetate} \\ \text{ion}}}{CH_3COO^-} + \underset{\text{proton}}{H^+} \qquad (6.5)$$

When a change occurs in the food that increases its acidity (which is really an increase in the concentration of protons or H^+ ions) the protons combine with the acetate ions to produce undissociated acid and the influence of these protons is therefore negated. Likewise when the food becomes less acidic, equation (6.5) is driven to the right and the acid dissociates to release protons and the pH is kept constant. In theory these systems offer a means of introducing into foods a large reservoir of undissociated acid that remains microbicidal at a range of pH values (Debevere, 1987), although the actual concentration range is restricted because of organoleptic implications.

An attractive feature of many mayonnaise-based salads is the incorporation of high protein ingredients such as cheese, chicken meat, corned beef, crab meat, egg, ham, herring meat, mycoprotein, prawns or sausage. These ingredients give significant added value to the product, but their inclusion usually results in a food that has a higher pH than if the protein ingredient were absent (Rose, 1984). For example, the pH of mayonnaise-based salads without protein ingredients is usually in the range of pH 3.2–4.5. The addition of cheese elevated this to pH 4.0–4.5, fish elevated this to pH 3.6–4.4, meat to pH 4.0–5.1 and seafood to pH 3.7–4.5. This has implications for the safety and microbiological stability of the products. There are suggestions that the protein components could confer some protection on the contaminating bacteria from the hostile environment of the dressing. For example, McKinley et al. (1974) showed that the food-borne pathogenic bacterium *Staphylococcus aureus* was protected from the acidic environment within the mayonnaise when it was inoculated into a mayonnaise-based salad as a contaminant of chicken meat.

Modified atmosphere packaging (MAP) of mayonnaise based salads has been introduced, although it is not used widely and published studies suggest that it is not always beneficial. For example, studies by Buick and Damoglou (1989) showed that a gaseous atmosphere of 20% (v/v) CO_2 and 80% (v/v) N_2 delayed the microbiological spoilage of a mayonnaise-based vegetable salad stored at 4°C, 10°C or 15°C by inhibiting growth of the spoilage yeasts. However, studies by Ahvenainen *et al.* (1990) that used a storage temperature of 5°C did not result in growth of spoilage microorganisms, but the use of gaseous atmospheres that contained concentrations of CO_2 greater than or equal to 20% (v/v) caused organoleptic deterioration of a mayonnaise-based potato salad during the shelf life. The CO_2 caused flavour changes described as 'oldish', 'sour', 'rancid' or 'oxidised off-taste' from the beginning of storage. These changes became more noticeable as the concentration of CO_2 was increased, and the flavour continued to deteriorate throughout storage.

Pasteurisation is a processing option that does not fit easily with the 'fresh' image of these products. Nevertheless, pasteurised salads have been marketed, although spoilage of these caused by acid-tolerant *Clostridium* spp. has been documented (Baumgart *et al.*, 1984). In addition, the flavour of the mayonnaise can deteriorate upon heating (Cerny and Hennlich, 1983), although developments have taken place that claim to overcome these changes by the use of thermostable mayonnaise ingredients (Galvin, 1991).

Market trends have resulted in the appearance of new dressings that reinforce the 'healthy eating' image of this product range. Dressings that have low oil content or that are 'virtually fat free' may appeal to the consumer, although work on the influence of these dressings on the organoleptic and microbiological quality of the salad products has not been published. Dressings based on yogurt or sour cream will probably also be reintroduced, and an interest in fermented dressings is emerging in the literature (Bonestroo *et al.*, 1993).

6.5.2 *Prepared fruit and vegetables*

Modification of the gaseous atmosphere of these products is applied quite widely in Europe and in the USA, although currently less so in the UK. The rationale behind MAP is to decrease the concentration of oxygen in the packs and poise it at a concentration that will diminish the extent of oxidative discoloration that leads to spoilage (McLachlan and Stark, 1985). MAP can also be used to retard ripening and senescence processes (Isenberg, 1979; Myers, 1989).

The concentration of gases within MAP products should be such that the production of CO_2 and consumption of O_2 by the respiring tissues is balanced by the gas transmission through the packaging material. The appropriate gas composition may be achieved by the respiration of the vegetable or fruit tissues or it may be imposed by flushing the pack with a suitable gas mixture. Although the future may see an expansion of MAP of these products it is true that MAP has severe limitations. Microorganisms of public health significance can multiply on vegetable tissues stored under MAP (Berrang et al., 1989a, 1989b), but potentially the most serious problem is the enhanced respiration rate of damaged vegetable and fruit tissues. This can cause overmodification of the gaseous atmosphere within the pack, leading to anaerobic respiration of the vegetable and fruit tissues and the development of associated taints. It also raises the spectre of the possible growth and toxin production by anaerobic bacteria such as Clostridium botulinum.

Close matching of the permeability characteristics of the packaging material and the respiration rates of the product is essential, therefore, if overmodified atmospheres are to be avoided. Huxsoll and Bolin (1989) emphasised that the optimum concentrations of O_2 and CO_2 must be established for each commodity and for each kind of degradative reaction, and be matched with the packaging material, the permeability of which is affected by storage temperature, polymer type, thickness and the surface area of the material available for gaseous exchange.

Interest in 'active' packaging may grow and an attempt may be made to address some of the difficulties encountered in packaging respiring foods. 'Active' films modify the composition of gas within a pack by chemical reaction and so create and maintain the correctly poised atmosphere (Ronk et al., 1989). For example, potassium permanganate has been used to absorb ethylene, calcium hydroxide to absorb CO_2, and O_2 scavengers based on the oxidation of ascorbic acid or ferrous compounds have also been available (Barmore, 1987). Although potentially useful, these films must be used cautiously. Chemical contamination of the fruit or vegetable tissue must be avoided, and it must be remembered that the capacity of the film to absorb gas is finite and the atmosphere will not be controlled once the active chemical agents are exhausted.

Microperforated films contain small pores, which allow mass transfer of gases to take place, so that movement through the film is not solely dependent upon diffusion. They can allow equilibrium concentrations of gases to be established in the case of rapidly respiring tissues, but their use tends to be somewhat by 'trial and error'.

Perhaps what all of this has identified as an urgent future requirement for these products is a comprehensive mathematical model encompassing tissue respiration rates and film permeabilities such that the composition of the gaseous atmosphere of these packs can be controlled reliably and safely. Future market trends will almost certainly see the introduction of products that are predominantly or solely fruit tissues. The technical difficulties in the manufacture of these products are great, but some producers are already trying out attractive packs of fruit pieces.

References

Adams, M.R., Hartley, A.D. and Cox, J.L. (1989) Factors affecting the efficacy of washing procedures used in the production of prepared salads. *Food Microbiology*, **6**, 69–77.

Ahvenainen, R., Skyttä, E. and Kivikataja, R-L. (1990) The influence of modified atmosphere packaging on the quality of selected ready-to-eat foods. *Food Science and Technology: Lebensmittel-Wissenschaft & Technologie*, **23**, 139–48.

Anon (1990) Statutory Instrument No. 1431. Food. *Food Hygiene (Amendment) Regulations*. HMSO, London.

Babic, I., Hilbert, G., Nguyen-The, C. and Guiraud, J. (1992) The yeast flora of stored ready-to-use carrots and their role in spoilage. *International Journal of Food Science and Technology*, **27**, 473–84.

Baird-Parker, A.C. (1980) Organic acids, in *Microbial ecology of foods. Vol. 1. Factors affecting life and death of microorganisms*, International Commission on Microbiological Specifications for Foods, Academic Press, London, New York, pp. 126–35.

Barmore, C.R. (1987) Packing Technology for fresh and minimally processed fruits and vegetables. *Journal of Food Quality*, **10**, 207–17.

Baumgart, J. and Hauschild, G. (1980) Enfluß von weinsäure auf die Haltbarkeit von feinkost-salaten. *Fleischwirtsch*, **60**(5), 1052–6.

Baumgart, J., Hippe, H. and Weber, B. (1984) Verderb pasteurisierter feinkostsalate durch *Clostridien. Chemie Mikrobiologie Technologie der Lebensmittel*, **8**, 109–14.

Baumgart, J., Weber, B. and Hanekamp, B. (1983) Mikrobiologisch stabilität von feinkosterzeugnissen. *Fleischwirtschaft*, **63**(1), 93–4.

Berrang, M.E., Brackett, R.E. and Beuchat, L.R. (1989a) Growth of *Aeromonas hydrophila* on fresh vegetables stored under a controlled atmosphere. *Applied and Environmental Microbiology*, **55**(9), 2167–71.

Berrang, M.E., Brackett, R.E. and Beuchat, L.R. (1989b) Growth of *Listeria monocytogenes* on fresh vegetables stored under controlled atmosphere. *Journal of Food Protection*, **52**(10), 702–5.

Bodansky, M. (1928) Lipoid solubility, permeability and hemolytic action of the saturated fatty acids. *Journal of Biological Chemistry*, **79**, 241–55.

Bolin, H.R. and Huxsoll, C.C. (1991) Effect of preparation procedures and storage parameters on quality retention of salad-cut lettuce. *Journal of Food Science*, **56**(1), 60 7.

Bolin, H.R., Stafford, A.E., King, A.D. Jr. and Huxsoll, C.C. (1977) Factors affecting the storage stability of shredded lettuce. *Journal of Food Science*, **42**(5), 1319–21.

Bonestroo, M.N., Kusters, B.J.M., de Wit, J.C. and Rombouts, F.M. (1993) The fate of spoilage and pathogenic bacteria in fermented sauce-based salads. *Food Microbiology*, **10**, 101–11.

Boyar, M.M., Kilcast, D. and Dodson, A.G. (1985) Physico-chemical changes in stored coleslaw. *Leatherhead Food R.A. Research Report*, No. 502.

Brackett, R.E. (1987) Microbiological consequences of minimally processed fruits and vegetables. *Journal of Food Quality*, **10**, 195–206.

Brocklehurst, T.F. (1984) A delicatessen problem. *Food Manufacture*, **April**, 65 and 67.

Brocklehurst, T.F. and Lund, B.M. (1984) Microbiological changes in mayonnaise-based salads during storage. *Food Microbiology*, **1**, 5–12.

Brocklehurst, T.F. and van Bentem, E. (1990) Packed freshness at your service. *Food Science and Technology Today*, **4**(3), 156–8.

Brocklehurst, T.F., White, C.A. and Dennis, C. (1983) The microflora of stored coleslaw and factors affecting the growth of spoilage yeasts in coleslaw. *Journal of Applied Bacteriology*, **55**, 57–63.

Brocklehurst, T.F., Zaman-Wong, C.M. and Lund, B.M. (1987) A note on the microbiology of retail packs of prepared salad vegetables. *Journal of Applied Bacteriology*, **63**, 409–15.

B.S.I. (1980) British Standards Institute, *Methods for Sensory Analysis of Food, Part 1*, BS 5929, BSI, London.

Buick, R.K. and Damoglou, A.P. (1989) Effect of modified atmosphere packaging on the microbial development and visible shelf life of a mayonnaise-based vegetable salad. *Journal of the Science of Food and Agriculture*, **46**, 339–47.

Carlin, F., Nguyen-The, C., Cudennec, P. and Reich, M. (1989) Microbiological spoilage of 'ready-to-use' grated carrots. *Science des Aliments*, **9**, 371–386.

Carlin, F., Nguyen-The, C., Chambroy, Y. and Reich, M. (1990) Effects of controlled atmospheres on microbial spoilage, electrolyte leakage and sugar content of fresh 'ready-to-use' grated carrots. *International Journal of Food Science and Technology*, **25**, 110–19.

Cerny, G. and Hennlich, W. (1983) Microbial stability of meat-salads at ambient temperatures. Part 2: Pasteurization of heat-sensitive mayonnaise with or without addition of preservatives. *Internationale Zeitschrift für Lebensmittel-Technologie und Verfahrenstechnik*, **7**, 610–16.

Chen, L.M. and Peng, A.C. (1980) Effect of acid dip on the shelf life of coleslaw. *Journal of Food Science*, **45**, 1556–8.

Christiansen, L.N. and King, N.S. (1971) The microbial content of some salads and sandwiches at retail outlets. *Journal of Milk and Food Technology*, **34**(6), 289–93.

CIMSCEE (1985) *Code for the Production of Microbiologically Safe and Stable Emulsified and Non-emulsified Sauces Containing Acetic Acid*, Comité des Industries des Mayonnaise et Sauces Condimentaires de la Communauté Economique Européenne.

Collins, M.A. (1982) Investigations on some factors affecting the keeping quality of coleslaw. *Record of Agricultural Research*, **30**, 53–60.

Corry, J.E.L., Walker, A.K. and Jarvis, B. (1980) The storage of perishable dairy-type products. Part I: Coleslaw salad, cottage cheese, strawberry yoghurt and pasteurised double cream. *Leatherhead Food R.A. Research Report*, No. 335.

Davies, A.M.C. and Brocklehurst, T.F. (1986) Near infrared reflectance analysis of oil concentration in an emulsion: a study of oil and water migrations in a mayonnaise-based salad. *Journal of the Science of Food and Agriculture*, **37**, 310–16.

Debevere, J.M. (1987) The use of buffered acidulant systems to improve the microbiological stability of acid foods. *Food Microbiology*, **4**, 105–14.

Dennis, C. and Buhagiar, R.W.M. (1980) Yeast spoilage of fresh and processed fruits and vegetables, in *Biology and Activities of Yeasts* (eds F.A. Skinner, S.M. Passmore and R.R. Davenport), Academic Press.

Dziezak, J.D. (1988) Monsanto's new product extends produce freshness. *Food Technology*, **September**, 98.

Eklund, T. (1983) The antimicrobial effects of dissociated and undissociated sorbic acid at different pH levels. *Journal of Applied Bacteriology*, **54**, 383–9.

Fowler, J.L. and Clark, W.S. Jr. (1975) Microbiology of delicatessen salads. *Journal of Milk and Food Technology*, **38**(3), 146–9.

Galvin, P.A. (1991) Pasteurized salads using ingredient blend retain fresh flavor. *Food Technology*, June, 110.

Garg, N., Churey, J.J. and Splittstoesser, D.F. (1990) Effect of processing conditions on the microflora of fresh-cut vegetables. *Journal of Food Protection*, **53**(8), 701–3.

Geeson, J.D., Brocklehurst, T.F. and Griffiths, N. (1987) Be prepared. *Food*, **February**, 49–53.

Goepfert, J.M. (1980) Vegetables, fruits, nuts and their products. in *Microbial Ecology of Foods. Vol. 2. Food Commodities*, International Commission on Microbiological Specifications for Foods, Academic Press, London, New York, pp. 606–42.

Gordon, N.E. and Reid, E.E. (1922) The solubility of liquids in liquids. The partition of the lower acids, particularly formic, between water and various organic solvents. *Journal of Physical Chemistry*, **26**, 773–89.

Goupy, P. (1989) Le brunissement enzymatique de la feuille de Scarole (*Cichorum endiva*):

composés phénolique et enzymes d'oxydation des feuilles chlorophyllienes et étiolées. *Ph.D. thesis*, Université des Sciences et Techniques du Languedoc, Montpellier.

Greenwood, M.H., Coetzee, E.F.C., Ford, B.M., Gil, P., Hooper, W.L., Matthews, S.C.W., Patrick, S., Pether, J.V.S. and Scott, R.J.D. (1975) The bacteriological quality of selected retail, ready-to-eat food products. *Environmental Health*, **93**(8), 208–11.

Hankin, L. and Ullman, W.W. (1969) Application of the oxidase test to refrigerated delicatessen foods. *Journal of Milk and Food Technology*, **32**, 122–5.

Harris, N.H., Martin, S.R. and Ellias, L. (1975) Bacteriological quality of selected delicatessen foods. *Journal of Milk and Food Technology*, **38**, 759–61.

Heaton, E.K., Boggess, T.S. Jr. and Li, K.C. (1969) Processing refrigerated fresh peach slices. *Food Technology*, **23**, 96–100.

Hilliam, M.A. (1986) *Chilled foods in the UK – second edition*, Leatherhead Food R.A. Information Group Services (Market Information Service), Food Market Update No. 14.

Holtzapffel, D. and Mossel, D.A.A. (1968) The survival of pathogenic bacteria in, and the microbial spoilage of, salads, containing meat, fish and vegetables. *Journal of Food Technology*, **3**, 223–39.

Horne, A.M.L. (1989) *Chilled foods in the UK – third edition*, Leatherhead Food R.A. Information Group Services (Market Intelligence Section), Food Market Update No. 33.

Huxsoll, C.C. and Bolin, H.R. (1989) Processing and distribution alternatives for minimally processed fruits and vegetables. *Food Technology*, **February** 124–8.

IFST (1990) *Guidelines for the Handling of Chilled Foods*, 2nd edn, Institute of Food Science and Technology, London.

Isenberg, F.M.R. (1979) Controlled atmosphere storage of vegetables. *Horticultural Review*, **1**, 337–94.

Kaufman, J. and Lutz, J.M. (1954) Lengthening the shelf life of packaged coleslaw. *Pre-Pack-Age*, **8**, 23–6.

King, A.D. Jr. and Bolin, H.R. (1989) Physiological and microbiological storage stability of minimally processed fruits and vegetables. *Food Technology*, **February**, 132–5.

King, A.D. Jr., Michener, H.D., Bayne, H.G. and Mihara, K.L. (1976) Microbial studies on shelf life of cabbage and coleslaw. *Applied and Environmental Microbiology*, **31**(3), 404–7.

Kirsop, B.H. and Brocklehurst, T.F. (1982) The spoilage of mayonnaise-based delicatessen salads. *Process Biochemistry*, **September/October**, 9–14.

Leo, A., Hansch, C. and Elkins, D. (1971) Partition coefficients and their uses. *Chemical Reviews*, **71**(6), 525–616.

Lueck, E. (1980) *Antimicrobial Food Additives: Characteristics, Uses, Effects*, Springer-Verlag, Berlin, Heidelberg, New York.

MAFF (1992) *Food Micromodel*, Ministry of Agriculture, Fisheries and Food, London.

Manvell, P.M. and Ackland, M.R. (1986) Rapid detection of microbial growth in vegetable salads at chill and abuse temperatures. *Food Microbiology*, **3**, 59–65.

McKinley, T.W., Henning, W.C. and McCroan, J.E. (1974) *Staphylococcal* growth and enterotoxin production in chicken and chicken salad. *Association of Food and Drug Officials Quarterly Bulletin*, **38**, 56.

McLachlan, A. and Stark, R. (1985) Modified atmosphere packaging of selected prepared vegetables. *Campden Food Preservation Research Association Technical Memorandum*, No. 412.

Myers, R.A. (1989) Packaging considerations for minimally processed fruits and vegetables. *Food Technology*, February, 129–31.

Nguyen-The, C. and Prunier, J.P. (1989) Involvement of pseudomonads in deterioration of 'ready-to-use' salads. *International Journal of Food Science and Technology*, **24**, 47–58.

Norberg, A.P. and Åkerstrand, K. (1980) Hållbarhetstider för färdigförpackade sallader. *Vår Föda*, **1**, 25–30.

O'Beirne, D. and Ballantyne, A. (1987) Some effects of modified-atmosphere packaging and vacuum packaging in combination with antioxidants on quality and storage life of chilled potato strips. *International Journal of Food Science and Technology*, **22**, 515–23.

Pace, P.J. (1975) Bacteriological quality of delicatessen foods: are standards needed? *Journal of Milk and Food Technology*, **38**(6), 347–53.

Ponting, J.D., Jackson, R. and Watters, G. (1972) Refrigerated apple slices: preservative effects of ascorbic acid, calcium and sulfites. *Journal of Food Science,* **37**, 434–6.

Priepke, P.E., Wei, L.S. and Nelson, A.I. (1976) Refrigerated storage of prepackaged salad vegetables. *Journal of Food Science,* **41**, 379–82.

Ranken, M.D. (1988) *Food Industries Manual,* 22nd edn, Blackie Academic & Professional, Glasgow.

Roberts, D. (1990) Sources of infection: food. *The Lancet,* **8719**, 859–61.

Robinson, J.E., Browne, K.M. and Burton, W.G. (1975) Storage characteristics of some vegetables and soft fruits. *Annals of Applied Biology,* **81**, 399–408.

Robinson, R.A. and Stokes, R.H. (1959) *Electrolyte Solutions,* Butterworths, London.

Rolle, R.S. and Chism, G.W. (1987) Physiological consequences of minimally processed fruits and vegetables. *Journal of Food Quality,* **10**, 157–77.

Ronk, R.J., Carson, K.L. and Thompson, P. (1989) Processing, packaging and regulation of minimally processed fruits and vegetables. *Food Technology,* **February**, 136–9.

Rose, S.A. (1984) Studies of the microbiological status of prepacked delicatessen salads collected from retail chill cabinets. *Campden Food Preservation Research Association, Technical Memorandum,* No. 371.

Rumpf, G. and Hansen, H. (1973) Gaschromatographische Bestimmung löslicher Inhaltstoffe in 'Controlled atmosphere' – gelagerten Möhren. *Gartenbauwissenschaft,* **38**, 281–5.

Shapiro, J.E. and Holder, I.A. (1960) Effect of antibiotic and chemical dips on the microflora of packaged salad mix. *Applied Microbiology,* **8**, 341–5.

Sizmur, K. and Walker, C.W. (1988) Listeria in prepacked salads. *The Lancet,* **8595**, 1167.

Sugiyama, H. and Yang, K.H. (1975) Growth potential of *Clostridium botulinum* in fresh mushrooms packaged in semi-permeable plastic film. *Applied Microbiology,* **30**, 964–9.

Tamminga, S.K., Beumer, R.R., Kiejbets, M.J.H. and Kampelmacher, E.H. (1978) Microbial spoilage and development of food poisoning bacteria in peeled completely or partly cooked vacuum packaged potatoes. *Archiv fur Lebensmittelhygiene,* **29**, 215–19.

Terry, R.C. and Overcast, W.W. (1976) A microbiological profile of commercially prepared salads. *Journal of Food Science,* **41**, 211–13.

Tunaley, A. and Brocklehurst, T.F. (1982) A study on the shelf-life of coleslaw. *Chilled Foods,* **November/December**, 12–13.

Tunaley, A., Brownsey, G. and Brocklehurst, T.F. (1985) Changes in mayonnaise-based salads during storage. *Food Science and Technology: Lebensmittel-Wissenschaft & Technologie,* **18**, 220–4.

Tuynenburg Muys, G. (1971) Microbial safety in emulsions. *Process Biochemistry,* **6**(6), 25–8.

von Schelhorn, M. (1951) Control of microorganisms causing spoilage in fruit and vegetable products. *Advances in Food Research,* **3**, 429–83.

von Schelhorn, M. (1964) Investigations of the distribution of preservatives between fat and water in foods. *Fourth International Symposium Food Microbiology,* Goteburg, Sweden, 1964, 139–144.

Wiberg, A.C., Larsson, B., Movitz, J. and Akerstrand, K. (1983) Hållbarhetstider för färdigförpackade sallader. *Vår Föda,* **35**, 404–16.

Williams, A.P. (1990) Chilled combined foods and chilled meals, in *Chilled Foods. The state of the art* (ed. T.R. Gormley), Elsevier Applied Science, London and New York, pp. 225–43.

Young, J.N. (1984) Delicatessen foods in the UK. *Leatherhead Food R.A., Food Market Update,* No. 33.

7 Chilled yogurt and other dairy desserts

M. LEWIS and R.H. DALE

7.1 Introduction

For many years the production of short-life perishable food products was organised and carried out on a regional or local level. This enabled products to be sold within a very short period following manufacture. However, since the Second World War a major revolution has taken place within the food industries of Europe, the USA and Japan. This has occurred in the chilled, short-life dairy products sector in particular.

Modern marketing methods and techniques have created ever increasing mass markets with an apparently insatiable appetite for new and novel products. The drive for increasing the efficiency of production plants in order to reduce costs and increase profits has led to a centralisation of production units. Major improvements in the ability of manufacturers and retailers to transport refrigerated products over long distances coupled with the lowering of trade barriers within the European Community have created export opportunities. All this now means that dairy desserts once considered perishable within very short periods are required for consumption many days after their manufacture. This tremendous change within the market both in volume and requirement has created immense technical problems and has led to a quiet revolution in the field of food technology.

Ensuring the safety of these products has of course been paramount, but to underwrite the commercial success it has been equally important to ensure that other product parameters remain good. Indeed, the sensory, visual and physical characteristics should exhibit the same quality of freshness at the end of the product's life as at the beginning.

This requirement for freshness (often associated by the consumer with healthiness and wholesomeness) together with the safety requirements have taken place in an environment where the removal of 'artificial' preservatives and other additives was also demanded. The challenge created for the food and dairy technologists has been enormous.

In order for the public to be confident of the quality of these products, the Government introduced mandatory date coding. Initially this was adopted by the food industry in the form of 'sell-by' dates. However, recent changes in UK and EC legislation require 'best before' dates for non-perishable products and a more definitive 'use-by' date for microbiologically unstable products such as dairy desserts. This legislation also requires manufacturers to be able to justify the codes which are applied to the products if requested to do so by the enforcement authorities. Therefore, it has been necessary for the food technologist, not only to extend the life of the products, but also to improve the methods by which the shelf life is determined.

This chapter will review many aspects of shelf life associated with dairy desserts, not in complicated scientific terms but in the practical language of the dairy industry. It will attempt to categorise dairy desserts into broad groupings and discuss key factors affecting shelf life from raw materials through to the consumer.

7.2 Products, product groups and characteristics

Over the last ten years, the sale of yogurt, fromage frais and other desserts has shown a steady growth, benefiting from market segmentation and the healthy eating trend. More recently, there has been an increasing trend for the more indulgent products containing higher fat levels, exotic fruits and the use of 'Bio' cultures.

The different varieties and percentages of sales by volume of yogurts, fromage frais and traditional desserts are shown in Figures 7.1–7.3.

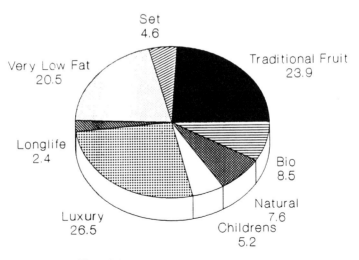

Figure 7.1 Yogurt – percentage of total sales.

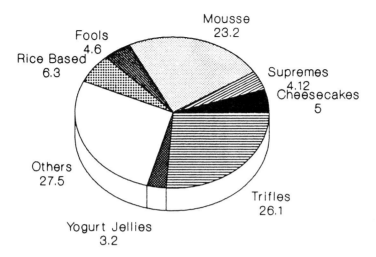

Figure 7.2 Traditional desserts – percentage of total sales.

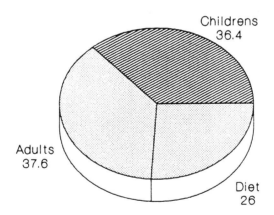

Figure 7.3 Fromage frais – percentage of total sales.

7.2.1 Product groups

For shelf life evaluation the products are classified into two main groups:

1. cultured products
2. desserts (un-fermented/blends)

The manufacture of cultured products involves the controlled use of lactic acid producing microorganisms for prescribed time and temperature combinations to achieve a final product with the desired characteristics of viscosity, texture, mouthfeel, flavour and acidity.

The desserts are either simple products such as custards and jellies or complex products including trifles, mousses and cheesecakes which are a mixture of textures, taste and acidity levels. General classifications of chilled yogurts, soft cheeses and desserts are given in Figures 7.4, 7.5 and 7.6.

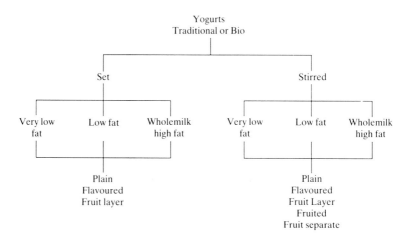

Figure 7.4 General classifications of chilled yogurts.

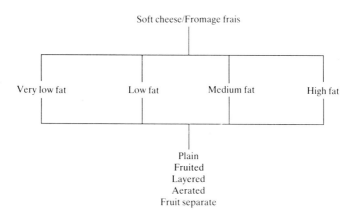

Figure 7.5 General classifications of chilled soft cheeses.

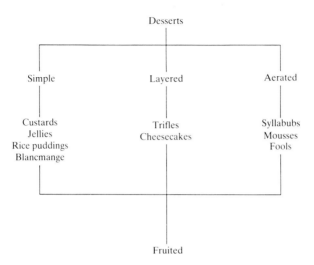

Figure 7.6 General classifications of chilled desserts.

7.2.2   Product characteristics

7.2.2.1   Yogurts

(a) Stirred yogurt. The texture should be smooth with a glossy appearance, thick and almost pourable, but must not be grainy or nodulated. The colour of natural yogurt should be creamy white. If fruited, it should represent the colour of the fruit without being too bright. The typical yogurt flavour – slightly acidic, clean, fresh with the acetaldehyde note, should be distinguishable and complementary to the fruit flavour.

(b) Bio yogurts. The Bio yogurts should be milder and creamier in taste than the traditional yogurts, but of similar colour and texture.

(c) Set yogurts. Set yogurts should have a glossy surface appearance without excessive whey. The texture is smooth and almost junket-like, giving a clean cut when spooned.

7.2.2.2   Fromage frais.
Natural low fat fromage frais is milky white in colour, has a smooth texture with a spreadable consistency. It is clean and mildly acidic in flavour with no appearance of syneresis.

7.2.2.3   Desserts

(a) Layered. Generally the layered products will have a spectrum of textures. Taste will range from sweet to acidic, strong to bland and the colours and flavours should complement the individual components. Cake and biscuit layers should retain their characteristic crunchy or open texture and not become wet and soggy.

(b) Custards. The texture should be smooth and thick with a glossy surface, but not gelatinous or grainy.

(c) Jellies. The gels should not be too brittle, but firm with 'melt-in-the-mouth' characteristics and a good fruity flavour.

(d) Mousses. Mousses may be whipped for varying periods to obtain either high or low overruns depending on the final textural characteristics required. In all cases a mousse should have uniform air cells. It should retain its texture and overrun without collapsing during its shelf life.

7.3   Factors affecting shelf life

Commercially the shelf life of a product may be defined as the number of days after production that the product can be consumed whilst still remaining safe, retaining its quality appeal, and meeting customer expectations. In other words, it should remain microbiologically safe and organoleptically acceptable within its stated shelf life.

To evaluate the shelf life of any product it is first necessary to identify which characteristics of the ingredients, the process and the storage conditions are responsible for, or will have an influence on, its shelf life.

The life of short chilled dairy desserts is influenced by:

- raw materials;
- product formulation;
- processing parameters;
- implementation of Good Manufacturing Practice;
- filling and packaging;
- storage and distribution;
- consumer usage and handling.

Measurement, monitoring and control of the above are of paramount importance in the evaluation process. The point at which the product becomes unacceptable either organoleptically or microbiologically, whichever manifests itself first, is the ultimate end point from which the life can be established.

Table 7.1 Raw materials commonly used in the manufacture of chilled yogurt and other dairy desserts

Yogurt	Soft cheese/ fromage frais	Desserts
Milk	Milk	Milk
Cream	Cream	Cake/sponge/biscuits
Sugar	Sugar	Stabiliser: gelatine, starch, pectin, gums
Cultures	Cultures	Sugar
Milk concentrates	Fruit/fruit conserves	Fruit/fruit conserves
Milk powders	Flavours	Cream
Fruit/fruit conserves	Colours	Flavours
Stabilisers		Colours
Flavours		Decoration: cherries, nuts, vermicelli
Colours		

7.3.1 Raw materials

The raw materials most likely to be used for the production of yogurt, fromage frais and desserts are given in Table 7.1. All the listed ingredients introduce microorganisms and chemicals which may affect the quality of the final product. Partnerships with approved suppliers and agreed specifications will help the dessert manufacturer to consistently supply a product which remains acceptable within the determined life. Changes in source and supply of these ingredients will result in a variation of factors which influence shelf life and is not to be recommended.

7.3.1.1 Milk. This ingredient, which is common to all the products, is variable in all the main constituents – protein, lactose, fat and in the microbiological flora.

The variability occurs between different breeds of cattle, different geographical regions and is seasonal. The control of the type and level of microorganisms, together with the monitoring of the protein content, is essential as these significantly affect the texture and stability of the final product.

The microorganisms can gain access to the milk from the cow, personnel or equipment used during milking, or during transportation to and storage at the processing dairy. To keep the microbiological flora to a minimum it is essential to cool the milk to below 5°C directly after milking. This temperature should be maintained until the milk is processed at the manufacturing site.

Recent trends have been towards larger dairy units having milk collection every other day or even twice a week. This has encouraged dairy farmers to invest in more hygienic equipment and increased awareness of health and quality issues, but has increased the potential for microbial growth and enzyme activity.

Modern methods of manufacture, plus quality standards demanded by national legislation, EC Directives and the dairy industry in general, have ensured that the raw milk on receipt at the processing factory tastes good, has a low bacterial count and is free from impurities. This quality is maintained by heat processing followed by cooling to 5°C as soon as possible after receipt of the milk.

Milk used for the manufacture of the dairy products should therefore have low bacterial counts, no off-flavours and minimal enzymic degradation. Stock rotation and control of temperatures will help to ensure a good quality basic raw material for all short shelf life dairy products.

7.3.1.2 Cream. The quality of the cream will be dependent on the quality of the milk used for separation and the method of handling before and after pasteurisation. Being high in fat the cream is more susceptible to enzyme degradation from lipase which splits the triglycerides into fatty acids, mono and diglycerides and glycerol. This will result in extreme cases in a rancid taste being evident in the final product. Lipase is inactivated to a greater extent by pasteurisation. However, as many microorganisms produce lipase, this can still be a problem if the cream is handled unhygienically after processing.

If milk is to be held for a prolonged period prior to separation it is often pasteurised immediately on receipt. Microbiological quality is monitored by testing for total viable count (TVC) and coliforms.

7.3.1.3 Concentrates. The two methods generally used for the concentration of milk solids are:

1. removal of water by evaporation;
2. removal of water by membrane filtration.

For both methods the quality of the concentrated milk is dependent on the quality of the raw milk used, and the handling techniques before and during processing.

The microbiological flora should be low in heat resistant bacteria (thermodurics) and low in spore formers. Chemically, milk which is to be evaporated must be heat stable in order to withstand the pre-heat treatment process.

After concentration, the temperature of storage and handling methods are critical to the microbiological quality. Depending on the rate of cooling and the concentration factor, lactose crystallisation may occur, which could adversely affect the flavour and textural characteristics of the final product.

Quality is monitored microbiologically by checking for spore formers and coliforms and chemically for fat, lactose, protein, total solids and pH.

7.3.1.4 Cultures.   Culture management and the activity and viability of the organisms is vital to final product quality, and to the shelf life of fermented products.

Culture preparation and handling demands the highest standards of hygiene combined with attention to detail in the manufacturing techniques and in the selection of plant. The risk of airborne contamination by yeast, moulds, bacteria and bacteriophage must be eliminated.

The cultures, when used, must contain very high numbers of viable and active bacteria in the correct ratio to achieve the desired pH in the appropriate time.

The quality of the bulk culture is maintained by storage at below 5°C for a maximum of 48 hours. The quality is monitored by testing for yeasts, moulds, cell balance and culture activity.

For direct vat inoculation, frozen cell concentrates are used and it is essential that these are stored at very low temperatures and used in accordance with the manufacturer's instructions.

7.3.1.5 Fruit.   After harvesting, fruit will remain acceptable for only a limited period of time. The time varies considerably by fruit type and variety, country of origin, harvesting methods and the method of storage employed by the grower.

Spoilage is caused mainly by microbiological activity (especially when fruit has been damaged), and chemical reactions catalysed by enzymes which occur naturally in the fruit.

To assure good quality fruit for further processing it is necessary to either destroy the factors responsible for spoilage or to inhibit them. This is achieved by either heat sterilisation (canning) or deep freezing. The processed fruits (canned or frozen) are all regarded as raw materials to produce conserves for inclusion in dairy desserts.

A major area of concern, not directly associated with shelf life but of paramount importance, is the presence of pesticides and other agrochemicals, which are used during growth and post-harvest storage. All fruits should be screened for these. They must be controlled within the limits specified in the legislation governing agrochemical residues.

7.3.1.6 Other ingredients.   As for any of the other raw materials used, the source of the ingredient, approval of supplier, the identification of critical control points (CCPs), and hygiene standards are all important factors in the shelf life of the final product.

7.3.2 Processing

An understanding of the synergistic and antagonistic reactions that take place with different processing methods when a variety of functional ingredients are used is necessary when a formulation is being developed. This may have a very important influence on the stability of the final product.

7.3.2.1 Yogurt. Having specified the microbiological, physical and chemical qualities and the accepted tolerances of the ingredients, the basic yogurt mix is subjected to a relatively severe heat treatment. This achieves four objectives:

1. Destruction of any undesirable organisms including pathogens.
2. Formation of physico-chemical complexes and denaturation of the whey proteins which ultimately affect the texture and water binding capacity of the coagulum.
3. Reduction of dissolved oxygen.
4. Formation of amino acids, peptides and other factors which enhance the growth of the culture organisms.

After addition of the culture, which is traditionally thermophilic, it is essential that the organisms (typically *Lactobacillus delbrueckii* subsp. *bulgaricus* and *Streptococcus salivarius* subsp. *thermophilus*) have ideal conditions in which to grow, i.e.: optimum temperature and a medium with all the desired factors, but without any inhibitory substances. The influence of cultures on final product quality and their susceptibility to outside influences must not be underestimated.

After fermentation to the desired pH the yogurt is cooled to below 20°C and often stored for a short period prior to filling.

It is essential that the pumps, heat exchangers, pipelines and storage tanks are cleaned and sterilised before use. Samples of the yogurt base from each batch should be checked for viscosity, texture, flavour and the presence of coliforms, yeasts and moulds. Coliforms will not normally survive in the low pH medium, but if initially present will indicate poor or inadequate cleaning of the plant. A typical manufacturing scheme for yogurts is given in Figure 7.7.

7.3.2.2 Fromage frais. Many of the manufacturing principles that apply to yogurt also apply to the manufacture of fromage frais. As with yogurt production, the solids level of the milk is increased and the mix is heat treated and held before cooling to incubation temperatures.

However, the lactic acid producing cultures used are different. These being mesophilic organisms, they require a lower incubation temperature and give fromage frais its distinct flavour and texture. As the incubation temperature is much lower than that for yogurt, and could also be suitable for the growth of undesirable organisms, great care must be taken in ensuring that the vats and associated equipment are all clean and sterile.

After incubation the coagulum is cooled to inactivate the cultures and

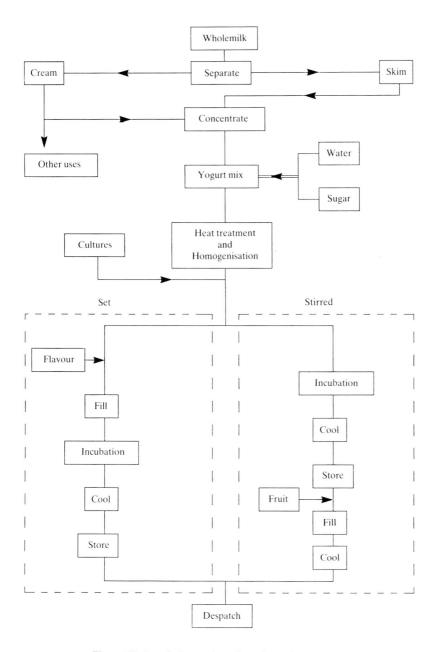

Figure 7.7 A typical manufacturing scheme for yogurts.

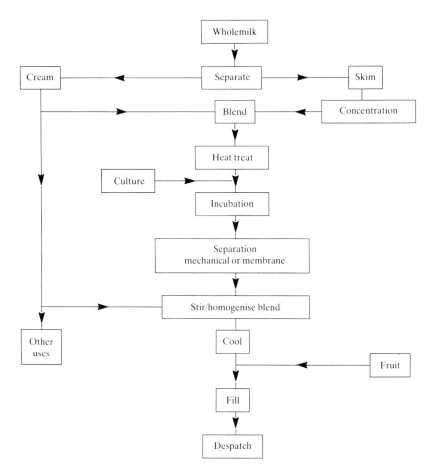

Figure 7.8 The manufacturing process for fromage frais.

prevent a further decrease in pH. At this stage, if the desired texture and viscosity have not been optimised, a further concentration of total solids is necessary. This is achieved by firstly re-heating the mix followed by either mechanical separation or membrane filtration.

Having achieved the correct viscosity and total solids, cream can be blended into the base (i.e. the plain curd, also known as 'fromage blanc') to give the required fat level. Fruit is normally added prior to filling.

At each critical stage of the process samples are taken and checked for the presence of coliform, yeast and moulds. The final product is also checked for viscosity, texture and flavour. The manufacturing process for fromage frais follows the general scheme shown in Figure 7.8.

7.3.2.3 Desserts. Desserts range from the relatively simple jellies, mousses and custards to layered products such as trifles, cheese cakes and complex continental desserts such as tiramisu. This combination gives a variety of textures, tastes, colours and appearances. For shelf life evaluation it is important that these attributes are maintained through life, e.g. crunchy texture, stability of aeration, absence of syneresis and leaching of colour.

Microbiologically the desserts are more vulnerable to contamination from spoilage organisms which may include pathogens due to the more neutral pH of the product and increased handling.

Processing methods for individual components are relatively simple; a simplified trifle-making process is represented in Figure 7.9.

(a) Mousse. Traditionally a mousse is high in fat with a high overrun, and this foam must be stable for the duration of its shelf life. Modern trends however, are for low fat mousses.

The structure of a mousse is normally maintained by the use of stabilisers or whipping agents. With advancements in functional and novel ingredients different structures can be achieved ranging from a soft open texture with large air cells to a strong almost rubbery texture with very small air cells.

(b) Custards. The selective use of stabilisers and starches will ensure that the desired texture is achieved – ranging from creamy to light and short to gelatinous.

The starch and other hydrocolloids must be well dispersed and fully hydrated before being heat treated to the desired temperature. The time and temperature used must ensure that the starch is cooked and the custard is pasteurised. The product can either be filled hot, or if used in combination with other ingredients, cooled to a temperature slightly above the gelation point. This prevents damaging the structure of the other ingredients in the multi-layered product.

(c) Jellies. Gelatine can contain a relatively high level of spore formers and the processing conditions must ensure that these are destroyed. The critical area is the storage temperature of the mix prior to filling, or in the case of complex desserts before addition to the other components of the product. This temperature must be sufficiently high to prevent the growth of microorganisms, but must not adversely affect the colour and flavour of the jelly and other components.

The most important aspects of desserts manufacture are the implementation of good manufacturing practices, personal and plant hygiene, and training. Implementation of aseptic techniques during processing,

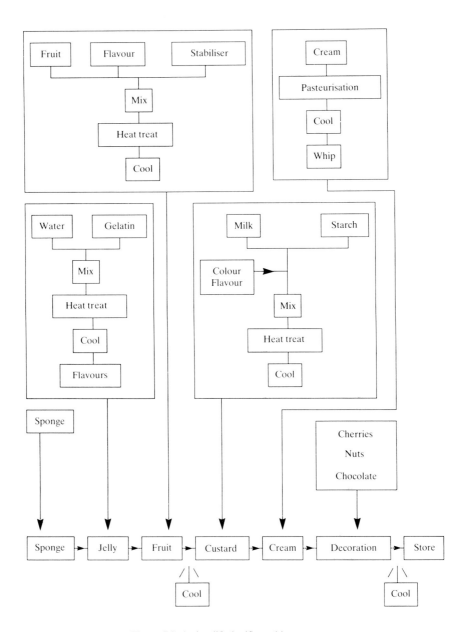

Figure 7.9 A simplified trifle-making process.

handling and filling is vital to ensure that the full shelf life potential of the product is realised. Critical control points should be identified and appropriate testing regimes be in place to ensure that the key standards are met.

7.3.2.4 Fruit conserves.
These will be specific for the product in terms of flavour, viscosity, pH and colour. The conserve chosen will depend upon the pH level, sweetness, and the addition rate to the final product.

To produce a fruit conserve which is stable for use in dairy products and free from yeasts, moulds and other undesirable organisms, the mix should be heated to 85°C or more for several minutes.

The fruit conserve will contain stabilisers (starch, pectins, gums) to give the desired viscosity, enhance mouthfeel and ensure that an even distribution of the fruit throughout the mix is maintained. Sugar is added to improve flavour and in some cases reduce the water activity.

The heating process may damage the colour of the mix and the flavour profile of the fruit. Therefore, colour and flavouring is usually added aseptically at the end of the process.

It is important to note that the shelf life of the fruit conserve as an ingredient will have a bearing on the shelf life of the final product. The normal shelf life of the conserve is 6–8 weeks, however, the microbiological stability is often significantly greater. The limiting factors are the colour and flavour changes. Therefore, if a yogurt is to have a shelf life of 2 weeks, then the fruit conserve must be used at least 2 weeks before the end of its own shelf life.

For large-scale manufacture the fruit conserve is normally delivered in 800 kg–1000 kg stainless steel vessels, for smaller processing operations in 25 kg–40 kg poly bags. The methods adopted to fill these containers, the heat treatment given during processing and the positive release systems in place by the fruit supplier should ensure that the fruit conserves arrive at the processing factory free from any yeast and mould contamination.

The same standards of hygiene and handling of the container must be implemented at the processing factory when the fruit vessels are connected to, and disconnected from the blending station. Similarly the poly bags must be emptied into pre-sterilised vessels where plant hygiene is of paramount importance.

The fruit vessels may be used in production several times within the shelf life of the conserve. Each time the vessel is used a risk of contamination from yeast and mould occurs. To manage the risk factor, good manufacturing practices should be adopted and operators instructed on handling methods, food safety issues and hygiene.

A further safeguard is achieved by measuring the carbon dioxide level within the headspace of the conserve vessel before initial use and at each subsequent visit to the filling area. An increase in carbon dioxide level may indicate activity of yeasts and the vessel should be rejected.

7.3.3   Filling and packaging

The filling operation and choice of packaging materials are critical to the ability of almost all food products to achieve their potential shelf life. In the case of short shelf life products such as yogurt and dairy desserts, this part of the process is critical due to the relatively delicate physical nature and microbiological sensitivity of the products. The filling and packaging operation is the last direct contact that the manufacturer has with the product.

The incorrect choice of filling mechanism, poor hygiene practices and the inability of packaging materials to protect the product can result in premature shelf life failure and customer dissatisfaction. Therefore, all the effort put into the selection of raw materials and developing the correct processing conditions can be wasted by injudicious actions in the final stages of production.

7.3.3.1   Filling.

The most important aspect of the filling operation with regard to shelf life is hygiene – the filler must be capable of being thoroughly cleaned and sterilised prior to the commencement of the filling operation. Failure to do this will inevitably result in, at best, a reduced shelf life of a product and, at worst, a food poisoning incident.

Most modern, high throughput fillers are capable of being fully cleaned in place. However, many older, small scale fillers need to be stripped down and manually cleaned. With this manual operation it is essential that the filler is reassembled with great care, and that a sterilising rinse is given prior to the commencement of the filling operation.

Most microbiological shelf life failure is caused by post-processing contamination at the filling stage either due to poor cleaning, poor design or environmental factors.

In the case of products such as yogurt and fromage frais which are of relatively low pH (<4.6) the most common spoilage organisms are yeasts. The yeasts involved in the spoilage of dairy products are commonly the lactose fermenting genera. However, due to the levels of sucrose incorporated into many products, other genera may also be found. Typical spoilage yeasts may be *Saccharomyces* and *Candida* spp. Moulds can also cause the premature spoilage of yogurts and fromage frais. However, as yeast and mould contaminations often occur together, it tends to be the production of gas by yeasts which is first noticed as a 'blowing' pack, and therefore, the yeast is identified as the spoilage organism.

The more neutral desserts (pH >4.6), whilst being subject to premature spoilage by yeasts and moulds, are also an ideal medium for bacterial growth. The bacteria most frequently found to contaminate desserts at the filling stage are members of the *Enterobacteriaceae* group, *Pseudomonas* spp., and *Bacillus* spp. (in particular *B. cereus*) which is commonly associated with cream products.

Bacterial spoilage may take two forms:

1. The souring of products due to the production of acid and off-flavours.
2. The enzymic breakdown of the structure of products due to the activities of exo-enzymes.

7.3.3.2 Packaging. Packaging, both in design and material terms, can have a major influence on the shelf life of the product. Packaging fulfils a number of functions which may include:

- protection of the product from physical damage;
- protection of the product from the environment;
- protection of the product from changes in the environment;
- provision of attractive marketing designs to convey information including the date code to the consumer;
- presentation of the product in an easy to handle and store format for distribution to the retailer and consumer.

The packaging of product can therefore influence the shelf life in a number of ways:

(a) Microbiologically. Packaging can carry microorganisms, and therefore must be manufactured and stored hygienically to ensure a minimum microbial loading. This is particularly important in the case of preformed pots which must be stored in a clean, dry, pest-proof environment. Ideally the outer cases should only be removed prior to the containers being taken into the filling room.

For 'form-fill-seal' packaging which is wound on a spool, again the outer packaging should only be removed immediately prior to entering the filling room. Additionally a substantial amount of the reel should be discarded before the material is fed into the pot-forming chamber of the filler. Lidding materials should be treated similarly to minimise any microbiological contamination.

For heat sealed containers where the lid is bonded to the pot the most common sealing problem is caused by product contaminating the lip of the pot and interfering with the bonding process.

'Snap-on' lids must be produced to tight tolerances to ensure an effective seal is obtained. Often a plastics tamper evident ring or other secondary packaging will assist in maintaining the integrity of the pack.

The seal of the pack must be secure in order to exclude environmental contamination, particularly during the cooling phase when a partial vacuum may be formed.

(b) Organoleptically. The most common 'off-flavour' associated with yogurts and dairy desserts which develops with time is caused by the oxi-dation of the milk fat. Flavour degradation also occurs with time and very often is an oxidative change.

Utilising the correct type of packaging material which reduces the level of oxygen permeability and light penetration can help to minimise changes induced by these environmental factors.

In neutral, or near neutral pH desserts, the shelf life is significantly shorter due to microbiological considerations, and therefore, oxidation is unlikely to be critical.

In some high fat desserts, with fat levels in excess of 5%, the flavour changes due to oxidation may be the determining factor.

(c) Visual. As with flavours, colour fade or change may occur over a prolonged period. This is particularly noticeable with natural red colours such as beetroot red (betanin). Many factors can influence colour change, including oxygen, pH and the presence of sulphur dioxide, which may be carried over in small quantities from any fruit that is added to the yogurt or desserts.

7.3.4 Storage and distribution

All foods, and dairy desserts are no exception, may spoil during storage and distribution. In general this may be due to:

- growth of microorganisms;
- biochemical and chemical changes such as oxidation, rancidity develop-ment and moisture migration;
- attacks by vermin, birds or other pests.

Physical damage of products is prevented by enforcing good standards of storage, handling and pest control within the distribution network. However, this is outside the scope of this book.

The microbiological and biochemical changes are greatly reduced by storing products at low temperatures. Effective temperature control is, therefore, a critical factor in preventing the development of spoilage organisms and ensuring that dairy desserts achieve their potential shelf life, as well as minimising any food poisoning risk.

The Food Hygiene (Amendment) Regulations 1990, as amended by the Food Hygiene (Amendment) Regulations 1991, formalised this require-ment for the industry, by including dairy desserts with a pH >4.5 in the list of foods which must be stored and distributed at temperatures of less than 8°C. However, the regulations failed to include any temperature requirements for desserts with a pH of 4.5 or below, and therefore, many yogurts and fromage frais products escape this mandatory requirement. It is therefore left to responsible companies to set and achieve their own temperature standards for this category of product. The maximum recommended temperature for storage and distribution of all dairy desserts is below 5°C.

In order to achieve the desired temperature standards within the distribution chain the following is recommended.

1. Products should be stacked in such a way that the cold air can circulate freely.
2. Product should be pre-cooled before entering the cold store.
3. Opening of the store or vehicle doors should be minimised.
4. Efficient temperature monitoring and alarm systems should be installed and maintained.
5. A high air flow/velocity within the store should be employed.
6. Products should be loaded on to vehicles via an air lock system wherever possible and under no circumstances should be left out on a loading bank.
7. Vehicles should be pre-cooled prior to loading the products.

The other major factor that can influence shelf life during the storage and distribution operation is light. This is most likely to be a critical factor in the display cabinet. However, it can be suitably restricted by the choice of packaging as discussed in the previous section.

7.3.5 Consumer storage

When determining the shelf life of a product, which in the main depends upon the integrity of the 'chill-chain' to maintain its desirable properties, full account must be given for the potential abuse of product by the retailer and consumer. During recent years surveys have been commissioned by industry, research bodies and government agencies to provide accurate data on the way the general public handle and store chilled products after purchase. The most recent of these is *Consumer Handling of Chilled Foods*, published in the UK by the Ministry of Agriculture, Fisheries and Food (MAFF, 1991), which investigated many factors associated with shopping, consumer handling and attitudes to chilled products.

The temperature regime used for establishing product shelf life must therefore be designed to take into account:

1. The time that the product may be out of refrigeration, between being removed from the retailer's chill cabinet and being placed in the consumer's refrigerator.
2. The number of days it will be stored in the consumer's refrigerator.
3. The likely position in which it will be stored within the consumer's

refrigerator (dairy products are often placed near the top or in the door, both of which are relatively warm positions).
4. The temperature range at which domestic refrigerators operate.

Education of the consumer about the product is important. Clear instructions of storage conditions should be given on the pack, and advertising information can be used to emphasise the importance of temperature control.

At the end of the day, however, it must be accepted that the last link in the 'chill chain' for any product is probably the weakest and all the efforts of a manufacturer can be confounded, if the product is handled badly by the consumer.

7.4 Evaluation methods

There are no absolute tests to evaluate shelf life. The methodology used and the process for evaluation will depend on the product, the quality criteria and the expertise within the company.

Before attempting to evaluate the shelf life it is important to have an understanding of the product composition, and the changes that may be induced by various processing conditions.

Different testing regimes will be required for:

1. low pH products;
2. neutral pH products;
3. those with high risk ingredients;
4. low water activity products.

In terms of microbiological spoilage it is important to establish which organisms are likely to be present in the final product, which are likely to affect safety or cause spoilage during shelf life, and the possible sources of contamination.

Microbiological, chemical and physical changes which affect final product quality can in many instances be detected by sensory analysis. These changes should be either evaluated or considered during the development process.

Sensory analysis, although subjective can play a major role in evaluating shelf life (caution must be exercised to ensure that no microbiological safety risk is present if the technique is employed).

It is essential that sufficient shelf life data are collected during the pilot and scale-up trials to identify the CCPs and the factors that will affect the stability of the product. It is recommended that a minimum of three full evaluation tests is carried out on product from factory scale pre-production trials to confirm the shelf life prior to launch of the product

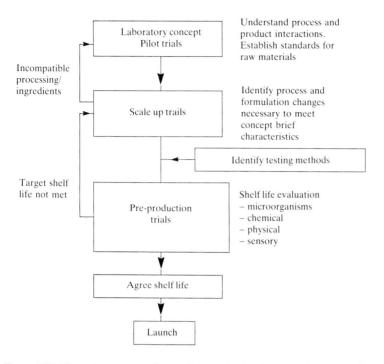

Figure 7.10 The main sequence of operations in the development of a new product.

Figure 7.10 shows the main sequence of operations in the development of a new product.

Many complicated cycling regimes to imitate the temperature patterns to which products may be subjected have been suggested and indeed are used for shelf life determinations. However, for simplicity it is often better to use a two-step system ensuring that the temperatures chosen allow sufficient room for abuse and are not idealistic.

A typical regime for dairy desserts would be storage for 2 days at 4°C followed by storage at 8°C for a period exceeding the target shelf life.

7.4.1 Shelf life determination – yogurt

The critical factors to consider are:

1. target life;
2. temperature of storage and distribution;
3. yeast and mould contamination;

Table 7.2   Testing schedule – shelf life determination

No. of days		0	1	2	3	4	7	14	21	28
Coliforms		*								
Y & M Colony count		*						*	*		
Incubated samples	7°C				*	*	*	*	*	*
checked for gas	21°C		*	*	*	*	*	*	*	*
production	30°C		*	*	*	*	*	*	*	*
Texture and Viscosity			*					*	*	*	
pH/acidity		*	*				*	*	*	*
Flavour profile			*					*	*	*	*

Storage temperature: 7°C unless indicated.
Target shelf life: 21 days.
Day of production: day 0.
* = Sampling occasion.

4. syneresis and texture;
5. degradation of flavour and colour.

The methods described can be used for shelf life evaluation of existing products as well as new products. In the case of new products however, it is recommended that a hazard analysis based on the Hazard Analysis Critical Control Point (HACCP) concept is carried out at the development and pre-production stages.

Sufficient samples must be taken to cover all the planned tests. Samples are stored in temperature-controlled rooms operating at 7°C, 21°C and 30°C. These are checked at regular intervals through to the target shelf life and beyond as illustrated in Table 7.2.

Microbiologically all samples are checked for coliforms, yeasts and moulds. Although coliforms do not survive for much longer than 24 hours due to the low pH, their initial presence in the product gives an indication of poor plant hygiene and the possibility of other contamination. The testing for coliforms using Violet Red Bile Agar is regarded as a useful check in establishing the shelf life of the product.

The number of yeasts and moulds present in the product can be detected by plating on Rose-Bengal Chloramphenicol Agar where individual colonies can be counted.

Due to the small quantity of product needed to carry out these tests (1 ml or 0.1 ml) the results tend to be unreliable especially when only low levels of yeasts are present. The tests are however a useful step in the identification of yeasts and moulds, and hence in establishing the possible cause of contamination.

Storage of yogurt at 21°C and 30°C for shelf life evaluation evolved as a result of the difficulties experienced with the plate count method. The presence of yeasts can be detected by gas formation when the product is stored at these temperatures. Gas formation in a pot of yogurt is evident by doming of the lid, or if the product is heavily contaminated or incubated for a longer period, by the gas forcing the lid clear of the rim of the pot. Storage at 21°C and 30°C also enables the factory to react quickly to any potential problems.

The 21°C and 30°C tests were developed following trials where samples of 'clean' uncontaminated product were inoculated with yeasts from several pots of yogurt known to be contaminated.

From these trials it was concluded that the time taken for the yeasts to produce sufficient gas to dome the lid was an indication of the severity of the contamination. The shorter the time to 'gas' the more contaminated the product. The results are summarised in Table 7.3. It was also established that different species of yeasts had different rates of gas production as indicated by the hours before doming in the three trials. These differences should be taken into account in the shelf life evaluation process.

The differences in the time taken to blow (gas formation between samples incubated at 21°C and 30°C) have also been investigated. Some discrepancies between the results were found, nevertheless, storage of samples at 21°C and 30°C forms an essential part of the shelf life evaluation of yogurt and indeed of factory control measures.

The investigation was carried out at a yogurt production site covering a period of three months and involving 5760 samples (samples were taken every 30 minutes from each filling machine during the production cycle). The results of the investigation are shown in Figures 7.11 and 7.12. The

Table 7.3 Yogurt inoculated with spoilage yeasts and samples incubated at 30°C

	No. of yeasts/pot	Hours before doming
Trial 1	60 000	40
	6000	48
	600	63
	6	76
	Control (Nil)	> 168
Trial 2	360 000	15
	36000	24
	360	46
	4	96
	Control (Nil)	> 144
Trial 3	260 000	24
	26000	46
	260	96
	26	120
	Control (Nil)	> 144

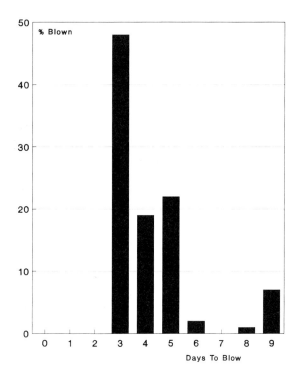

Figure 7.11 Storage of yogurt samples – comparison of gas formation at 30°C and 21°C (223 samples blown in 2 days at 30°C).

charts show, based on the total number of samples that were found to blow in 2 days at 30°C (Figure 7.11) and in 3 days at 30°C (Figure 7.12), the percentage breakdown of samples kept at 21°C, that were found to blow during storage. For example (Figure 7.11) 233 samples were found to blow after 2 days at 30°C. Among the duplicate samples stored at 21°C 46% was found to blow after 3 days, 19% after 4 days and so on.

A comparison of 'blowing' times at 21°C and 7°C demonstrates a clear correlation between the two. The shelf life of the refrigerated product can therefore be predicted by the time taken for samples stored at the elevated temperature to 'blow'. Results are shown in Figure 7.13.

The majority of short shelf life yogurts are 'live', i.e. the culture organisms are still viable. Although their metabolic rate at 7°C is relatively low there is nonetheless some activity. This can be determined during shelf life by pH measurement (see Figure 7.14), by titratable acidity determination and by taste.

The increase in acidity can alter the flavour profile and if combined

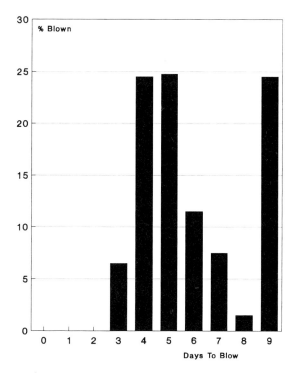

Figure 7.12 Storage of yogurt samples – comparison of gas formation at 30°C and 21°C (341 samples blown in 3 days at 30°C).

with degradation of fruit flavours, it can often become manifested as off and stale taints. To establish the extent of flavour degradation, trained assessors are used.

The deterioration can be noted and the assessors are able to rank the product according to age fairly consistently. The chemical and biochemical changes that occur over time show that the product does decline with age. From a sensory point of view the shelf life is set at least one day prior to the product changes becoming so evident that they are judged to be unacceptable to the consumer. Spider plots (Figure 7.15) can be used to highlight differences between fresh and stored samples.

7.5   Current developments and the future

During the last two decades many developments have been made by both industry and research organisations to extend the shelf life of many types of foods. These have included techniques and aids such as:

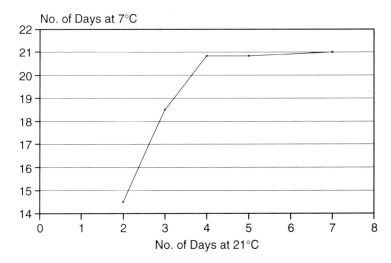

Figure 7.13 Storage of yogurt samples – comparison of blowing times at 21°C and 7°C.

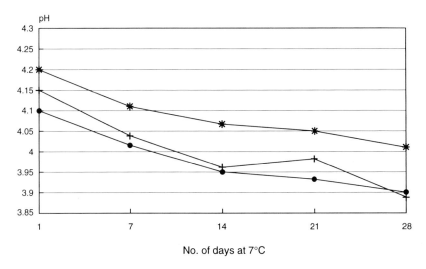

No. of days at 7°C

Figure 7.14 Storage of yogurt samples – pH change with time. Series 1, •; series 2, +; series 3, *.

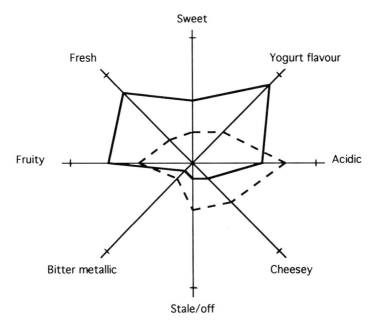

Figure 7.15 Spider plots – differences between fresh and stored samples. —, day 1; – –, day 28.

- irradiation;
- modified and controlled atmosphere packaging;
- oxygen absorbers;
- aseptic processing and packaging developments.

Few of these developments have, however, been of use in the extension of shelf life of fresh dairy desserts due to cost, adverse effects on the food or consumer attitudes.

Most progress in this product sector has been achieved by better practices and attention to detail. The key areas have been:

- improved selection and quality of raw materials;
- greater knowledge and utilisation of functional ingredients;
- improved process plant design and hygiene;
- the use of techniques such as HACCP and challenge testing to establish safe and quality related shelf life;
- greater use of rapid method techniques for analysis and hygiene monitoring;

- improved cooling and refrigeration;
- the selection of technologically advanced packaging materials.

One area which has been the subject of much recent work and debate is the use of time–temperature indicators (TTIs). These are markers which may be applied to the outer packaging, which will indicate to the reader the 'temperature history' of the product. Clearly they have the potential to indicate the residual safe shelf life of desserts, either to the retailer or the consumer. However, current costs are relatively high and some reliability problems exist.

The changes within the desserts market have been so great within the last twenty years that no one in the 1960s could have foreseen or predicted the size and scope of this market in the 1990s. Equally it is difficult to envisage what further changes will occur during the next twenty years. Certainly for the short term, growth both in terms of volume and variety, and the drive for improved quality and safety will inevitably continue. However, it can be predicted confidently that consumers will also demand:

1. Less wastage in packaging. Tertiary and possibly even secondary packaging will be gradually reduced unless they are biodegradable or can be recycled.
2. Improved safety and freshness. These are likely to become more important than a long shelf life.
3. Better value for money than in the affluent 1980s.
4. Greater attention to nutritional and health aspects. Low cholesterol, low fat, high in unsaturates, low sugars, high fibre, added vitamins and health promoting minerals.

All of these requirements will place further demand on the food technologists as they attempt to meet industry's needs and the consumer's wants.

Bibliography

Birch, G.G. and Parker, K.J. (eds) (1984) *Control of Food Quality and Food Analysis*, Elsevier Applied Science.

Campden Food and Drink Research Association (1990) *Evaluation of Shelf Life for Chilled Foods*, Technical Manual No. 28

Campden Food and Drink Research Association (1991) *Shelf Life Problems, Technology and Solutions*, Symposium Proceedings.

Dennis, C. and Stringer, M.F. (eds) (1992) *Chilled Foods – A Comprehensive Guide*, Ellis Horwood.

Marth, E.H. (1978) *Standard Methods for the Examination of Dairy Products*, 14th edn, American Public Health Association.

Ministry of Agriculture, Fisheries and Food (1991) *Consumer Handling of Chilled Foods: A Survey of Time and Temperature Conditions.*

Shapton, D. and Shapton, N. (eds) (1991) *Principles and Practices for the Safe Processing of Foods*, Butterworth and Heinemann.

Sutherland, J.P., Varnam, A.H. and Evans, M.G. (1986) *A Colour Atlas of Food Quality Control*, Wolfe Publishing Limited.
Walker, S.J. (1988) Major spoilage micro-organisms in milk and dairy products. *Journal of Society of Dairy Technology*, **41**, 91–92.

8 Modified-atmosphere-packed ready-to-cook and ready-to-eat meat products

R.C EBURNE and G. PRENTICE

8.1 Introduction

There have been tremendous changes in all aspects of the meat and meat products group in the last few years. These changes encompass the development, production, distribution and storage of product, legislation and, last but not least, changes of attitude by the consumers. The consumers of today want convenience; convenience in preparation, packaging, portion control and convenience in serving whether cooking is required or not. They also want, and take for granted, product safety. The 'use by' or 'best before' date on any product is regarded as a guaranteed date of safe quality, and if any other attitude is taken, it is more likely to be one of regarding it as a minimum date with one or two extra days to be taken without any decline in quality or safety.

Changes in food legislation have been fast and furious in the last ten years. The Food Safety Act 1990, the Food Hygiene Regulations and all their associated codes of practice and amendments have set the scene for improvement of good manufacturing practice. EC legislation on food safety has been reflected and often anticipated in UK legislation. In the meat products group there now exists comprehensive legislation on fresh meats and meat products, which governs all aspects of the hygienic manufacture of these products. The Food Hygiene Regulations have stipulated lower temperatures for refrigerated food distribution, and now most chilled meat products are distributed at temperatures of less than 5°C in the UK.

These changes in legislation have been paralleled by an even greater activity within the legislative and technical committees of the various food trade associations who have published an enormous number of authoritative standards and codes of practice to help their members stay at the forefront of hygienic and safe manufacture. Two associations in particular are of importance to the meat manufacturers, namely the British Meat Manufacturers' Associations (BMMA) and the Chilled Food Association (CFA). Both of these associations have published standards in 1993 on the production of 'high risk' foods. A high risk food is a cooked food which is sold ready to be eaten by the ultimate consumer without any further cooking and, as such, requires great care to ensure that no contamination occurs after cooking, during the final processing and packing stages.

Complementing the activity of the manufacturers' trade associations an equal input of authoritative codes of practice from the major retailers for the guidance of their 'own label' suppliers, from the Food Research Associations (particularly Campden Food & Drink Research Association) and also from the food scientists and technologists' professional body, the Institute of Food Science and Technology (UK), has also been seen.

These efforts have contributed in their various ways to safer products with reliable and accurate shelf lives. However, at the same time, there have been many changes which have made the shelf life evaluation of meat products a more difficult and hazardous process.

It has already been mentioned that customers regard 'use by' dates as a guaranteed date of safety. The food technologist has to be absolutely sure his shelf life recommendation is correct. He has to make sure his experimental methodology is sound and reliable and resist the commercial and customer pressures for longer shelf lives which he cannot guarantee. He has to bear in mind there are many changes occurring in the marketplace, which are not positive factors in the maintenance of good shelf life. An example of this is the increasing use of microwave ovens for reheating foods. The uneven heating by many of the early models coupled with incorrect use by some customers can result in an unacceptable end product. Another example is the variations in temperature of household refrigerators. Only the very latest models have automatic defrost and a thermometer permanently installed, and many food manufacturers do not help themselves by just stating 'keep refrigerated', on their pack labels.

Meat products have also suffered, perhaps more than other foods, from the attack on additives, whose addition prevents the development of an unsafe product but are now being limited both in range and in quantity. Chief amongst these are common salt, nitrites and sulphites. The desire to reduce sodium in the diet, the cation common to all three additives, again contributes to a reduction in shelf life because there is a concomitant reduction in the levels of the preservative. Many bacon and sausage packs are now marketed with low salt where salt is less than 1%. This contrasts with a salt level in mild cured bacon of 2%, a level of 4% plus in Wiltshire bacon and a minimum of 1.5% salt in pork sausage.

Finally, the newly identified microbiological hazards should be mentioned, which continue to surface and require a rethink on shelf life evaluation. *Listeria monocytogenes*, first discovered in 1924, took nearly sixty years to make its effect, but what an effect that has been! Shelf life evaluation of every cooked, ready-to-eat product must now take account of this ubiquitous organism. More recently, the verotoxigenic *E. coli* type 0157:H7 has been identified as the culprit in a case of food poisoning and

T E M P	T I M E	O P E R A T I O N	T R A N S P O R T	D E L A Y	I N S P E C T I O N	S T O R A G E	N U M B E R	PRODUCT : WILTSHIRE HAM PROCESS : MANUFACTURE COMMODITY No. : TECHNOLOGIST : DATE : 23/08/93	
								DESCRIPTION	HAZARDS
<5°C							1	REMOVE MEAT FROM CHILL	1,2
							2	WEIGH ALL MEATS TO APPROPRIATE FORMULATION	
							3	TRANSFER TO CONTAINER	3,4
							4	TRANSFER TO CHILL IF APPROPRIATE	
-2°C							5	HOLD UNTIL REQUIRED	5,6
<5°C							6	REMOVE FORMULATED MEAT FROM CHILL, IF APPROPRIATE	1,2
							7	TRANSFER MEATS TO MINCER	
							8	MINCE AS APPROPRIATE	3,7
							9	TRANSFER TO CONTAINER	4
							10	TRANSFER CONTAINER TO CHILL, IF APPROPRIATE	
-2°C							11	HOLD PRODUCT IN CHILL, IF APPROPRIATE	5,6
							12	MAKE PICKLE	8,3,7,9
							13	HOLD PICKLE UNTIL REQUIRED	5,2
							14	TRANSFER PRODUCT TO CHURN	
							15	TRANSFER PICKLE TO CHURN	
							16	CURE TO APPROPRIATE PROCESS	3,8,7,10
							17	HOLD PRODUCT UNTIL REQUIRED	6,5
							18	TRANSFER PRODUCT TO BANK	
0°C							19	TRANSFER PRODUCT VIA REFRIGERATED VEHICLE TO COOKED CUTS PLANT	5,6
							20	REMOVE PRODUCT FROM LORRY	1
-2°C							21	TRANSFER TO CHILL AND HOLD UNTIL REQUIRED	5,6
							22	REMOVE FROM CHILL	1,2
							23	TRANSFER TO TIPPER	
							24	TIP INTO ALTERNATIVE CONTAINER	3,4,10
							25	TRANSFER CONTAINER TO FILLER	
							26	TIP PRODUCT INTO FILLER HOPPER	3,10
							27	FILL INTO POLYTHENE LINED MOULD	3,7,11
							28	FOLD OVER LINER	
							29	INSERT BLOCK	
							30	PLACE SPRING AND TENSION	
							31	LOAD MOULDS ONTO TREE	
	4hr						32	HOLD TREES UNTIL REQUIRED	12
							33	LOAD INTO COOKER	
>72°C							34	COOK TO APPROPRIATE PROGRAMME	13

Figure 8.1 A HACCP process flow chart.

must be added to the list of pathogens which meat product manufacturers now monitor.

The scientific factors, however, that have to be considered in evaluating shelf life are still basically the same, namely microbiological, sensory and chemical. Any one factor may terminate a shelf life, but more often than not, it will be a combination of the first two. Every food product made and marketed must have a known and safe shelf life.

The design of the procedure to establish this must not only take into account all these factors but must be carefully designed to suit the product, the process and the distribution and final storage conditions. It must be carried out on samples which are known to be representative of actual production. It is essential that a hazard analysis (based on the Hazard Analysis Critical Control Point (HACCP) principles) is carried out on the product and process, so that the evaluator is well aware of the intrinsic hazards and, therefore, is able to look specifically for those spoilage organisms which are likely to develop.

The first stage of such an analysis is to construct a process flow chart. The first page from a three page flow chart is shown in Figure 8.1. It follows the flow of the meat and other materials from intake right through to final product despatch.

It is a graphic presentation of the sequence of events in the meat product manufacture being analysed. Some charts use symbols, i.e. a circle for 'operation', a square for 'inspection' and an arrow for 'transport'. Others prefer to describe in full the various parameters, e.g. temperature, time, operation, inspection. Each item of the process is described and the hazards linked with that item denoted by a number.

In a second spreadsheet (an example of which is given in Table 8.1 which is page 1 from a 7 page analysis), the hazards are described together with the actions required, the frequency of checking and the person responsible. There is a final column in which the demerit points are listed. These are determined according to the seriousness of the hazards and are rated 1000 for critical, 100 for serious, 10 for major and 1 for minor. They are allocated by the Hazard Analysis team which in NewMarket Foods is made up of the Product Development Manager, the Food Safety Officer, and a Production Manager and the team is chaired by the Quality Services Manager. All these personnel have attended recognised training courses on HACCP and its implementation. The demerit points remain unchanged unless the process is altered, and are used as reference by the HACCP auditor when auditing the process.

8.2 Meat product groups and their basic characteristics

The group of meat and meat products is very diverse, and when coupled with the variety of preservation and packaging methods, becomes extremely diverse indeed. In this chapter, the basic product groups and their packaging formats together with the preservation methods as they apply within these groups will be briefly considered. These basic groups are fresh/frozen meats, cured meats (e.g. bacon), cooked meats (e.g. ham, pork luncheon meat) and prepared meat products. The last group is probably the most variable in that it encompasses sausages, burgers, hot and cold pies, pizzas and 'ready meals'; in fact anything containing more than 10% meat.

Tables 8.1 A table of identified hazards and their associated control

Item No.	Item description	Hazard No.	Hazard nature	Action required	Frequency	Responsible person	Demerit points
1	Remove product from chill	1	Product out of temperature specification	Target temperature less than 5°C. If temperature between 5° and 10° return to chill. If temperature >10°C reject	Each batch	Production	
		2	Product not within life	Maximum 4 days. Reject product not coded or outside life	Each batch	Production	
3	Transfer to container	3	Poor cleaning of containers	Clean as per hygiene operating instructions	As per hygiene schedule	Production services	
				Monitor ATP level (soiling and microbial loading). If high levels regularly found, review cleaning procedures/schedules (continue to monitor)	As per micro. schedule	Micro. lab	
		4	Use of soiled containers	Visual inspection before use. If soiled reject for washing			
5	Hold until required	5	Chill not running within specified limits	Target −2°C +/− 2°C	Each batch	Production Refrigeration engineers	
		6	Foreign body contamination	Cover all product. If uncovered, inspect, reject/cover	Each batch	Production	
6	Remove product from chill	1	Product out of temperature specification	Target temperature less than 5°C. If temperature between 5° and 10°C, return to chill. If temperature >10°C reject	Each batch	Production	

Step	Process step	No.	Hazard	Control / corrective action	Monitoring	Responsibility
		2	Product not within life	Maximum 4 days. Reject product not coded or outside life	Each batch	Production
8	Mince as appropriate	3	Poor cleaning	Clean as per hygiene operating instructions	As per hygiene schedule	Hygiene dept.
				Monitor ATP level (soiling and microbial loading). If high levels regularly found, review cleaning procedures/schedules (continue to monitor)	As per micro. schedule	Micro. lab
		7	Foreign body contamination from equipment	Check all equipment on assembly	Each piece of equipment	Engineers
9	Transfer to container	4	Use of soiled containers	Visual inspection before use. If soiled remove for washing	Each batch	Production
11	Hold until required	5	Chill not running within specified limits	Target $-2°C +/- 2°C$		Refrigeration engineers
		6	Foreign body contamination	Cover all product. If uncovered, inspect, reject/cover	Each batch	Production
12	Make pickle	3	Poor cleaning	Clean as per hygiene operating instructions	As per hygiene schedule	Hygiene dept.
				Monitor ATP level (soiling and microbial loading). If high levels regularly found, review cleaning procedures/schedules (continue to monitor)	As per micro. schedule	Micro. lab

Table 8.2 Typical gas mixtures used for meat and meat products

| Product | Gas types and percentages | | |
	Oxygen	Carbon dioxide	Nitrogen
Bacon	<0.1	35–45	55–65
Cooked cured meats	<0.1	35–45	55–65
Cooked cured meats	<0.1	0	100
Fresh meats*	–	100	–
Fresh meats*	–	40	60
Fresh meats	80	20	–
Fresh sausage	<1	100	–
Fresh offal	60–80	0–20	0–20
Fresh poultry	–	35	65

*Bulk master packs

The packaging gas mixtures used for preservation are basically nitrogen and carbon dioxide mixtures (see Table 8.2), although there are some variations in use for 'master packs' or when colour development/preservation is a priority. 'Master packs' is a term used to describe the transport of several retail meat packs, usually air packed in PVC films, or several fresh meat primal joints in one large bulk pack. The gas is usually 100% carbon dioxide which gives a maximum antimicrobial effect. Colour of the meat is restored on removal from the master pack by atmospheric oxygen.

In other cases e.g. bacon, ham and cooked meats, a mixture of 60% nitrogen and 40% carbon dioxide has been shown to be an optimum combination. Higher levels of carbon dioxide have not been proved to extend the shelf life further.

However, the critical gas level, as always in cured meats, raw or cooked, is that of oxygen where the lowest possible level is used. Modern thermoforming packaging equipment, with the correct film and settings, can consistently achieve levels of less than 0.1% residual oxygen in the pack.

The basic product group characteristics can be best described as in taste panel assessments, i.e. appearance, texture and flavour.

8.2.1 Appearance

One of the most important attributes of meats and meat products is colour. If the colour is not protected during shelf life, the well-known brown colour in fresh meat and greying in cured meat will ensue as a result of oxidation. The basic pigment of raw meat is myoglobin. This, for example, in the case of vacuum-packed raw beef would be a purple/red colour (reduced myoglobin). The pigment deteriorates to the brown oxidised form of myoglobin (metmyoglobin) when the meat is exposed to low levels of oxygen and enzymic activity, and the meat is said to have lost its 'bloom'. The bright red colour so desirable of fresh red meats is due to the oxygenation of myoglobin to oxymyoglobin at high levels of oxygen (e.g. >20%). Cured meats owe their colour to the action of nitrite on the myoglobin pigment to produce nitrosylmyoglobin. Those cured meats which are partially or fully cooked develop nitrosylhaemochromogen, the characteristic pink colour of ham. This colour can be achieved with very low levels of nitrite, and is a hazard to be aware of when producing non-nitrited products like roast turkey and roast pork in the same processing area.

8.2.2 Flavour

The most important off-flavour from a shelf life standpoint is that of rancidity due to the oxidation of fat. The high fat contents, the presence of unsaturated fats and salt, comminution and frozen storage, all tend to increase the likelihood of rancidity development.

8.2.3 Texture

Tenderness is probably the most significant characteristic in fresh meat followed closely by succulence. The former is influenced by the initial age of the slaughtered animal but is greatly affected by the handling, slaughtering, chilling and maturation treatments as well as the control of temperature during processing to the final cut of meat. Fat levels are the obvious contributor to succulence but water retention in the meat is also significant. In trying to retain this textural quality through the shelf life, it is important to prevent the gain or loss of moisture or water vapour, and avoid unacceptable levels of 'drip' in the final pack.

8.3 Factors affecting shelf life

The factors which affect shelf life can be divided according to whether they are causes or effects. The latter may be determined by laboratory tests when the shelf life is evaluated and can themselves be split into three sub-categories, i.e. microbiological, chemical and sensory. In the case of meat and meat products the following are some of the elements which would be included depending on the product and pack type:

1. Microbiological: total viable count (TVC), *Lactobacillus* spp., *Enterobacteriaceae*, *E. coli*, *Pseudomonas*, *Brochothrix thermosphacta* and yeasts.
2. Chemical: acidity, peroxide value (PV), water loss.
3. Sensory: odour, flavour, texture and appearance.

Table 8.3 Factors affecting shelf life – a list of intrinsic and extrinsic factors

---

Intrinsic factors
Type of animal, e.g. porcine, bovine
Breed and feed regime
Age of animal at time of slaughter
Initial microflora
Chemical condition, e.g. peroxide value, pH value
Water activity (a_w)
Basic meat product make-up, e.g. recipe, preservatives, antioxidants
Availability of oxygen

Extrinsic factors
Processing, heat treatments, time control
Hygiene, standard of personnel and equipment cleaning
Quality Management System, HACCP procedures
Temperature control
Packaging system, materials, equipment, gases
Storage

However, a more useful approach in evaluating the factors is to consider the causes, and, in this approach, to further separate them into intrinsic and extrinsic factors. A general list of these factors is shown in Table 8.3.

8.3.1 Intrinsic factors

Whilst all these factors are important and must be taken into account when evaluating shelf life, arguably the most important is the initial microflora and its level. Every attempt should always be made to keep this to an absolute minimum. Modern abattoirs are designed principally to achieve this, and if proper care is taken to avoid contamination from the gut and its natural high levels of bacteria, there is no reason why the carcass should not be nearly sterile. Thus counts of less than 1000 cfu/g can be expected. If counts are maintained at this level, rather than, say, 10^5 on fresh meats under aerobic conditions, a doubling of the shelf life is possible, before a cut off of 10^7 is reached.

Of the microflora on fresh meat, the Gram-negative aerobic rod-shaped bacteria, e.g. *Pseudomonas* spp., predominate. In anaerobic conditions, the slower-growing lactic acid bacteria, *Lactobacilli* spp., come to the fore.

The type of animal is only relevant in respect of its relative proneness to harbour pathogenic bacteria. The presence of *Salmonella* is more likely in poultry, but less so in pork and beef. The breed may also be a factor. For example, in pigs some breeds are more stress-susceptible and give rise to pale, soft and exudative (PSE) meat. This, if used in a cured product, would result in disintegration of the texture of the product.

The age of the animal at time of slaughter is a very important factor.

Tenderness of the meat improves with maturation but bacterial counts also increase and drying out occurs.

Water activity (a_w) is a measure of the amount of water available that will support microbial growth. In meat and meat products a normal level is 0.97. Unfortunately most pathogens find this a very acceptable level for growth. It can be reduced by the addition of salt and, of course, drying through heat treatment. A good example of a cured meat product is salami, where a very low water activity is achieved, although the true version of this product would not be a suitable candidate for modified atmosphere packaging (MAP) as it usually has moulds on the surface, which would be degraded by such a packaging method.

The final intrinsic factor worthy of mention in meat products is the presence or otherwise of preservatives, namely sodium nitrite and sulphur dioxide. Both are essential. Nitrite is used in cured meats and cured meat products, e.g. bacon, ham; and sulphur dioxide in prepared meat products, e.g. sausages, burgers, where a reasonable length of shelf life is required (see Figure 8.2). A minimum nitrite level of 30 ppm must be achieved at the end of the manufacturing process, with a desirable level of 100 ppm residual for both raw and cooked cured meats.

Sulphur dioxide levels have a legal maximum of 450 ppm in meat products and formulations are usually developed to achieve this. During a typical nine-day life of a fresh pork sausage this will drop by approximately 50%. The incorporation of antioxidants such as ascorbic acid and its salts, alpha-tocopherol and ascorbyl palmitate will have the effect of

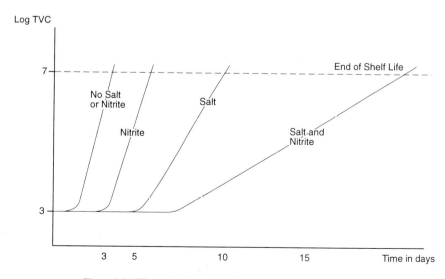

Figure 8.2 Effects of salt and nitrite on gas packed pork meat.

mopping up the oxygen and is very effective in increasing shelf life by preventing rancidity development and maintaining the colour of cooked cured products.

8.3.2 Extrinsic factors

All the extrinsic factors are the basic requirements of good manufacturing practice. Their degree of importance depends on whether the meat product is a raw meat or a partially prepared meat product which has to be cooked by the consumer; or a fully cooked ready-to-eat product. It is essential that a meat manufacturer can ensure that his products are made to a recognised standard such as the BMMA standard for the Hygienic and Safe Manufacture of Meat and other Food Products before he considers an evaluation of shelf life. It is also a prerequisite that the manufacturer operates a Quality Management System. This could be to British Standard 5750 Part II (ISO 9002) but if not, any other quality system would still need to have a clear company quality policy, and procedures covering document control, product traceability, process control, hygiene procedures, calibration of measuring instruments and staff training.

It is important to know all the factors that have to be taken into account, and therefore a detailed product specification which would include its process flow and hazard analysis must be available.

8.3.2.1 Processing. Processing can take many forms, from simple butchery into joints or minced meat to full curing and smoking and smoking treatments in ham production.

In fresh meat the size reduction of the meat is an important factor, as is the time taken to process the meat. Mincing or dicing, with the consequent increase in surface area plus the opportunity for microbiological contamination, will decrease the potential shelf life. In cooked or smoked meats the time and temperature settings of the cooking programme must be designed to reduce the microbiological load so that the product is safe to eat without further cooking. A typical TVC for a cooked meat product at the ex-factory stage would be $< 10\,000$ cfu/gram.

8.3.2.2 Hygiene. The basic requirements of hygiene are set out in the EC and UK legislation on meat and meat products, e.g. design, layout, interior finishes, and the movement of materials and operators through the plant.

Procedures must be in operation specifying cleaning methods, schedules and frequency for the structure and the equipment in the factory. There must be adequate laboratory facilities for monitoring the efficiency of cleaning, e.g. by swabbing and plating or by such methods as ATP bioluminescence.

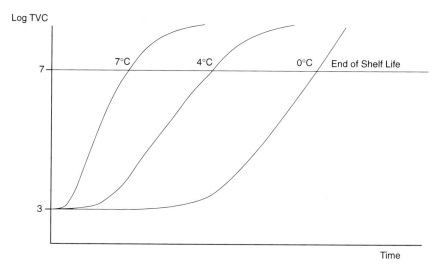

Figure 8.3 Effect of temperature on storage of raw meat.

The important specific aspects of hygiene in raw meat shelf life are the cleanliness of cutting boards and the sterilisation of boning knives in hot water pots (set at +82°C). Cutting boards should not be used for more than 4 hours without cleaning or turning.

Ready-to-eat chilled meat products must be processed after factory cooking in a 'high risk' area. This concept is now well established and a detailed specification can be found, for example, in the BMMA Standard for High Risk Operations (No. P005, dated 1.10.93). The cookers should form a barrier between the low and high risk areas. No personnel can enter or leave the area without passing through a sanitisation area which has cloakrooms, washroom and boot wash. Protective clothing must be distinctive and restricted for use in the area only. When carrying out a shelf life evaluation on cooked meat products all of the hygiene data on the high risk area, e.g. environmental swabbing, deep cleaning of equipment, organisation of raw materials and packaging and staff movement must demonstrate compliance with the specification; the objective of which is to minimise post-cooking microbiological contamination.

8.3.2.3 Temperature. The temperature of chilled meat products is legally specified. Packing rooms have to operate at room temperatures of 12°C. Product temperatures vary from offal 3°C, poultry 4°C and fresh meat 7°C. Distribution temperatures are 5°C but many major retailers specify temperatures of <3°C for cooked meats and for fresh meats. These temperatures have to be regularly measured and recorded, and also,

Table 8.4 Effect of different packaging formats on the shelf life of various meat products

(a) *Air pack*

	Days from manufacture to arrival in shop (maximum)	Days from arrival in shop to 'Use By'
Pork sausage	5	8
Skinless sausage	5	7
Sausagemeat	5	8
Stuffing	5	8
Pork chops	2	5

(b) *Modified atmosphere pack or vacuum pack – uncooked*

	Days from cure to pack (maximum)	Days from pack to 'Use By'
Mild cure back bacon	7	21
Wiltshire back bacon	7	28
Mild cure shoulder steaks	7	24

(c) *Modified atmosphere pack or vacuum pack – cooked*

	Days from cook to pack (maximum)	Days from pack to 'Use By'
Roast ham	7	21
Cooked ham	7	21
Pork luncheon meat	7	21
Hot dogs	4	24

(d) *Fresh meat – primals/cuts – bulk pack*

	Type	Days in pack (maximum)	Days from retail packing to 'Use By'
Bone-in pork (primal)	MAP	10	4
Boneless pork	MAP	9	4
Offal	VP	7	3
Dusted products	VP	7	4
Poultry	MAP	11	3

(e) *Other packaging types*

	Packaging type	Days from manufacture to 'Use By'
Paté	Chub	24
Black pudding	Chub	21
Pork pie	Bunchwrap	9
Pizzas	Overwrap	9

MAP = modified-atmosphere-packed.
VP = vacuum-packed.

equally important, the thermometers have to be calibrated. The temperature history of any product to be evaluated for shelf life obviously must be known and be within specification. Figure 8.3 shows the effect of temperature on the storage of raw meat.

8.3.2.4 Packaging. The effects of various packaging formats on meat product shelf life can best be seen in Table 8.4a–e.

8.4   Determination of shelf life

8.4.1 Procedures

The usefulness of any shelf life determination is entirely dependent on the conditions under which the determination is carried out. Ideally, any such trial would give information as to (1) the shelf life under ideal storage, (2) the shelf life under poor storage conditions and (3) the shelf life under the conditions likely to be met during normal distribution and storage and use in the consumer's home.

It would seem that (3) would be the most informative as this time, with a little extra as a safety margin, and would give an adequate shelf life. This however is not as straightforward as it may appear because 'normal' distribution and storage temperatures do not exist. Thus it is better to decide on a set of conditions for determination and keep them constant. Additionally, although in practice temperatures experienced during distribution, retail and storage by the consumer may all be different, if the temperature profile of storage in a laboratory determination is too complex, it may be impossible to gain an adequate understanding as to the microbial changes that are taking place. Also it would be most unlikely that the results obtained could be compared with those obtained in other laboratories.

8.4.2 Temperature

For the determination of the shelf life of new products, NewMarket Foods has chosen systems which are as straightforward as possible while closely reproducing the conditions likely to be met in practice. Every sample tested throughout the study is subjected to the appropriate temperature/time regime as shown in Table 8.5.

8.4.3 Test frequency

Microbiological examination and sensory analysis are carried out throughout the expected life of the product and beyond. For short life

Table 8.5 Microbiology laboratory – shelf life storage conditions

Product type	Storage temperatures		
	Bulk storage	Retail storage	Customer storage
Fresh pork	0°C	5°C	8°C (1)
Sausage	NA	5°C	8°C (1)
Cooked/uncooked retail pack	NA	5°C	8°C (4)
Cooked bulk pack	5°C	5°C (3)	8°C (1)
	Sealed	Opened	Opened

Where appropriate, figures in brackets refer to the number of days the samples are held at the stated temperature. NA = not applicable

products, e.g. fresh meats, these tests can be as often as daily with the time beyond the expected life being a day; but for fresh meats containing preservatives, tests are usually at intervals of 2 to 3 days, up to a maximum of 12 days.

Products should be tested on day of production and on at least three further occasions during the projected shelf life. Ideally these should be followed by tests at the end of the projected shelf life and two days immediately before and after that.

It is important that tests are frequent enough so as not to miss any turning points in the determination, but with most products, testing every day throughout the determination would be unnecessary and excessive. It must be remembered when setting test dates that the purpose of the exercise is to set a shelf life for the product, which is both safe and realistic. Careful preparation in setting test days will be necessary if the laboratory working week is only Monday to Friday.

8.4.4   Storage atmosphere

During shelf life determination products are stored in the sealed finished packs in which they are to be sold. To mimic usage in the retail delicatessen counter, after storage in the original packaging, bulk cooked meats are stored open for the last 4 days of their shelf life.

8.4.5   Sample numbers

In general, the more samples are examined on a sampling occasion, the more accurate the results obtained. However, the number of samples tends to be governed by practical considerations. In the case of a bulk food destined for sale from a delicatessen counter, for example, it may be appropriate to return to the same pack for sampling throughout the entire evaluation. However, it is usually necessary to store the product being studied in its final retail packaging.

A separate set of samples must therefore be used on each sampling occasion. On each such occasion there must be enough replicates taken to give a good representation of the general state of the product under test. A high level of replicate samples could however put considerable demands on both the resources and incubation space. Testing five replicate samples on each occasion is a good compromise as the means obtained from the samples give a sound basis for comparison. Additionally, the results from five samples can easily be applied to a number of sampling plans which may be used to generate useful information about the batch from which the samples have been taken.

From time to time however, either because of scarcity of the product or other restrictions, it is not always possible to test five samples on each occasion and lower numbers of samples must suffice. The results obtained under such circumstances must be treated with caution and are only meaningful if the batch being examined is uniform. For products with a wide variation in quality within the batch the information obtained could be of limited value. Basing shelf life estimations on tests carried out on a single sample on each sampling occasion could therefore be grossly misleading.

8.4.6 Sensory analysis

As described above, a shelf life determination should give information as to the length of time a product will remain wholesome, i.e. acceptable both from a safety and an organoleptic point of view. The most effective way of determining the sensory end point of a product under storage is for a panel of trained assessors to examine the product at regular intervals.

It is not always possible for formal taste panels to be used in shelf life determinations and frequently it is left to the experience of a few individuals to determine whether a product is 'acceptable' or not. This is only possible if the individuals carrying out the assessment are highly skilled with considerable experience of sensory analysis techniques.

8.4.7 Laboratory analysis

In addition to sensory analysis during the shelf life study, it is almost always necessary to carry out microbiological analysis of the product. This provides greater understanding of the changes taking place during storage. It is also possible to carry out chemical analyses during storage – examples of these are peroxide values (assessing the development of oxidative rancidity), reduction in nitrite levels, and volatile nitrogen levels (giving some indications of proteolysis of meat). In general however, chemical analysis is not sensitive enough to demonstrate the changes taking place during storage and the product has usually deteriorated to such an extent that it is organoleptically and/or microbiologically unacceptable before chemical analyses can detect any changes.

8.4.8   Microbiological examination

The microbiological examination of products during a shelf life study can give some information on both the time taken for the spoilage organisms to reach a level where they affect the sensory properties of the product, and, though less usefully, the likelihood of any pathogenic microorganisms present (immediately after production/packing) attaining levels during storage which would create a health risk to the consumers.

8.4.8.1   Microorganisms affecting product keeping quality. The main spoilage organisms during aerobic, low temperature storage are *Pseudomonas* spp. whereas under vacuum storage, the major spoilage organisms are *Lactobacillus* spp. and yeasts. MAP may involve spoilage by a combination of the above, i.e. *Lactobacillus* spp., *Pseudomonas* spp. and yeasts and in addition may support the growth of *Brochothrix thermosphacta*. These organisms tend to affect the sensory properties of product at levels in the region of 10^7 cfu/g. Therefore the end point of the shelf life is generally considered to be reached when microbial counts reach this level. Useful information regarding the end point can of course be obtained from sensory analysis carried out in parallel with microbiological examination.

Since the initial shelf life determination is an opportunity to gain as much information as possible about the microbial flora of the product, a wide range of organisms are frequently examined throughout the storage. Not all of these play an important role in spoilage at chill temperatures, however they may give some idea of the hygienic conditions under which the product has been prepared or the microbiological risks associated with the product (e.g. the presence of coliforms could indicate the presence of pathogenic organisms). Figures 8.4, 8.5 and 8.6 show changes that were observed in the spoilage flora of sausage, cooked meat and fresh pork respectively, under various storage conditions.

8.4.8.2   Pathogens. A shelf life determination should give information as to the likelihood of any pathogen, which survives the manufacturing process or gains access to the product after processing, to develop in the product to such a level that it would become a health risk to the consumer. This is most desirable, however, in practice there are many hurdles in the way of achieving this. These include the following:

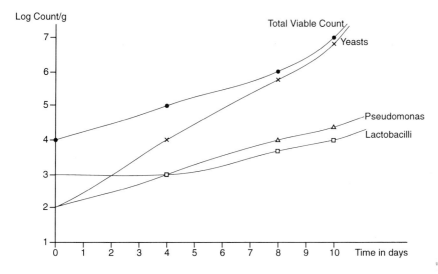

Figure 8.4 Spoilage flora of sausage – aerobic storage at 5°C.

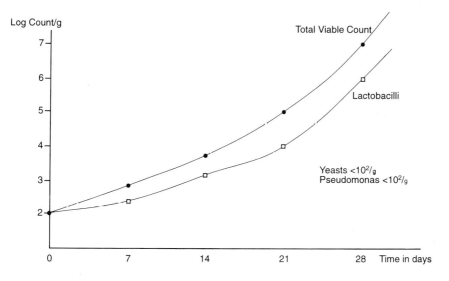

Figure 8.5 Spoilage flora of cooked meat – MAP storage at 5°C.

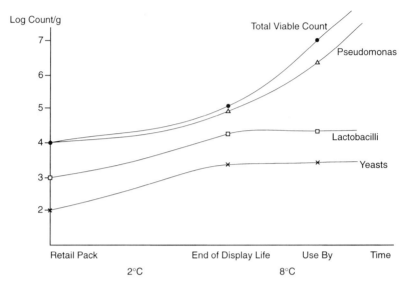

Figure 8.6 Spoilage flora of fresh pork – aerobic storage at 2°C, followed by storage at 8°C.

1. It is not possible in practice to investigate all of the organisms of concern.
2. From experience, the presence of pathogens in the product should be very infrequent. However, their absence from the shelf life results is no absolute guarantee that they will not be present in the product.
3. Inoculating the product with pathogens at the beginning of its shelf life and following their development is never straightforward. The inoculum is unlikely to bear any relationship to the microorganisms that might gain access from the environment. It would not be possible either to investigate all the strains or to reproduce exactly the growth conditions found in practice.

Shelf life determinations nevertheless do frequently include a search for pathogens of concern, e.g. *Salmonella* spp., *Listeria* spp. This does provide some information at the time but gives very little assurance that the pathogens in question are absent or that if present, will fail to multiply. Thus although shelf life determinations can give some ideas as to how long a product takes to spoil in a given storage condition, they give little assurance of safety.

8.4.8.3 Standards. There are very few authoritative statements on what is an acceptable microbiological quality for foods. A most useful docu-

Table 8.6 Microbiological quality of ready-to-eat foods sampled at point of sale

	Microbiological Count (cfu/g unless otherwise stated)			
	Satisfactory	Fairly Satisfactory	Unsatisfactory	Unacceptable (potentially hazardous)
Aerobic plate count				
Cooked pies, pasties	$< 10^4$	$10^3 – 10^5$	$> 10^5$	
Cooked meats	$< 10^4$	$10^4 – 10^6$	$> 10^6$	
Salmonella spp.	not detected in 25 g			present in 25 g
L. monocytogenes	not detected in 25 g	present in 25 g $< 10^2$	$10^2 – 10^3$	$> 10^3$
E. coli	< 20	$20 – 10^2$	$10^2 – 10^4$	$> 10^4$
S. aureus	< 20	$20 – 10^2$	$10^2 – 10^4$	10^4
C. perfringens	< 200	$200 – 10^3$	$10^3 – 10^4$	$> 10^4$
B. cereus and other *Bacillus* spp.	< 200	$200 – 10^4$	$10^4 – 10^5$	$> 10^5$

ment on this topic has been produced by the UK Public Health Laboratory Service: *Provisional microbiological guidelines for some ready-to-eat foods sampled at point of sale* (PHLS, 1992). These criteria are given in Table 8.6. The figures are given with the understanding that they may be altered as more information is obtained. No recommendations have been made concerning faecal streptococci, *E. coli* 0157 or *Yersinia enterocolitica* as insufficient information was available to deduce satisfactory levels.

8.5 Current trends

Some of the current trends in the manufacture, marketing and consumption of meat and meat products have been highlighted in the introduction to this chapter. With regard to the evaluation of shelf life, the trends can be classified into three categories:

1. microbiological safety and quality;
2. packaging and packaging techniques;
3. quality and safety management.

8.5.1 *Microbiological safety and quality*

New and significant relevance has had to be given to certain pathogenic bacteria for which tests were not carried out routinely a few years ago.

Examination for *Listeria monocytogenes* is now routine in any meat factory microbiological laboratory. New, faster and more reliable methods are becoming available. *E. coli* 0157:H7 is another which will require greater attention by the meat microbiologist to ensure it will not become a threat to otherwise safe meat products.

Laboratory accreditation to a recognised national standard such as that of the National Measurement Accreditation Service (NAMAS), or other similar accreditation schemes, e.g. those run by Campden Food and Drink Research Association (CLAS) and LawLabs (LABCRED), will become a prerequisite of a factory laboratory. This will entail substantial changes in laboratory design, methodology and personal and environmental hygiene.

A recent development in determining the shelf life of products with special reference to safety is mathematical modelling. Here, a large bank of information is built up about the growth and survival of specific microorganisms under a variety of conditions. A computer program is then developed which will allow the growth or otherwise of these microorganisms in any given environment to be predicted. To use the program, the physical and chemical characteristics of the food under investigation are defined, e.g. pH, a_w, nutritional composition. The program then calculates the growth characteristics under any particular storage condition. Modern models are extremely sophisticated and can give a good estimate of the growth of a particular microorganism in a given food under defined conditions. The data on which they base their predictions, however, are of necessity incomplete and the results must, therefore, be interpreted with care.

No laboratory test or mathematical modelling can be comprehensive enough to reproduce the storage of a product under every circumstance. The information which can be obtained from them *vis-a-vis* the safety of the product after storage is, therefore, limited. A comprehensive knowledge of the shelf life of any product can only be obtained after the product has been in production for some time and its storage characteristics monitored regularly.

8.5.2 Packaging and packaging techniques

Probably the most important factor in maintaining the assigned shelf life using modified atmosphere packaging is the integrity of the seal. The seal area immediately prior to sealing must be free from contaminants such as fats/grease to prevent the subsequent formation of leakers. It is now recognised that a good seal should be at least 5 mm wide.

Packaging film manufacturers are researching the so-called 'smart' films which can change their permeability properties under adverse conditions, e.g. misuse of the pack resulting in microbiological spoilage. An example is the aluminium oxide coated polyester film which has good clarity and oxygen barrier characteristics that are not influenced by the thickness of the coating. The latter can be as thin as 20–30 nm (200–300 Å). This layer is not sensitive to humidity changes (as is EVOH) and although, like other barrier layers, it tends to crack under extreme conditions during packing, the rupture will 'heal' itself by absorbing moisture from the atmosphere causing the oxide crystals to swell. This effect restores the film's oxygen barrier to almost its original value.

Other factors which affect the overall residual O_2 content of MA packs and therefore shelf life are:

1. machine cycles that alternately evacuate/back gas flush the pack several times prior to sealing;
2. optimisation of the headspace to product ratio to allow a sufficient amount of the modified gas mixture to reduce the percentage of residual O_2.
3. temperature of the product at point of packing. Since the solubility of air increases significantly at low temperatures, and the percentage of O_2, compared with N_2, is much higher in solution (33–35%), packing of product that is too cold can result in a higher than expected residual O_2 level as the gases in the final pack eventually reach an internal equilibrium.

There will obviously be further developments to reduce fogging, to increase barrier and to improve sealability whilst still allowing easy opening for the consumer and to satisfy the environmentalists with respect to environmental friendliness.

New systems for extended MAP storage of raw meats are on offer and being actively developed by Captech and Chill-tec. Both systems, initially developed in New Zealand, claim to markedly extend the shelf lives of products, particularly meat, by similar means. Hygienically prepared products are sealed in very high barrier, multilayer pouches in combination with Snorkel and Chamber machines. Very powerful vacuum pumps effectively remove all the air, including oxygen, which is then replaced with oxygen free CO_2. This in combination with a high degree of temperature control throughout subsequent storage and distribution (typically $-1 \pm \frac{1}{2}°C$) can, it is claimed, extend the life of pork up to 10 weeks, with additional benefits of product tenderness and colour in the ultimate retail pack.

Gas exchange preservation (GEP) involves pumping air out and replacing it by a series of gases in quick succession, each with a different role to play, e.g.

- CO – to inhibit enzymes;
- SO_2 or ethylene oxide – to kill bacteria;
- N_2 – to flush out the system.

Such a technique is unlikely to have a future because of the toxicity of carbon monoxide and the banning of ethylene oxide in food.

Gas mixtures must strike a balance between the bacteriostatic effects of increased CO_2 level and the exudation problems associated with the resultant drop in pH of the meat.

Oxygen scavengers have been around for some time. New developments are expected to use them as an integral part of the pack so that they cannot be inadvertently eaten by the consumer.

8.5.3 Quality and safety management

The trend in the meat industry of companies seeking certification to ISO 9002, the international standard for Quality Management System (or its British equivalent BS 5750), will continue. With its emphasis on process control, calibration of all measuring instruments (temperature measurement being a critical factor), document control and training, such a system will ensure, in the future, more accurate setting of product shelf life.

Similarly the use of HACCP will also continue to identify the hazards and assess the degree of risks inherent in any process. A shelf life determination will not be carried out unless a detailed hazard analysis of the product and process has been made and the critical control points understood and established.

References

Advisory Committee on the Microbiological Safety of Foods (1992) *Report on Vacuum Packaging and Associated Practices*, HMSO, London.

British Meats Manufacturers' Association (1993) Accredited Standards BMMA.

Campden Food & Drink Research Association (1992) *Guidelines for the Good Manufacturing and Handling of Modified Atmosphere Packed Food Products*, Technical Manual no. 34.

Code of Practice for Suppliers of J. Sainsbury Own-Label Foods (1993).

Institute of Food Science & Technology (UK) (1993) *Shelf Life of Foods – Guidelines for its Determination and Prediction*.

Public Health Laboratory Service (1992) Provisional microbiological guidelines for some ready-to-eat foods sampled at point of sale. *PHLS Microbiology Digest*, **9**(3).

9 Ambient packaged cakes

H.P. JONES

9.1 Introduction

The market of 'ambient packaged cakes' covers the range of cakes sold through the supermarket rather than the baker's shop. The major distinction between the two categories is the difference in shelf life requirements. The small baker makes most goods daily and more complex confectionery products with a shelf life of several days, once or twice a week. The packaged cakes sold in the supermarket today normally have a minimum shelf life of three weeks. The need for longer life is necessary because of the time required to distribute to stores with a subsequent requirement for a reasonable period of display on the shelves. Additionally, supermarket products have to be properly packaged to protect them through distribution and in-store handling.

The ambient packaged cake market is served by a few manufacturers who can produce large quantities of cakes to consistent standards. These companies must have the technical resources to design products with the required attributes. The term 'ambient' is necessary to distinguish this market sector from the 'frozen' and 'chill' sectors which operate with very different shelf life requirements. Chilled cakes, in particular fresh cream filled ones, normally have one or two days' life and are merchandised in refrigerated display cabinets. Frozen cakes usually have a shelf life of many months whilst in the freezer but only one to two days at ambient once thawed.

A wide range of ingredients and manufacturing techniques are used in the production of cakes. Besides the many ingredients and different processes employed to make cakes such as sponges, fruit cakes and pastries, flour confectionery overlaps with other product sectors of the food industry, namely, chocolate and sugar confectionery. The latter have very different composition and product characteristics; and as such can complicate shelf life considerations when combined with flour based products.

One of the key tasks of the cake/food technologist, therefore, is to design cakes in which the characteristics of individual components are not adversely affected during distribution and subsequent storage.

Table 9.1 Classification of ambient cakes

Type	Main feature
Sponge cake	Low fat level
Fruit cake	Medium fat level and fruit
Plain cake, e.g. Madeira	High fat level
Chocolate-coated cake	Moisture barrier present
Fruit pies	High and low moisture components
Pastries	Multi-component products

9.2 Product classification

Ambient cakes may be classified in several ways such as by formulation or process type, but for the purpose of shelf life evaluation, the classes listed in Table 9.1 will be used.

One of the challenges of the ambient cake technologist is to formulate products which will retain their moistness, texture and appearance for as long as possible. To do this, an in-depth and up-to-date knowledge of ingredients, packaging materials, production processes and the technology of moisture control is necessary.

Ambient cakes belong to the category of intermediate moisture food products, i.e. with about 20% moisture, and water activities (a_w) within the range 0.65–0.90. With these water activities cakes can be preserved for many weeks in a variety of ways, i.e. canning, vacuum packaging, gas flushing and alcohol injection. Canning is sometimes used and will preserve cake for many months but there are drawbacks which limit its use. The high product temperature reached in the canning process excludes all but the simplest of oven finished cakes, as it can result in pudding-like eating quality. Vacuum packaging can damage the fragile structure of most cakes and so only the very robust type can be packed this way. The preservation of cakes therefore relies mainly on formulation and control of the inside-pack atmosphere by the use of suitable packaging, and in certain 'long life' applications, modified atmosphere packaging. The modern cake factory and the systems employed in it are designed in such a way that only raw materials of the right and specified quality are used and that production processes are carried out correctly and hygienically, so that finished products have the specified moisture content and a_w, ensuring the assigned shelf lives are achieved consistently.

9.3 Equilibrium relative humidity and mould-free shelf life

The growth of microorganisms in foods is, in part, determined by the availability of water that will support microbial growth. This is measured

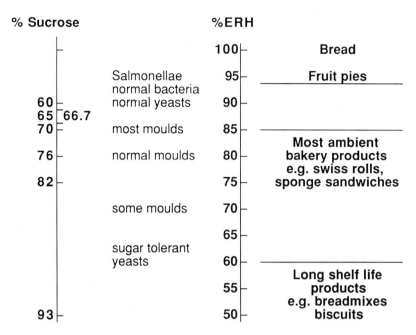

Figure 9.1 Minimum ERHs (and their approximate corresponding sucrose concentrations), permitting growth of microorganisms.

by the 'water activity' (a_w) of the food. The 'equilibrium relative humidity' (ERH) of a cake is the humidity at which rates of evaporation and condensation of water are equal. It is the relative humidity which is eventually reached in the atmosphere surrounding the cake when it is closely enclosed by a perfect water barrier. At this equilibrium, the terms ERH and a_w are interchangeable. In the bakery trade, the term ERH is more appropriate and preferred to a_w since microbial growth tends to develop on the exposed surface of the product. The minimum ERHs (and their approximate corresponding sucrose concentrations) permitting growth of microorganisms are shown in Figure 9.1. As can be seen, most moulds are only able to grow at an ERH above 80%. Table 9.2 shows a range of bakery products and their approximate ERHs (Cauvain and Seiler, 1992).

Using experimental data, the Flour Milling and Baking Research Association (FMBRA) in the UK was able to demonstrate the relationship between ERH and the mould-free shelf life (MFSL) of cake at various storage temperatures (Figure 9.2). It is apparent that there is a linear relationship between ERH and the logarithm of the MFSL within the range 74–90% ERH. This relationship is given by the following expressions for the storage temperatures of 27°C and 21°C respectively (Seiler, 1976).

Table 9.2 A range of bakery products and their approximate ERHs

Product	ERH%
Biscuits	5–15
Bread crumb	96–98
Bread crust	30–50
Plain cakes, e.g. Madeira	80–90
Fruited cakes	73–75
Christmas puddings	70–77
Jam	70–80
Marzipan	70–80
Dried fruit	65–70
Glacé cherries	75

Source: Cauvain and Seiler, 1992.

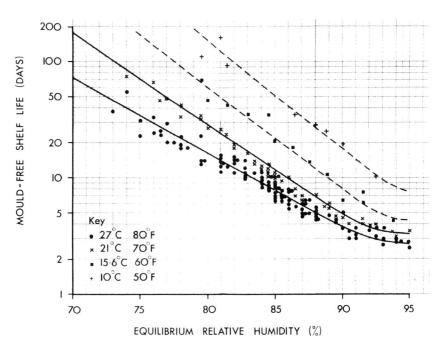

Figure 9.2 MFSL, in days, at various storage temperatures in relation to the ERH of the product. (Source: Cauvain and Seiler, 1992).

$$\text{Log}_{10} \text{ MFSL (days at } 27°C) = 6.42 - (0.065 \times \text{ERH\%})$$
$$\text{Log}_{10} \text{ MFSL (days at } 21°C) = 7.91 - (0.081 \times \text{ERH\%})$$

From this work it has been possible to estimate the MFSL of cakes based on their formulations, using the above relationship and since 1990, with the help of FMBRA's recently developed ERH CALC (see section 9.6).

9.4   Product characteristics

9.4.1   Sponge cakes

This product group is made up of lines such as Swiss rolls, sponge sandwiches, and the foundations for a variety of gateaux. The formulations are usually very low in fat, often containing no added fat. This is necessary to enable the sponge to be rolled, cut and assembled into a variety of shapes without cracking or breaking. Though the fat content of the sponge is low the final product may be enriched with buttercream or synthetic cream, with fat contents of around 45%. The characteristics of a sponge are light texture, delicate flavour and good cutting properties.

As well as the total product ERH that needs to be controlled, it is important to ensure that the ERHs of individual components in a multi-component product are also balanced as far as possible to minimise moisture migration from one component to another, unless this is desired. Sponge products lose moisture very rapidly when exposed to the atmosphere because of the large surface area to weight ratio and low fat contents. To prevent moisture loss, they are usually wrapped in films that can provide a good moisture vapour barrier, as soon as they are sufficiently cooled. This ensures that the correct moisture level is retained in the product. A shelf life of three weeks can usually be obtained by optimising the formulation and choosing the correct wrapping material.

9.4.2   Fruit cakes

The rich fruit cake eaten at Christmas and the more humble slab cake are British specialities noted for their moistness and good keeping qualities. Fruit contents can range from 30% to 100% of the batter weight and consequently a strong cake structure is required to support the fruit and prevent it from sinking during baking. High protein flour, egg and the judicious use of fat provide the crumb strength to maintain an even distribution of fruit and to hold the cake together when cut. Both defatted soya flour and egg albumen can be used to supplement the protein levels.

The addition of dried fruit helps to increase the shelf life by reducing the ERH of the cake. Dried fruit contains only 16% moisture but in combination with the reducing sugars in it produces very moist eating quality, characteristics of a cake with a much higher moisture content. A shelf life of many weeks can be obtained because of this and it can be significantly extended by adding alcohol to the product before or after baking. Alcohol has been shown to act as a mould inhibitor and retard crumb staling (Guy *et al.*, 1983; Ooraikul, 1991).

Fruit cakes lose moisture slowly even when unwrapped and it is normal practice to leave slab cakes to stand overnight to allow moisture to equilibrate and fats to set before cutting and wrapping. Heavily fruited cakes soaked in alcohol will remain in good condition for one year or more if stored in an airtight container.

9.4.3 Plain cakes

This group comprises many typically British cakes such as Madeira, Battenburg and Victoria sandwich. There are also many American formulations which are popular today such as 'Death by Chocolate' and 'Fudge Cake'.

The inclusion of chocolate in a formulation increases the fat content further. High fat levels result in lower volume cake than sponge cake but produce a richer, moister eating cake which can be eaten without the addition of buttercream or other fillings. It is common for cake foundations of this type to have ingredients added such as nuts, cherries, chocolate chips and so on. They are often used as a base for converting into Battenburg, fondant fancies and iced celebration cakes. Special account needs to be taken of the ERH of post-bake finishes as moisture migration can spoil the appearance and eating characteristics of decorations.

9.4.4 Chocolate coated cakes

Chocolate coated cakes have become a significant sub-sector within the ambient cake market and they do have particular technical properties in respect of shelf life. Any of the cake formulations so far discussed can be used as a foundation over which chocolate can be enrobed. Chocolate not only adds a unique flavour and texture but also encloses the product in a fatty barrier which reduces the rate of moisture loss from the cake and thereby assists in shelf life extension. There are a number of special considerations to be taken account of when developing cakes for chocolate coating. Firstly, there is the need to avoid 'crumbing' as it will contaminate chocolate circulating in the enrober. Secondly the foundation must not shrink excessively during life as this will leave a fragile chocolate shell which is likely to disintegrate in the pack or when the product is cut or eaten. It is necessary to use a chocolate coverture which will cut cleanly without shattering and yet not be too soft to handle in warm weather.

9.4.5 Fruit pies

Fruit pies form the largest single product sector within the ambient cake market and are mainly produced in the mini pie format. The product make-up is approximately 50% pastry and 50% fruit filling and products are formulated to keep the pastry dry and crisp eating, and the filling moist.

Fruit pies are normally oven finished and packed directly after cooling. They are not film wrapped but packed into cartons thereby allowing a gradual loss of moisture to the atmosphere through life.

9.4.6 Pastries

This product group encompasses a wide variety of products which include:

- jam tarts
- puff pastries
- Danish pastries
- Viennese tarts
- cherry Bakewell tarts

Pastries come in many shapes and sizes and their make-up is often complex, as they can have up to six different components. The following fillings and decorations are commonly applied:

- synthetic creams
- jams and jellies
- cake fillings, e.g. Bakewell
- icings
- chocolate
- nuts
- glacé cherries

The complex nature of their composition poses particular problems in preserving the texture and appearance of components throughout the life of the product. Most of the products mentioned in this group are usually wrapped in impermeable films.

9.4.7 Product characteristics – a summary

From the previous outlines of product characteristics and past experience, a few generalisations can be made concerning product factors that are conducive to longer shelf life. While these are probably not new, it is useful to put them together so that they may help future product design.

1. complete enrobing in chocolate or chocolate coverture helps to retain quality inside (e.g. chocolate covered Swiss rolls vs. ordinary Swiss rolls).

2. High fruit content: the low ERH and the presence of hydroxymethyl furfural (HMF) in dark fruit cakes contribute to a longer shelf life.
3. Low moisture content (e.g. Jaffa cakes)
4. Jam and cream fillings are better than jam alone or cream alone (e.g. in sponge sandwiches).
5. High sugars content (e.g. Jamaica ginger cake).

9.5   Factors affecting shelf life

The most common causes of quality deterioration of ambient cakes are:

- microbiological spoilage (visual growth or fermentation);
- crumb staling (dryness and the development of off-flavours);
- rancidity (off-flavour development);
- crystallisation of sugars (e.g. grittiness in cream fillings);
- syneresis of jams and jellies;
- off-flavours and odours other than rancidity;
- chocolate bloom (or loss of gloss in baker's coatings);
- structural weakness;
- colour fade, change and transfer;
- moisture migration and loss.

9.5.1   Microbiological spoilage

The microorganisms most commonly found in ambient packaged cakes are moulds and yeasts. The ability of these microorganisms to grow and spoil the food is determined by a number of factors such as the availability of water, the environmental temperature and the pH of the system. In general, the risk of microbial spoilage can be significantly reduced by (a) developing formulations to an appropriate ERH, (b) using a suitable mould inhibitor and (c) optimising the pH where possible (Cauvain and Young, 1990).

There are few ingredients used in the manufacture of ambient cakes, which are generally recognised as actual or potential sources of harmful organisms; the most common potentially 'sensitive' ingredients are eggs, cocoa powder and desiccated coconut. However, these are usually pasteurised, dehydrated and subsequently baked in the products which render them microbiologically safe. Also, they are carefully controlled by the suppliers and manufacturers who ensure they remain uncontaminated. When coconut products and cocoa powder are used in 'cold' processes to make coatings and fillings for instance, the cake manufacturer is well advised to have them checked for pathogens by a competent laboratory.

9.5.2 Crumb staling

Staling is a phenomenon related to changes in the state of cooked starch and recognised in baked products as a dry crumbly texture, often accompanied by an unpleasant flavour and odour (Guy et al., 1983).

9.5.3 Rancidity

The oxidation of fats can lead to off-flavours and odours but this has not been a major problem for the ambient cake manufacturer whose products have in the main three weeks' shelf life, provided the fats used are fresh and have been stored correctly. However, increase in the use of butter/butter oil over the years has resulted in a higher incidence of hydrolytic rancidity (Bennion, 1972). Furthermore, some cakes (also from Continental Europe) are now sold with shelf lives of 3 to 6 months, which tends to increase the potential for oxidative rancidity.

9.5.4 Crystallisation of sugars

This fault may occur in jams, icings, caramel, various cake decorations and fillings. The causes are frequently related to incorrect formulation and poor processing. Basically, if moisture is free to migrate from a layer of caramel, for example, into an adjoining component, it can result in graining in the caramel (Lees, 1973). Likewise, the loss of moisture from jams and icings can lead to coarse crystal growth in them (Paul, 1972). Indeed, even in the absence of any free moisture transfer, water vapour will migrate as long as there is a sufficient gradient. Of course, moisture migration can generally be minimised by judicious formulation, reducing as far as practicable the difference between the ERHs of the various components.

9.5.5 Syneresis of jams and jellies

This phenomenon can often be seen in jam-filled cakes and manifests itself as a dark, moist syrupy area above or below the jam layer. It is caused by the liquid phase in the jam separating from the gel structure and migrating into the cake crumb. The appearance is unsightly and the eat, cloying and unpleasant. The main causes are normally due to the wrong choice of gelling agents or incorrect processing during jam boiling (Anon, 1984). Excessive pumping of bulk jam after it has set damages the gel structure and encourages syneresis.

9.5.6   Colour fade, change and transfer

The widespread rejection of artificial colours in foods in the late 1980s has increased the use of natural colours in the baking industry. Many of the food colours now used are derived from plants, e.g. anthocyanins, which are unstable under certain processing and/or environmental conditions. Ultraviolet barrier films or cartons can be used, for example, to overcome instability to light. Some natural colours are unstable in acid environments and the original colours can be significantly changed as shelf life progresses (Newstubb and Henry, 1988).

9.5.7   Off-flavours and odours other than rancidity

Off-flavours and odours in cakes can be caused for a variety of reasons, some of the most common ones being:

1. The use of old or badly stored ingredients (e.g. dried fruit) can introduce stale/unpleasant flavours which will accentuate as the product ages.
2. Packaging odours can be transmitted to products from printing inks, recycled board and so on (Anon, 1960).
3. Jam fermentation due to microbial contamination produces alcohol notes which are unacceptable.
4. Taints can come from cleaning chemicals if hygiene procedures are incorrectly carried out.

9.5.8   Chocolate bloom

This is a common fault in chocolate confectionery products and may also be found in chocolate-covered cakes. It is recognised by the dull greyish appearance of the chocolate coating. The four most frequent causes are: poor chocolate tempering, incorrect cooling causing condensation and subsequent sugar crystallisation, incompatibility between fats in the chocolate and the product enrobed, and temperature abuse during storage of the finished product (Minifie, 1988).

9.5.9   Structural weakness

Many cake formulations are designed to produce light, tender cakes, e.g. Swiss rolls, Madeiras and Victoria sandwiches. These products are often described as 'whole cakes' because they are sold as single products for portioning by the end user. If the structure of the cake is too weak so that it crumbles when cut it will be unacceptable to the consumer. Such a fault may not be apparent when the cake is first produced but develops as moisture redistributes within the product. There are several causes for this but the most common ones are protein deficiency in the flour, insufficient egg and/or excessive fat in the formulation and incorrect processing.

9.5.10 Moisture migration

Moisture in ambient cakes will migrate, if permitted to do so, whenever a moisture gradient exists, until equilibrium is eventually reached. This can be demonstrated by examining a freshly baked Madeira cake where the moisture contents of the top crust and the core are typically 10% and 25% respectively. After cooling and wrapping in a barrier film, moisture will migrate from the core to the top crust and into the air space inside the pack until equilibrium is attained. Similarly, migration will also occur between adjacent components. This is most commonly seen in fruit pies where the pastry is softened by moisture coming from the filling. Excessive moisture transfer can spoil the desired characteristics of a product by making, for example, the pastry in a fruit pie soft and soggy, and the filling dry and stale. Moisture migration can be minimised by careful formulation with a view to balancing the ERHs of the various components but this may not be feasible technically or acceptable organoleptically. An alternative solution would be to introduce a moisture barrier which inevitably incurs additional cost and may not always be practicable.

9.6 ERH CALC

ERH CALC (Cauvain and Young, 1990) is the first part of a computer-based 'Cake Expert System' for the baking industry produced by the UK Flour Milling and Baking Research Association (FMBRA), which enables the technologist to run formulation simulations and rapidly calculate theoretical ERH of the products and hence estimate their MFSL. The benefits of this computer tool are threefold. Firstly, it saves considerable time and effort in determining MFSL compared to trial and error methods. Secondly, it enables many more theoretical formulation options to be tried in a limited amount of time. Thirdly, it is an excellent training aid for new development staff who are unfamiliar with cake technology.

The main features of ERH CALC are (Figure 9.3):

1. It has a customised ingredient database which is tailored to the user's requirements thereby avoiding the need to occupy computer memory with irrelevant data.
2. It permits ingredient details to be input manually which is essential for trying out new ingredients.

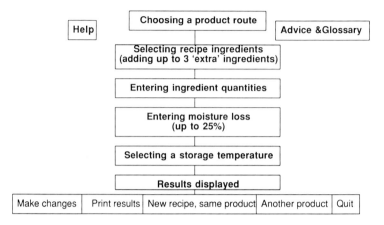

Figure 9.3 Main features of ERH CALC. (Source: Cauvain and Young, 1990).

3. It permits a range of process moisture losses to be input, e.g. baking, cooling and storage, which is essential for accurate ERH calculation.
4. ERH and MFSL can be calculated at either of two storage tempera- tures, 21°C and 27°C, which cover adequately the temperature range normally found in retail and domestic situations in the UK.
5. Component and product formulations are classified according to whether they are baked or unbaked, because of the effects of this on sugar solubility and the final ERH.
6. At the end, the system produces an overall ERH and MFSL prediction for the composite product, with the overall ERH being a weighted average of its components.
7. Also included are an 'advice' and a 'glossary' section. The 'advice' section contains information on possible changes to the formulation or production conditions and their effects on MFSL. For example, there are tables to help evaluate the effect of using the mould inhibitor, potassium sorbate and tables to show how shelf life can be increased further by lowering the product pH.

To get the most out of ERH CALC it is necessary to understand the design assumptions and to compare predictions with actual measured results. By reconciling differences, the user will develop skills in interpret- ing the information produced. ERH and MFSL predictions are made on the assumption that the product is wrapped in an impermeable film and that moisture will equilibrate within the pack. In practice, this is not always the case. For example, fruit pies are not usually film-wrapped and are free to lose moisture to the atmosphere. Also, assumptions are made about solubility levels of sugars whereas in practice, process conditions can greatly affect the amount of sugar which finally goes into solution.

The effects that mould inhibitors, e.g. sorbic acid, and others have on extending shelf life are not computed within the system but reference tables previously mentioned enable manual adjustments to be made. It is therefore possible for the user to formulate for specific shelf life requirements. By using ERH CALC the newcomer to cake technology quickly understands the role and significance of humectants in increasing cake shelf life as well as the importance of accurate control of moisture loss in baking and cooling.

The FMBRA team who developed the software is currently preparing the second edition incorporating cake formulation balance and fault diagnosis. Considerable experience gained in the use of ERH CALC since it was first launched has confirmed that it is an extremely useful tool, one that can be highly recommended to anyone involved in industrial cake development and manufacture.

9.7 The determination of product shelf life

The theoretical estimation of shelf life through ERH CALC is a very valuable tool in formulation design but there are many other factors that have to be considered. The quantitative and qualitative data collected during concept life tests relate to a development product manufactured under tightly controlled conditions. It is necessary however to take a broader view and consider external factors which may put the product at risk.

Hazard Analysis Critical Control Point (HACCP) is a system designed to identify potential hazards and their associated risks, allowing appropriate controls to be introduced and monitored (CFDRA, 1992).

9.7.1 Product data

The product data required for making shelf life decisions are derived from:

- sensory analysis
- laboratory analysis (chemical analyses and physical tests)
- microbiological examination
- travel test

9.7.1.1 Sensory analysis. The following are some of the most common quality attributes assessed in the sensory analysis of cakes:

- moistness
- crumb firmness
- colour
- flavour

- texture
- mouthfeel
- odour

Products should be assessed by trained assessors who have been selected for flavour sensitivity, colour identification and their ability to recognise consistently a range of quality attributes and assess their intensity reliably. The analyses are usually carried out at weekly intervals until the product has achieved its desired shelf life or until it becomes unacceptable. Each attribute is judged on a qualitative or numerical scale so that results can be tabulated or plotted as they become available. The information obtained can be used to make comparisons, identify trends and set product standards.

The sensory analysis environment should ensure that assessors are not distracted or influenced by one another, or affected by any external factors, and that the correct lighting is used for colour evaluation. The importance of correct experimental design and proper data analysis cannot be overemphasised. Further information on sensory analysis of foods can be found in BS 5929 Parts I–VI (BSI, 1982, 1984, 1986, 1989).

9.7.1.2 Laboratory analysis. Analyses and tests (other than microbiological examination) commonly used include:

- moisture content;
- peroxide value/free fatty acid;
- titratable acidity;
- pH value;
- refractometric solids % (RS %);
- ERH %;
- specific volume of cake (to identify possible shrinkage);
- product weight loss;
- moisture/fat migration into packaging;
- travel test and package performance.

It is necessary to carry out ERH measurement on individual components as well as on the complete product for it is possible to have an apparently safe ERH for the comminuted product but an unacceptably high ERH for one of the components. The MFSL of a cake is usually governed by the component which has the highest ERH and hence the need to determine the ERH of individual components. Big differences between the ERHs of various components also tend to suggest that moisture/water vapour migration (and other related deterioration) is likely to be a problem.

Additional chemical analysis may be carried out for nutritional labelling purposes. If a customer has specific nutritional requirements it would be sensible to ensure that they are met at an early stage of the development programme as changes that have to be made later may affect the shelf life of the product.

9.7.1.3 Microbiological examination.   Moulds and yeasts are the most common organisms that are likely to grow in packaged cakes although total viable counts and presumptive coliform counts are monitored routinely. In certain intermediate products whose manufacture involves only the mixing of ingredients (e.g. synthetic filling creams), it is necessary to check for the presence of pathogenic organisms. Although the ERH of most packaged cakes is too low to support the growth of pathogens (Parry and Pawsey, 1984), this procedure is useful to confirm that the formulations have been correctly weighed and processed.

9.7.2   External factors

The following external factors are usually considered during shelf life determination of cakes:

- plant hygiene;
- process control;
- storage of intermediate products;
- environmental and human factors;
- historical data from similar products;
- information from external sources;
- consumer use.

9.7.2.1 Plant hygiene.   It is necessary to ensure that plant and machines are capable of being cleaned to a satisfactory standard and if there are potential problems they must be identified and resolved as early as possible. Some of the more common problems encountered are:

- poor access to machines;
- inefficient use of cleaning chemicals, e.g. poor control of detergent and disinfectant concentrations;
- inadequate supply of water at the desired temperature and pressure;
- inadequate hygiene specifications;
- poorly trained staff.

Regular environmental monitoring (e.g. using air sampling, swabbing of machine parts and surfaces and so on) during factory trials can provide early warnings of such problems.

9.7.2.2 Process control.   It is necessary to establish at an early stage the actual process capabilities during plant trials as over-scaling of liquids, under-scaling of powders, inaccuracy in depositing and inconsistency in baking and so on are problems which can result in unacceptable variations in product moisture content and ERH.

9.7.2.3 Storage of intermediate products. Many cakes use intermediate products that are not heat-treated (e.g. filling creams for Swiss rolls), and control of such intermediate products can be crucial to the maintenance of the assigned product shelf life. Control should include a maximum holding period, the conditions of storage, handling procedures and if appropriate positive release based on a practical and meaningful sampling plan.

9.7.2.4 Environmental and human factors. Past experience has indicated that MFSL of cakes can be extended by 10–15% simply as a result of better hygiene, improved housekeeping and more effective pest control in the bakery. It has been shown that MFSLs of certain cakes increased significantly, the main reason being the production of these cakes had been transferred from an old and poorly maintained factory to one which was purpose-built and had a superior environment in respect of general hygiene.

Poor personal hygiene can cause high levels of microbiological contamination at start of life, which can result in reduced product shelf life. The importance of personal hygiene cannot be overemphasised, this being especially critical in labour-intensive bakery operations.

9.7.2.5 Historical data from similar products. Information from similar products and processes can be very useful in shelf life evaluation. It is not uncommon for similar products that are manufactured on the same plant to be grouped together because they are similar and have the same shelf life, for production/distribution planning and scheduling purposes. Historical data and information are particularly useful to newcomers in product development as well as the more experienced product developers who are working on shelf life extension.

9.7.2.6 Information from external sources. Ingredient and packaging suppliers are good sources of technical data and often have relevant application experience which can assist in the setting of product shelf life. They may also have specialist instrumentation and product testing 'know-how' and be prepared to help in certain aspects of shelf life evaluation.

Research Associations (e.g. FMBRA) are an invaluable source of scientific and technological expertise. this is particularly true for medium to small sized companies who do not have a central research and development function. They can provide information/legislation services, private consultancy as well as a wide range of analytical services. It is reassuring to know when one is venturing into a new product or process area, one can turn to the RAs for informal advice or consultancy on a confidential basis.

9.7.2.7 Consumer use. It is important to give some thought to the product end-use environment (i.e. the climate and the way the product may be stored and consumed), particularly if the product is destined for export. Temperature has a significant effect on the shelf life of ambient packaged cakes and any shelf life determination must take this into account. It is also important to consider at a very early stage the legal status of any additives such as preservatives (e.g. mould inhibitors) that may have to be used to achieve the target shelf life, especially when the product is being developed for the export market.

9.8 Shelf life determination

A possible decision process for determining product shelf life is outlined in Figure 9.4. The process not only utilises product data but also requires relevant information from the process and the environment in which the product is to be manufactured, distributed, stored, merchandised and consumed. There may also be a need for information from specialist/ external sources (e.g. Research Associations and suppliers) when new materials (edible and/or packaging), new product types or new processes are involved. The decision requires judgements to be made about the robustness of the formulation, the microbiological profile, the process and end-use conditions. The setting of a product shelf life is usually a joint effort from among Product Development, Laboratory Service and Quality Assurance management.

9.8.1 Product development activities

The following represents the sequence of activities for the determination of product shelf life of ambient packaged cakes.

(a) Concept stage (development bakery):
  1. Formulation development.
  2. Estimation of baking and cooling losses.
  3. Calculation of theoretical ERH and prediction of MFSL using ERH CALC.
  4. Further formulation development if necessary.
  5. Production of samples for shelf life and other evaluations.
  6. Analysis of samples at start of life.
  7. Sampling for analysis at pre-determined intervals.
  8. Comparison of preliminary shelf life with prediction.

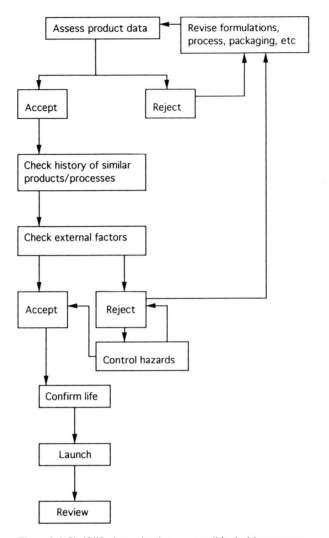

Figure 9.4 Shelf life determination – a possible decision process.

    9. If necessary, further formulation adjustments and life tests.
   10. Setting of provisional product shelf life.
(b) Factory stage (plant bakery):
    1. Identification of food safety hazards (HACCP).
    2. Scale-up of formulations and processes, with modifications where appropriate.
    3. Shelf life determination using samples made from pilot or full scale plant.

4. Comparison of shelf life results with those obtained using concept samples.
5. More full scale factory runs (and shelf life determinations) especially if pilot plant only was used in (3) above.
6. Confirmation of product shelf life (issuing of finalised and approved complete 'product–process–packaging' specifications).
7. Product launch and shelf life validation and monitoring using samples from production runs.
8. Follow-up actions and investigations if necessary.

9.8.2 *An example – a white chocolate mini sponge roll*

The following information was obtained during the development of a new packaged cake which was a chocolate buttercream-filled mini roll completely covered in white chocolate. This was the first white chocolate cake from an industrial cake manufacturer in the UK. Little was known of the performance and potential problems associated with the handling of white chocolate although the latter is more widely used in the biscuit and chocolate confectionery industry. The sponge and buttercream on the other hand were components in everyday use. White chocolate is more prone to rancidity development than normal chocolate and therefore PV and FFA determinations were carried out on both the stored chocolate and the finished product. Sensory profiles of the white chocolate and of the whole product were obtained and recorded using 'star' diagrams or 'spider' plots. The product was produced using a well established process and standard plant and equipment with the exception of the chocolate enrober and its associated storage tanks. A standard pack format was used and as anticipated the 'travel test' gave satisfactory results and revealed no major potential problems in distribution.

9.8.2.1 Sensory data. Nine quality attributes were evaluated and the data presented (Table 9.3) were the ratings of the final product. The attributes assessed were: chocolate colour and opacity, chocolate melt and mouthfeel, chocolate flavour, sponge texture, sponge crumbliness, sponge toughness, product moistness, buttercream flavour and overall product flavour (see Table 9.3). 'Spider plots' of the white chocolate and the total product were produced based on the data obtained, using a sensory panel of six assessors (Figure 9.5 a and b).

9.8.2.2 Other data. Other relevant product data obtained are summarised in Table 9.4. The dedicated white chocolate enrober and storage tanks required special control and monitoring to minimise the risk of ran-

Table 9.3 White chocolate mini sponge roll – sensory analysis results

Quality attribute	Rating		Total score	Mean score
Chocolate opacity	Translucent	(1)		
	Opaque	(10)	31	5.2
Chocolate melt	Slow	(1)		
	Fast	(10)	43	7.2
Chocolate flavour	Weak	(1)		
	Strong	(10)	50	8.3
Sponge texture	Compact	(1)		
	Open	(10)	46	7.6
Sponge crumbliness	Crumbly	(1)		
	Firm	(10)	36	6.0
Sponge toughness	Tough	(1)		
	Soft	(10)	32	5.3
Overall moistness	Very dry	(1)		
	Very moist	(10)	32	5.3
Buttercream flavour	Weak	(1)		
	Strong	(10)	45	7.5
Overall chocolate flavour	Weak	(1)		
	Strong	(10)	30	5.0

The panel consisted of six assessors.

cidity development and colour contamination. The rest of the process was well established and controlled in the normal way. The product was eventually assigned a shelf life of 3 weeks.

9.9   Current developments

Two important issues in the packaged cake industry today are:

1. shelf life extension
2. shorter lead time to market

both of which have implications for shelf life evaluation.

9.9.1   Shelf life extension

The demand for packaged cakes with a longer life is driven by the need to export as well as to remain competitive in the home market. Extending shelf life requires new technologies (e.g. new processes and techniques) which must be evaluated by the methods described, but if shelf life is to be extended to months then the process of shelf life evaluation will

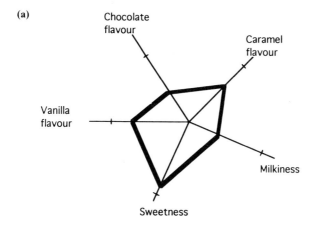

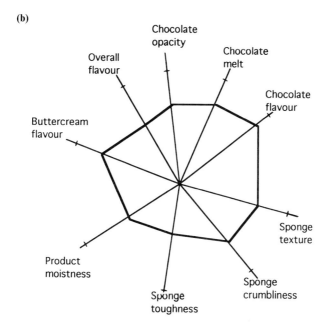

Figure 9.5 Spider plots of the white chocolate (a) and the enrobed mini sponge roll (b).

need to be speeded up. Accelerated shelf life determinations are being successfully used in certain applications and there is now a wide variety of instruments available, which will carry out chemical and micro-biological analyses faster than conventional methods.

Table 9.4 Shelf life determination of white chocolate mini sponge roll – a summary of some relevant product data

Component	Moisture content%	ERH%	TVC[a] (cfu/g)	Yeasts/g[a]	Moulds/g[a]
Total product	17.3	78.5	280	10	< 10
Golden sponge	20.3	79.2	–	–	–
Buttercream	15.4	77.4	150	20	10
White chocolate	1.6	70.1	–	–	–

[a]Results after 5 weeks' storage.

9.9.2 Shorter lead time to market

International competition and competition within the Single European Market in foods are demanding faster entry into the marketplace with new products. Capital investment must begin to pay back earlier to improve profitability which in turn can be used to finance business expansion. All this has meant that the development process must be shortened without compromising product safety and quality. In addition food legislation demands that food must be safe and wholesome and, should a 'due diligence' defence be used, evidence must exist to prove that 'all reasonable precautions' have actually been taken. In this context, the process of shelf life determination must not only be quicker but also more rigorous, comprehensive and well documented. The route to achieving greater speed and reliability can be facilitated through the use of predictive computer models such as the ERH CALC and where appropriate the 'Food Micromodel' (MAFF, 1992) which is the UK Ministry of Agriculture, Fisheries and Food's microbiological predictive program. Much benefit can also be gained by the implementation of techniques like HACCP as well as judicious introduction of modern sophisticated analytical instruments and data handling and analysis capabilities.

References

Anon (1960) *Odour in Packaging*, The Institute of Packaging Conference Technical Papers, UK.

Anon (1984) *The Handbook for the Fruit Industry*, Section 14, Genu Pectins Skensued, Copenhagen Pectin Factory Limited, Denmark.

Bennion, M. (1972) Fats as cooking media, shortening agents and components of pastry, in *Food Theory and Applications* (eds P.C. Paul and H.H. Palmer), Wiley, London, pp. 213–50.

BSI (1982, 1984, 1986, 1989) *Methods for Sensory Analysis of Food*, BS 5929, part 1–6, British Standards Institution, London.

Cauvain, S.P. and Young, L.S. (1990) *ERH CALC*, Computer Software Package, Flour Milling and Baking Research Association, Chorleywood.

Cauvain, S.P. and Seiler, D.A. (1992) *Equilibrium Relative Humidity and the Shelf Life of Cakes*, Flour Milling and Baking Research Association, Chorleywood.

CFDRA (1992) *HACCP: A Practical Guide* (ed. S. Leaper). The Campden Food and Drink Research Association, Chipping Campden.

Guy, R.C.E., Hodge, D.C. and Robb, J. (1983) *An Examination of the Phenomena Associated with Cake Staling*, Report 107, Flour Milling and Baking Research Association, Chorleywood.

Lees, R. (1973) *Sugar Confectionery and Chocolate Manufacture*, Leonard Hill, London, pp. 191–205.

MAFF (1992) *Micromodel*, Ministry of Agriculture, Fisheries and Food, UK.

Minifie, B.W. (1988) *Chocolate, Cocoa and Confectionery: Science and Technology*, 3rd edn, Van Nostrand Reinhold Inc., New York.

Newstubb, C.J. and Henry, B.S. (1988) Natural colours – a challenge and an opportunity. *Food Technology International Europe*, Sterling Publication Ltd.

Ooraikul, B. (1991) Modified atmosphere packaging of bakery products, in *Modified Atmosphere Packaging of Food* (eds B. Ooraikul and M.E. Stiles), Ellis Horwood, Chichester, pp. 49–115.

Parry, T.J. and Pawsey, R.K. (1984) *Principles of Microbiology for Students of Food Technology*, 2nd edn, Hutchinson, London.

Paul, P.C. (1972) Basic scientific principles, sugars, and browning reactions, in *Food Theory and Applications* (eds P.C. Paul and H.H. Palmer), Wiley, London, pp. 1–76.

Seiler, D.A.L. (1976) The stability of intermediate moisture foods with respect to mould growth, in *Intermediate Moisture Foods* (eds R. Davies, G.G. Birch and K.J. Parker), Applied Science, London, pp. 166–80.

10 Potato crisps and savoury snacks

A. REILLY and C.M.D. MAN

10.1 Introduction

Potato crisps and related savoury snacks such as extruded products, belong to a highly competitive, innovative and growing sector of the food market. In the UK, they are categorised as snack products which are generally understood as ready-to-eat ambient, 'shelf stable' (6–12 weeks) savoury products, prepacked and offered through a variety of outlets including supermarkets and other food retailers as well as catering establishments (Blenford, 1990). This then is the definition of snack products for the purpose of this chapter although it is understood that the term 'snack products' can mean very different products in different countries within the European Community, and indeed in North America. In 1991, the UK consumed some 234 k tonnes of snacks which equated to just over 4 kg per head per annum. In financial terms, the UK snack market is worth more than £3 billion a year and is still growing (Euromonitor, 1992).

10.2 The product group

Broadly speaking, snack food products may be divided into the following categories based on the process technology associated with their manufacture (Burdon, 1989):

1. *Deep fat fried.* This includes potato crisps and potato strips/sticks/rings, and represents by far the major portion of the snack food business.
2. *Quick fried.* Pre-formed partly cooked pellets derived from potato, potato starch and/or other cereal materials are fried at high temperature (i.e. of the order of 200°C) for a short time (10–15 seconds) giving expanded, light-textured products.
3. *Extrusion-cooked.* Cereal/potato powder mixes are extruded through dies at high pressure and temperature to give an expanded base which, after further drying, is enrobed with oil and flavour. A large number of products are available in this category and they display varying sizes, shapes, textures and flavours.

4. *Roasted.* This is primarily represented by nuts, particularly in the form of dry roasted peanuts.

The primary raw materials for snacks are therefore potato, either fresh or dehydrated, cereals (maize, rice, wheat, etc.) and nuts. Notwithstanding the important influence these raw materials have on the quality of the final products, by far the most important ingredient that can affect shelf life is the oil used, either in frying or as a carrier for seasoning. Snack products as a group can be said to be consumed principally for pleasure, because of their unique texture and the enormous variety of flavours available. As such, well planned and conducted consumer acceptability tests in the form of appropriate sensory analysis, are an important part of the shelf life evaluation of any snack product.

10.3 Factors affecting shelf life of potato crisps and savoury snacks

In general, the factors that can influence the shelf life of foods are (IFST, 1993):

Intrinsic

- raw materials
- product formulation and composition
- product make-up
- water activity value
- pH value and acidity
- availability of oxygen and redox potential

Extrinsic

- processing
- hygiene
- packaging materials and system
- storage, distribution and retail display

Whilst all the relevant factors undoubtedly have their influence on the shelf life of a snack product, some do have greater effects and deserve more attention.

10.3.1 The oil

Although the oil is primarily used as a heat transfer medium during the frying process, it does get absorbed and becomes a major part of the finished product. Ordinary potato crisps contain as much as 35–40% edible oil and even in reduced fat crisps, the level of oil can still be significant (typically less than 25%). It is imperative therefore that care must be taken in the selection, transport, storage, handling and use of frying oils since any abuse would most certainly result in reduced product shelf life (e.g. as a result of rancidity and off-flavour development) and in customer complaints.

Thus, a heavy duty frying oil, probably the most demanding use of any edible oil product should have the following properties (Hunt, 1989):

1. Resistance of chemical breakdown such as oxidation, polymerisation, or hydrolysis at temperatures up to 180°C.
2. Colour stability so as not to discolour food.
3. Pourability, pumpability at ambient temperature.
4. Nutritional characteristics.
5. Oil stability not only at the high temperature of the frying process, but also during the prolonged life of the fried food when this oil may be exposed to air, for example, on the large surface area of the crisps.

10.3.2 The process

Frying, be it deep fat frying or quick frying, is probably one of the most severe tests to which one can subject an oil in the manufacture of snack products. Since the quality of the frying oil is of paramount importance in determining the shelf life of fried foods, it is important to control the quality of the oil during use. In practice, the quality limits for a frying oil during use will depend on the food being fried, as different components can leach out of the food and lead to different characteristics in the oil. Although most snack product manufacturers now use fairly sophisticated continuous fryers with indirect heating systems, automatic filtration, balanced steam stacks, controlled oil flow and efficient controls and instrumentation, all of which are aimed at keeping the oil in good condition, a few basic rules based on the principles of 'Good Manufacturing Practice' (GMP), can help to maintain the quality of the oil during use (McGill, 1986; Burdon, 1989; Neilsen, 1993).

1. Turnover period (the time taken for the food to absorb the oil capacity of the fryer): Generally, as long as the recommended frying conditions are closely adhered to, the lower the turnover period, the less the oil will be degraded.
2. Specified frying temperatures: Temperatures higher than those specified promote oil degradation, and lower ones result in excessive oil uptake by the product.
3. Planned production: It is important to ensure by careful planning, a good, steady product throughput to avoid dramatic temperature changes as well as to reduce the risk of holding the oil idle in the fryer at frying temperature.
4. Cleaning: Appropriate and efficient cleaning regimes should be employed to minimise the risk of contamination by cleaning materials or as a result of poor cleaning techniques, either of which can cause deterioration in the quality of the oil.
5. Plant maintenance: A preventive maintenance programme should be

operated, that can greatly reduce the risk of contamination of the oil by metals, in particular copper (e.g. from pumps, pipes, valves, fittings or paddle shaft wear), which may act as powerful catalysts of oil oxidation.

As an indication of oil degradation, one can measure the free fatty acid (FFA) level in the oil in the fryer on a regular basis (Burdon, 1989). Determination of the FFA level is a useful check, as it is an objective measurement that can be carried out easily during production runs, and can be automated. Experience has shown, however, that there can be big differences in the levels of FFA accepted in different production processes without indicating any difference in quality of the finished products. These differences more or less reflect the differences in the type of frying oil as well as fryer used, and the product being processed. Leatherhead Food Research Association in the UK has developed a rapid method based on measurement of the viscosity of the frying oil. A good correlation has been achieved between the rheological properties measured and the quality of the oil expressed by the content of the polymers, which are being formed as the oil decomposes (Gillat et al., 1991).

10.3.3 Packaging materials

One of the most important functions of food packaging is the protection of the product from environmental factors (see section 10.3.4 for further discussion) such as light, water vapour, gases and odours during its shelf life. The exact protection required, however, depends on the nature of the product. In respect of the shelf life of snacks, the following are the main properties of flexible packaging materials (e.g. coextruded OPP), which can affect the storage quality of a product.

1. Water vapour transmission rate (WVTR): For a given material such as coextruded OPP, this is primarily a function of film thickness (Figure 10.1). The lower the WVTR of a film, the better is the moisture barrier. Moisture barrier of a packaging film, of course, may be further enhanced by various processes such as coating with an additional barrier material, lamination and metallisation (Table 10.1).
2. Oxygen transmission rate (OTR): Similar to WVTR, OTR of clear OPP decreases as the thickness of the film increases (Figure 10.2). Permeability to oxygen is substantially reduced by coating with a suitable barrier material (e.g. acrylic) and by metallisation (Table 10.1).
3. Optical density (OD): This is defined as OD $= \mathrm{Log}_{10}$ (incident light/ transmitted light). Determined using a suitable densitometer (at $23 \pm 2°C$, $50 \pm 5\%$ RH), it is a measure of the light barrier property of a film (Figure 10.3). The greater the OD of a film, the better is the

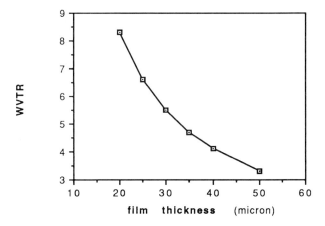

Figure 10.1 Permeability of coextruded OPP films to water vapour. (Source: CFP, UK.)

Table 10.1 Typical water vapour transmission rates and oxygen transmission rates of some biaxially oriented polypropylene films used for snacks

Material type	OTR ($cm^3/m^2/24h/atm$ at $23 \pm 2°C$ and 90% RH)	WVTR ($g/m^2/24h$ at $38°C$ and 90% RH)
Clear (CFP), 30 μm	<1500	<5.5
Opaque voided (CFP), 35 μm	1550	5.2
White pigmented (CFP), 30 μm	<1500	<5.5
Metallised (CFP), 30 μm	<120	<0.8
PVdC coated 2 sides (ICI), 28 μm	16	5.0
PVdC coated 2 sides (ICI), 39 μm	5	2.3
PVdC/acrylic coated (Mobil), 26 μm	23	4.2
Acrylic coated 2 sides (Mobil), 30 μm	650	4.0
Metallised/acrylic coated (Mobil), 21 μm	1–2	1.0–1.5

Sources: various technical data sheets, Courtaulds Films Polypropylene (CFP), ICI 'Propafilm' and Mobil Plastics Europe.

light barrier and hence protection against light-induced changes (e.g. oxidation and bleaching).

4. Flavour/odour barrier property: The significance of flavour/odour barrier performance of a packaging film lies in its practical importance in relation to the flavour retention of packaged foods such as snacks, and also with respect to protection against tainting by extraneous sources. Snack products are usually highly flavoured and contain an appreciable amount of oil, making them susceptible to contamination by taints; flavour retention and taint protection over relatively long shelf lives are therefore an important consideration. However, it has been shown by British Cellophane Limited (1982) that the odour

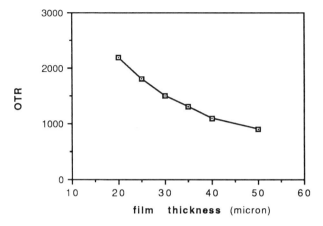

Figure 10.2 Permeability of coextruded OPP films to oxygen. (Source: CFP, UK.)

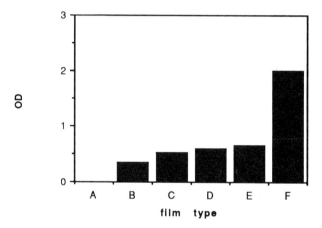

Figure 10.3 Optical densities of some coextruded OPP films. A: clear; B: opaque voided (35 micron); C: white pigmented (30 micron); D: white pigmented (35 micron); E, white pigmented (40 micron); F: metallised (20 and 30 micron). (Source: CFP, UK.)

barrier performance of coextruded OPP films should not be assessed on the basis of oxygen permeability. Indeed because of the very many flavours that can be used and odours that may be encountered potentially, there is no general measure of the odour barrier property of a packaging film. Specific storage tests and/or calculations (Zobel, 1988) have to be carried out to assess this barrier property with respect to the flavour/odour in question (see Appendix for more information on flavour loss calculations).

During the shelf life of a snack, two main deterioration processes take place together, one being texture loss due to moisture pick-up, the other being rancidity development which requires oxygen and may be light-induced. Although both need to be controlled, relatively speaking, the former is more important to potato crisps and related snacks and the latter to nuts, because of their compositional differences. Thus, currently biaxially oriented polypropylene (OPP) films are the most commonly used packaging materials for crisps and snacks within Europe, while nuts are usually packaged in, for example, PVdC coated OPP/LDPE laminate or metallised polyester/LDPE laminate, depending on the value of the product. OPP has qualities of toughness (against puncture and abrasion) and clarity and is rendered heat sealable by coextrusion with polyolefin copolymers (polypropylene co-ethylene) or by off-line coating (e.g. with PVdC).

Table 10.1 lists typical WVTRs and OTRs of some OPP films used for crisps and snacks packaging within Europe. It must be stressed that these values are flat sheet permeability values; the protection of the product depends on the total barrier provided by the film pack. The sheet barrier properties may be altered by bad conversion techniques, or by mishandling such as scratching by poorly maintained packaging machines. Moreover, the seal integrity of the pack must be good enough to prevent leakage during the shelf life of the product. Pack barrier for snacks is thus a combination of:

- film barrier
- maintenance of film barrier
- seal integrity.

In practice, to achieve the required level of protection of a snack, it does not necessarily follow that the highest barrier material is the best choice of packaging. The packaging material that is chosen will be a compromise between protective requirements, shelf life, aesthetics and cost. In the crisps sector, at present, a 30 micron clear OPP film is the most cost effective form of packaging for commodity products with short shelf life (12 weeks or less) while metallised OPP laminates are used for larger family packs, sensitive products and high added value products. In the nuts sector, commodity products with short shelf life requirements are packed in nitrogen gas flushed PVdC coated OPP/LDPE laminates while higher value added products and those with longer shelf life requirements are packed in nitrogen gas flushed metallised polyester/LDPE laminates.

10.3.4 Environmental factors

Fatty food products such as crisps can become unacceptable through the formation of rancid off-flavours due to oxidation of the oil content of the product through the process of oxidative rancidity. It is known that this reaction may be catalysed by light and heat. Two previous investigations carried out by BCL in the 1980s looked at crisp rancidity in relation to the light barrier properties of various packaging films. The first study (1983) employed very severe test conditions where the test packs were exposed to fluorescent lighting continuously, i.e. 24 hours a day, giving a light intensity of 1000 lux on the packs which were stored flat. The second study (1985) was designed to simulate more closely the storage and display conditions to which commercial packs of crisps were usually subjected. It also used a different type of fluorescent tube giving an intensity of 1700 lux, on a 12 hours 'on'/12 hours 'off' basis. Overall, useful conclusions have been drawn from these two studies and are summarised below:

1. Improved light barrier properties of packaging films give extended shelf life of crisps in respect of rancid off-flavours. Thus, printed metallised OPP films give longer shelf life than printed OPP films which in turn give longer life than unprinted OPP films.
2. Prolonged storage under fluorescent lights (24 hour continuous exposure) at ambient humidity can cause crisps to become rancid before any texture changes due to moisture uptake are detected.
3. The incorporation of a clear window in a metallised pack significantly reduces the acceptable shelf life of the crisps in respect of rancid off-flavours.
4. Shingle storage of packs offers a longer shelf life than packs stored flat (Figure 10.4).
5. Metallised films also prolong the shelf life of crisps in respect of moisture uptake.

10.3.5 Legal standards

Within the European Community, the need to achieve harmonisation of legislation in member states in respect of materials and articles destined for use in contact with foods and the need to protect the consumer from risks associated with the migration of harmful substances from packaging materials, have meant that food packaging migration is now under the control of the relevant legislation (Ashby *et al.*, 1992). The EC 'plastics' directive 90/128/EEC as amended by directive 92/39/EEC, sets an overall migration limit for all plastics food contact materials and articles of 10 mg/dm^2 (or 60 mg/kg of food), and lists monomers and other starting substances approved for use in the manufacture of plastics, with restrictions where necessary. In the UK, the implementation of this directive and two other directives, i.e. 82/711/EEC on test conditions and 85/572/EEC on use of simulants, has now been achieved by the Plastics Materials

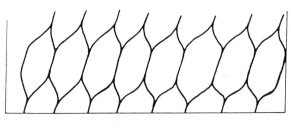

SHINGLE STORAGE

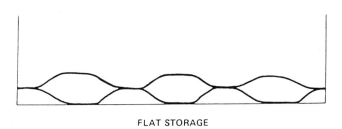

FLAT STORAGE

Figure 10.4 Shelf life of crisps: type of pack storage. (Source: BCL, 1985; CFP, UK.)

and Articles in Contact with Food Regulations 1992. This piece of legislation applies to all in the chain from the plastics manufacturer, through
the plastics converter, the food packer/manufacturer, to the food retailer.
All have a definite role to play in the compliance of the overall migration
and where appropriate, specific migration limits, though each may have a
slightly different responsibility to bear. Regarding overall (global) migration values from coextruded OPP films, the following are typical results
(Surman, 1993):

1. <1 mg/dm^2 using distilled water or water of equivalent quality;
2. <1 mg/dm^2 using 3% acetic acid (w/v) in aqueous solution;
3. <1 mg/dm^2 using rectified olive oil.

The snack manufacturer obviously has a responsibility to ensure that
all the information supplied to him by the packaging film supplier in
respect of migration into food simulants is appropriate to his actual snack
product, and this does not take into consideration any sensory analysis
required additionally. Furthermore, since the snack manufacturer may

also be expected to supply the retailer with compliance statements, it seems therefore some migration testing by the former cannot be avoided. This is particularly relevant in the case of a new/novel product and film combination, where migration testing can well be an important part of the shelf life evaluation programme.

10.4   Shelf life determination

The nature and characteristics of snack products are such that the most common tests employed in the determination of their shelf life are:

- chemical tests
- physical tests
- sensory tests

One method for ready salted potato crisps (BCL, 1985) involves storing sufficient packs of the products under controlled conditions of temperature (e.g. 25°C) and relative humidity (e.g. 75%) for a period of 12 weeks. Packs of the same products are also stored in a deep freeze to act as controls in subsequent sensory analysis. Stored products are tested at the start of the storage period and evaluated at weekly intervals until the products are regarded as no longer acceptable by a trained taste panel of 8–10 assessors. Panel assessors are asked to give their opinion of the grading of the crisps for flavour and texture directly against a control on a scale of 1–10 where:

10	= equal to control;
9	= slight difference to control;
8	= more distinct difference but still acceptable;
7	= beginning to lose acceptability;
6	= more distinct loss of acceptability;
5	= very distinct loss of acceptability;
4 or less	= unacceptability.

In addition to sensory tests, crisps are used for chemical tests at every sampling occasion. To do these, the oil is extracted from the crisps and the peroxide value and free fatty acid value of the extracted oil are determined. Moisture uptake of the packs is monitored by weighing the packs immediately before submission to the taste panel. Figures 10.5, 10.6 and 10.7 show changes in flavour, peroxide value and moisture uptake of crisps packed in printed metallised OPP, during a shelf life study in which the packs were stored flat and subjected to a 12 hour cycling exposure to fluorescent lights (BCL, 1985). It was found that the crisps began to lose acceptability after about 8 weeks of storage. Since peroxide value gives a

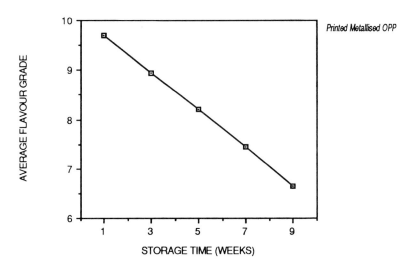

Figure 10.5 Flavour assessment of crisps (stored flat) exposed to fluorescent lighting (1700 lux). (Source: BCL, 1985; CFP, UK.)

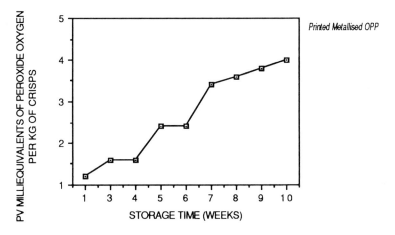

Figure 10.6 Peroxide value of crisps (stored flat) exposed to fluorescent lighting (1700 lux). (Source: BCL, 1985; CFP, UK.)

measure of the primary oxidation products which normally decompose quickly to secondary and tertiary oxidation products, it is apparent that changes in PV did not correlate as closely as changes in moisture uptake, with the gradual loss in product acceptability.

Besides laboratory tests, packs taken from production trials should be examined for seal integrity which can be a major factor limiting shelf life. Careful visual examination of returned packs from a 'travel test' through

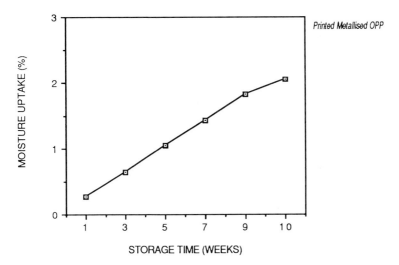

Figure 10.7 Moisture uptake of crisps (stored flat) exposed to fluorescent lighting (1700 lux). (Source: BCL, 1985; CFP, UK.)

the distribution and storage chain, is also important to reveal transit hazards due to various mechanical stresses and pressure, which can cause premature termination of product shelf life. Experience has shown that the level of sophistication of a distribution system (including handling, transport and storage) can have considerable influence on the shelf life of snack products.

It is also possible to predict ambient shelf life of snacks from accelerated shelf life tests, i.e. storage at elevated temperature and humidity. Despite obvious benefits, such tests tend to be very product-specific and require experience and care in the interpretation of results. An alternative approach to accelerated tests would be to model shelf life and pack performance, using appropriate computer programs (Oswin, 1983; Hayes, 1992). For snack products, and potato crisps in particular, there exist, as discussed previously, two competing deterioration mechanisms, i.e. oxidative rancidity and moisture uptake. Regarding moisture uptake, the information required for modelling is well known (Labuza, 1982; Hayes, 1992):

1. the moisture-sorption isotherm data for the temperature in question;
2. the packaging film properties such as WVTR;
3. the storage conditions anticipated.

Armed with other film properties, e.g. OTR and permeation data, it is conceivable that chemical changes can also be modelled using similar computer techniques. This perhaps will be one of the many technical challenges facing the industry for the immediate future.

Acknowledgements

Grateful thanks are expressed to Mr E.D. Surman, Development Manager of Courtaulds Films Polypropylene UK, for various shelf life reports and information on polypropylene films provided in this chapter.

Appendix – Flavour loss calculations

Work carried out by BCL (1984) resulted in the derivation of a simple equation which can be used to estimate the likely permeation coefficients of a wide range of chemical substances through coextruded OPP as well as polyethylene, at low odourant concentrations. In the SI system, permeation coefficients have the unit $g\ mm^{-2}\ Pa^{-1}\ s^{-1}$, which represents the weight of flavourant/odourant permeating a polymer specimen one metre thick, one square metre in area, per second, with a vapour pressure difference across the specimen of one Pascal ($=$ 10 ppm vol/vol). The permeation data, together with information relating to the pack contents and storage/display environment, provide a convenient method for estimating the transfer rates of flavours or contaminants through commercial flexible packs. Zobel (1988) has shown that the rate of transmission (R in $g\ s^{-1}$) of flavourant (e.g. vinegar flavour measured as acetic acid) through a packaging film is given by the following formula:

$$R = (PC \times VP \times A)/L$$

where PC = permeation coefficient ($g\ mm^{-2}\ Pa^{-1}\ s^{-1}$)
VP = vapour pressure of flavourant (Pa)
A = area of film (m^2)
L = thickness of film (m)

Strictly speaking, VP should be the difference in vapour pressure of flavourant between the inside and the outside of the pack; but for practical purposes, the inside pack vapour pressure, as measured by headspace gas chromatography, will suffice. Using this formula, it is possible, in the event that highly flavoured snacks are being packaged, to conduct flavour loss calculations, thereby providing the reassurance that the chosen OPP film, for example, will give an adequate barrier.

References

Ashby, R., Cooper, I., Shorten, D. and Tice, P. (1992) *Food Packaging Migration and Legislation*, PIRA International, UK.
BCL (1982) *An Investigation into the Odour Barrier Properties of Coextruded Polypropylene Film*, Courtaulds Films Polypropylene, UK.

BCL (1983) *A Study of the effect of Light Barriers on the Onset of Rancidity in Crisps*, Courtaulds Films Polypropylene, UK.

BCL (1984) *Determination of the Odour Barrier Performance of Coextruded Packaging Films*, Courtaulds Films Polypropylene, UK.

BCL (1985) *Crisp Rancidity – the Effect of a Clear Window in Metallised Film on Crisp Shelf Life*, Courtaulds Films Polypropylene, UK.

Blenford, D.E. (1990) Satisfying a growing appetite for snacks. *Food Technology International Europe*, Sterling, London, pp. 145–9.

Burdon, T.A. (1989) Rancidity in Snack Foods, in *Rancidity in Foods*, 2nd edn (eds J.C. Allen and R.J. Hamilton), Elsevier Applied Science, London, pp. 161–9.

Courtaulds Films. Technical Information Leaflets: SCB, SWH, SHP, SHM. Courtaulds Films Polypropylene, UK.

Euromonitor (1992) Savoury snacks – Euromonitor Market Direction.

Gillat, P., Kress-Rogers, E. and Rossell, B. (1991) A novel sensor for the measurement of frying oil quality. *Lipid Technology*, **3**(3), 78–82.

Hayes, G.D. (1992) The modelling of food shelf life and package performance, using computer spreadsheets, in *Food Engineering in a Computer Climate*, 215–223. Institution of Chemical Engineers, UK.

Hunt, R.W. (1989) Oils and fats, in *Food Processing – Proceedings of the Ninth British Nutrition Foundations Annual Conference* (ed. R. Cottrell), The Parthenon Publishing Group, UK.

IFST (1993) *Shelf Life of Foods – Guidelines for its Determination and Prediction*, Institute of Food Science and Technology, UK.

Labuza, T.P. (1982) Moisture Gain and Loss in Packaged Foods. *Food Technology*, **36**(4), 92–94, 96, 97.

McGill, E.A. (1986) Deep Frying, in *Impulse Foods*, Volume one (ed. D.E. Blenford), Food Trade Press, UK.

Mobil Plastics Europe. Product Information Sheets : Bicor[®] MB 666, MB 777, MM 778. Mobil Plastics Europe, London.

Nielsen, K. (1993) Frying Oils Technology. *Food Technology International Europe*, Sterling Publications Limited, London, pp. 127–32.

Oswin, C.R. (1983) Isotherms and Package Life: Some Advances in Emballistics. *Food Chemistry*, No. 12, 179–88.

Propafilm. Product Information Sheets: Propafilm C, Propafilm CB. ICI, Herts.

Surman, E.D. (1993) Personal communication, CFP, UK.

Zobel, M.G.R. (1988) Packaging and Questions of Flavour Retention. *Food Technology International Europe*, Sterling Publications Limited, London, pp. 339–42.

11 Chocolate confectionery

A.V. MARTIN

11.1 Introduction

The shelf life of chocolate is the period of time during which it will retain acceptable appearance, aroma, flavour and texture.

Chocolate is a high energy foodstuff with a complex nutritional profile, containing 28–40% lipids (cocoa butter, possibly other vegetable fats and milk fat), 50–70% carbohydrates, and 4–8% proteins. It is also an important source of mineral salts (Ca, Mg, Fe, Na, K) coming from cocoa liquor, and vitamins (riboflavin, vitamin A, vitamin E).

Despite this complexity, chocolate is very shelf stable due principally to the unique properties of cocoa. Cocoa solids contain a natural antioxidant in the form of tocopherol and cocoa butter breaks down to inoffensive short chain fatty acids.

As a result, most chocolate products can be classified as 'medium' or 'long life' products which, when packaged, should have a storage life under normal conditions of temperature and humidity of nine months or longer. In the UK 'normal' conditions are probably represented by a temperature of 20°C and 60–65% relative humidity.

Nevertheless, degradation of the product can occur at earlier stages whereby its physical and/or organoleptic characteristics no longer correspond to the parameters set by the manufacturer's quality standard and so are unacceptable.

It is the purpose of this chapter to examine the attributes of chocolate which provide this stability and how product degradation can occur. The various forms which chocolate confectionery can take will be considered and factors influencing their shelf lives. Methods of determining shelf lives will also be examined.

11.2 Composition of chocolate

The precise composition of chocolate varies throughout the world due to differing national tastes and varying legislation which is mainly concerned with the percentages of cocoa and added milk solids, and amounts and types of permitted vegetable fats.

In many countries chocolate production is strictly controlled by law, in most cases restricting ingredients to sugar, cocoa butter, cocoa solids and milk solids. Some countries such as the UK allow a percentage of cocoa butter to be replaced by vegetable fat, and others permit the use of nutmeat, whey and so on.

11.2.1 Cocoa liquor

Cocoa beans comprise approximately 88% nibs, 11% shell and 1% germ. Once harvested the beans are fermented, cleaned, roasted and the nibs separated from the beans. The nib is a cellular mass containing about 55% cocoa butter locked within the cell structure. Grinding breaks down the cell walls releasing the fat which, as it is liquefied by frictional heat, becomes a continuous phase in which the disintegrated cell particles are suspended. This fluid paste is called 'cocoa liquor' or 'cocoa mass'.

11.2.2 Fats

The fats found in chocolate include cocoa butter, milk fat and, in the UK, non cocoa butter vegetable fat. This last group is commonly known as 'cocoa butter equivalents' or 'CBEs'.

11.2.2.1 Cocoa butter. To meet legal requirements most chocolates contain at least 20% cocoa butter which has properties unmatched by any other fat. It is the cocoa butter which gives chocolate its unique flavour and exceptional shelf life through its oxidative stability. The characteristic physical properties of cocoa butter which give chocolate its special texture lie in its unique melting properties, i.e. it remains solid at room temperature up to 28°C yet melts fully and completely at 36°C (below mouth temperature). Cocoa butter is expressed from cocoa liquor leaving cocoa powder. From certain sources it must be deodorised to remove potentially harsh flavour tones and this process may reduce its antioxidant properties.

11.2.2.2 Milk fat. This is used for four reasons:

- for taste;
- as a texture modifier – to soften chocolate;
- as a fat bloom inhibitor;
- to reduce cost.

Two main processes exist for the incorporation of milk into chocolate, which confer quite different tastes on the resultant products:

- the continental process using milk powder added to cocoa liquor;
- the crumb process used in the UK and frequently in the US and certain European countries whereby milk, sugar and cocoa liquor are con-

densed under vacuum and the resultant solid ground to a powder which is then added to the cocoa mass.

11.2.2.3   CBEs (Cocoa Butter Equivalents).   These are prepared from illipe, shea and palm oils. They have a fatty acid composition almost identical to that of cocoa butter so that the physical properties of a mixture with cocoa butter in any proportion are practically the same as those of cocoa butter itself.

11.2.3   Sugar

Sugar is used to offset the bitterness of cocoa solids in plain chocolate. In milk chocolate, sugar, particularly in crumb form, has a great influence on the ultimate flavour – the combination of milk proteins and sugar through Maillard, or browning, reaction leads to the caramelised flavour characteristic of most UK milk chocolate.

11.3   Manufacture of chocolate

11.3.1   Mixing

Sugar (and crumb or milk powder for milk chocolate) is added to the cocoa liquor (or cocoa mass) and the preparation is thoroughly mixed.

11.3.2   Refining

This enables the smooth texture of the chocolate to be achieved initially by reducing the particle size. The cocoa liquor/sugar paste is passed through a series of roller refiners with extra cocoa butter being added to maintain its flow properties as the surface area of the solid particles increases.

11.3.3   Conching

Conching is the working of chocolate, milk crumb and added fats in the form of cocoa butter, CBEs (if required), lecithin (emulsifier) and any flavours such as vanilla, into a fluid paste.

This operation further refines the texture of the mixture through continuous agitation in a large tank and coats all the particles produced in the earlier processes with fat to give the smooth mouthfeel characteristic of good chocolate. Conching also has the effect of modifying the flavour of the chocolate mass by reducing astringency and allowing the more muted and subtle pleasant flavour notes to develop.

11.3.4 Tempering

Before chocolate can be used for moulding or enrobing (coating) it must be tempered so that it can set rapidly and uniformly with good permanent colour, texture and gloss. Chocolate can set in six states, only the more stable of which gives the desired gloss and snap. To achieve this stability it is necessary to cool down the chocolate with continuous mixing to produce a multitude of 'seed' fat crystals and distribute them uniformly throughout the mass of liquid chocolate thus providing nuclei for subsequent crystallisation. During this operation changes in viscosity can be used to obtain a measure of the condition of the chocolate.

11.3.5 Uses of chocolate

There are two principal ways in which chocolate is used:

11.3.5.1 Moulding. This is the process in which tempered chocolate is deposited in warmed polished metal or plastics moulds, then cooled by passing through a cooling tunnel to give rapid setting and good appearance. Good tempering will ensure that the cocoa butter will shrink in the mould and demould cleanly. In general metal moulds may be more effective in that cooling can be transmitted readily through the mould whereas with plastics, cooling takes place primarily through the chocolate surface. Good mould design and moulding procedure, however, should minimise this potential problem and enable the full benefits to be derived from plastics, i.e. lightness, quietness in operation and flexibility which assists in demoulding. Combination moulds are now available in stainless steel with polycarbonate carriers which give the best of all worlds, but at extra cost.

11.3.5.2 Enrobing. This is the process in which centres are passed through a curtain of tempered chocolate and over a chocolate bottoming device to coat the bases. Sometimes the product is 'double' enrobed to ensure extra coating if the centre is especially vulnerable to external influences, or to complete covering of awkward surfaces. In these instances the first coating may not require to be well tempered provided it is set before the second coating is applied. The property of shrinking on cooling of cocoa butter, essential for moulding, must be taken into account in enrobing. If enrobed centres cool too rapidly the chocolate could crack but on the other hand if it cools too slowly it could end up discoloured and soft – in either case the problem might not be apparent at the packaging stage and only emerge when the pack is opened.

11.4 Types of chocolate confectionery

11.4.1 Moulded blocks

11.4.1.1 Milk or plain chocolate. This may contain:

- roasted nuts, e.g. hazelnuts, almonds, peanuts
- unroasted nuts/fruit, e.g. raisins
- fondant cream/praline
- layered wafer/biscuit
- cereal, e.g. crispies

11.4.1.2 Moulded aerated blocks. Aerated chocolate has been a very popular product for many years. The principal manufacturing processes are:

- 'vacuum aeration' in which the tempered chocolate is subjected to a vacuum under which microbubbles of entrapped air expand leading to a cellular texture. Cooling then takes place, still under vacuum to avoid collapse of the aeration.
- 'gas injection' where inert gas, generally CO_2, is injected into the chocolate under pressure. The product is then moulded under atmospheric pressure.

11.4.2 Filled blocks

Moulding of filled chocolate blocks can be done in two ways, each of which has its adherents. In straight moulding the product is deposited into the mould in its entirety in one operation or a centre is pushed into a mould full of chocolate. In 'shell' moulding the inside of the mould is in effect lined with a solid coating of chocolate to form a shell into which the centre, be it a cream or a solid such as a biscuit, is filled or inserted, with additional chocolate to provide backing cover. This operation can be described as 'fill-cool-tip-cool'.

11.4.3 Count lines

While moulded blocks or bars are generally segmented so that they can be eaten over several occasions or shared, count lines are intended to be eaten in one go and by one person. They are usually, but not exclusively, enrobed and can contain:

- wafer – layered with fondant cream or praline
- cereal, e.g. rice crispies
- biscuit

- fruit and/or nuts
- caramel (toffee)
- butterscotch
- cracknel
- nougat
- peanut butter

The above list is not exclusive and it can be seen that most, if not all, of the ingredients can also be found in one form or another in moulded products. It is, perhaps, worth mentioning that in moulded lines caramel is a centre in its own right whereas in a count line, it performs the secondary function of holding nuts, cereal and other components together.

11.4.4 Assortments

These comprise a number of different sweets which can be enrobed or moulded and may be miniature versions of the products already described. They frequently also include fondant cream centres which have been deposited in liquid form into shapes formed in starch, allowed to solidify and then brushed out and enrobed. Often the centres are formulated so that after covering they revert to a semi-liquid form. This method of producing centres has been superseded in many cases by 'starchless moulding' in which the fondant, for example, is deposited into plastics moulds. This involves the use of release oil in the moulds which must be carefully specified and controlled to avoid possible contamination of the enrobing chocolate and consequent loss of shelf life.

11.4.5 Straight lines

These comprise small sweets similar to those in an assortment but all one type in a pack. Sometimes this is done when sweets are unsuitable for mixing in an assortment where they could transfer flavour to others. This was originally the case with chocolate peppermints, but specialised 'After Dinner' mints are now branded lines in their own right.

11.4.6 White chocolate

This consists mainly of deodorised cocoa butter, sugar and milk powder and is produced in a modified version of standard milk chocolate manufacture. It can be moulded or enrobed and used wherever normal chocolate would be found but as it lacks the antioxidant properties of cocoa liquor, and as the deodorising process can reduce those of cocoa butter, it is much more susceptible to oxidative rancidity.

11.5   Attributes of milk chocolate

11.5.1   Texture

1. Hardness: This characterises the hardness of the chocolate. It is assessed by its resistance to a point and can be scored on a scale from 'soft' to 'hard'.
2. Snap: This represents the sound intensity produced when breaking the piece of chocolate and can be scaled from 'low' to 'high'.
3. Melting: Melting is the assessment of a solid product which quickly changes into a liquid or semi-liquid state under the action of saliva in the mouth. It can be scored from 'slow' to 'quick'.
4. Sticky or Claggy: This describes the texture of chocolate that remains soft, sticks to the teeth and persists in the mouth. Scoring scale is from 'very sticky' to 'non-sticky'.
5. Smoothness: Smoothness describes chocolate particle size and texture by the impression of more or less coarseness in the mouth when eating the product. Scoring is from 'very gritty' to 'very smooth'.

11.5.2   Flavour

1. Sweet is a basic taste whose reference is saccharosis. It is scored from 'not sweet' to 'very sweet'.
2. Cocoa flavour is a specific complex flavour which refers to the basic note of the product. It is scored from 'no cocoa flavour' to 'very strong cocoa flavour'.
3. Milky flavour is a general term designating the presence of a pure flavour or odour of milk. It is scored from 'no milky flavour' to 'very strong milky flavour'.
4. Toffee flavour describes the flavour associated with specific sweets. It is scored from 'no toffee flavour' to 'very strong toffee flavour'.
5. Cream/butter flavour designates the presence of pure flavour of cream or butter in a chocolate. It is scored from 'no cream or butter flavour' to 'very strong cream or butter flavour'.
6. Acid represents the elementary taste caused by diluted aqueous solution of acids such as citric or lactic. It is scored from 'no acid taste' to 'strong acid taste'.
7. Astringent refers to the ability of certain substances to cause contraction of tissues in the mouth and especially at the back of the throat. Scoring is from 'no astringent sensation' to 'very strong astringent sensation'.
8. Rancid applies to fatty substances degraded by oxidation or hydrolysis releasing short-chain fatty acids, aldehydes and ketones.
9. Butyric describes a piquant cheese odour deriving from fat lipolysis.

10. Cardboardy is a generic, ill defined taste developed by oxidation of old cocoa and chocolate.

11.6   Causes of deterioration in quality

Chocolate, when stored under the correct conditions of temperature and humidity, is a very stable product due to its low moisture content (1.0%–1.9%) and its high fat content (28%–35% including 1.4%–1.6% of poly-unsaturated fatty acids). The presence of tocopherols (vitamin E) in cocoa liquor and cocoa powder provides a high degree of protection against oxidative rancidity. Nevertheless, severe degradation may occur – fat bloom, sugar bloom, rancidity and loss of texture can result if proper manufacturing and storage procedures are not followed.

The factors causing deterioration of chocolate products can be divided into two main classes: those which are inherent in the product itself and cannot be prevented by packaging alone and those which are dependent on the environment and may be controlled to a greater or less degree by choice and effective use of packaging.

11.6.1   Product factors

11.6.1.1   Quality of raw material.   It goes without saying that the quality of the raw materials has a major bearing on the quality of the finished product and strict quality control must be exercised.

11.6.1.2   Quality of chocolate.   Improperly tempered chocolate will continue to stabilise after the product is wrapped and has left the factory, leading to soft texture and the appearance of fat crystals, particularly on the surface of the product, causing the greyish, mouldy appearance known as 'fat bloom'. This unsightly blemish can also be caused by incompatible oil or fat used as a lubricant in the manufacture of centres migrating through the chocolate or by the release of oil from high fat centres such as roasted nuts, coconut, truffle, and so on. Injudicious use of 'rework' in a product can also affect the quality of temper of the chocolate.

11.6.1.3   Oxidative deterioration.   In the short term oxidative rancidity is unlikely to occur in appreciable concentration with plain or milk choco-late but it can relatively rapidly affect other ingredients such as high fat centres or roasted nuts which do not have a full covering of chocolate. This can be the result of inadequate coating on enrobed centres or poor backing off on moulded products. With milk or plain chocolate, after the lapse of a considerable period of time, staling or a 'cardboardy' flavour can become apparent. White chocolate does not have the antioxidant protection of cocoa liquor and so is prone to oxidative rancidity, particularly light induced. Even with light barrier packaging its shelf life is shorter than that of milk or plain chocolate. The cost of eliminating oxygen from the packaging of chocolate would be prohibitive and not generally worthwhile in view of the relatively limited increase in shelf life which would result. It could only be justified if particularly sophisticated ingredients used in the product recipe were especially susceptible to oxygen and where the product could stand the oncost of oxygen scavengers and barrier packaging.

11.6.2   Environmental factors

11.6.2.1   Temperature. Temperature, especially high and fluctuating conditions, has a marked effect on the quality and shelf life of chocolate products with the potential to cause loss of temper, fat bloom and accelerated staling. Although low temperatures will preserve flavours and the textural quality of the chocolate, bars containing wafers, and expanded centres, can crack under low temperature storage. If the packaging of the bar is not moisture vapour proof the cracks will permit the entry of moisture to the centre with consequent rapid deterioration.

11.6.2.2   Humidity. Storage in damp conditions, condensation due to packaging in damp conditions, or condensation of moisture in coolers or fondant centres with high relative humidity (RH) giving off moisture which is then trapped in the package can all cause 'sugar bloom'. This is similar in appearance to fat bloom but with a rough rather than greasy feel and is the result of the moisture extracting soluble sugar from the chocolate and then depositing it in the form of large granules on the chocolate after re-evaporation. Certain centres, such as cracknel or 'honeycomb' are particularly hygroscopic and require extra protection against moisture pick up compared with conventional chocolate products. This could involve the use of double chocolate coating to minimise the possibility of cracks through which the moisture could be drawn into the centre. Other centres can lose moisture and dry out under some, not necessarily particularly extreme, conditions. In both these instances packaging plays a vital role in affording a reasonable shelf life to the product.

11.6.2.3   Off-odour/loss of flavour. This can be caused by external influences permeating the packaging material or, indeed, emanating from it. Storage of inadequately wrapped chocolate near strong smelling chemicals or display in shops close to strongly flavoured sweets such as poorly wrapped mints can all cause unacceptable flavour pick up. Some plastics packaging materials can cause flavour loss or 'scalping' by absorbing the 'high notes' but this is not likely with the materials most commonly used for packaging chocolate products.

Odour transfer from the inks used on packaging can cause taint but modern water or alcohol based formulations, properly applied, should minimise this risk. The increasing use of reclaimed board, for environmental reasons, on intermediate and outer packaging leads to a greater risk of taint which must be countered by enhanced barrier primary packaging.

11.6.2.4 Insect infestation. Chocolate products are very attractive to several varieties of insect and if storage or transit conditions are likely to be such as to result in infestation very careful consideration must be given to the packaging employed. It must be effectively sealed and resistant to creeping insects penetrating through folds and boring species which can drill through aluminium foil but fortunately appear to be frustrated by the flexible plastics in common use.

11.6.2.5 Light. As mentioned earlier, light-induced rancidity can be a problem with certain products such as white chocolate and chocolate containing poorly coated roast nuts. Although outer packaging should protect a product for most of its life, even short exposure on a shop counter or shelf can be sufficient to cause unacceptable deterioration.

11.7 Control of shelf life by packaging

11.7.1 Heat

Normal chocolate confectionery packaging is not designed to withstand high temperatures which are best avoided by storage and transit in controlled conditions. High temperature, approaching the melting point of cocoa butter (36°C), causes the chocolate to soften, drastically reducing its shelf life and no amount of subsequent cooling can reverse the process of deterioration.

A certain amount of insulation can be built into outer packaging by using foil lined or metallised board or expanded polystyrene, but experience shows that at best this is a short-term remedy. It is more likely that insulation only delays the effect of heat and in fact it may retain it after the pack is put into cool conditions.

11.7.2 Moisture

It is possible, by careful use of packaging material, to protect a product from external moisture almost indefinitely. The traditional foil and paper wrap used for blocks of chocolate is adequate for most products of this type, stored, transported and sold under temperate, well regulated conditions; but if moisture protection is likely to be required and traditional appearance retained, the foil must be heat sealed. This requires the use of special machinery and the foil to be coated with either a heatseal varnish or low density polyethylene film. The latter is to be preferred as it gives a better seal and provides the foil with added protection against tearing, piercing by the corners of the product, projecting nuts and similar kinds of physical damage, and insect penetration.

By contrast, the irregular shape of most count lines does not lend itself to the foil and paper band format while the nature of the product is generally such that more protection is required against moisture, even in temperate conditions, than is the case with block lines. For this type of product the horizontal form-fill-seal (HFFS) wrap, also known as 'pillow pack', 'fin seal' and 'flow wrap', has been devised. This method takes a continuous web of flexible material, supplied on reel, and forms it into a tube around the product, sealing its edges together by heat and/or pressure as it progresses through the machine. This tube, containing the product, is then cut to a predetermined length and the open ends sealed, again by heat and/or pressure. This continuous flow wrap, by careful choice of the materials used, can give a very wide range of properties to the package. In particular it can provide a complete barrier to moisture vapour – indeed most materials which are capable of being heat sealed will also give an adequate barrier against moisture.

Where an unusually high degree of protection against moisture is required, either to keep it out of or to retain it within the product, it may well be necessary to use a laminate, e.g. of polyester and aluminium foil with polyethylene, as a heat sealant. The foil could be replaced by metallisation of the two plastics films.

11.7.3 Oxygen

The flow wrap which provides an excellent barrier to moisture can also protect its contents against oxygen, provided the appropriate material is chosen. This would generally incorporate a PVdC (polyvinylidene chloride) coating which could also be used for heat sealing. The addition of a layer of aluminium either as foil or as a coating applied by a metallisation process, will also enhance the oxygen barrier properties of a wrap.

Oxygen barrier materials are constantly being developed and PVdC can be replaced, if its chlorine content is considered to be environmentally undesirable, e.g. by silicon oxide or EVOH (ethylene vinyl alcohol), although these do not have the wide range of properties available from PVdC and are considerably more expensive.

Oxygen scavengers are available which can eliminate the oxygen contained within an oxygen barrier package. These have not been considered necessary for ordinary chocolate confectionery but have been used on occasion in Japan. Flow wrap equipment can be modified to gas flush a package, replacing air with nitrogen or carbon dioxide. This operation slows down the machine and necessitates the use of a heat seal medium, generally polyethylene, to obtain a sufficiently gas tight closure.

11.7.4 Taint/loss of flavour

The film most used to flow wrap confectionery, coextruded, cavitated or pearlised biaxially oriented polypropylene (OPP) is a good barrier to external taint or product flavour loss. This property can be enhanced by coating the film with PVdC or acrylic instead of coextruding it with polyolefin copolymer. The latter is more common and cheaper but rather less efficient as a barrier, particularly to oxygen.

It should be noted that although materials which are good oxygen barriers are also good odour barriers it is possible to have good barrier to odour without necessarily having a corresponding oxygen barrier. Some OPP films are coated with acrylic on one side and PVdC on the other, thus giving heat sealability with a wide temperature range and protection against moisture, oxygen and taint. Any film can have its barrier properties further improved by metallisation and/or lamination, both of which, incidentally, can be said to give the wrap an extra 'quality' appeal.

There is always the possibility that ink from the upper surface of the wrapping material can transfer to the inside in the reel and thence to the product. Correct procedures at the packaging converter should eliminate this but it is a potential source of taint which must be considered. The choice of inks and varnish must also be carefully made in order to eliminate the possibility of taint.

Residual solvents resulting from incomplete drying or oxidation of printing inks, varnishes and sealants are the most likely offenders in this respect. Their presence can generally be detected by simple smell and taste testing but GLC procedures should be used to identify the source of the taint.

Over the years some plastics materials have caused tainting through the incomplete conversion of monomers or the use of softeners or plasticisers and others have absorbed volatile flavours from the product. These problems should have been overcome by the plastics processors and certainly have been in the case of OPP but nevertheless it is essential that packaging materials, especially those coming into contact with the chocolate, are thoroughly checked for potential taint and flavour loss before they are used.

11.7.5 Light

Pearlised OPP has been given a degree of opacity through a process of cavitation which is adequate to eliminate the 'show through' or 'optical staining' which was a feature of chocolate wraps made from clear film, albeit heavily printed. It is not, however, sufficiently opaque to provide much protection against light for particularly susceptible products such as white chocolate. For these products a lamination of film and aluminium foil, or at least a lamination of two metallised films plus a solid background print, is required to give sufficient protection for a reasonable shelf life to be achieved.

11.8 Determination of shelf life

As the basic forms of chocolate confectionery have been on the market for many years it has been possible to assign reasonably accurate shelf lives for most products under varying climatic conditions. The most generally specified conditions are 'Temperate' and 'Tropical' although it is difficult to classify individual countries rigidly into these categories because of seasonal and regional variations. In addition, the quality of the conditions under which products are distributed and sold should be taken into account when determining shelf life.

Table 11.1 lists what may be regarded as representative shelf lives, characteristic of products adequately wrapped to withstand the effects of high relative humidities and to exclude light. These shelf lives must be regarded as the longest that can be assigned for the purpose of 'Best Before' date on packaging materials. If there is any likelihood of the product being exposed to adverse conditions for an appreciable length of time, e.g. in the unrefrigerated hold of a ship in tropical waters, the shorter life appropriate to 'Tropical' climate should be chosen.

Table 11.1 Representative shelf life (in months) of some chocolate confectionery

Category of product	Temperate conditions	Tropical conditions
Milk chocolate	16	12
Plain chocolate	24	24
White chocolate	16	12
Fondant cream filled chocolate	18	12
Chocolate with nuts	12	9
Count lines and wafer/cereal centred products	12	9
Fat filled chocolate	12	9

11.8.1 Shelf life of new products

In general a shelf life can be assigned to a new product by analogy with an existing product, using the knowledge of the development confectioner and packaging technologist to choose the most appropriate reference.

Nevertheless it is essential to confirm this judgement by checking the performance of a new, or altered, product under a variety of conditions as well as normal storage.

11.8.1.1 Testing products for shelf life.
A suitable range of conditioned cabinets should be available, for example:

Ambient 20°C 65% RH
Ambient 25°C 80% RH
Ambient 32°C 60% RH
Ambient 32°C 80% RH

Local circumstances may make other conditions more appropriate, e.g. the cold dry conditions of a Canadian winter, or cycling of temperature and humidity to promote the development of bloom to be expected under unregulated storage and thus the development of means to retard it.

11.8.1.2 Procedures.
Samples should be kept in these cabinets together with a standard reference product of a similar nature, either an 'own company' product or a competitor's product which is known to have a satisfactory shelf life and performance in the appropriate market and whose age can be established. Consideration should be given to the nature of the product and package and a decision taken as to whether additional tests, e.g. for light fastness, cold storage or cyclical temperature or humidity changes are desirable and if they are, arrangements should be made to incorporate them into the test schedule.

Initially keeping tests are only intended to compare the keeping properties of a new or amended product with those of a standard product. With this in mind, it should be possible for product knowledgeable personnel to use their judgement and give a reasonably accurate shelf life based solely on an accelerated keeping test, confirmed by a long-term keeping test and long-term storage trial.

It is essential that all assessments of keeping tests should be made by expert staff. The standard product and its known response to test conditions will indicate to the expert any cabinet unreliability. Such a guide as to the reliability of storage conditions is particularly important when a new product is on test. A minimum of three assessors is required at the time of tasting.

New products may require a 'fresh' sample for comparison at the time of tasting and this would be obtained by remaking.

11.8.2   Types of test

11.8.2.1   Accelerating keeping test.   This test should last 6–8 weeks with the samples being examined weekly. The accelerated deterioration is caused by elevated temperature and increased humidity. A revised product deteriorating more than standard on this test should not usually proceed to production. Where a revised/new product keeps better than, or as well as the standard it is assumed that it will have an equivalent shelf life. This, however, must be confirmed by a long-term test.

11.8.2.2   Long-term keeping test.   This test would last up to 18 months and take place under ambient conditions (20°C and 60% RH) with 4-weekly examinations. Standards would again be used and this test should confirm the accelerated keeping test with which it initially runs concurrently. The range of keeping cabinets listed previously can be used for long-term testing to give a more detailed profile of the product's keeping characteristics.

11.8.2.3   Long-term storage test.   This test would use production-made samples of the revised/new product, and would eventually supersede the long-term keeping test in confirming its shelf life.

11.8.3   Results of keeping test – scoring system

Chocolate products should be scored by the five characteristics or attributes listed below, although (4) and (5) will not always be needed.

1. appearance
2. flavour/taste
3. texture
4. colour
5. others (specified, e.g. odour)

11.8.3.1   Determining the attribute score.   Only the test product is scored, and the score depends on its comparison with the standard as shown in Table 11.2.

11.8.3.2   Overall product score.   The product should also be given an overall product score (1–5) based on the agreed attributes and the above criteria. One attribute having a reject score means that the whole product must have a reject score. Using the keeping test scoring forms, each assessor (minimum of three) should independently taste the test and standard products, individually score the attributes and overall score and make appropriate comments on a keeping test form (Figure 11.1).

Table 11.2 Determining the attribute score in a keeping test

Test product score	Result	Score criteria
5	Acceptable	The test product has kept better than the standard product
4	Acceptable	The test and standard products are of equal quality. They have deteriorated at the same rate
3	Reassessment is an option	Test product is slightly inferior to standard but nothing undesirable has developed
2	Reject	Test product is inferior to standard, but further work may be recommended
1	Reject	Test product is much inferior to standard and further work is not recommended

The person coordinating the keeping test should then collate the results and, in conjunction with the assessors, come to an agreed result. This agreed result, including comments, should be entered on a keeping test summary form (Figure 11.2), after each tasting session.

The test ends either at a pre-arranged time or when the product is judged to have reached the end of its acceptable shelf life.

PRODUCT: PRODUCT REFERENCE(S): REASONS FOR TEST: ADDITIONAL SAMPLE NOTES:	DATE OF TASTING	SAMPLE AGE WEEK/MONTHS:
	CABINET DESCRIPTION: TEMPERATURE: HUMIDITY:	

ATTRIBUTE	COMMENTS		TEST SCORE	NOTES
	STD PRODUCT	TEST PRODUCT		
APPEARANCE				
FLAVOUR/TASTE				
TEXTURE				
COLOUR (IF APPLICABLE)				
OTHER (SPECIFY)				
TOTAL PRODUCT				

RECOMMENDATION/ACTION AT THIS SAMPLING	FINAL RECOMMENDATION - TEST COMPLETE	SCORE GUIDE
1. Continue test as trial product: satisfactory: Y/N 2. Comments:		5. Better than standard 4. Same as standard 3. Slight difference, nothing undesirable 2. Inferior to standard 1. Much inferior

Figure 11.1 A keeping test form.

		CABINET																													
Date of Tasting	Age of Sample Weeks/Months (Delete as Necessary)	Description				Description				Description				Description				Description			
		°C		% RH		°C		% RH		°C		% RH		°C		% RH		°C		% RH	
		Attributes - Score																														
		1	2	3	4	5	6	1	2	3	4	5	6	1	2	3	4	5	6	1	2	3	4	5	6	1	2	3	4	5	6

Figure 11.2 A keeping test summary form.

11.9   Packaging materials – taint testing

As mentioned earlier, packaging materials can be a source of contamination leading to the early deterioration of chocolate. Milk chocolate in particular is very susceptible to taint resulting from inadequately controlled packaging.

Modern methods of printing and the use of, for example, water or alcohol based inks, together with a heightened awareness of the need for very strict quality control at all stages of the production and packaging of chocolate products has greatly reduced the likelihood of taint from packaging.

Nevertheless incoming packaging materials should be regularly checked and three principal methods of testing are available.

11.9.1   Robinson test

This test is widely used throughout Europe. A piece of the test material, 20 cm × 22 cm, folded and perforated, not in contact with the product, is kept in a jar with 15 g of grated fresh milk chocolate, in the dark, for 48 hours at 20°C and 75% RH. A control is set up either without the material being tested or, if the material is printed, with an unprinted version of the material.

The evaluation of the test is carried out by a panel of assessors who compare blind the chocolate from the test with that from the control. The intensity of any off-flavour is evaluated on a numerical scale as follows (scored by half points):

0 No difference in flavour
1 Just perceptible difference in flavour
2 Just definable off-flavour
3 Definite off-flavour
4 Strong off-flavour

The scores given by the assessors are added and the total divided by the number of assessors: e.g. eight assessors with scores of 2.5, 3.0, 2.0, 1.5, 2.0, 2.5, 1.5, 3.0 giving a total of 18; dividing the total by 8 gives 2.25 which on rounding up to the nearest 0.5 becomes 2.5. Acceptance levels are generally taken as 1.5 for unprinted material and 2.5 for printed.

11.9.2 Gas liquid chromatography (GLC)

By this method levels of residual solvents in printed materials can be monitored against agreed standards such as a global maximum of 20 mg/m^2 with a sub-total of hydrocarbons not to exceed 10 mg/m^2.

11.9.3 Aroma index

This method uses a Buchi Vapodest 100 or similar steam distiller to determine the presence and level of taint in packaging materials. Filtered condensate from the distiller is measured in a spectrophotometer at 280 nm and the absorbance multiplied by 100 to give the aroma index.

Packaging for chocolate products should be rejected if it has an aroma index higher than 35.

11.9.4 General

It should be mentioned that there are occasions when analytical instruments fail to pick up taints which are readily detected by a well trained human nose or palate. For this reason the availability of a Robinson type test with experienced assessors is an essential backup to any form of scientific taint testing of packaged materials.

While it must be the responsibility of the material supplier to ensure that his product meets the agreed scientifically quantified criteria of GLC and/or aroma index testing, it is ultimately the chocolate manufacturer who must ensure that the consumer receives a product free from any contamination from the packaging designed to protect it.

Not all confectionery manufacturers can equip themselves to carry out all the appropriate scientific tests for taint, although all suppliers should, yet all must ensure that they have the trained staff for organoleptic checking of the materials which they use. Indeed the same staff could well be those who carry out the analysis of keeping tests.

Bibliography

Beckett, S.T. (ed.) (1987) *Industrial Chocolate Manufacture and Use*, Blackie Academic & Professional, Glasgow.

Briston, J. (1983) *Plastics in Packaging – Properties and Applications*, Practical Packaging Series, The Institute of Packaging, Melton Mowbray.

Minifie, B.W. (1988) *Chocolate, Cocoa and Confectionery: Science and Technology*, 3rd edn, Van Nostrand Reinhold, New York.

Oswin, C.R. (1983) *Package Life – Theory and Practice*, Practical Packaging Series, The Institute of Packaging, Melton Mowbray.

Paine, F.A. and Paine, H.Y. (1992) *A Handbook of Food Packaging*, 2nd edn., Blackie Academic & Professional, Glasgow.

Saxby, M.J. (ed.) (1993) *Food Taints and Off-flavours*, Blackie Academic & Professional, Glasgow.

12   Ready-to-eat breakfast cereals
J.A.K. HOWARTH

12.1   Introduction

Ready-to-eat breakfast cereals belong to the category of foods that are inherently stable and have a long shelf life. Thus, the requirements for determining shelf life are quite different from products which have a short shelf life, for example, chilled foods which may only be stable for three to four days. The factors affecting the shelf life are also quite different; deterioration during life will probably not affect the safety of a breakfast cereal but will have an impact on consumer satisfaction.

Ready-to-eat breakfast cereals are designed to be eaten straight from the packet, requiring no preparation, and so do not include breakfast items such as porridge. It is therefore important for the manufacturer to identify the parameters most critical to consumer satisfaction and ensure that these are the characteristics preserved throughout the life of the product. This chapter gives a broad outline of the means of determining cereal shelf lives and includes some pointers and general guidelines for methodology which could also be applied to other 'long life' products.

If determination of shelf life is new within an organisation then one of the first steps is to ensure that the senior management fully understands the implications of the work. There must be clear standards laid down as to what denotes acceptable quality at the end of shelf life and everyone must be aware of these and accept them. Failure to do this at an early stage could lead to difficulties when trying to implement any new standards.

There are two main areas of interest when looking at stability of breakfast cereals – organoleptic properties and analytical values. Appearance, flavour and texture of the product are important, as are analytical values such as vitamin/mineral content where the product has been fortified and a claim made. These areas are legally binding and it is important to have evidence to back any claims made regarding stability and analytical data (IFST, 1993).

Although it is not necessary with products like cereals to put a date of manufacture on the product (although a 'lot' code is required), there is a 'Best Before' date and consumers now expect there to be a fairly long time remaining after they have purchased the product before it becomes unacceptable. In particular, major retailers are now demanding that 75%

of the shelf life is still available when the product is delivered to their depots.

Shelf life testing and date-marking of the product can only give information on the stability of a full, sealed package – it cannot give information relating to the consumer who keeps an open carton in the cupboard for six months (IFST, 1993). Laboratory testing can give an indication of what could be expected but cannot be solely relied upon in setting the shelf life.

The manufacturer cannot be expected to guarantee a shelf life once the pack is opened, and when the product has been abused in some way.

12.2   The products

The product group of 'breakfast cereals' contains a wide range of products as can be seen on the supermarket shelves. These products can have quite different characteristics, while all being expected to have a similar shelf life.

The products can be separated into five groups which may need slightly different treatments.

12.2.1   Uncoated cereals

Examples of these are flakes, crisp rice, shredded bran. These products are typically low in moisture content – usually below 4% – and are inherently stable if not exposed to the environment. These would traditionally be expected to have a long shelf life with very little change in product characteristics.

12.2.2   Coated products

Examples of coated products are sugar coated flakes, honey nut flakes, coated extruded products. These products still have a relatively low moisture content, usually below 5%. They tend to be more hygroscopic than uncoated products and depending on the type of coating, a potentially unstable ingredient may be present. For example, a cereal with a nut based coating can suffer from rancidity problems if not handled in the correct way.

12.2.3   Products with added components

Examples are flakes with raisins, flakes with mixed fruit. The moisture content of the whole cereal may be around 7%; however this could be made up of cereal at 3% and fruit at 12%; these are products which will show very different storage characteristics. Moisture transfer between cereal and fruit can be the critical factor in determining shelf life rather than the ingress of moisture from the environment. A product with a higher moisture content will generally be less stable than the one with a lower moisture content (Labuza, 1982).

12.2.4 Muesli products

These products have a fairly high moisture content, so moisture pick-up from the environment is not as critical as the stability of the ingredients themselves. A muesli product can only be acceptable for the time its least stable ingredient remains acceptable.

12.2.5 New products

These can take any form, or could be a combination of any of the particular cereal types mentioned above. If the product is a new combination then the shelf life must be determined, although previously gained experience can be used to give some guidance.

As discussed above, moisture content plays an important role in determining the shelf life of breakfast cereals. Since most products do not usually support microbial activity, microbial spoilage of the food is not a critical factor. Changes in moisture content can affect the organoleptic properties and this is the main criterion to be used.

Most cereals will reach an equilibrium moisture content naturally, which will remain stable for many years if stored in a relatively constant environment. Examples of this have been cereals which were discovered after 40 years and showed no signs of spoilage. The moisture content is usually higher than would be acceptable organoleptically. This only serves to emphasise the importance of organoleptic characteristics in storage testing.

12.3 Factors affecting shelf life

There are a number of factors which will affect the shelf life of a breakfast cereal and these will have differing degrees of influence. All must be taken into consideration and as with most foods, the better the control in all the areas, the greater the confidence in achieving the shelf life required. The main factors which affect shelf life have been identified as:

• raw materials
• processing

- packaging materials
- climate and storage conditions.

The first three are within the control of the manufacturer and although the fourth cannot be controlled, the effects can be predicted to some degree.

12.3.1   Raw materials

The majority of raw materials used to manufacture breakfast cereals are to be processed in some way – the main exceptions to this being fruit/nut additions to products and muesli type products. As mentioned earlier in this chapter, microbial spoilage of breakfast cereals is very rare and the use of Hazard Analysis Critical Control Point (HACCP) technique can ensure that major hazards are either eliminated or controlled.

The main factor therefore concerning raw materials is that of consistently high quality and each material must have the critical factors identified which will allow manufacture of a high quality product.

Materials which may cause some concern microbiologically are ingredients such as milk powder, cocoa powder, dried fruits, nuts – particularly coconut, and any which do not undergo a sufficiently high temperature processing. The specifications for these materials should lay down stringent standards and the quality system must ensure that these requirements are met before the materials are used.

Potential causes of rancidity in a product can originate from nuts, and their quality must be carefully controlled to ensure that these materials do survive the long shelf life in an acceptable state.

Moisture content and equilibrium relative humidity (ERH) of fruit are critical, and depending on the quantity of fruit added to the cereal, they will affect the overall acceptability of the product.

High-quality consistent raw materials will ensure that the required shelf life will be met.

12.3.2   Processing

As with most foods, heat treatment extends the life of the materials and also ensures a minimum of microbial contamination.

Most breakfast cereals, after processing, have virtually no microbial count, but a low moisture content and an ERH which will not support any microbial growth.

Although breakfast cereals are processed, the conditions of processing are not as severe as those in the canning industry for example. Cereals are manufactured to an image, the main criteria for acceptance being organoleptic properties, moisture content and bulk density. That image will also have an acceptable range within which variation is acceptable. And so, whilst processing does have a definite influence on the shelf life, its main function is to convert the raw materials into highly palatable food products, with the production of certain distinct characteristics in the foods, such as attractive colour, pleasant flavour and crunchy texture.

12.3.3 Packaging materials

Packaging used for breakfast cereals serves two purposes – protection from spoilage and protection from physical damage. The most common form of packaging in use is that of a paperboard carton with an inner liner containing the food. The inner liner will provide most of the protection to the food while the outer carton provides protection from physical damage and also from potential tampering.

The main purpose of the inner liner is to protect from moisture transfer so as to preserve the product characteristics. The most effective type of liner will be determined during shelf life testing. A liner which has barrier properties which are too effective can give other problems in storage, for example, the generation of unpleasant odours in the headspace. This is therefore a major consideration. Antioxidants can increase the expected shelf life and in some countries can be used in the liner material for this purpose (Labuza, 1982). As will be discussed later, compromises may have to be made on some occasions to allow for these factors.

12.3.4 Climate and storage conditions

As previously discussed, the liner type is crucial to preserving the shelf life of the product and the external conditions can have a considerable effect on the product. During determination of shelf life the climate of the market must be taken into account; for example, the requirements of products stored in Mediterranean/tropical climates are quite different from those destined for Northern Europe.

The destination country of the product is also of importance as transport facilities and hence the potential for picking up taints during transport and storage must be considered and, if possible, minimised. If there are poor standards of warehousing then the risk of infestation may be high. This knowledge may mean that a shorter shelf life is appropriate for some markets.

All the factors which may contribute to the length of acceptable shelf life in the product cannot be listed here. However, an attempt has been made to highlight the major areas. The most important factors will depend on the specific product and market, and the areas considered above will assist in identifying the most critical ones for that particular product. Methodology and useful checklists are available in other texts (IFST, 1993).

12.4   Determination of shelf life

The initial determination of shelf life may have been carried out on a development product which will have given an indication of the expected shelf life. A product which remains on the market for a long period of time may need to have its shelf life re-evaluated periodically as changes are made to raw materials, processing, or packaging materials. This emphasises that once the life has been determined, this is not the end of the story – monitoring on a regular basis must continue to ensure confidence in the product.   The methodology for determination and monitoring of shelf life of breakfast cereals can be divided into a number of areas all of which are important:

1. Initial determination of shelf life:
    (a) identification of critical product characteristics;
    (b) break point analysis (critical moisture content determination).
2. Shelf life testing:
    (a) samples;
    (b) storage conditions;
    (c) assessment of results.
3 Monitoring activities:
    (a) new markets;
    (b) packaging materials changes;
    (c) processing/raw material changes.

12.4.1   Initial determination of shelf life

Before beginning a shelf life test there are some basic pieces of information which must be sought. These will set the ground rules for a particular product and will ensure that the correct test is set up to provide useful data.

12.4.1.1   Identification of critical product characteristics.   When planning a test to determine or confirm the shelf life of a product, it is important to ensure that the most critical factors have been identified.

With breakfast cereals, each product can be quite different and the characteristics which are important for the acceptability of the product are those which must be tested.

Selection of the factors will also depend on whether the test is an initial determination or a confirmatory test when a fair amount of information about the product has been obtained.

For all breakfast cereals sensory attributes are most important as it is unlikely that any harmful substances will be generated during processing and storage. If this is to be the main guide, then the selection of assessors for sensory evaluation is critical. Details about this can be found in many relevant texts (Amerine *et al.*, 1965). One of the most important flavours/ off-flavours is that of rancidity and it is well known that some people are more sensitive to it than others and the use of trained assessors may be useful.

Analytical data can also be used to evaluate changes occurring in the product and appropriate parameters should be selected – the most common of these being:

- moisture
- vitamins
- rancidity measures

If there is no on-site laboratory, a reputable laboratory may be used. The same laboratory should be used throughout the testing period to maintain consistency.

Analytical tests together with sensory evaluation can give an accurate determination of shelf life, and it is important that both these are used (Birch *et al.*, 1977).

12.4.1.2 Break point testing. The purpose of break point testing is to determine the moisture level at which a product is no longer acceptable.

Samples of different moisture levels are prepared and presented to selected assessors in a random order. The samples can be prepared in a laboratory or by selecting suitable samples from production runs. The target moisture levels should be determined and samples close to these selected. The amount of water to be added to the product is calculated and weighed into trays. These trays are placed in a plexiglass chamber with the required quantity of product. The chamber should be sealed and allowed to stand until all the water has been absorbed – usually 4–7 days. Once the water has been absorbed the product should be allowed to equi- librate for one week in glass jars. After checking of moisture content the samples can be submitted to the sensory panel. The assessors rate the samples organoleptically and the moisture level at which the product is not acceptable is determined. This procedure should be agreed by a number of senior personnel within the organisation as this will form the basis for determining the acceptable shelf life of all products.

Different products will have different break points depending on their composition and end use.

12.4.2 Shelf life testing

The specific methodology used for a shelf life test will depend on the type of product and the resources available. However, there are some general rules which will help to ensure that the data collected provide a realistic assessment of product shelf life.

12.4.2.1 Samples. The specific arrangements for sensory testing will depend on the available resources, but in general, a minimum of six experienced assessors is needed to give a meaningful result.

Accelerated tests require at least 18 cartons of cereal packaged in the same packaging as intended for storage. It is not usually necessary for each assessor to have a full carton, a bowl for each will be sufficient.

Ambient testing will also need at least 18 cartons of cereal which should be stored under typical conditions, e.g. in a distribution warehouse.

If enough food is envisaged to be left over after sensory evaluation for the analytical work, then one carton per assessor is sufficient. Otherwise a second carton may be needed for the analysis.

Results plotted graphically are more easily interpreted and trend lines can be drawn.

The shelf life determination should extend beyond the proposed life of the product as this will give extra information concerning what may happen once the product is in the home of the consumer.

During testing, a reference sample available to compare with the sample under test is desirable. However, no acceptable method of preserving a cereal for this purpose is known (Stone *et al.*, 1985). A freshly made sample will provide some reference, and the use of an experienced panel should be adequate.

12.4.2.2 Storage conditions. Storage under a number of different environmental conditions (including the use of accelerated storage) can give some predictive results.

In general, there are three types of testing conditions that can be used which have different purposes (see Table 12.1).

The most suitable conditions should be selected depending upon the product and the time available before shelf life must be established. For example, in the development of a new product it may not be possible to complete an 18 month ambient test; an accelerated test could be used to give an initial prediction, followed by a full test afterwards.

Table 12.1 Types of storage conditions and their uses

Test	Suitable for	Not suitable	Time
Ambient	All products	–	18 months
Accelerated 38°C	Flaked/puffed products	Fruit products, coated	18 weeks
Tropical 38°C 90% humidity	Investigating packaging	General shelf life prediction	Variable

Table 12.2 Appearance scores for a
product stored under ambient conditions

Month	Appearance
0	7.2
1	6.2
2	5.8
3	6.5
4	5.3
6	6.2
7	6.2
8	5.8
9	5.7
10	5.7
11	5.7
12	7.3
13	6.0
14	6.0
15	6.2
16	6.0
17	7.5
18	6.3

12.4.2.3 Assessment of results.   Data collected during a shelf life test will
consist of sensory as well as analytical data. Analysing the data and
looking at the correlation coefficient, percentage fit and slope to assess for
trends from the sensory scores and analysis results will give an effective
prediction. The correlation coefficient between, for example, sensory
scores and analytical results gives a good indication of whether or not
there has been significant quality deterioration over time. In general, it is
accepted that the higher the correlation coefficient, the more significant
the observed change.

In the example shown in Table 12.2, there is little change in the
appearance scores against time reflected in a slope of 0.01, a correlation
coefficient of 0.12 and a percentage fit of 1.5.

Results plotted graphically are more easily interpreted and trend lines
can be drawn as in Figure 12.1 (the higher the score, the higher the
acceptability).

Using the results from the break point analysis, it can be determined
when the product becomes unacceptable.

For analytical data, the critical point may be when a vitamin falls
below the intended nutritional claim.

Addition of some vitamins, in particular vitamin C, can give some stability problems and this is affected by the method of application and
storage conditions (Labuza, 1982).

Figure 12.2 shows little loss of vitamin C when applied to the product,
in this case, separately from other vitamins.

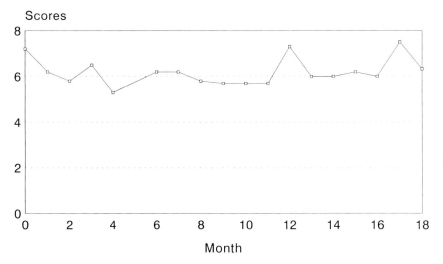

Figure 12.1 Appearance scores plotted to show trends more clearly.

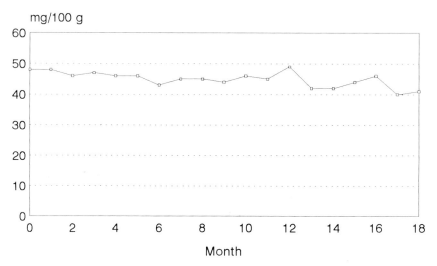

Figure 12.2 Vitamin C added as a separate spray showing little change on storage.

This, however, changes when vitamin C is added together with other vitamins. While the vitamins are stable in solution, once on the product some changes are observed (see Figure 12.3). The graph shows a rapid initial loss and this could also result in development of off-flavours and odours.

In general, one result showing a marked adverse trend would not

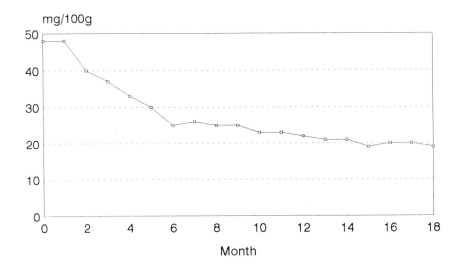

Figure 12.3 Vitamin C added as one spray with other vitamins, showing changes of vitamin C with storage.

indicate a definite cause for concern, as this could be a one-off sample with a fault. in the packaging. Two consecutive results which show marked vitamin degradation would however need investigation.

The following examples illustrate the methodology of testing and how the shelf life can be determined.

12.4.3 Example 1 – flaked/puffed product

The steps involved in testing this type of product, assuming it is a new product are:

1. identification of critical attributes;
2. break point analysis;
3. test conditions;
4. interpretation of results.

12.4.3.1 Critical attributes. As the product does not have any 'high risk' ingredients, there are no specific factors which may need specialist assessors.

The most critical factors for this type of product are:

- appearance
- flavour/off-flavour
- texture (crisp/crunchy)

- moisture
- vitamins/minerals if fortified

12.4.3.2 Break point analysis.   This identifies the moisture content at which the product quality becomes unacceptable from a sensory point of view. It is assumed that for this product the break point moisture level is 6%. This will be used to confirm the final shelf life.

12.4.3.3 Test conditions.   In the initial determination of shelf life, both accelerated and ambient testings are useful if run parallel to one another.

The accelerated test will give a prediction of the full shelf life and may highlight any early problems.

12.4.3.4 Interpretation of results.   Figures 12.4 and 12.5 show data from storage of a product under ambient conditions. The test ran for 18 months and Figure 12.4 demonstrates that the product reached its break point in 16 months. This would suggest that the product should not have a shelf life longer than 16 months.

Figure 12.5 confirms the product acceptability by sensory evaluation. For example the data for texture yield:

Intercept	8.25
Slope	– 0.09
Correlation coefficient	0.72

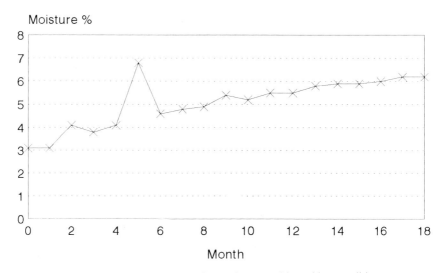

Figure 12.4 Moisture content of a product stored in ambient conditions.

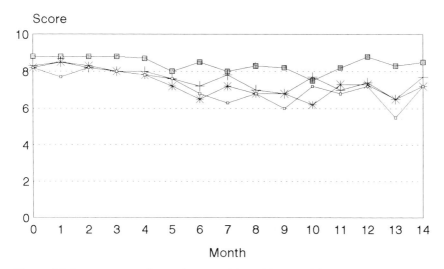

Figure 12.5 Sensory scores of a product stored in ambient conditions. □, Appearance; +, texture; *, flavour; ■, off flavour.

It may be concluded that there were no real trends in the reduction of acceptability.·

The same product tested under accelerated conditions showed little deterioration in product quality (Figure 12.6) and little increase in moisture (Figure 12.7).

From these results the predicted shelf life from accelerated testing would be 18 months (based on one week accelerated life being equivalent to one month ambient life). However, with the ambient results the acceptable recommendation would be 16 months.

The results of the test can only be used to predict the expected shelf life when using the same product formulation, manufacturing process and packaging materials. Any major changes will invalidate the prediction based on accelerated test alone.

Break point testing/tropical conditions can be used to assess different packaging materials without doing a full test.

12.4.4   Example 2 – Cereal with added components

Combining two or more materials together which have very different storage properties can give rise to complex shelf life problems. All constituent parts must be acceptable at the end of the shelf life and the percentage combination can have a marked effect. A good example is flakes with raisins.

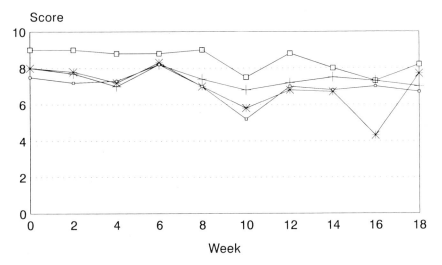

Figure 12.6 Sensory scores of a product stored under accelerated conditions. □, Appearance; +, texture; *, flavour, ■, off flavour.

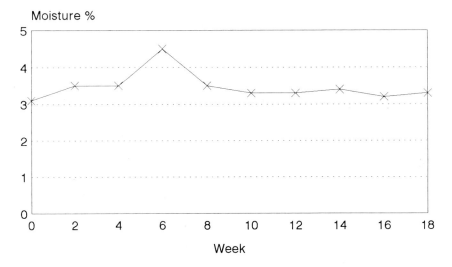

Figure 121.7 Moisture content of a product stored under accelerated conditions.

12.4.4.1 Identification of critical attributes. The following are identified as critical attributes:

- Appearance – plump, glossy fruit, 'bright' flakes.
- Texture – crisp flake/soft fruit.
- Flavour – fresh, fruity flavour, fresh bran flavour.
- Analytical parameters will include:
  - moisture of flakes and fruit
  - vitamins/minerals.

12.4.4.2 Break point analysis. Taking a homogeneous product, the overall moisture can be determined when the product is no longer acceptable. However, in this case, the 'total' moisture is not the critical parameter, but the values for the individual parts of the product are.

The break point for this type of product would have a maximum and minimum value, for example, a minimum of 2.0%, a maximum of 8.0% with a maximum for cereal at 7.0%.

12.4.4.3 Test conditions. Only ambient test conditions are suitable for products with fruit added. Accelerated tests, i.e. at high temperature, will cause premature hardening of the fruit and will not give an accurate prediction. Accelerated tests may be used to look at the stability of nutrients but not organoleptic properties.

For sensory assessment, information should be obtained separately for fruit and flake texture.

12.4.4.4 Interpretation of results. In Table 12.3 it can be seen that there is little change in the organoleptic properties of the product. However, there are clear trends in the moisture contents of the flakes and fruit. The previously determined break point of the product would, from these figures, suggest an acceptable shelf life of about 14 months, based on moisture content. The organoleptic properties confirm this. However, with this type of product experience has shown that organoleptic properties are more critical.

Another example (Table 12.4) shows a marked deterioration in fruit texture and for this product a shelf life of only 8 months would be acceptable.

In this situation, a decision then has to be made as to whether to modify the product or packaging or offer a reduced shelf life. Any changes to the product/pack should require re-testing.

Table 12.5 shows the effects of different levels of fruit addition. The higher level affects flake quality whilst the lower level results in deterioration of the fruit.

With other materials, e.g. nuts, it is likely that oxidative change rather

Table 12.3 Data from the shelf life test of a product over 13 months showing organoleptic properties and moisture content

Month	Appearance	Texture fruit	Texture flake	Flavour	Off flavour	Moisture flake	Moisture fruit
0	7.5	7.25	6.5	7.5	8.5	4.1	11.4
1	7.5	7.33	6.33	7.17	8.6	4.1	9.3
2	7.17	7.17	6.0	7.17	9.0	4.3	8.7
3	8.17	6.5	5.67	7.17	8.3	4.6	8.3
4	7.8	6.2	6.8	7.6	9.0	5.0	8.8
5	7.33	6.67	6.5	7.5	8.6	5.0	8.1
6	7.67	7.17	6.17	7.5	8.1	5.4	8.8
7	7.83	5.67	6.33	7.17	8.1	6.7	8.5
8	7.4	6.2	6.0	7.4	9.0	6.6	8.1
9	7.6	5.6	5.6	7.2	9.0	6.5	7.0
10	7.4	6.2	6.0	7.4	9.0	6.6	7.9
11	7.6	6.6	6.2	7.0	8.6	6.9	8.2
12	8.0	6.5	6.0	6.5	8.3	7.2	8.4
13	7.5	6.17	5.33	6.17	7.5	7.2	8.2

Table 12.4 Texture scores for a product stored under ambient conditions

Month	Texture of fruit
0	7.3
1	7.3
2	7.2
3	6.5
4	6.2
5	6.2
6	6.2
7	6.0
8	5.7
9	5.3
10	5.3
11	5.3
12	5.0
13	4.8

than moisture transfer will be critical. In this case, either the quality of the nuts or oxygen availability, or both will be the life controlling factor.

12.4.5   Example 3 – Coated products, e.g. extruded, coated cereal

This type of product can consist of any kind of 'base' material, e.g. corn, oats, wheat, rice, and can have various coatings, from a simple sugar coating to one consisting of honey, nuts, cocoa powder and so on.

Table 12.5 Effects of different levels of fruit addition on fruit and flake texture

Month	15% fruit Flake texture	15% fruit Fruit texture	25% fruit Flake texture	25% fruit Fruit texture	40% fruit Flake texture	40% fruit Fruit texture
0	7.5	7.7	7.2	7.2	7.9	7.7
1	7.7	7.6	7.7	7.2	7.7	7.5
2	7.8	7.3	7.3	7.5	7.5	7.5
3	7.6	7.4	7.3	7.0	7.5	7.6
4	7.5	7.4	7.6	7.2	7.2	7.6
5	7.6	7.0	7.5	7.3	7.0	7.4
6	7.7	7.0	7.4	7.2	6.8	7.4
7	7.8	6.8	7.2	7.7	6.4	7.5
8	7.3	6.8	6.8	7.3	6.4	7.3
9	7.5	6.7	7.5	7.2	6.2	7.6
10	7.7	6.4	7.4	7.2	6.1	7.7
11	7.3	6.2	7.0	6.5	6.0	7.5
12	7.6	6.0	6.7	7.3	5.6	7.5

12.4.5.1   Identification of critical attributes.   An oat based product with a honey and nut coating is taken as an example.

The most critical attributes will include:

- Appearance: dullness/glossiness
- Flavour: rancidity and other potential off-flavours; loss of honey/nut flavour
- Texture: stickiness, softness
- Analytical parameters: moisture
                         PV (peroxide value)
                         FFA (free fatty acid)
                         vitamins/minerals

12.4.5.2   Break point analysis.   As an increase in moisture content can cause changes other than softness, the break point for this type of product is usually lower than for other cereals. For this example a maximum moisture content of 5.0% is assumed to be the critical value.

12.4.5.3   Test conditions.   Ambient conditions are most suitable; accelerated tests (high temperature) may cause some unusual effects, e.g. increased stickiness, which would not be seen in ambient conditions.

12.4.5.4   Interpretation of results.   Figures 12.8 and 12.9 show clear trends in increase in moisture content and reduction of texture quality. Using the break point analysis moisture level, the product would no longer be acceptable after 8 months. The decision must then be made as to whether this life is acceptable. If the alternative is to reformulate then the product must have a full storage test before the shelf life can be confirmed.

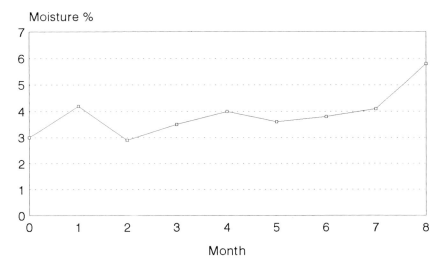

Figure 12.8 Moisture content during storage. Break point level 5%.

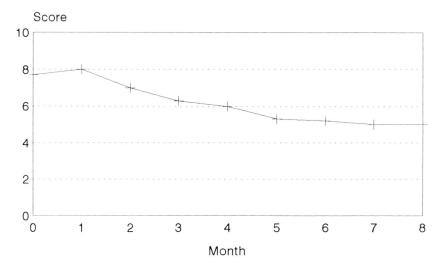

Figure 12.9 Texture scores during storage. Break point level 5%.

Figure 12.10 shows a clear trend in FFA and PV results which would suggest potential rancidity and off-flavour development.

However, in this case there has been no deterioration in the assessors' rating of flavour (Figure 12.11) which suggests that the increases in PV

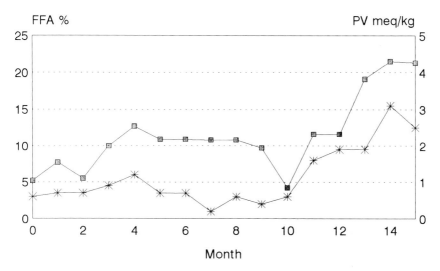

Figure 12.10 PV and FFA levels during storage. *, FFA; ■, PV.

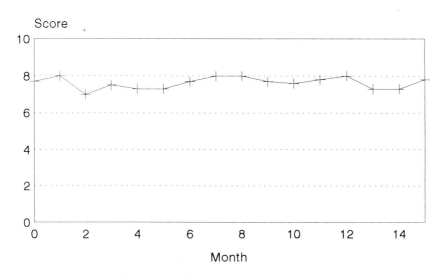

Figure 12.11 Flavour scores during storage.

and FFA are not reflected in the acceptability of the product. This again emphasises that both sensory and analytical data should be used together as they provide complementary information.

12.4.6 Monitoring activities

Once the shelf life has been initially determined, it should be monitored on a regular basis to take into consideration changes in raw material/processing which might not be major changes, but could over a period of time cause a drift in product quality.

The frequency of re-testing will depend on the facilities available and the complexity of the product. For example a product containing 'high-risk' ingredients may need to be re-tested every 2–3 years whereas a relatively stable product may only need to be re-tested every 5 years.

A programme should be set up to ensure all products are re-examined on a regular basis. This will also give some confidence against the risks in shelf life testing of looking at a typical situation rather than the worst case (Paine, 1992). Mathematical models can be used to predict shelf life from currently available data which can help to minimise repeat testing (Labuza, 1982).

If there are any changes to raw material or, more critically to packaging materials, then a full test should be carried out before the change is confirmed. This will minimise the risks involved.

12.5 Conclusions

In this chapter the main criteria for consideration when evaluating the shelf life of breakfast cereals have been discussed. As indicated, there are some points for general consideration which relate to all types of cereals. However the wide diversity of cereal products means that each product should be treated on an individual basis. Lessons learned from other products can be used, but this information should not be treated as absolute. Small changes in processing or raw materials can have a serious effect on storage life.

Each product category and individual company facilities must determine the exact nature of the testing carried out, and the examples quoted should give an indication of how the data collected can be analysed and interpreted to provide useful storage information. It is important to design the programme to suit individual requirements.

References

Amerine, M.A., Pangborn, R.M. and Roessler, E.B. (1965) *Principles of Sensory Evaluation*, Academic Press, New York, pp. 275–304, 321, 377, 494, 510.
Anderson, R.H., Maxwell, D.L., Mulley, A.E. and Fritsch, C.W. (1976) Effects of processing and storage on micro-nutrients in breakfast cereal. *Food Technology*, **30**(5), 110, 112–114.

Birch, G.G., Brennan, J.G. and Parker, K.J. (1977) *Sensory Properties of Foods*, Applied Science, Barking, Essex, Ch. 8, p. 113, Ch. 13, p. 213.

Borenstein, B., Caldwell, E.F., Gordon, H.T., Johnson, L. and Labuza, T.P. (1990) Fortification and Preservation of Cereals, in *Breakfast Cereals and How They are Made* (eds R.B. Fast and E.F. Caldwell), St. Paul, Minnesota.

Fast, R.B. (1987) Breakfast cereals: processed grains for human consumption. *Cereal Foods World*, **32**(3), 241–4.

IFST (1993) *Shelf Life of Foods – Guidelines for its Determination and Prediction*, IFST, London, pp. 3–5, 35.

Labuza, T.P. (1982) *Shelf Life Dating of Foods*, Food and Nutr. Press, Westport, Connecticut, pp. 101, 107, 108, 115, 149.

Maxwell, D. (1990) *Prepared Foods*, **159**(2), 87–88.

Paine, F.A. (1992) *What is Shelf Life*, Food Technology International Europe, Sterling, London.

Seiler, D.A.L. (1988) *Food Science and Technology Today*, **2**(1), 37–41.

Stauffer, J.E. (1991) *Cereal Foods World*, **36**(1), 11–12, 14, 16, 19–20, 23, 26.

Stone, H. and Sidel, J.L. (1985) *Sensory Evaluation Practices*, Academic Press, London, pp. 264, 265.

13 The storage of thermally processed foods in containers other than cans

M.R. GODDARD

13.1 Introduction and background

The market for thermally processed foods presented in containers other than the traditional can is, in commercial terms, a relatively young one. All common packaging materials, board, glass and plastics as well as metal, are now represented in this market, the most recent entry being plastics.

In the case of these heat-stable high-barrier plastics containers both Maskell (1991) and Seldman (1992) give good accounts of the history of this market, showing how the first products were test marketed as recently as 1983 and how it was not until 1987/88, when a number of both major branded food manufacturers (General Foods, Batchelor Foods) and high street retailers (Boots, Marks & Spencer) entered the market, that the area started to grow. Growth however has been rapid, and, for the most part, sustained through the 1980s and into the 1990s. This is demonstrated quite vividly by figures on the amount of retortable plastics barrier containers sold in the UK over the period 1988–1992 (Wendt, 1992) (Table 13.1). Other figures reflect this trend with the area continuing to show a value growth of around 8% pa to an estimated total value of £26 million in 1992 (Anon, 1992c).

Other major packaging formats for ambient stable moist/liquid products are the board/foil laminate TetraPak and Combibloc containers, dominated by the fruit juice and dairy markets, and the glass jar.

Despite the fact that glass has a considerable history as the packaging for heat processed products (Appert's original experiments in 1809 used corked jars), usage has been declining until relatively recently. Fuelled by the growth in the pasta ('pour over') sauce market and more recently in the conversion of the 'cook-in' sauce market from cans and board/foil laminates to glass, the format has gained favour again, partly due to its 'green' image and recyclability.

The non-pasta sauce market in the UK started with the launch of a range of canned cook-in sauces under the RHM 'Homepride' label in 1974. The first launch in carton (Colmans) took place in 1987 and since then growth has been rapid (around 20% pa in terms of volume) with the

Table 13.1 Growth of retortable plastics barrier containers in the UK (1988–1992)

Year	1988	1989	1990	1991*	1992*
Containers used (million units)	5.0	9.3	19.5	24.0	30.7

*Estimated.
Source: Wendt, 1992.

market having an estimated market value in the UK of around £60 million (Anon, 1992a). The pasta sauce market is somewhat younger having started in the UK with the launch of Campbell's 'Prego' range in 1981. This market is almost entirely glass based and has also shown very rapid growth (21% volume increase in 1991) with an estimated UK market value of £65 million in 1992 (Anon, 1992b).

None of these product areas has any appreciable showing in cans. This review therefore, focuses on these product areas and concentrates on the shelf life of heat processed foods, packed in plastics packaging. It is the case however that many of the observations and procedures will be equally applicable to other packaging formats, differences in shelf life between packaging formats being related, in the most part, to variation in permeability of the actual packaging materials and their sealing systems to external factors affecting product stability, primarily light and oxygen.

13.2   Product groups and their characteristics

The products covered under the heading of this chapter can all be described as 'meal components in sauce'. The reason that such a blanket description can be applied to pasta sauces, stir fry vegetable mixes, ready meals and so on is that all of these products need the application of an accurate thermal process to provide stability while optimising quality. This requirement dictates that, although the ratio of sauce to components may vary and the components themselves be many and diverse, the presence of a continuous liquid phase is common to all.

In all these moist, ambient-stable, processed food systems a combination of an applied heat process, product formulation and suitable packaging is used to confer microbiological safety and stability by either (a) producing and maintaining a microbiologically sterile system or (b) reducing microbial counts to an acceptable level and producing and maintaining a bacteriostatic system.

In the case of the product groups covered in this chapter these two categories are usually differentiated by the pH of the foods concerned. High pH products (pH $\geqslant 4.5$) are generally cream sauces, gravy based meals or sauces, or occasionally low water activity 'dry' packed meal components such as potato products. Low pH products (pH $\leqslant 4.5$) are generally tomato based or of the 'sweet and sour' type with high levels of natural acidulants such as vinegar, fruit juice or fermented sauces.

High pH products have to be subjected to a thermal process sufficient to destroy all microorganisms and in general terms this means a heat treatment equivalent to at least 3 minutes at 121°C ($F_0 = 3$). For low pH foods, with a pH of 4.5 or less, a less severe thermal process will achieve ambient stability as the pathogenic organisms of greatest concern – *Clostridium botulinum* – cannot grow under these conditions.

These basic microbiological rules hold regardless of whether the product is packed in glass, high-barrier plastics or foil laminates and determine that quality change on storage due to microbial activity (i.e. spoilage) should not be a shelf life factor in these products.

13.3 Specific factors affecting shelf life

In thermally processed ambient-stable foods deterioration is restricted, for the most part, to that caused by (i) enzyme activity, (ii) chemical reaction and (iii) physical breakdown of components.

13.3.1 Enzymic activity

In general terms the thermal processes to which these products are subjected during manufacture are sufficient to inactivate all enzymes and it is rare for residual enzymic activity or enzyme regeneration to cause storage problems.

The possible exception to this is in the case of UHT High Temperature Short Time processes. Here enzyme reactivation has been noted, the most commonly quoted example being the reactivation of alkaline phosphatase, lipase and protease in UHT processed milk (Kikakis, 1986). Possible storage effects are gelation due to protease activity and the introduction of off-notes in the flavour due to lipase action on milk fat. Such problems are however uncommon and are rarely if ever observed in retort processed systems due to the longer periods of heating involved.

13.3.2 Chemical changes

Chemical changes that take place in such systems are those related to either oxidation, non-enzymic browning (i.e. Maillard reaction) or resulting from nutrient breakdown.

13.3.2.1 Oxidation. Oxidation reactions are many and complex. They can use either headspace oxygen, trapped oxygen or free radical oxygen released by enzymic activity or thermal treatment. They can be initiated photochemically; they are, in common with all chemical reactions, very dependent on temperature and time, and are often catalysed by common food constituents such as trace metals. The results of these reactions are similarly varied but most commonly are observed as 'off' colour and flavour development resulting from the oxidation of lipids, colours and other reactive species. Under normal ambient storage conditions, i.e. 15–25°C, oxidation reactions are probably the most common cause of quality deterioration during storage.

Mogensen and Poulsen (1980), in a study comparing different packaging materials on the shelf life of UHT milk, showed a strong dependence of flavour quality on storage time and temperature and, most significantly, whether or not the packaging was permeable to oxygen.

Colour changes however, although similarly dependent on storage temperature and time, did not show this link with oxygen and were concluded to be related to non-enzymic browning reactions (see below) rather than oxidation reactions. Trammell *et al.* (1986) demonstrated similar results for pasteurised orange juice where both the loss of ascorbic acid and, in this case, browning could be related to initial headspace oxygen concentration but where flavour change could not be related to oxygen concentration, implicating once again, Maillard type reactions.

13.3.2.2 Non-enzymic browning or Maillard reaction. In general terms this reaction takes the general form of a condensation reaction between amino acids and reducing sugars and has the potential to occur in any system where these two substrates are present. Although the Maillard reaction is extremely complex the factors which control it are reasonably well understood. The application of thermal energy has a complex effect on the reaction. In general, as with all chemical reactions, heat accelerates and in many cases initiates the reaction, but due to the complexity of the sequence of the reaction steps the relationship is not a clear one (Benzig-Purdie *et al.*, 1985). Moisture content is an important controlling factor. Very low (approaching 0%) and very high (greater than 90%) moisture systems show little or no non-enzymic browning, but few foods fall into these categories. pH has an inhibitory effect on the Maillard reaction when low and accelerates the reaction when high but there is little or no effect between pH values of 3 and 8, i.e. at the pH values of most foods. The nature of the substrate materials also affects the reaction. Proteins are less reactive than pure amino acids, polymeric carbohydrates such as starch do not take part in the reaction but pure reducing sugars such as lactose are very reactive. Many other chemical constituents of foods have either positive or negative effects on non-enzymic browning and this complex series of reactions can affect food quality in three ways. Firstly it can produce undesirable 'off'-colour and flavour – the brown discoloration and bitter notes in sterilised milk are usually quoted as an example of this. Secondly the condensation reaction can lead to a reduction in nutritive quality of the food as it consumes carbohydrate and amino acids, and thirdly it has been suggested that some of the compounds produced by the latter stages of the reaction may be anti-nutritional in nature.

13.3.2.3 Nutrient breakdown.   Loss of nutrients from a processed food is strongly influenced by the severity of the applied heat process and by the time and temperature of storage. The effects of thermal processing have been well reviewed by Harris and Karmas (1975) who provided a detailed compilation of available kinetic data relating rates of loss of a range of nutrients to thermal processes. A general conclusion is that 'High Temperature Short Time' (HTST) processes and low storage temperatures favour nutrient retention but that all processed foods exhibit some degree of nutrient loss. Similarly Kramer (1977) reviewed the available literature on the effects of storage on fresh, frozen and canned foods and concluded that in all cases the lower the storage temperature the better for not only the nutrient retention, but also the 'aesthetic' properties of the food, i.e. appearance, taste, and so on.

13.3.3   Physical breakdown

Although there is the potential for physical change in many of the components of thermally processed ambient stable products, e.g. texture change in meat, softening of vegetable components, these are rarely a problem. The major reason for this lies in the fact that the initial heat process to which the food has been subjected, particularly if this is a sterilisation process, has already effected far more change on the system than that possible by even the most elevated storage time/temperature combination.

The two main physical factors influencing the shelf life of these foods relate therefore to the continuous aqueous sauce phase rather than to the discontinuous component phase and to two phenomena, namely starch retrogradation and emulsion breakdown.

13.3.3.1   Starch retrogradation.   As previously mentioned most thermally processed foods contain an appreciable percentage of water-based sauce or gravy both to add taste to the other components and to facilitate the heat processing operation. In many cases the texture of this sauce component is controlled by the addition of thickening agents such as edible gums and starches. In actual fact careful selection of these thickeners can also improve the efficiency of the applied thermal process by providing a system with heat transfer properties optimised for each stage of the process through control of the temperature/viscosity profiles (Whistler and Paschall, 1967). The most commonly used thickeners are those best suited to this purpose – chemically modified starches.

A great deal has been written regarding the physical and chemical nature and behaviour of starch and it is not within the remit of this chapter to go into this topic in any detail. For a very complete reference work on this subject the multi-volume treatise *Starch: Chemistry and Technology* by Whistler and Paschall is recommended. There is one property of cooked starch systems which is of importance in the storage stability of many ambient-stable moist foods and that is the phenomenon known as 'retrogradation'. To understand this phenomenon a little further explanation of the physico-chemical properties of starch is necessary.

Starches are the favoured thickeners for savoury foods because of the short and clean texture generally desired in such systems, but, because of the relatively delicate nature of cooked native starches such as cornflour or potato starch, chemical modification is required to give the starch the necessary stability to processing.

In most applications the thickening and texture-giving properties of starch are due to its presence in the hydrated form as swollen granules entrapping concentrated aqueous biopolymer solutions. These biopolymers comprise repeating anhydroglucose units either linear in nature and connected by alpha 1-4 glycosidic links (amylose) or with a branched structure, the anhydroglucose units being again connected by alpha 1-4 links but also having an alpha 1-6 link at selected sites (amylopectin). In the presence of heat and water these glucose polymers move from a crystalline to a solution state, binding water of hydration and 'swell'. Starches are chemically cross-linked to 'toughen' the granules and to prevent (or at least reduce) granule disintegration through the application of heat, shear, extremes of pH or ionic change. Cross-linking is achieved by treatment of the native starch with di- or polyfunctional reagents capable of reacting with the hydroxyl groups in and between both the amylose and amylopectin molecules to form chemical bridges which restrict swelling of the hydrated polymers and hence of the starch granules.

'Retrogradation' is a phenomenon related to the tendency for dissolved starch molecules, particularly the linear amylose molecules, to move from a disordered to a more ordered state, but one quite different from that found in the uncooked starch granules. In solution the hydroxyl groups on parallel amylose molecules exert attractive forces (hydrogen bonding) and molecules line up into a network structure. This restructuring in solution manifests itself initially as the formation of a gel structure but with time, or when exacerbated by freeze–thaw cycling, the gel contracts and water is expelled (so-called 'weeping'). In extreme cases this 'dehydration' will result in amylose being precipitated out of solution as insoluble, high melting point granules, giving rise to a rough or grainy texture. This phenomenon is not entirely restricted to amylose. Amylopectin will also exhibit a form of retrogradation, giving rise to weak gels; but the strength of these is weak and as the melting point of crystalline amylopectin is below the serving and eating temperature of most savoury products, this is not considered to be a problem.

The 'toughening' of the starch granules or immobilisation of polymeric material by chemical crosslinking also serves to reduce the amount of free starch molecules, in particular the amylose, which leaches out of swollen or broken granules and hence acts to reduce the chance of retrogradation. This is not a total solution however, since the percentage of starch molecules which can be cross linked without giving rise to unacceptable reduction in thickening power of the starch is low – a maximum of one crosslink per 100 starch molecules and often as low as one link per 2000 molecules. This still leaves a very high percentage of 'free' molecules and an appreciable risk of retrogradation taking place, particularly in systems which have been subjected to extremes of heat and shear, e.g. sterilised systems. In order to overcome this, most modified starches are based on native starches low in amylose (and hence high in amylopectin) – the so-called waxy starches – and a second modification is applied to remove the unacceptable 'long' or 'slimy' texture associated with amylopectin.

In most cases therefore the tendency for heat processed foods to exhibit retrogradation has been formulated out but the growing need for 'clean labels' and the progressive removal of chemical additives from foods is forcing a return to native starch and flour based systems which may well result in a resurrection of the problem.

13.3.3.2 Emulsion stability. Many heat processed foods, particularly those containing cream style sauces, contain appreciable levels of fat in the form of an oil-in-water emulsion.

In order to maintain the fat in this state the system requires the presence, at the oil/water interface, of an emulsifier – a material with both hydrophilic and lipophilic properties, which stabilises the fat droplets against coalescence. If this material is not present at a sufficiently high level to stabilise the emulsion throughout the thermal process, or if its emulsifying properties are damaged by the applied heat, the emulsion will 'break' and the oil and water phases will separate into two distinct layers.

The most common emulsifiers used in food systems are proteins – particularly milk proteins – and fat derivatives, both naturally occurring and synthetic, where hydrophilicity is derived from the presence of polar species attached to the non-polar glyceride moieties.

Fat-derived emulsifiers are in general stable to the time and temperature combinations that most conventional thermally processed foods experience. Proteins are considerably more heat labile, denaturing (changing structure) and changing functionality in the presence of heat. Proteins are also sensitive to chemical factors such as pH and free ion concentration, and, under certain conditions in aqueous solutions will, often as a function of time, denature and change in functionality. The most common visible result of protein denaturation is a loss of emulsifying properties, reflected in emulsion breakdown, and a textural change, such as gelation or granularity, in the aqueous phase. Any or all of these changes may be important factors in shelf life determination.

13.3.4 Other factors influencing shelf life

Two other factors may affect the shelf life of thermally processed ambient stable foods, both of which primarily influence the flavour of stored products. Firstly, there is the possibility, particularly in plastics laminate packaging but also to a lesser extent in other laminate materials, of flavour migration into the packaging material or partitioning between product and packaging and secondly, the much more common effect of flavour transfer between product components.

The latter effect is only really a problem in mixed component systems (such as fruit salads and ready meals) where, over a period of time, individual components start to lose their own flavour characteristics and to take on an 'average' taste. It is rare for this phenomenon to produce truly negative quality attributes but, in order to maintain high quality in these products, it is often monitored as a guide to establishing optimum shelf life.

Flavour and colour migration into packaging tends to be more of an aesthetic problem than a quality issue. The levels of loss of flavour and colour into the packaging are very low and are more likely to result in discoloration of the inside of the pack rather than a significant loss of colour or flavour in the product. What is of more concern is the possibility of constituents of the packaging material, e.g. plasticisers, migrating into the food. Of particular concern regarding the potential quality issues associated with the presence of these materials in processed foods are systems where the food has been subjected to high or prolonged thermal treatment whilst in contact with the packaging material, e.g. during a post-packaging pasteurisation or sterilisation process or during regeneration for consumption in either a conventional or a microwave oven.

In 1973 the EEC adopted a resolution to initiate a programme for the harmonisation of legislation on food contact materials in order to remove technical barriers to intra-community trade and to protect consumers from any risk arising from the migration of packaging components into foods. The first part of the legislation on this issue related to plastics was completed in 1990 and issued as Directive 90/128/EEC, the so-called 'Plastics' Directive.

The legislation prescribes in some detail test methods for measuring the migration of packaging material components into foodstuffs and the maximum permitted levels of these components. It further spells out the nature of the tests required to be made with reference to the food simulants which should be used to replace actual foods, the temperature regimes to which the test materials should be subjected and the number of replicates/frequency of testing.

Although this type of testing is unlikely to form part of shelf life evaluation, as all packaging or potential packaging materials should have already passed through this protocol, the methodologies included within it can often be usefully applied to the determination of specific storage problems, e.g. related to flavour loss or colour migration into packaging, and the reader is directed to the official EC publications for details.

13.4 Determination of shelf life

From the information given above it can be seen that the storage changes which dominate in heat processed ambient-stable foods such as sauces and ready meals are mainly changes in flavour and colour. Textural changes can occur in such foods but by and large these are insignificant when compared to the textural changes imposed on the system by the initial thermal process. Changes in colour and flavour, therefore, are the major determinants of shelf life. This then governs the way in which changes are monitored and shelf life is set.

Textural change is limited and if it does occur, is usually restricted to the aqueous phase. Rheological measurements, such as the measurement of viscosity under specific conditions, can be used to monitor such change. In most instances however, if such change is to be a controlling factor in shelf life determination, it will be easily recognised without the need for instrumental analysis.

Colour change also tends to be relatively easy to recognise as a shelf life determinant but in this case instrumental measurement is favoured as a means of quantifying the change and finding the point of unacceptability.

Flavour change is the most common and most difficult shelf life controlling factor to quantify in thermally processed ambient-stable products. Instrumental analysis of flavour change is very difficult. Food flavours, particularly natural food flavours, are complex and subtle, often comprising many hundreds of chemical constituents, many at extremely low levels. Many and various attempts have been made to measure flavour. Chromatographic methods such as HPLC (high performance liquid chromatography) and GC (gas chromatography) have been widely used

(Barberio, 1986), both as means of producing a 'fingerprint' of the flavour and, when coupled with mass spectroscopy, as means of identifying change in specific aroma compounds. Experience suggests however, that such techniques are best suited for the examination of specific problems (for example, the plasticiser migration problem outlined above), and are not suitable as quality control tools to be used in the setting of shelf life criteria.

In summary therefore, the best approach to use in the storage testing and shelf life determination of thermally processed ambient-stable foods is to rely on the human senses, using carefully controlled sensory analysis techniques, augmenting these, if necessary, with analytical or instrumental analyses.

The following sections describe a protocol for the storage, sensory testing and shelf life determination of an ambient-stable pasta product, a protocol which can be adapted to suit any of this type of product.

13.4.1 Storage protocol

The two major factors to take into consideration in setting up a storage trial for any product are the anticipated time and temperature of storage.

13.4.1.1 Time. As previously mentioned the microbiological storage life of thermally processed products that have been processed and handled correctly is indefinite; which is why the determination of shelf life is based on the maintenance of acceptable sensory quality. A realistic assessment of the period between manufacture and consumption for this type of product gives a total life of 18 months. This figure is based largely on experience with other ambient-stable products, e.g. canned products, jams and preserves and dry mix products, and probably errs on the side of caution for this new generation of thermally processed foods. Although it is known from in-home audits that canned and dry mix products may reach this age (or even older) before consumption, it is likely that there is less chance of this being the case with modern packaging formats, particularly with respect to the plastics laminate pack, the 'technicalities' of which are less well understood by the consumer. Nevertheless, based on this assessment, storage testing is generally set to run for a minimum of 12 months. 'Take offs' – the intervals at which samples are removed from storage for analysis – are usually scheduled at monthly intervals although it is common practice to sample at, for example, 0, 1, 2, 3, 6 and 12 months, only testing at the remaining take-off points if problems are becoming apparent.

13.4.1.2 Temperature. It is important to remember that an estimate of the temperature of storage of ambient-stable products is probably very different from the average ambient temperature they actually experience in practice. Temperatures within the distribution chain are likely, in Northern Europe, to range from zero in an unheated warehouse at night to in excess of 30°C in a truck in mid-summer. Because of this it is common to store at two temperatures – an 'average' temperature, usually taken as 25°C, and an 'abuse' temperature, usually taken as 35°C. It must also be noted that these are Northern European criteria. For tropical climates higher temperatures, e.g. 30°C average, 40°C abuse are usually used.

One final point regarding temperature of storage is that if it is known that the product is likely, when in the distribution chain, to experience severe and regular temperature cycling, this should also be built into the storage protocol.

13.4.1.3 Other factors. Two other factors may need to be considered when setting up a storage protocol. Firstly, there may be a need to consider and allow for the effect of light. This is certainly the case for products packed in glass or other transparent materials but may also be important for products packed in translucent plastics. If light is a factor, it is normal to set up two parallel exercises, with one set of samples being stored under suitable illumination, and a control set being stored in the dark.

Secondly, certain packaging materials are permeable to water vapour. This should not be the case for the materials used for thermally processed foods but needs to be taken into consideration if the protocol is to be extended, e.g. to dry mixes. In the case of moisture vapour transfer being suspected as a contributing factor to storage stability, a control experiment needs to be set up storing samples in both high and low relative humidity environments.

13.4.2 Sensory analysis

The definition of the shelf life of a food product in respect of sensory changes as a function of storage is based on the answering of one or more of the following questions:

1. How long can the product be stored without noticeable change in its sensory attributes?
2. How do sensory attributes change on storage?
3. How long can the product be stored before changes in sensory properties render it unacceptable?

The first two questions relate to objective analysis of the product – no qualification is required and no subjective assessment of quality is required. If question (1) is used to set shelf life a simple 'yes/no' response to a discrimination test will suffice. There is no need for highly trained sensory assessors but a large number of people are required to ensure a statistically robust answer. Triangular tests and paired comparison tests will give a simple yes/no answer; ranking and magnitude estimation tests will add some measure of the degree of difference.

If question (2) is used then shelf life will either be estimated from determining the point at which selected sensory attributes of the product approach predetermined unacceptable levels or by the application of a secondary test which will answer either question (1) or (2). A descriptive test based on assessment of samples by a highly trained sensory panel is required to provide this sort of 'magnitude' data and a profiling method such as Quantitative Descriptive Analysis (QDA) is often used.

The third question is rather different. Changes in sensory properties are expected and a subjective assessment of the degree of change considered acceptable is required. Typical tests are based on either comparison, presenting paired samples (e.g. the test sample against a control) and seeking an absolute preference, or ranking, presenting samples either singly or in sequence and seeking a degree of preference. For this latter approach the 'Hedonic' rating scale, derived by Peryam and Pilgrim (1957) in the 1950s is still the most widely used (Figure 13.1).

If this approach is used it is most important that the panel be composed of untrained 'consumers' – to ensure a subjective rather than an objective assessment – and number at least 50 people to ensure statistical reliability. This approach is commonly used as an 'in-house' evaluation technique and in this case it is unlikely that the panel will truly represent the consuming public. Sensory quality assessments of this sort should therefore be regarded as giving guidance rather than absolute results. The only way to obtain the latter is via full consumer research.

Detailed guidelines for all of the methodologies outlined above together with a wide range of less widely used and more sophisticated tests are given in the book *Guidelines for Sensory Analysis in Food Product Development and Quality Control* (Lyon *et al.*, 1992). For our test case, the

Nine point Hedonic rating scale

Like extremely
Like very much
Like moderately
Like slightly
Neither like nor dislike
Dislike slightly
Dislike moderately
Dislike very much
Dislike extremely

Figure 13.1 Nine point Hedonic rating scale (Peryam and Pilgrim, 1957).

ambient-stable pasta in sauce product, we will focus on the use of QDA to produce sensory 'fingerprints' coupled with a hedonic ranking to obtain estimates for both shelf life and the sensory characteristics which govern it.

13.5   An example – pasta shapes in savoury tomato sauce

13.5.1   Protocol

The test product is a simple ready meal consisting of pasta shapes in a minced meat and tomato sauce, the following being a summary of the manufacturing and distribution process.

> The product is packed, as a two shot fill (pre-cooked drained pasta followed by hot sauce) into preformed polypropylene trays, lidded with a polyethylene/aluminium foil laminate and retort sterilised to a F_0 value of 3.
>
> The product is for distribution at ambient, the individual trays being overwrapped with a printed paperboard sleeve and shrink-wrapped in dozens in cardboard trays. The desired storage life (manufacture to consumption) is one year.

From this information a storage protocol can be developed to determine the shelf life of the product.

1. The product is fully sterilised so that microbiological stability will not be a shelf life determinant. Past experience suggests however that the sauce containing meat and tomato may give rise to colour changes on storage and further, it is possible due to the acidic nature of tomato, that changes in meat texture may occur. Furthermore pasta tends to soften in time due to water pick-up and starch loss, so textural changes in both pasta and sauce are possible. This combination of possible changes suggests that a QDA test, coupled with a simple monadic liking test (i.e. samples are presented one at a time) is probably the best approach for this product. Although instrumental measurements may be considered to provide further information on colour change, experience also tells that the heterogeneous nature of the product (coarse textured sauce, meat particles, pasta) will give poor reproducibility. Colour analysis will therefore have to rely on sensory estimation.
2. The product will be stored, transported and displayed at ambient temperatures. A Northern European environment is assumed and storage trials at $+25°C$ and $+35°C$ will be conducted, in order to assess the product's tolerance to abuse conditions. A control sample will be stored at $+2°C$, the assumption being that any change over the storage trial at this temperature will be minimal.
3. The product is packed in an opaque primary packaging and over-

Table 13.2 Storage protocol for pasta in savoury tomato sauce

Take off point	Date	Storage temperature	Testing required	Number of samples required
Time zero	Jul 1993	n/a	QDA + Colour	10 + 2
One month	Aug 1993	+2°C, +25°C and +35°C	QDA + Colour	10 + 2 for each temperature
Two months	Sep 1993	+2°C, +25°C and +35°C	QDA + Colour	10 + 2 for each temperature
Three months	Oct 1993	+2°C, +25°C and +35°C	QDA + Colour	10 + 2 for each temperature
Six months	Jan 1994	+2°C, +25°C and +35°C	QDA + Colour	10 + 2 for each temperature
One year	Jul 1994	+2°C, +25°C and +35°C	QDA + Colour	10 + 2 for each temperature
Eighteen months	Jan 1995	+2°C, +25°C and +35°C	QDA + Colour	10 + 2 for each temperature

wrapped with a paperboard sleeve. For this protocol, the packaging is assumed to be lightproof and there is no need to build a light sensitivity test into the trial.

4. The product is expected to have a storage life of one year. To add a margin of safety, storage trial will continue for 18 months. Take-offs however will be staggered – time zero, one month, two months, three months, six months, one year and eighteen months but a 'safety factor' of extra samples will be included to allow for intermediate take-offs and testing if necessary.

The test protocol can therefore be summarised as in Table 13.2. This protocol allows the scheduling of the testing and gives an estimate of the total number of samples required. The ten samples retained for the QDA analysis at each 'take off' point is based on the need for 40 replicates and the assumption that each pack will provide four portions. It can be seen that a minimum of 72 samples should be stored at each temperature with a further 12 samples available for the time zero testing. Bearing in mind that these are minimum figures, the number should be increased by 50% for the storage samples and at least doubled for the time zero samples to allow for the training of the taste panel, i.e. a total requirement of some 350 samples.

13.5.2 QDA/Liking testing

For the purpose of this example it is assumed that a suitable sensory analysis facility is available and that an experienced taste panel has been selected. If this is not the case then the reader is directed again to the book *Guidelines for Sensory Analysis in Food Product Development and Quality Control* (Lyon *et al.*, 1992), where the authors give in some detail

Table 13.3 Attribute list for pasta in savoury tomato sauce

Pasta	Code	Sauce	Code
Colour intensity	PASCOL	Thickness	THICHN
Intactness	INTACT	Colour intensity	SAUCOL
Firmness	PASFIR	Glossiness	SAUGLO
Smoothness	PASSMO	Smoothness	SAUSMO
Sliminess	PASSLI	Chewiness (of meat)	CHEWIN
Starchiness	PASSTA	Overall strength	
		of flavour	FLAVST
		Tomato flavour	TOMFLA
		Meat flavour	MEAFLA
		Herbs	HERFLA
		Spiciness	SPIFLA

the requirements for the design and development of such facilities and panels.

The first step in the QDA methodology is to develop a descriptive vocabulary to describe the sensory attributes of the product in question. This is done as a group exercise and after due discussion an attribute list is generated. This lists all the sensory parameters, appearance, aroma, flavour and texture, by which the assessors can describe any given sample in terms of a set of scores. Table 13.3 gives the full attribute list for the test product and Figure 13.2 shows the scoring sheet relating to the pasta attributes.

With these attribute lists and a score sheet a trained assessor can produce an accurate and reproducible 'fingerprint' of a sample. To ensure statistical confidence each sample is tasted blind in the order of 40 times. A QDA taste panel usually has 12 to 15 assessors and each assessor is presented randomly with each sample two or three times. A carefully randomised design for sample presentation coupled with internal replication and random coding of samples ensures that the sample analysis is free from order effects and other subjective parameters.

As stated previously, QDA analysis is, if correctly applied, entirely objective. In order to assess changes in product quality, an acceptability question, based on hedonic rating, is added to the end of the QDA scoring sheet.

Each storage sample is tested at each take off and an average score calculated for every sensory attribute. With this information a sensory 'fingerprint' can be constructed for each sample. Typically this information is represented graphically as a simple line or bar graph showing sensory scores as a function of attribute. Using this method a graphical representation of the sensory properties of the product may be produced and comparisons made between samples by simply overlaying plots. Figure 13.3 represents sensory plots for the control sample stored at $+2°C$ compared with the sample stored at $+35°C$ after one year.

Attribute	Low									High
	1	2	3	4	5	6	7	8	9	10
COLOUR INTENSITY	--									
INTACTNESS	--									
FIRMNESS	--									
SMOOTH-NESS	--									
SLIMINESS	--									
STARCHI-NESS	--									

Figure 13.2 Scoring sheet for pasta.

Although these graphical representations show changes in sensory properties quite clearly they do not, in their own right, give any estimate of the statistical significance of these differences. It is usual therefore to couple this simple graphical approach with a statistical analysis of the raw data. Once again there are a number of methods available, which mostly rely on the analysis of variance to give a measure of confidence intervals between samples on the basis of their individual attributes. Such information may be superimposed on the plots, using asterisks to highlight those attributes which show significance at the various confidence limits.

Similarly this information gives no indication as to the effect that any changes are having on product acceptability. The liking scores, averaged in the same way from the hedonic data, give this information (albeit in a crude form). Such information is usually expressed in the form of a simple line graph as shown in Figure 13.4.

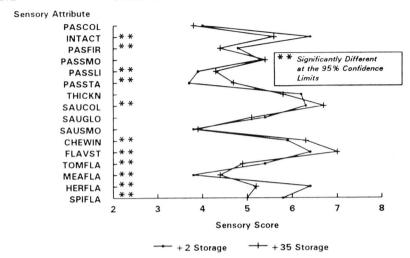

Figure 13.3 Comparison of sensory scores for 'control' and 'abuse' stored samples. ., +2°C storage; +, +35°C storage.

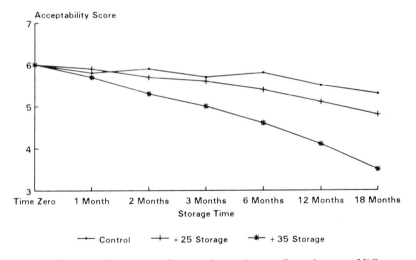

Figure 13.4 Hedonic liking scores for stored samples. ., Control; +, +25°C storage; *, +35°C storage.

13.5.3 Interpretation of results

13.5.3.1 Basic analysis. The simplest way of using the results produced by a storage study such as this is to use the hedonic liking scores to determine product shelf life and the sensory analysis results to determine which factors are controlling the shelf life.

To determine shelf life from acceptability data a threshold liking score is set, either by a suitable 'expert' panel or from data gained from full consumer testing. The shelf life is set based on the period and conditions of storage which will reduce the acceptability score of the product to this point.

Assuming all other factors being equal, i.e. that the sensory and acceptability tests have been properly controlled and carried out, any changes in liking must be linked to changes in sensory properties. Sensory data can therefore be used to determine the factors responsible for changes in acceptability by analysing the sensory data for statistically significant changes in attributes.

In the above example expert assessors have set a threshold acceptability score of 5.0 for the product. Shelf life for the product stored under normal conditions is therefore between 12 and 18 months but any temperature abuse will shorten this considerably.

The major attribute changes as a function of storage time, and temperature detected in the sensory analysis can be seen to be related to pasta texture (intactness, firmness and starchiness), sauce appearance (colour, glossiness) and flavour (all attributes), and meat chewiness. Although it is not possible to draw definite conclusions from this analysis it is likely that the loss of 'freshness' of flavour from the sauce coupled with the loss of texture in the pasta are the prime determinants of shelf life and the first problems to be addressed if a longer shelf life is to be sought.

13.5.3.2 Predictive analysis. This simplistic approach to the determination and rationalisation of shelf life from the interpretation of storage results is usually sufficient for most products. This is particularly the case where the foods, such as the example in this chapter, have relatively short shelf lives and where storage conditions, although variable, are reasonably well controlled. In the case of products with longer shelf lives, or where for example storage temperatures may be subjected to wide variations, shelf life prediction may be preferred to simple shelf life determination. This approach is based on the building of quality kinetics equations, which are derived from detailed study of the effects of a carefully controlled matrix of storage parameters (time, temperature, light and so on) on the perceived quality of a specific product. This information allows the construction of a predictive equation which includes these parameters as variables and which can be used to model and predict quality performance on storage. This approach to shelf life testing has been the subject of much and varied work and a detailed review is beyond the remit of this chapter. There may however be occasions when such an approach will need to be considered and interested readers are directed to *An Illustrated Approach to Food Chemistry* (Labuza, 1985) for a complete review of the subject.

Acknowledgements

The author would like to thank Mr R. Howker and Miss S. Butler of Unilever Research, Colworth House for their assistance in sourcing the references quoted in this chapter.

References

Anon (1992a) *The Grocer*, August 10th, p. 35.
Anon (1992b) *The Grocer*, September 14th, p. 98.
Anon (1992c) *Supermarketing*, September 18th, p. 22.
Barberio, G.C. (1986) in *The Shelflife of Foods and Beverages* (ed. G. Charalambous), Elsevier, London.
Benzig-Purdie, L.M., Ripmeester, J.A. and Ratcliffe, C.I. (1985) *Journal of Agricultural Food Chemistry*, **33**, 31–3.
Harris, R.S. and Karmas, E. (1975) in *Nutritional Evaluation of Food Processing*, AVI, Westport, Connecticut.
Kikakis, J.P. (1986) in *The Shelflife of Foods and Beverages* (ed. G. Charalambous), Elsevier, London.
Kramer, A. (1977) *Journal of Food Quality*, **1**, 23–55.
Labuza, T.P. (1985) in *Food Chemistry* (ed. O.R. Fennema), Marcel Dekker, New York.
Lyon, D.H., Francombe, M.R., Hasdell, T.A. and Lawson, K. (1992) *Guidelines for Sensory Analysis in Food Product Development and Quality Control*, Chapman & Hall, London.
Maskell, A.J. (1991) *Packaging Technology and Science*, **4**, 21–8.
Mogensen, G. and Poulsen, P.R. (1980) *Milchwissenschaft*, **35**(9), 552–4.
Peryam, D.R. and Pilgrim, F.J. (1957) Hedonic scale method for measuring food preferences. *Food Technology*, **11**(9), 9–14.
Seldman, J.D. (1992) *Packaging Technology and Science*, **5**, 154.
Trammel, D.J., Dalsis, D.E. and Malone, C.T. (1986) *Journal of Food Science*, **51**(4), 1021–3.
Wendt, C.H. (1992) *Packaging Technology and Science*, **5**, 159–63.
Whistler, R.L. and Paschall, E.F. (1967) *Starch: Chemistry and Technology*, Academic Press, London.

14 Ambient-stable sauces and pickles

A.A. JONES and C.M.D. MAN

14.1 Introduction

The product group of sauces and pickles comprises a very wide range of traditional as well as more modern fruit/vegetable products. To examine these products will necessitate subdividing the group and dealing with each subgroup in turn. Different subgroups have their own particular modes of deterioration but they all rely wholly or primarily on the use of acetic acid for preservation.

In this chapter, sauces are taken to include the emulsified sauces such as mayonnaise and salad dressings, and the non-emulsified condiment sauces such as tomato ketchup, brown sauce, mint sauce, and so on as well as the sweet sauces such as topping syrups and fruit-based sauces. Pickles are interpreted to include those products traditionally regarded as pickles, such as pickled onions, pickled cabbage, pickled gherkins and so on and also products which are in the grey area between pickles and sauces, such as sweet pickles, piccalilli and chutneys.

The major similarity among all these products, as pointed out earlier, is that traditionally (albeit less so these days) they belong to the category of compositionally-preserved foods since they rely in the main on acetic acid (or sugar) for self preservation. In more recent times, dependence on the traditional method of preservation has been reduced, due to consumer demand for less acidic or less sweet products, making some of these products potentially vulnerable to microbiological spoilage. Consequently the use of alternative preservation methods, such as the inclusion of chemical preservatives (e.g. the organic acid preservatives), thermal processing (e.g. pasteurisation), and aseptic processing and packaging has increased. Moreover, greater emphasis has been placed increasingly on preventive tools such as the one based on the 'Hazard Analysis Critical Control Point' (HACCP) system, for the assurance of safety and quality in foods (CFDRA, 1992).

It is intended to examine briefly the scope of sauces and pickles and in more detail the main factors affecting shelf life and the way they can influence microbiological as well as physico-chemical changes in these products. Once the relevant shelf life determining factors and modes of deterioration have been established, the exact methodology for shelf life determination usually follows logically. Current practice in the shelf life determination of these products, including the use of challenge testing and mathematical models, will be outlined together with a worked example. Reference will be made to previous chapters regarding areas which should be considered but have already been covered elsewhere in this book.

Finally a section will examine current developments within this product sector as well as the industry at large, which may have an impact on the shelf life of these products and the methods by which their shelf lives are determined in future.

14.2   The products

As discussed in the introduction, this product group comprises two major areas, of which sauces can be subdivided into at least three subgroups.

14.2.1   Sauces

Sauces may be defined as a range of formulated liquid or semi-solid food products, which when added to a food, alter or enhance the sensory appeal of that food, by adding richness of flavour and/or enhancing the mouthfeel.

Sauces may be used at the preparation stage of a meal. Marinades are examples of products which may be included in this category, where a certain degree of flavour needs to be introduced into the food before cooking. Sauces may be added at the cooking stage; products in this category range from simple sauces used for their flavour, such as chilli sauce, added to spice a meat dish (e.g. chilli con carne), to more complicated savoury cooking sauces such as creamy mushroom sauce, which when added to a basic commodity such as chicken, converts it into an exotic recipe dish. These sauces also include the 'make-a-meal' and pasta sauces. The main subgroup is represented by the 'pour-over' sauces which are added to a complete meal as an accompaniment (e.g. a salad meal or a convenience food such as pizza) in order to enhance or alter its sensory characteristics according to the consumer's preference. This subgroup of sauces is by far the biggest subgroup and includes the emulsified salad dressings (e.g. mayonnaise, salad cream, French dressing and so on), other emulsified sauces containing particulates (e.g. sauce tartare and horseradish sauce), non-emulsified sauces (e.g. tomato ketchup and brown sauce), the more exotic 'ethnic' type sauces (e.g. satay sauce) and fruit-based sauces for use with savoury products (e.g. cranberry sauce and red-currant jelly). 'Pour-over' sauces may also include the sweet (topping) and fruit-flavoured sauces used to add flavour and variety to desserts such as ice-cream, pudding and yogurt.

While sauces can be subdivided according to their culinary uses, from the point of view of shelf life consideration, the approach that subdivides them into emulsified, non-emulsified and fruit-based sauces will be more useful. Also, for the purpose of this chapter, only ready-to-use ambient-stable sauces will be considered and no reference will be made to products preserved other than by acetic acid or by acetic acid in conjunction with a mild heat treatment.

14.2.1.1 Emulsified sauces. These, as their name suggests, are a group of sauces which consist of a viscous oil-in-water emulsion, stabilised primarily by egg yolk and normally containing vinegar. The level of oil ranges from the 80% plus level found in mayonnaise (this being very close to the maximum possible level of oil for an oil-in-water emulsion, higher levels would normally result in inversion to a water-in-oil emulsion), to the 'virtually oil free' sauces (e.g. low-calorie dressings) containing only a few percent oil. Emulsified sauces, therefore, may have widely varying oil contents, with the mouthfeel and texture possibly being modified by the inclusion of various fat mimetics or substitutes. The emulsion is usually formed by high shear mixing which reduces the oil into minute droplets of a uniform size distribution of about a few microns in diameter and distributes them evenly in the water phase of the product. Stability of the emulsion is then maintained by the inclusion of emulsifiers and stabilisers, either natural or chemically derived. Thus, a mayonnaise emulsion may rely solely on the emulsifying properties of the egg, or include additional ingredients such as polysaccharide gums (e.g. guar gum, xanthan gum) which are often used in commercially available mayonnaise.

Some of the emulsified sauces have been carefully defined, although definitions may vary from authority to authority. A mayonnaise, for example, has been defined by the European Codex as containing a minimum oil content of 78.5% w/w (from all sources) , and a minimum technically pure egg yolk content of 6% (WHO/FAO, 1989). It should be mentioned that, however, at the time of writing, this standard is being considered for international rather than regional status, and as part of the consideration, the details of the standard are also under review. The Association of the Mayonnaise and Condiment Sauce Industry of the EC, however, has agreed a voluntary standard for mayonnaise which requires a minimum oil content of 70% w/w and a minimum technically pure egg yolk content of 5% w/w (CIMSCEE, 1991). 'Technically pure egg yolk' is defined as the composition of egg yolk commercially available, and is assumed to contain about 25% of egg white. The US Standards define mayonnaise with yet another set of criteria.

Other than mayonnaise, there is currently no further legal or informal agreement for emulsified sauces within Europe, since the repeal of the UK's Salad Cream Regulations. However, in the USA, a salad dressing is defined as 'an emulsified semi-solid food prepared from vegetable oils, vinegar, lemon juice and/or lime juice, egg yolk, and starchy paste'.

There are also emulsified sauces which contain added particulates. An example of these is sauce tartare, an emulsified dressing-based sauce containing particles of vegetables, usually gherkins and capers. Another sauce group which is important in the UK and Germany (but perhaps less well known in other countries) is that of the horseradish products. These again are based on salad dressing/cream, with the inclusion of grated horseradish (and perhaps turnip), giving a distinctively flavoured product for use with cooked meats and fish.

14.2.1.2 Non-emulsified sauces.   These, as their name suggests, are non-fat based sauces, and are often manufactured by a process that may include a heating stage. Of such sauces, the classic example is tomato ketchup. The European trade association has put forward proposed standards for tomato ketchup, which require a minimum tomato solids content, and limit the addition of other ingredients (CIMSCEE, 1992). Other sauces falling within this subgroup include brown sauce, various other ketchups (e.g. mushroom ketchup), and the 'ethnic' style sauces that are now coming onto the market. Like emulsified sauces, they may be smooth, or contain particulates. The range of sauces is again very wide, but the technological problems associated with shelf life are very similar, as discussed later in this chapter.

14.2.1.3 Fruit-based sauces.   These may be further subdivided into 'savoury' fruit-based sauces such as redcurrant jelly, cranberry sauce or the sweet confectionery sauces, such as flavoured topping syrups. The former group usually relies on sugar, and sometimes vinegar for preservation, having a high soluble solids content which inhibits most spoilage organisms. The process of manufacture often includes a heating stage which has a pasteurisation effect. The sweet topping syrups rely on a high soluble solids content and adequate thermal processing to inhibit microbial growth, with a low pH (e.g. due to the use of citric acid) also playing a minor part in maintaining the assigned shelf life.

14.2.2   Pickles and other related products

Pickles consist of vegetables preserved in vinegar or vinegar-based sauce, a traditional method of preservation which has been practised in many countries for centuries. Traditionally, pickling is one of the ways of ensuring that perishable fruit and vegetables would be available for periods outside their normal harvesting seasons. The major varieties consumed in the UK are pickled onions, pickled beetroot and piccalilli. The products are further divided into sweet and sour categories, with sour pickles being the predominant category. Chutneys and relishes are frequently included in this category.

The traditional pickling process involves a number of stages: the brining of vegetables for storage, brine removal prior to preservation (freshening) and the preservation in vinegar or vinegar-based sauce (the pickling proper). The vegetables are often entire but usually processed to make them suitable for protracted storage. Thanks to efforts of J.C. Dakin and others for their work carried out at the Leatherhead Food Research Association over some 30 years, virtually all aspects of traditional pickle manufacture were scrutinised with the result that many practical problems were tackled and solutions found (Kilcast, 1984).

Chutneys and relishes are similar products, relishes often having smaller pieces of vegetables than chutneys. They basically consist of vegetable and/or fruit pieces suspended in a thick vinegar-based sauce. Their process of manufacture often includes a boiling/heating stage which reduces the moisture content of the mix, softens the fruit/vegetables and pasteurises the product. Examples of these products include familiar brands such as Branston Pickle, and products such as mango chutney.

14.3 Factors affecting shelf life

Many of the products within the area of ambient-stable sauces and pickles are well established and the specific factors that affect their shelf life are well known and documented. A very useful and comprehensive review on pickles and sauces is available and has recently been up-dated (Broomfield, 1993). Nevertheless, it is useful to review some of these factors as a good understanding of how they influence product shelf life will be important to product developers who are newcomers to this field as well as those who are trying to develop modern versions of these products.

14.3.1 Raw materials

The importance of quality and consistency of the raw materials used in the maintenance of the shelf life of sauces and pickles cannot be overemphasised. From a microbiological safety point of view, pasteurised egg is a must wherever it is used. All raw materials should be handled according to Good Manufacturing Practice (Anderson and Blanchfield, 1991) and if necessary, any sensitive ingredients should be decontaminated before use. Because of the long shelf life of products in this group, the quality of the raw materials is crucial if the assigned shelf life is to be met the first time and every time. For example, even the slightest signs of

browning in the dehydrated horseradish flakes for use in various horseradish sauces could mean that the end product would not survive its stated shelf life as a result of colour deterioration.

14.3.2   Composition and formulation

This is perhaps the most important factor that influences the shelf life of ambient-stable sauces and pickles. This is because the exact composition and formulation of a product will have profound influence on possible changes that may occur during the storage of the product. These changes can be microbiological, physical, and chemical/biochemical in nature. Such changes, of course, can have safety and/or quality implications which are intimately linked to the shelf life of the product.

In the case of emulsified sauces (i.e. oil-in-water emulsions), the oil droplets are discrete and distributed throughout the continuous aqueous phase. This structure tends to preclude the spread of lipolytic spoilage organisms in the product. Furthermore, there is little indication that industrially produced oils (and fats) have a significant role to play in food-borne diseases. The oil phase can therefore be disregarded at least from a food safety point of view. For sauces (emulsified and non-emulsified) and pickles, therefore, the product safety determining factors are associated with the (continuous) aqueous phase. This aqueous phase contains the necessary ingredients that can support microbiological growth, e.g. sugars, water and certain micronutrients. However, it also contains invariably the components that either kill these organisms or inhibit their growth. Thus, the factors in the aqueous phase that determine the microbiological safety and stability of the product are:

1. Acetic acid (used as such or derived from vinegar). The level of acetic acid is the single most important factor in determining microbiological safety and quality in sauces and pickles (see section 14.4.2). Its efficacy as a preservative agent, measured by the percentage of undissociated acetic acid, is affected by the pH of the aqueous phase and its own dissociation constant. Acetic acid has the characteristic that at the pH of many sauces and pickles it is mainly in the undissociated form, thereby exerting maximum anti-microbial effect. Moreover, the fact that acetic acid has a very low oil:water partition coefficient (compared with sorbic and benzoic acid) means that to all intents and purposes, all its preservative effect is retained in the aqueous phase of an emulsified sauce (for further discussion see Chapter 6).

2. pH of the aqueous phase. Figure 14.1 gives the approximate pH growth ranges for some microorganisms important in food spoilage. As in other foods, *Clostridium botulinum* is unable to grow in a sauce or pickle with a pH value below 4.5

3. Salt and sugar content. Too high a salt content (e.g. $>3-4\%$) is unacceptable from a sensory point of view. Beyond a certain point, sugar

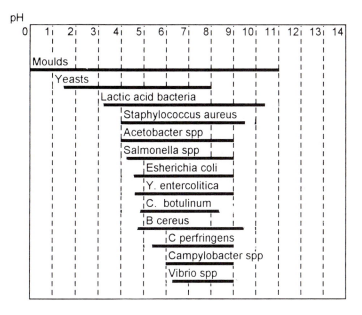

Figure 14.1 Approximate pH growth ranges for some microorganisms important in food spoilage.

and salt most certainly contribute some preservative effect (e.g. through the reduction of water activity as the total solids increase) and their contribution is indeed included in the CIMSCEE formulae (see section 14.4.2).

4. The presence of preservatives (either naturally present or added). Isothiocyanates in horseradish and the volatile 'oil of mustard' (allyl isothiocyanate) in black mustard are good examples of naturally occurring preservative agents that more or less make these materials self-preserving. An example of added (permitted) preservative is potassium sorbate (e.g. in some tomato sauce and cranberry sauce), and where they are used, acidulants such as citric acid, lactic acid and tartaric acid may also play a minor preservative role.

The synergistic effect of acetic acid, pH, salt and sugar on the microbiological safety and stability of mayonnaise and similar products has been studied and defined empirically by a mathematical model which will be discussed more fully in the next section of this chapter.

Composition and formulation are also crucial to the physical stability, and hence consumer acceptability and shelf life of emulsified as well as non-emulsified sauces. In mayonnaise and salad dressings, the egg protein plays a vital role in the stability of the oil-in-water emulsion. The transient stability of the emulsion depends on factors like the efficiency of the mechanical emulsification, the size distribution of the oil droplets, the intrinsic viscosity of the mix and so on. The long-term stability of the emulsion however depends also on the use of suitable emulsifiers and stabilisers. The egg protein remains the effective emulsifier (surfactant) and stabilisers such as guar gum and xanthan gum are commonly employed to ensure the long-term stability of the product. In some non-emulsified sauces, modified starch is often used to give a texture and to confer the long-term stability of the product. In addition to selecting the right starch (one that can withstand low pH, high shear, heat treatment and one that is less likely to retrograde and 'weep'), correct processing is important to ensure that the texture benefits of the starch are realised (Figure 14.2).

	Under-cook	Optimal cook	Over-cook
Appearance	Cloudy	Clear	Clear
Texture	Thin, starchy taste	Heavy bodied short textured	Cohesive, long textured
Stability	Poor	Good	Fair
Viscosity	Low	Good	Viscosity drop

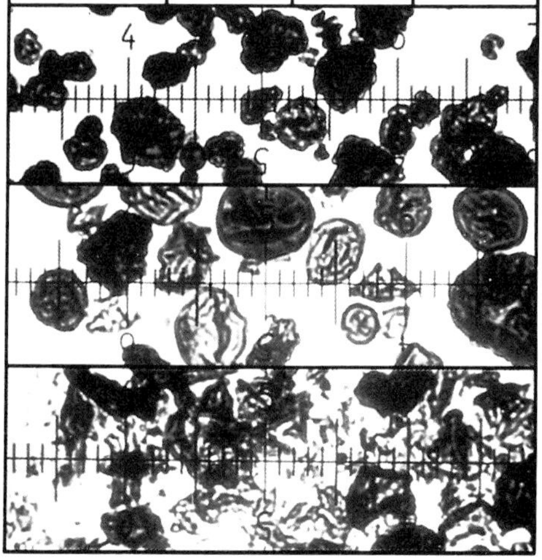

Under-cooked

Optimal

Over-cooked

Figure 14.2 Characteristics of under-cooked, optimal, and over-cooked starch slurries. (Source: Food Starch Technology. National Starch & Chemical.)

14.3.3 Availability of oxygen

For long shelf life products such as sauces and pickles, oxygen can be an important factor that affects shelf life. In emulsified sauces, the choice of vegetable oils can have a major influence on the development of oxidative rancidity. Table 14.1 lists the iodine values of some common edible vegetable oils. As can be seen from this table, the more stable oils include rapeseed oil and soya oil, which is one reason why these two oils tend to be the most used in the sauces industry. Sunflower oil has been marketed as being beneficial to health, and whilst it is not in the remit of this chapter to discuss the nutritive aspects of various oils, its use has been seen as desirable, but its greater susceptibility to rancidity development limits the shelf life of products containing it.

Vegetables and fruit used in the manufacture of sauces and pickles often contain enzymes that have not been inactivated. In the presence of oxygen, grated fresh horseradish will brown very quickly due to its polyphenols content. Fresh horseradish should be handled and processed with the minimum of delay and sulphur dioxide (as an anti-oxidant) may also be used to control browning if the shelf life of the end product is not to be reduced.

Table 14.1 Iodine values of vegetable oils – an indication of their susceptibility to oxidative rancidity

Vegetable oil	Iodine value
Rapeseed oil	97–107
Soya oil	125–136
Sunflowerseed oil	125–140
Corn (maize) oil	110–128
Olive oil	80–88

14.3.4 Processing

It is possible to produce microbiologically stable sauces and pickles based on a cold process provided certain criteria are satisfied (see section 14.4.2). Indeed for emulsified sauces, it is neither necessary nor desirable to use a hot process. In recent years, however, consumer demand for milder products has meant that a pasteurisation stage (or alternatively hot-filling not less than 80°C in some cases) is included to achieve an acceptable shelf life for many pickles and some sauces.

Pasteurisation of pickles involves the controlled and limited thermal processing of the final product within its container. Pasteurisation has three possible advantageous effects in respect of product shelf life, namely (Broomfield, 1993):

1. Thermal destruction of spoilage microorganisms, permitting a lower acetic acid content to be used.
2. Total or partial thermal inactivation of enzymes of vegetable or of microbial origin, thus preventing deteriorative changes caused by enzymes.
3. In the case where self-venting closures are used, removal of air during pasteurising and retention of headspace vacuum on cooling, thus minimising oxygen-dependent and oxidative changes (e.g. darkening and softening).

Hygienic design and practices are the cornerstones of Good Manufacturing Practice and they are fundamental to sauces and pickles manufacture as they are to other food products, irrespective of whether the sauce or pickle is pasteurised or not.

14.3.5 Packaging

The traditional packaging material used for sauces and pickles is glass which provides practically a perfect gas as well as water vapour barrier. In addition, where necessary, hot-filling is possible with glass containers, which can be a useful alternative to in-container pasteurisation. Recent developments in packaging materials, in particular plastics materials, have led to the introduction of the multilayer 'squeezable' bottles for sauces. A typical structure for this type of bottle is: inside PP/adhesive/EVOH/adhesive/outside PP, EVOH being the gas barrier layer and PP the water vapour barrier layer. While this type of container offers the consumer convenience in use, it is not commonly filled hot although it can withstand hot-filling up to 70°C. Moreover, because of its multilayer structure, barrier properties of the container depend on EVOH and PP being present throughout the container. The oxygen barrier property of EVOH is affected by the relative humidity of the environment and this has to be taken into account when designing storage trials for products packaged in this container. Finally, both the packaging supplier and the sauce manufacturer have a responsibility to ensure, particularly for any new sauce/bottle combinations, that the legislative standards in respect of food packaging migration are complied with, and in the UK, as detailed in the Plastics Materials and Articles in Contact with Food Regulations 1992.

14.3.6 Consumer use

Consumer use of multi-use products like sauces and pickles has always been an uncertain factor in respect of product shelf life. Although it is generally believed that many mayonnaises and dressings are sensitive only to typical acetic acid resistant organisms which are not widespread in the consumer's home, it is important that the possibility of spoilage during use should be considered during the development of mild formulations. Spoilage may be controlled to a certain extent by limiting the shelf life of opened product at room temperature and/or recommending refrigerated storage once the product has been opened. In fact yeast contamination has been known to cause some tomato sauce to ferment and the pack to explode; the use of precise label instructions is very important for micro-biologically vulnerable products.

14.4 Challenge testing and the use of mathematical models

14.4.1 Challenge testing

To establish the microbiological safety and stability of sauces and pickles, challenge testing may be used. Challenge testing is a technique which yields information to the manufacturer as to the microbiological status of a product during its 'normal' or expected life before consumption. To the food microbiologist it is the most direct evidence of product safety and stability (Shapton and Shapton, 1991). In practice, challenge testing com-prises the direct inoculation of a food with microorganisms. When carried out for safety purposes, the microorganisms will be pathogens which are likely to be associated with the product being tested. For the purpose of stability testing, those spoilage organisms are selected which are known to cause problems in the particular type of food under investigation. The choice of microorganisms for inoculation, their culture and method of inoculation are therefore important considerations for challenge testing. The organisms chosen also require to be 'trained' to be able to survive under adverse conditions (e.g. the presence of acetic acid, low pH, high sugar and so on). Ideally, organisms likely to be used should be cultured from within the sauce plant, however, certain indicator organisms have been identified and specified in the 'code for the production of micro-biologically safe and stable emulsified and non-emulsified sauces contain-ing acetic acid' produced by the Comité des Industries des Mayonnaises et Sauces Condimentaires de la Communauté Economique Européenne (CIMSCEE, 1991). This code states that an intrinsically stable sauce is one where acetic acid tolerant organisms will not grow. Of the organisms iden-tified, the mould *Moniliella acetoabutans* is considered the organism most resistant to acetic acid, but is easily eliminated by satisfactory hygiene and/ or pasteurisation. Contamination due to this mould within the food industry is considered rare. This organism may be a useful reference, but as it is easily eliminated, it is not usually used in challenge testing.

EE code recommends a twofold examination, covering stability. Product safety requires that pathogens cannot uce, the major hazard being due to salmonellae. However risk of possible contamination where the laboratory is υased at a factory, challenge testing is not carried out using *Salmonella* spp. but an indicator organism is used which has been shown to be killed in a similar manner to salmonellae, this being a strain of *Escherichia coli* (NCTC 5933 or VBEEs 01-03). Product stability on the other hand requires that the sauce does not support the growth of spoilage organisms. Several organisms considered to be indicators of resistance to the conditions likely to be present in sauces are (CIMSCEE, 1991):

Moulds: *Monascus ruber* (Van Tieghem), (VMEuMO 01-02) resistant to 1.8% acetic acid;
            Penicillium roqueforti (VMMoPe 16-07) resistant to 1.2% acetic acid;
            Penicillium verrucosum (VMMoPe 20-07) resistant to 1.2% acetic acid.
Yeasts: *Pichia membranaefaciens* (Hansen) (VYAPi 01-02 and 01-04) resistant to 2.5% acetic acid;
            Zygosaccharomyces bailii (VYASa 07-01 and 07-05) resistant to 3.0% acetic acid.
Lactobacilli: *Lactobacillus buchneri* (VBLLa 18-01) resistant to 2.5% to 3.0% acetic acid.

The organisms must be adapted gradually to acetic acid before use, as detailed in the code, or as described originally by Tuynenburg Muys (1971).

Challenge testing, as can be seen, is extremely time-consuming and more importantly requires laboratory skills which may not always be available. Time is a crucial factor in today's product development programmes and as an alternative approach to challenge testing, mathematical models are often used to predict microbiological safety and stability before embarking on a shelf life determination for a new or revised product.

14.4.2 Mathematical models

The CIMSCEE code outlined in section 14.4.1 also includes a model which can be used to establish safety and stability for sauces containing acetic acid derived from vinegar or directly used. This model was developed from research into the Microbiological Composition Analysis (MCA) of edible emulsions carried out by G. Tuynenburg Muys at the Unilever Research Laboratory in the Netherlands in the 1960s. The model takes into account the acetic acid content, its degree of dissociation (this being dependent on the pH of the food), the salt content, the disaccharide content and the hexose content of the sauce. The contents (percentages) of these ingredients are expressed on the weight of aqueous phase, i.e. water plus acetic acid (or vinegar) plus salt plus sugars. Because the partition coefficient for acetic acid in oil:water systems is very low, for practical purposes it is assumed that all the acetic acid will be available in the aqueous phase. This model which describes the relationship between the above-mentioned ingredients and the potential for microbiological growth has been expressed by the following formulae:

$$15.75 \ (1 - \alpha) \ (\text{total acetic acid } \%) + 3.08 \ (\text{salt } \%) +$$
$$(\text{hexose } \%) + 0.5 \ (\text{disaccharide } \%) + 40 \ (4.0 - \text{pH}) = \Sigma_s \quad (14.1)$$

For any sauce based on acetic acid, if the value of this formula (Σ_s) exceeds 63, safety from microbial pathogens is assured.

$$15.75 \ (1 - \alpha) \ (\text{total acetic acid } \%) + 3.08 \ (\text{salt } \%) +$$
$$(\text{hexose } \%) + 0.5 \ (\text{disaccharide } \%) = \Sigma \quad (14.2)$$

For any sauce based on acetic acid, if the value of this formula (Σ) exceeds 63, microbial spoilage should not occur.

$(1 - \alpha)$ is the proportion of the total acetic acid which is undissociated and is related to the pH of the sauce and the pK_a of acetic acid.

The model has certain limitations, for example, it does not take into account the effects of any other anti-microbial ingredients, such as preservatives, or any anti-microbial agents naturally present in the foods (e.g. as in horseradish and mustard). Also care must be exercised when particulates are present, as no allowance is made for slow acid equilibration in sauces such as sauce tartare. Furthermore the code does not apply to pickles or dressed salads, and on the whole it badly needs updating.

The inclusion of preservatives can improve the preservation of the sauce, thus allowing an apparently low stability value which might otherwise suggest instability when interpreted on its own. Work by Dakin (Dakin, 1968) suggests that an 800 mg/kg level of sorbic acid in a pickle or sauce has the equivalent effect of 1.0% acetic acid. Care however should be taken in the use of this finding as the partition coefficient for sorbic acid is such that the preservative will be distributed throughout a sauce which has an oil phase, and not be restricted to the aqueous phase of the sauce. This will result in a significantly reduced level of sorbic acid in the aqueous phase of an emulsion, especially in high oil systems, making the preservative action somewhat less effective than would otherwise be expected.

Another empirical model that can be used to predict the stability of unpasteurised pickles and sauces is the 'Preservation Index' put forward by Dakin (Binstead et al., 1971). This model or rule basically states that

Table 14.2 A comparison of CIMSCEE values against Preservation Index values for various sauces

Sauce	Intrinsic safety	Stability	Preservation Index
Mayonnaise	75.7	75.7	4.6
Sweet and sour	66.9	66.5	4.5
Sauce tartare	89.7	57.7	3.3
1000 Island dressing	66.7	66.7	3.7
Ranch dressing*	66.4	52.2	2.9
Hot horseradish	76.5	56.5	3.6

CIMSCEE code has the value 63 as the cut off point. Preservation Index has the value of 3.6 as the cut off value.
*Preserved with potassium sorbate.

the minimum acetic acid content necessary to achieve the satisfactory preservation of all pickles and sauces is 3.6%, calculated as a percentage of the volatile constituents of the product. Thus,

$$\text{Preservation index} = \frac{\text{Total acetic acid acidity} \times 100}{(100 - \text{total solids})} \qquad (14.3)$$

Like the CIMSCEE formulae, the Preservation Index has to be interpreted carefully since an Index lower than 3.6% does not always mean instability, as in the case of mango chutney. A comparison of the stability values of some sauces based on the CIMSCEE formulae and their corresponding values of Preservation Index is given in Table 14.2.

14.5 Shelf life evaluation

The shelf life of sauces and pickles is somewhat difficult to establish predictively, or by accelerated methods. Other than the microbiological mathematical models previously described, there is no known model that can be applied to the more modern varieties of sauces and pickles. In products such as sauces and pickles, composition and formulation play a cardinal role in determining the shelf life of the product and interactions between ingredients can prove very difficult to model. Accelerated tests, for example, may speed up some changes, but others may proceed at the same rate. Since accelerated tests are usually taken to mean storage at elevated temperatures, with or without cycling, they almost always tend to select for a different microflora which would not be representative of what may be present under ambient conditions. Other factors too will be of major relevance in sauces and pickles. Factors such as availability of oxygen, susceptibility to oxygen and to light, barrier properties of the packaging used and so on may all play a part and contribute to limit the usefulness of any predictive or accelerated methods.

Fortunately, the product group of sauces and pickles is still largely a traditional one, and consequently useful information regarding shelf life is available in the literature as well as within the manufacturing companies. Similar products are often available with which to compare for an estimation of shelf life. Such comparisons must, however, be treated with caution, as subtle changes in formulation and/or packaging format could have a major effect on the shelf life of the product.

Frequently, initial shelf life estimations may be based upon knowledge of the deterioration associated with individual ingredients. For example, in helping to decide the best oil to use in the formulation of an oil-in-water emulsion from a quality standpoint, the resistance of a vegetable oil to rancidity development can be assessed using a FIRA-Astell or Rancimat apparatus (Rossell, 1989). Similarly, the knowledge that a formulation contains materials that are prone to browning will prompt the product developer to pay particular attention to probable colour changes during shelf life determination.

Once the critical factors have been identified, storage trials will be possible with tests designed to detect the potential deteriorative changes that are likely to limit the product life. It must be said therefore, there is yet no substitute for the direct approach to shelf life determination whereby the sauce or pickle being studied is stored under defined and controlled conditions for the whole of the expected shelf life of the product in order that the correct life can be assigned.

14.5.1 Shelf life determination

The first stage in a shelf life determination must be the assessment of microbiological safety. Fortunately, past experience and historical data coupled with the use of HACCP and the CIMSCEE code have meant that microbiological safety can be quickly established for sauces and pickles. A product failing to satisfy the CIMSCEE's criteria for safety and stability for instance, will require further investigation (e.g. challenge testing), or else alternative methods of preservation (e.g. pasteurisation) may be necessary.

Once microbiological safety (and stability) has been established, storage trials can be carried out. From past experience, it can be said that most quality deteriorations tend to manifest themselves as sensory changes so that shelf life tests are usually selected to monitor them. Different conditions of storage may be used and the following are the more common conditions:

chill   0–4°C
ambient (UK)   15–25°C
                     (temperate: 25°C, 75%RH)
accelerated   30–37°C
                     (tropical: 37°C, 95%RH)

Temperature cycling (important for studying emulsion stability and/or effects of temperature abuse) may be superimposed on these conditions, depending on the purpose of the trial. Other variations in conditions may also be included such as storage in the dark or under artificial light, with or without cycling, and different packaging.

For sauces and pickles, sampling for analysis is normally carried out on a monthly basis, and where appropriate, samples stored under different conditions are compared. The following are examples of the more common tests that are carried out for shelf life determination of sauces:

- Sensory analysis: aroma, flavour, colour, texture, mouthfeel, visual appearance (signs of separation and apparent viscosity and consistency).
- Chemical analysis: pH, total volatile acidity, peroxide value and free fatty acid content of extracted oil, specific components such as the volatile and pungent isothiocyanates in horseradish.
- Instrumental analysis: viscosity measurement using a Brookfield viscometer or Boswick consistometer and colour measurement using a Minolta Chroma Meter (based on the L*a*b* colour notation system).

These tests can be used to give some indication of the rate of change, and help to locate the end-point of the shelf life. The aim of any shelf life determination is to find the level of change in respect of each critical quality attribute beyond which the product is regarded as unacceptable. Some products will start to change from day one. A horseradish product, for example, will begin to brown, and lose its pungency (or 'heat') immediately after packing. Shelf life studies must inevitably include a degree of judgement regarding the level(s) at which the deteriorative changes have become unacceptable. Such decisions are usually made jointly by the technical, sales and marketing (including the customer where appropriate) departments.

14.5.2   A worked example

An example to show the process of shelf life determination is given in this section. The product chosen is an own-label horseradish sauce product, with its compositional standards shown in Table 14.3. The initial study

Table 14.3 Composition of 'hot horseradish sauce' and CIMSCEE calculation of safety and stability values using a spreadsheet program

Ingredient	% Recipe components	% Water phase
Acetic acid 80%	2.6	3.2
Hexose	0.0	0.0
Sucrose	4.6	5.7
Salt	1.6	2.0
Water	71.4	89.0
(pH 3.5)		
Dissociation constant	0.948	
Microbiological stability	57.4	
Intrinsic safety	77.4	
Preservation index	3.6	
pH	3.5	

included an assessment of microbiological safety and stability of the concept product. As can be seen, the preservation values indicate the product is microbiologically safe, but that its microbiological stability is in doubt (Table 14.3). These results, produced using a popular spreadsheet program, prompted a challenge test on the product. It was believed that the product should be stable, as certain natural constituents in horseradish are bactericidal (i.e. the isothiocyanates). This was confirmed by the challenge testing, results of which are shown in Table 14.4. A comparison with existing products also suggested that the product would remain in an acceptable condition for at least 10 months, but after that, loss in 'heat' and browning could reach unacceptable levels. Storage trials were then carried out to confirm this. Important quality attributes were identified as colour, 'heat' intensity, flavour and viscosity. These parameters were examined over a period of time, by sensory as well as appropriate chemical analyses. Results of these tests are shown in Table 14.5. These results indicate that the product would remain acceptable for a period of about 11 months, and consequently a 10 months life was recommended, which satisfied the customer's requirements and gave a good margin of safety of about a month.

Similar methods of determination can be applied to most, if not all of the ambient-stable sauces and pickles. The value of a mathematical model (e.g. the CIMSCEE model) as a first step in the development process is that it gives the development personnel an opportunity to fine tune the formulation before going to a full shelf life determination. The model also enables decisions to be made early in the product development programme as to whether or not a pasteurisation stage is required as part of the manufacturing process.

Table 14.4 Results of the challenge testing on hot horseradish sauce

Time	Media	Control	Lactobacillus buchneri	Zygosacch-aromyces bailii 07-01	Zygosacch-aromyces bailii 07-05	Pichia membranae faciens 01-02	Pichia membranae faciens 01-04	Penicillium roqueforti	Penicillium verrucosum	Monascus ruber
24 hours	L agar	400	400	20	40	70	50	70	50	30
	L agar + 1% acetic acid	<10	<10	<10	<10	<10	<10	<10	<10	<10
8 days	L agar	200	<10	<10	<10	<10	30	20	<10	<10
	L agar + 1% acetic acid	<10	<10	<10	<10	<10	<10	<10	<10	<10
22 days	MRS	200	60	<10	<10	<10	<10	<10	<10	140
	MEA	<10	<10	<10	<10	<10	<10	<10	<10	<10
	MRS + acetic acid 1%	<10	<10	<10	<10	<10	<10	<10	<10	<10
	MEA + acetic acid 1%	<10	<10	<10	<10	<10	<10	<10	<10	<10
32 days	MRS	150	<10							
	MEA	20	<10							
	T.V.C.	400								

Table 14.5 Changes in mustard oil content (as allyl iso-thiocyanate) and assessor's perceived 'heat' of hot horseradish sauce over a 12 months' period

Product age	Mustard oil content (%)	Perceived heat*
1 month	0.81	10
2 months	0.77	9
3 months	0.74	7
4 months	0.72	7
5 months	0.74	6
6 months	0.76	6
7 months	0.74	5
8 months	0.73	4
9 months	0.73	5
10 months	0.69	4
11 months	0.69	2

*The sensory heat level is judged on a subjective 1 to 10 scale.
10 is hot, 1 lacks heat.

14.6   Current developments

14.6.1   Alternative ingredients and packaging

Within the sauces sector, over the past few years there have been major moves to development of reduced fat, and even fat-free products (the so-called 'lite' products) as well as the use of alternative packaging formats. For example, products are being developed using various fat mimetics and replacers, based upon a number of raw materials. These are claimed by the suppliers to produce an acceptable product from a sensory point of view. Often, however, the system being sold does not completely provide all the characteristics associated with vegetable oils, when used in a sauce or salad dressing. Developers are therefore working on combining several of these systems in order to evaluate any possible synergistic effects, with a view to reproducing the quality characteristics of the product with a traditional oil content. Similarly, pickles containing less acid and/or sugar, albeit pasteurised, are becoming more popular as a result of consumer demand for milder products. Gas packaging (e.g. vacuum packing) in conjunction with plastics materials (Kilcast, 1984) has also been used to package pickles (e.g. sliced beetroot) for chill distribution, giving the products a novel and 'fresher' image. These developments have major ramifications for product shelf life. Some of the systems being used have been available for many years, but their effects in a sauce or pickle system are not well documented. Others are novel in their applications, and their effects under certain conditions are not known. Combining these systems (ingredients and packaging) to effect a synergistic outcome, with a view to producing a product of the required sensory characteristics and pack appeal, may result in some beneficial effects being realised initially, which cannot be sustained during the whole of the product shelf life. Consequently the product developer will need to consider carefully all aspects of potential product deterioration, without the luxury previously afforded to him of comparing with any existing products.

Differing process requirements (e.g. as a result of using emerging process technologies) also add to the complexity in developing new products and establishing their shelf lives. Well planned and conducted shelf life determinations involving relevant and meaningful physical, chemical, microbiological and sensory analyses must be carried out over time with these new products, to unequivocally establish their safety and acceptability.

14.6.2 New techniques in shelf life determinations

Whilst at the time of writing there are few novel approaches to shelf life determination of sauces and pickles, much research has been done and is still being carried out into the extension of mathematical modelling in food products in general (e.g. the UK's MAFF Micromodel). These models may, in the future, be more widely used by the food technologist in establishing the 'safe' life of sauces and pickles. These models, coupled with other intelligent knowledge-based (computer) systems being developed (see Chapter 3) will enable product development personnel to predict shelf life early in the development programme.

14.7 Conclusion

Sauces and pickles traditionally have relied on a combination of acetic acid, salt and sugar for their preservation. In more recent times, the use of thermal processing (pasteurisation), preservatives (e.g. sorbic acid) and other functional ingredients have enabled the food technologist to vary the composition of these products resulting in less salty and less acidic products, which are increasingly being demanded by the consumer. Even more recently the introduction of fat replacement systems has additionally offered the opportunity for further new product development for sauces. For the food technologist, the determination of shelf life has moved from simple monitoring of well known deterioration processes of the basic ingredients to more complicated investigations, concentrating not only on ingredient changes due to ageing, but also on the potential for microbiological changes as well as possible physico-chemical changes under many different conditions.

Some of the challenges for the food technologist have been highlighted in this chapter, and examples of probable degradation have been given. To be successful in this product group, the product developer must know the hazards and risks associated with the materials he is using, and be alert to any possible risks associated with changes in the product matrix brought about by the use of new formulations, novel ingredients and modern packaging formats.

References

Anderson, K.J. and Blanchfield, J.R. (eds) (1991) *Food and Drink – Good Manufacturing Practice: A Guide to its Responsible Management*, 3rd edn, IFST, London.

Anon (1987) *Food Starch Technology*. National Starch & Chemical, Manchester.

Binstead, R., Devey, J.D. and Dakin, J.C. (1971) *Pickle and Sauce Making*, 3rd edn, Food Trade Press, London.

Broomfield, R. (1993) Acid, Salt and Sugar Preserves, in *Food Industries Manual*, 23rd edn (eds M.D. Ranken and R.C. Kill), Blackie Academic & Professional, Glasgow, pp. 234–87.

CFDRA (1992) *Hazard Analysis Critical Control Points (HACCP) – A Practical Guide*, Technical Manual No. 38, Campden Food & Drink Research Association.

CIMSCEE (1991) *Code for the Production of Microbiologically Safe and Stable Emulsified and Non-Emulsified Sauces containing Acetic Acid*.

CIMSCEE (1991) *Code of Practice for the Production of Mayonnaise*.

CIMSCEE (1992) *Draft Code of Practice for the Manufacture of Tomato Ketchup*.

Dakin, J.C. (1968) *The Influence of Supplementary Preservatives on the Preservative Action of Acetic Acid*, Technical Circular No 401, Leatherhead Food R.A.

Kilcast, D. (1984) Preserved for the Future. *Food*, November, 28–29, 33.

Rossell, J.B. (1989) Measurement of rancidity, in *Rancidity in Foods*, 2nd edn (eds J.C. Allen and R.J. Hamilton), Elsevier Applied Science, Essex.

Shapton, D.A. and Shapton, N.F. (eds) (1991) *Principles and Practices for the Safe Processing of Foods*, Butterworth-Heinemann, Oxford.

Tuynenburg Muys, G. (1971) Microbial Safety in Emulsions. *Process Biochemistry*, 6, 25–8.

WHO/FAO (1989) Codex Alimentarius Regional Standard for Mayonnaise.

15 Frozen foods

H. SYMONS

15.1 How many industries?

As their name implies all frozen foods depend for their stability and hence an adequate shelf life on product temperature being maintained colder than the freezing point. For most foods the freezing point is around $-2°C$ (28.4°F). This superchill temperature is totally unsatisfactory for holding any frozen products, all of which demand far colder temperatures. This has led to prefixes being used in front of the adjective 'frozen' (such as 'quick' or 'deep') to make the point that merely being hard because it is cold is an inadequate safeguard for maintaining the quality of frozen foods.

15.1.1 Speed of freezing

The term 'quick' was introduced by Clarence Birdseye, the father of the retail frozen food industry. Birdseye had at least two reasons to select the adjective 'quick'. One was to distinguish the new industry he was struggling to develop, based on superior quality presented to the retail consumer, both from the frozen meat trade (which had adopted $-10°C$ (14°F) as its storage temperature) and also from the 'sharp' frozen industry in which the product to be frozen is placed in a chamber called the 'freezer' at -7 to $-10°C$ (19.4°F to 14°F) with no effort to separate already frozen product from ambient product introduced to be frozen in the same chamber. Not only is 'sharp' freezing very slow, taking days or even weeks rather than hours, but also the product may suffer frequent large temperature fluctuations as new batches of product at ambient temperature are introduced into the chamber for freezing. Much of the frozen meat in international trade is carried today in container ships at $-18°C$ (0°F) on account of the impracticability of providing different temperatures for various parts of the cargo. Enormous quantities of fish, fruits, vegetables and shrimps are now also traded internationally and these products all demand frozen food temperatures.

Birdseye's second reason for calling the new industry 'quick frozen' was to promote his recent invention, the multi-plate froster, which freezes product in a controlled and rapid fashion. Jul (1984) relates a discussion he had, in the late 1930s, with executives in Birds Eye Division of General Foods in the USA, who had purchased Birdseye's patents, when he was able to obtain their admission that the speed of freezing was not as important to product quality as the maintenance of adequately cold temperatures ($-18°C$ ($0°F$)) or colder during distribution.

Speed of freezing plays a part in determining shelf life. The first recognition of the importance of speed in freezing was probably due to experiments by Plank *et al.* (1916) who demonstrated superior product quality when the Ottesen method of freezing (patented in 1911) was employed and the product quality compared to 'sharp' frozen material. The 'Ottesen' method relies on intimate contact with the material to be frozen – generally fish – with cold sprays of isotonic sodium chloride. The Ottesen method was abandoned either because of the difficulty of maintaining the isotonicity of the sodium chloride solution or because, when the solution was not precisely isotonic, some salt would be picked up by the product leading to early onset of rancidity.

Rather than coin the adjective 'quick' it would have been more accurate if the experimenters had stressed the need for freezing to be carried out in a controlled fashion in a device designed to freeze product, entirely separate from any storage facility. Undue emphasis on the importance of freezing speed is misleading. Speed of freezing within the range normally encountered in practice has little, if any, effect on quality. Excessive freezing speeds can ruin product. An increase in volume of around 10% is associated with freezing most foods. The build up of internal pressure during very rapid freezing (such as obtained when product is immersed in total loss refrigerants such as liquid nitrogen or carbon dioxide), shatters the already frozen, and now supercooled and therefore brittle, external layers. Providing the speed is not excessively slow, days or weeks rather than hours, most products are comparatively insensitive to the speed of freezing. Broadly speaking faster is marginally better than slower in most products. This is particularly true for fruit and vegetable products, less so for animal tissue. Most of the advantages apparent immediately post freezing in plant tissue are however lost during subsequent storage, distribution and thawing. Current practice in the industry freezes product quickly but this reflects more the need economically to process a large quantity of product in as small a factory space as practicable rather than any obeisance to the demands of product quality.

The Codex Alimentarius Code of International Practice for Processing and Handling of Quick Frozen Foods requires freezing to be carried out in equipment designed to freeze product and at a speed appropriate to the product. Thawing is not the reverse of freezing, unless microwave thawing is used. It is far slower than freezing and is generally carried out by the consumer in an uncontrolled fashion.

15.1.2   Ice cream/quick frozen foods/frozen foods

If the frozen meat trade is defined as employing $-10°C$ ($14°F$) as its characterising storage temperature two other frozen food industries can also be defined. The ice cream industry requires temperatures as cold as $-20°C$ ($-4°F$) while the 'quick/deep frozen food' industry (colloquially referred to as 'frozen foods') demands $-18°C$ ($0°F$).

A distinction between 'quick frozen' and 'frozen' retail products is preserved in several European countries. 'Surgelé' contrasts with 'Congelé' products in France; 'Tiefgefroren' contrasts with 'Gefroren' in Germany, and 'Surgelato' with 'Congelato' in Italy.

The choice of zero Fahrenheit, which translates into $-17.8°$ on the Celsius scale, for quick frozen foods does not imply any magical properties for this temperature. Clarence Birdseye was an American who thought in Fahrenheit and advocated zero to minus five as an appropriate temperature, with the minimum of fluctuations, at which to hold and distribute quick frozen foods (Birdseye and Fitzgerald, 1932). In the 1950s a massive research programme into frozen food quality was undertaken by the Western Regional Research Laboratory of USDA/ARS in Albany, California. The results of this research (Van Arsdel et al., 1969), determined the answer to the question 'what happens, in microbiological, nutritional and sensory terms to the various products being frozen by the industry at different sub-freezing temperatures?' One outcome of this research was the reaffirmation of zero (forgetting the -5 advocated by Birdseye), as the industry norm by Harold Humphrey, then the General Manager of Birdseye Division of General Foods (Olson, personal communication). The concept of Time–Temperature Tolerance (TTT) to describe frozen food stability was developed by this programme.

15.2   Stability of frozen foods

15.2.1   Microorganisms

Microbiological growth overwhelms physico-chemical changes at around $-8°C$ ($18°F$) or warmer temperatures. Michener and Elliott (in Van Arsdel et al., 1969) list the maximum recommended storage temperatures at which microbiological spoilage ceases. Most authorities put this at between $-9°C$ ($16°F$) and $-12°C$ ($10°F$). The discrepancies in the minimum temperatures found can probably be ascribed to the short length of some of the experiments. Moulds can take months rather than weeks to develop substantially. Although microbiological spoilage can be discounted at frozen food storage temperatures it must be borne in mind that the enzymes in any microorganisms present in the product will still play a part in spoilage. Hence the point that a product produced under hygienic conditions or heat processed (blanched or cooked) will enjoy a longer shelf life than its unhygienic or raw counterpart. Many common pathogens (notably salmonellae, vegetative cells of *Clostridium perfringens* and *E. coli*) decline in numbers by several logs during prolonged cold storage but this must never be regarded as a substitute for good hygiene in processing.

15.2.2 Ice mobility

Ice, an inevitable concomitant of attaining temperatures as cold as −18°C in food systems, is restless, always responding to any vapour pressure differential created by any thermal gradient, which is the reason for demanding reasonably constant temperatures during distribution of frozen foods. Fluctuations in product temperature of 2–3°C, as are likely to be found in bulk cold stores maintaining −18°C (0°F) or colder, are unlikely to cause perceptible damage even over long periods. On the other hand frequent fluctuations in temperature, particularly large fluctuations at 'warm' temperatures (i.e. close to or in the zone of maximum crystal formation – between −1°C (30°F) and −5°C (23°F)), which can be experienced in retail display cabinets and during the 'carry home' period, cause ice crystals to ripen or grow, coalesce and move to the product surface or, if space allows, onto the inside of the packaging material. This leads ultimately to a freeze-dried product if the packaging is permeable to moisture allowing the sublimed or evaporated water vapour to escape. The loss of moisture results in toughening of animal tissue and greater exposure to any oxygen present.

Oxygen is the bugbear of almost all frozen foods, leading to oxidative rancidity if any unsaturated lipids are present, loss of colour and development of off-flavours. Moisture loss by sublimation from the surface of products leads to 'freezer burn', an unsightly, white colour which can be mistaken for mould but which is resolved on rehydration during cooking unless it is severe. A whitish surface appearance, sought after in some markets, can also be induced, in products such as poultry, by very rapid surface freezing (by liquid nitrogen or carbon dioxide), which produces very small crystals leading to scattering of incident light.

15.2.3 Physico-chemical reactions

The most important quality changes during frozen storage which determine shelf life encompass colour loss and colour change in vegetables. In green vegetables this is due to hydrolysis of chlorophyll to pheophytin, giving a dull khaki colour. Examples of the principal reactions occurring during storage are flavour loss, followed by the development of off-flavours; vitamin loss; retrogradation of starch; protein denaturation; hydrolytic (in milk) and oxidative rancidity; drip formation in animal tissues; crystallisation of sucrose (on the surface this gives rise to spectacular volcanic excrescences of sucrose hydrate, the formation of which proceeds fastest at $-23°C$ ($-10°F$)) and crystallisation of lactose (in ice cream this causes a grainy texture). Good accounts of these changes in the various product categories can be found in Jul (1984), Van Arsdel *et al.* (1969), and Mallet (1992).

Nucleation, crystal ripening, changes on thawing and associated quality defects peculiar to frozen products (Fennema, 1991; Bald, 1991; Jul, 1984; Van Arsdel *et al.*, 1969; Reid, in Mallet, 1992) are all important considerations in assessing shelf life and can affect formulation considerations in selecting ingredients and processes which minimise these induced changes.

15.2.4 Time–temperature tolerance (TTT)

The time–temperature tolerance concept, developed as a result of the massive programme of research into frozen food stability at Albany, postulated that quality loss in frozen foods is proportional to the reciprocal of the storage temperature. This programme was concerned with evaluating the quality stability of frozen products then being marketed in the US and paid relatively little attention to the suitability of different vegetable varieties for freezing, growing conditions, processing or packaging but concentrated on evaluating product stability taking for granted the current industry practices.

A survey of frozen food quality conducted in 1983/4 (Earl *et al.*, 1985) found frozen products in the distribution system as old as 840 days! Arrhenius plots on the assumption that quality loss is a zero order reaction fitted the data best. The reaction order of quality loss can in fact lie between zero and two but the data fitted best to zero order kinetics.

15.2.5 Product quality, processing and packaging (PPP) factors

Jul (1984) drew attention to the very profound effects that the level of intrinsic product quality (freshness, suitability of variety for freezing and so on), the processing (whether blanched or cooked, whole, sliced or comminuted, addition of antioxidants, etc.) and the packaging (presence of glaze, breading, batter or gravy, oxygen and moisture permeability of primary packaging, how close fitting to the contours of the product, whether evacuated or gas-flushed) all exert on the final product quality. These can overwhelm TTT considerations in determining shelf life. Figure 15.1 illustrates the values for shelf life at different temperatures for various frozen products, including the effects of different packaging on bacon.

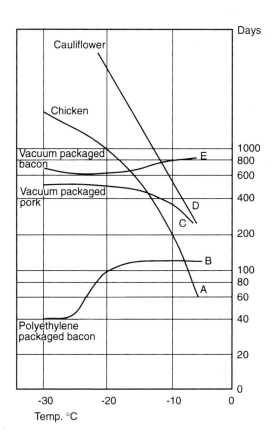

Figure 15.1 Estimate shapes of shelf life curves for various frozen foods. (Source: M. Jul, 1984. In: Thermal processing and quality of food, Zeuthen *et al.* (eds), 1984.)

15.2.6 Glassy state

The classic TTT concept, which has long served the frozen food industry well, especially after taking account of the modifications proposed by consideration of the PPP factors, has recently been refined by the recognition of the importance of the glassy state in frozen foods (Reid, in Mallett (1992) and Blond and Colas, in Bald (1991)). As an increasing proportion of water is converted to ice with decreasing temperature the remaining solutes become progressively more concentrated and exceedingly viscous until, in a maximally freeze-concentrated solution, the glass transition temperature $(T_{g'})$ peculiar to the food is reached. At this temperature, the material between the ice crystals becomes a glass: an amorphous meta-stable solid, but retaining the disordered structure of a liquid, with a high viscosity ($> 10^{13}$ Pa s). This change from a visco-elastic liquid (rubber) to a glass is accompanied by a dramatic decrease in mobility. All reactions slowed down as a consequence and hence quality loss greatly retarded, almost to the point of being suspended over the few years of interest to frozen foods. The $T_{g'}$ of ice cream varies between –23° to –43°C depending on formulation (Goff et al., 1993).

Moisture content has little influence on the $T_{g'}$; the presence of solutes of low molecular weight (such as sugars) lowers the $T_{g'}$; however substances of high molecular weight (such as starches) exert little effect. This has the consequence that increasing maturity in many vegetables (maturity being commonly associated with a decrease in sugars and an increase in starch) will result in raising the $T_{g'}$ as also will increasing blanching time in products such as French fries in which the cut surfaces allow the leaching of sugars. Reid (in Mallet, 1992) further suggests that, at frozen food temperatures warmer than the $T_{g'}$, the rate of quality loss may be dependent on the difference between the storage temperature and $T_{g'}$ rather than with the reciprocal of the storage temperature. Developing knowledge of the glass transition temperatures of materials commonly frozen and the factors which alter these temperatures will enable bio-technologists to manipulate plant genomes to achieve a warmer $T_{g'}$ and product developers to formulate products and adjust processes to give as warm a $T_{g'}$ as feasible. It is clearly advantageous to plan storage temperatures to take account of the $T_{g'}$ of the stored products, remembering that it is a waste of energy and money to store at temperatures colder than the $T_{g'}$ while, in the case of long-term bulk storage, the quality/cost equation is likely to favour attaining temperatures close to the $T_{g'}$.

15.2.7   Know your product

A prerequisite in planning any shelf life determination of a frozen product is to select the most thermo-labile important quality attribute, whether this be flavour loss, colour change, toughening, development of rancidity and so on. If experience is lacking in the likely stabilities of the various quality attributes help can be sought in the literature. A list of anticipated shelf lives for a number of products commonly frozen can be found in the literature, notably in Table 15.1 of practical storage life (PSL) taken from the International Institute of Refrigeration (IIF) (1986) where expected PSLs are tabulated for three temperatures, –12°C (10°F), –18°C (0°F) and –24°C (–12°F). The shelf lives given for –24°C (–12°F) are conservative, none more than 24 months because of a lack of published data since few investigators are concerned with longer storage periods for food products. Guadagni (in Van Arsdel, 1969) found no measurable changes over five years at –29°C (–20°F) in most frozen fruits. Jul (1984) quoting Bengtsson et al. (1972) makes the same point. Many meat products probably have a

Table 15.1 Practical storage life (months) at several storage temperatures

Product	−12°C (10°F)	−18°C (0°F)	−24°C (−12°F)
Fruits			
Raspberries/strawberries (raw)	5	24	>24
Raspberries/strawberries in sugar	3	24	>24
Peaches, apricots, cherries (raw)	4	18	>24
Peaches. apricots, cherries in sugar	3	18	>24
Fruit juice concentrate	–	24	>24
Vegetables			
Asparagus (with green spears)	3	12	>24
Beans, green	4	15	>24
Beans, lima	–	18	>24
Broccoli	–	15	24
Brussels sprouts	6	15	>24
Carrots	10	18	>24
Cauliflower	4	12	24
Corn-on-the-cob	–	12	18
Cut corn	4	15	>24
Mushrooms (cultivated)	2	8	>24
Peas, green	6	24	>24
Peppers, red and green	–	6	12
Potatoes, French fried	9	24	>24
Spinach (chopped)	4	18	>24
Onions	–	10	15
Leeks (blanched)	–	18	–
Meats and poultry			
Beef carcass (unpackaged)[a]	8	15	24
Beef steaks/cuts	8	18	24
Ground beef	6	10	15
Veal carcass (unpackaged)[a]	6	12	15
Veal steaks/cuts	6	12	15
Lamb carcass, grass fed (unpackaged)[a]	18	24	>24
Lamb steaks	12	18	24
Pork carcass (unpackaged)[a]	6	10	15
Pork steaks/cuts	6	10	15
Sliced bacon (vacuum packed)	12	12	12
Chicken, whole	9	18	>24
Chicken, parts/cuts	9	18	>24
Turkey, whole	8	15	>24
Ducks, geese, whole	6	12	18
Liver	4	12	18
Seafood			
Fatty fish, glazed	3	5	>9
Lean fish[b]	4	9	>12
Lobster, crab, shrimps in shell (cooked)	4	5	>12
Clams and oysters	4	6	>9
Shrimps (cooked/peeled)	2	5	>9

Table 15.1 *Continued*

Product	−12°C (10°F)	−18°C (0°F)	−24°C (−12°F)
Eggs			
Whole egg magma	–	12	>24
Milk and milk products			
Butter, lactic, unsalted pH 4.7	15	18	20
Butter, lactic, salted pH 4.7	8	12	14
Butter, sweet cream, unsalted pH 6.6	–	>24	>24
Butter, sweet cream, salted (2%) pH 6.6	20	>24	>24
Cream	–	12	15
Ice cream	1	6	24
Bakery and confectionery products			
Cakes (cheese, sponge, chocolate, fruit, etc.)	–	15	24
Breads	–	3	–
Raw dough	–	12	18

[a]Carcass may be wrapped in stockinette.
[b]The PSL for single fillets of lean fish would be 6, 9 and 12 months at −18°C (0°F), −24°C (−12°F) and −30°C (22°F) respectively.

Source: IIR (1986)

shelf life of over 2 years if **PPP** factors are well managed and the product held at frozen food temperatures. Winger (1984) found no loss in eating quality of grass fed lamb, hygienically processed and well packaged, after two years at –10°C (14°F). Anecdotal evidence tells us that the flesh of mammoths, after several thousand years in the permafrost in Siberia, was still recognisable and edible if not actually delicious! Help in determining what is the most thermo-labile attribute in a new product may be obtained by a judicious assessment of similar competitors' products. If date marking is practised it is a simple matter to search out both 'old' and recent production and assess the changes found. In the absence of date marking, production codes can often be broken since these are seldom cryptic.

Once the decision has been made as to which quality attributes are critical, a taste panel needs to be assembled and trained, selecting those who show reasonable sensitivity to the particular attribute and who can demonstrate consistent scores.

15.2.8 Objective tests

Objective tests are available for a number of quality attributes of frozen foods. These seldom faithfully reflect consumer preferences and are little used in day-to-day industry testing in the course of shelf life predictions or quality assurance. If a nutritional claim is made, then of course how that nutrient withstands prolonged cold storage and simulated thermal abuse is important. The loss of vitamin C and the ratio of chlorophyll to pheophytin in green vegetables can be a measure of thermal abuse (Olson and Dietrich in Van Arsdel *et al.*, 1969) as can the decrease in optical density of a muscle homogenate in cod (Love, 1962), the development of thiobarbituric acid (TBA) or peroxide value in products containing unsaturated lipids (Dalhoff and Jul, 1965), the development of cold store flavour in fish (McGill *et al.*, 1974) and a host of other indicators in various products. These objective tests may be useful to determine alongside sensory changes and may also be necessary in any claim or litigation alleging unsatisfactory product handling or failure to meet a quality specification by a third party. They have seldom, however, been found to reflect accurately, and with sufficient sensitivity, consumer preferences. In general they only confirm what is already abundantly apparent from taste panel assessments.

15.2.9 Accelerated testing

Seldom can the luxury be permitted of long-term assessment of product quality over the months or years of anticipated shelf life at frozen food temperatures. Some form of accelerated testing is necessary which is likely to result in sacrificing a degree of accuracy in the results obtained. This presupposes that all frozen products lose quality, at warmer temperatures than colder, i.e. possess a positive $Q_{10}(q_{10})$. ($Q_{10}(q_{10})$ is the ratio of quality loss at two temperatures in the range of frozen food temperatures, that are 10° apart: 10°C for Q_{10} and 10°F for q_{10}.) Not all frozen products exhibit a positive $Q_{10}(q_{10})$. Neutral stability, or a $Q_{10}(q_{10})$ of 1, is found in a few products, such as salami, which may be a component in a frozen product. The quality of this cured, fermented and dried product is temperature independent and it enjoys an equally long shelf life at frozen food temperatures as at chill or ambient. A negative Q_{10} is rare and was first described by Boegh-Sorensen (1972) who found reverse stability in frozen vacuum-packaged cured sliced pork products. Shelf life was almost independent of storage temperatures between −6 to −23°C (21 to −9°F) while one product, smoked streaky bacon, exhibited a longer shelf life at the warmest temperature. Lindeloev (1978) showed that at a storage temperature as cold as 25°C (−13°F) the shelf life of bacon is shorter than at −5°C (23°F). This is an example of the effect of concentration of catalysts of oxidative rancidity (sodium chloride, nitrate and nitrite) by the subtraction of ice from the solution overwhelming the effect of temperature reduction. Christensen and Jensen (in Zeuthen *et al.*, 1984) did not find reverse stability in cured fish.

Accelerated testing can usefully be carried out by holding control product at −40°C (−40°F) and exposing test samples to three or four different storage temperatures between −30°C (−22°F) and −10°C (14°F). For many products the reference samples may be held at −30°C (−22°F) since little change occurs in most products at colder temperatures.

15.2.10   Just noticeable difference

The goal of shelf life determination is to estimate the length of time during which the product under test will still be appreciated by the ultimate consumer as being of the level of quality expected for the product, that is to say for how long it will maintain 'practical storage life' (PSL). Loss of quality in frozen foods is a gradual process, the changes being slow or very slow, cumulative and irreversible. PSL is a highly subjective concept and difficult to measure by taste panel procedures. In the rarefied atmosphere of a taste panel, as opposed to a meal situation, the trained assessors are likely to discriminate between nuances of quality unlikely to be appreciated by the consumer. A way out of this difficulty is to measure the time to 'just noticeable difference' (JND) or 'high quality life' (HQL) by a trained taste panel and then multiply this by an arbitrary figure, generally between 2 and 5, to arrive at PSL. In products peculiarly sensitive to colour loss (peaches, cauliflower, red pigmented fish) PSL may be close to JND.

JND is conveniently defined as the moment during storage at the expected temperatures of the cold chain at which a proportion (generally 70%) of the trained assessors can correctly distinguish the product under test from the control (held at −30°C (−22°F) or −40°C) using a triangular or duo–trio test. It can be argued that the proportion of assessors able to discriminate successfully should be much lower, say 25%, on the basis that a small proportion of consumers is likely to be highly discriminatory concerning the particular quality attribute deemed to be critical. Anyone with experience of taste panels knows how very sensitive individuals can be to particular sensory attributes and sometimes surprisingly insensitive to others.

Dalhoff and Jul (1965) preferred a sensory scoring system (−5 equals dislike extremely, 0 neither like nor dislike, +5 like extremely) to determining JND by triangular or duo–trio testing. A decrease of 1 point on the scale would equate to JND. An advantage of this procedure is that fewer replicates are required than the four replicates for each time/temperature stipulated by Guadagni (in Van Arsdel et al., 1969). An objection is that the preference scoring system is likely to be population specific. For instance quality expectations for fish flavour would be very different between a Danish population (who expect their fish to be alive when purchased) and an English population accustomed to fish held in ice for several days. The English taste panel would probably score the Danish fish as lacking in fish flavour whereas the Danes would score the English fish as partly rotten at best!

15.2.11 $Q_{10}(q_{10})$

Most frozen products enjoy shelf life measured in many months or even years. During product development answers as to the likely shelf life of a new or modified product are required in weeks or a few months to be of any use. Hence there is the need for accelerated shelf life determinations. Accelerated shelf life tests aim to establish the *rate* of quality loss with temperature change and hence to enable PSL at conventional distribution temperatures to be assessed far more rapidly than the long-term tests at the anticipated storage temperature. This rate can be expressed as the ratio of the shelf lives found at two different temperatures, generally 10°C (Q_{10}) or 10°F (q_{10}) apart. For instance, Guadagni (in Van Arsdel *et al.*, 1969) found stabilities of strawberries, assessing both colour and flavour, held at three different temperatures, −18°C (0°F), −12°C (10°F) and −7°C (20°F) to be 360, 60 and 10 days respectively. The q_{10} is therefore 360/60 or 6 and 60/10 or 6 again for the respective 10°F differences measured. Not all rate determinations work out as neatly as strawberries and it is probably futile to try to fit quality loss determinations to a particular mathematical formula. Foods are complicated biological systems and do not lend themselves to convenient mathematical expressions which can be applied to a wide variety of products.

15.3 Product characteristics

15.3.1 Fruits and vegetables

Most fruits freeze well; that is to say the thawed product is barely distinguishable from the raw fruit before freezing. Although strawberries do not fall into this category, losing texture during freezing and thawing, the early days of the frozen food industry saw strawberries dominating the market for frozen fruit. The fruit was mixed with sugar in wooden barrels placed in a frozen food warehouse and rolled periodically to mix the fruit and sugar. The frozen product was used in preserves and ice creams. Heat inactivation of the enzymes that cause rapid discoloration by enzymic browning leads to a cooked flavour which is unacceptable and the addition of syrups with ascorbic acid as an antioxidant is used instead. q_{10}s for frozen fruit, measured on flavour and colour, have been found to range from 2.2 for blueberries to 6.0 for strawberries in dry sugar (Guadagni in Van Arsdel *et al.*, 1969).

Frozen vegetables have enjoyed enormous success in many different parts of the world. Since many vegetables do not can well, the introduction of frozen vegetables has meant populations living in high latitudes can enjoy summer vegetables all year round instead of having to rely largely on root crops in the winter. Properly blanched vegetables have a long shelf life at frozen food temperatures enabling them to be exported all over the world to remedy crop shortfalls and to span the seasons. During storage chlorophyll is converted to pheophytin, with loss of green colour and introduction of a khaki hue, and this can be used as an objective test for quality loss in green vegetables. Vitamin C can also be used as an objective indicator of quality loss. The most sensitive quality attribute is a diminution of flavour accompanied by a loss of colour.

15.3.2 Seafood

Microbiological spoilage is the principal cause of quality loss in seafood at temperatures above chill; around 0°C (32°F) enzymic breakdown of protein becomes the principal cause of quality loss; below –8°C (18°F) microbiological spoilage ceases and protein denaturation coupled with oxidative rancidity in fatty species become the chief factors affecting quality.

Figure 15.2 illustrates the stabilities at various temperatures of several species of commonly consumed finfish. Lane (1984) pointed out that sensory characteristics of frozen fish change in intensity during storage rather than in character. The development of rancid flavours and progressive toughening accompanied by the development of cold store flavour are the principal sensory changes. In the case of young fish (e.g. codling) the initial stages of cold store damage may give rise to an increase in acceptability scores. The 'firming' of the soft texture characteristic of young fish by the early onset of protein denaturation is preferred by most taste panellists (Kelly, 1969). Assessing codling in storage trials may therefore result in an initial rise in preference for texture before the expected decline sets in. Flavour is probably more critical than texture (Connell and Howgate, 1971) since this tends to be lost before protein denaturation is appreciable. Formaldehyde is formed during cold storage by enzymic decomposition of trimethylamine oxide (TMAO). Formaldehyde content is a good objective criterion of time/temperature exposure in frozen gadoid species (Boeri et al., 1993). This formaldehyde reacts with proteins, thereby decreasing their solubility in salt and buffer solutions (Rehbein, 1971). Quality loss during cold storage of fish is characterised by increasing loss of water-holding capacity, decrease in protein extractability and a slight loss in ATPase activity (Reid et al., 1985). Much colder temperatures than –18°C (0°F) are useful for bulk storage of seafood. In Japan the retention of a pristine white colour in surimi

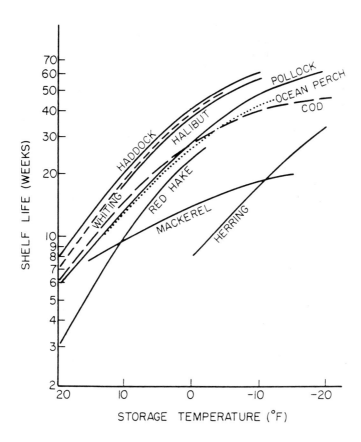

Figure 15.2 Average shelf life values for selected finfish based on literature reported values. (Source: IIR, Proceedings of 'storage lives of chilled and frozen fish and fish products', 1985.)

demands storage temperatures as cold as −60°C (−6°F). Magnussen (1992) reviews the use of such temperatures on mackerel and salmon. Steynor (1992) describes a 2000 tonnes chamber holding −60°C (−6°F) in South Africa.

Of all seafood species, squid (*Loligo duvaucelli*) probably is most sensitive to lack of product freshness leading to reduced stability in subsequent storage. Squids held for two days in ice lose flavour and the cold storage life is dramatically shortened (Jose Joseph *et al.*, 1985).

15.3.3 Meat

Meat, whether it be lamb, venison, beef or poultry all freeze well. Consumer preference is for chilled meat. Some 80% of the chilled beef purchased at supermarkets in the USA is subsequently frozen by the

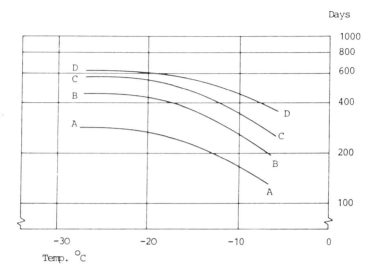

Figure 15.3 Examples of the influence of PPP factors on shelf lives of frozen foods. A. Pig meat with high iodine number in fat; B. Pig meat with low iodine number in fat; C. Same meat as B, but cooked; D. Same as C, but vacuum packaged. (Source: M. Jul, 1984. In: Thermal processing and quality of foods, Zeuthen *et al.* (eds), 1984.)

housewife at home. This reaction against purchasing frozen beef probably reflects a desire on the part of the purchaser to assess quality (ratio of bone to muscle, degree of marbling, presence of excess fat and so on) rather than any prejudice against the frozen beef processor. Stability of frozen meats can be affected by the diet of the animal. Pigs reflect in their depot fat the degree of unsaturation of the fat component of their diet. Figure 15.3 gives examples of the influence of the degree of unsaturated fat on shelf life of pig meat. Grass fed frozen lamb is recognised as having a greater stability in the frozen state than its grain fed counterpart. Rapidly chilled muscles become tough on freezing and thawing, a phenomenon known as 'cold shortening', which scarcely affects poultry. This applies with especial severity to small animals such as lamb, as the sheer bulk of the beef carcass precludes all but superficial muscles from chilling with sufficient rapidity to undergo 'cold shortening'. Electrical stimulation post-slaughter can reduce the time the carcass needs to spend above 10°C (50°F) to avoid 'cold shortening'. Eating quality of electrically stimulated grass fed lamb, processed to strict hygiene standards and wrapped in plastics, is essentially unchanged for at least two years storage at 10°C (14°F) (Winger, 1984). In ground beefburgers the critical quality attribute may be a lack of balance in the spices present. Pepper flavour persists well in cold store whereas other spices diminish in intensity. A high pepper note may indicate this lack of balance long before rancidity sets in. The lack of clear and unambiguous data on the shelf lives of meats, which is ascribed to differing definitions of the end of storage life, is clearly seen in a review by Evans and James (1993).

15.3.4 Bakery products

If seafood loses quality within days of capture bakery products lose freshness within a few hours of being removed from the oven. Freezing is an obvious method to preserve 'fresh from the oven' characteristics were it not for the need to traverse the chill temperature zone twice, on freezing and again when thawing. Quality loss, through starch retrogradation, occurs most rapidly at chill temperatures in baked goods. Slow freezing is to be avoided in order to reduce the time spent at chill temperatures. Despite this constraint a well formulated, frozen, stored and refreshened bakery product (regardless of the time spent in frozen storage) has sensory properties comparable with the same (unfrozen) product less than one day after baking (Stauffer, 1992). Amylase is a useful antidote to bread staling. Moisture migration during frozen storage is the principal cause of staling in general. With careful formulation, strict regard for the first 'P' coupled with modifying production and handling techniques, the second 'P', can guard against these defects. Cooling before freezing is important for stability: a hot bakery product placed in a blast freezer will result in an ice rind formed just below the crust surface, which will become detached on slicing. Some bakery products, notably croissants, are difficult to formulate to enable them to be frozen without becoming leathery and losing their fresh aroma. The open interior of the product mitigates against rapid freezing.

Yeast cells do not withstand freezing well. Yeast raised products have some of the lowest stabilities of any frozen foods. This can be partially compensated for by increasing the amount of yeast used in the formulation; new and improved yeast strains exhibit a better survival rate in freezing.

15.3.5 Prepared products

Complex multi-component products not only bring all the problems of the stability characteristics of each component but a few extra, such as aroma migration between the components and the likelihood of spaces being present in the package, leading to easy access for oxygen. If fluctuating temperatures are encountered moisture migration from a high water activity component to a low one may result in grave quality defects. A common complaint concerning frozen multi-component prepared foods is a lack of, or 'sameness', of flavour. This is probably due to the beginning of aroma migration between the components, the more highly flavoured component transmitting flavour to the bland ones so that a depressing

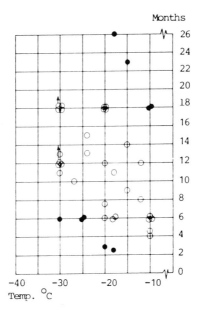

Figure 15.4 Shelf life data for ready-to-eat meat dishes as reported by various authors, as collected by Spiess, and quoted by Jul (1984). (Source: M. Jul, 1984. In: Thermal processing and quality of foods, Zeuthen *et al.* (eds), 1984.)

uniformity in flavour results. 'Sameness' of flavour should be noted as possibly the first perceptible difference in many products. Otherwise the rule of assessing stability of multi-component products is to identify the most thermo-labile component and its most sensitive quality attribute and concentrate on assessing this as an indicator of JND. Figure 15.4 illustrates the enormous degree of variability reported by various authors in the shelf life of ready-to-eat frozen meat dishes.

15.4 The cold chain

The final decision as to the likely shelf life of a given frozen product must take account of the fact that the product is not going to be stored at a steady temperature of –18°C (0°F) from the end of freezing until thawing for consumption or during end cooking. A typical frozen product will spend part of its shelf life in a bulk cold store, a refrigerated vehicle or container, a distribution store, a retail display cabinet or institutional frozen food storage cabinet, a period out of refrigeration during the journey from the retail outlet to home and time in a home freezer or star-marked frozen food storage compartment, before being consumed in the

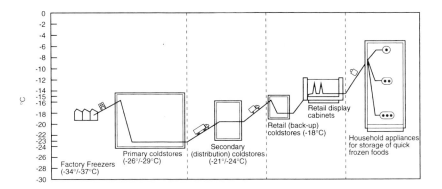

Figure 15.5 Temperature profile of the cold chain. (Source: Sanderson-Walker, 1984. In: Thermal processing and quality of foods, Zeuthen *et al.* (eds), 1984.)

frozen state, thawed or end cooked. Figure 15.5 illustrates the various components of a typical cold chain in Europe where 'star marked' frozen food storage compartments are common in household refrigerators.

An essential part of any shelf life determination in markets where 'star marked' frozen food storage compartments are in use is to assess the shelf life at the relevant temperatures for '1-Star', −6°C (21°F) and '2-Star', −12°C (10°F).

15.4.1 Temperature monitoring

There is a plethora of indicating and recording devices to enable product temperatures to be monitored throughout distribution; from simple indicating thermometers to computerised recorders which can be buried in loads where they record temperature every 15 minutes, the complete record being read out on a computer within a minute or so at the end of the journey or period in storage. Refrigerated vehicles can be fitted with transmitters which enable the dispatcher to call up the vehicle at any time and discover its location and load temperature without any need for intervention by the driver.

15.4.2 Time–temperature indicators

The literature is replete with over five hundred patents for freeze–thaw indicators and temperature limit indicators as well as time–temperature integrators. Few have been brought to market and none has achieved an enduring success. Some are unwieldy or expensive; the best are inexpensive, costing a few pennies each, but, despite numerous trials in products as diverse as cut flowers, vaccines, ice cream, frozen military rations or frozen sous vide products, no sustained successful use has yet been announced. Trials seem always to be abandoned even if the device itself performs its task adequately.

More attention is being paid to frozen food temperatures in Europe in the wake of the EC Directive that mandates specific temperatures for various commodities throughout the cold chain. The need for this law was long disputed on the grounds that such temperatures have little, if anything, to do with health, are only concerned with quality and that temperature at any particular moment is an imperfect indicator even of quality.

15.4.3   Control of time in storage

Frozen foods, well formulated, correctly processed and adequately packaged have a very long cold storage life at sufficiently cold temperatures but nothing is for ever. Some system of control is required over the time spent in the various segments of the cold chain. This calls for control over pallets, control over the cases of product and, finally, over the individual packages.

Control over pallets is generally achieved by the computerised recording system of the producer in concert with the bulk storage facility. Control over cases is achieved in Europe by printing the mandatory open shelf life date which is demanded on individual packets on the outer case in standard format. In the USA no such assistance is provided to the supermarket store clerk who may have to choose between two identical cases to be placed in the display cabinet. Production codes in cryptic form do not help much. In countries where open shelf life dating is mandated, such as in the EC, a minimum durability, 'best before' or final consumption date is printed on the consumer package together with the relevant 'star marking' storage instructions. In the USA some producers give a shelf life date on individual packets but, over the years, there seems to have been little consumer reaction. Labuza (1982) gives the rationale for open shelf life dating on consumer packets as an aid to engendering consumer confidence and supplying the consumer with useful information. In the absence of a temperature history this information can be misleading. Opponents to mandatory open shelf life dating on consumer packets allege that this will give undue prominence to time to the detriment of maintaining adequate temperatures which is immeasurably more important to frozen food quality. Also when more than one date is on display very few, if any, prospective customers will select the earlier date; most will ignore the date while a few will 'rummage' for the latest date, upsetting the 'FIFO' (first in, first out) principle of stock rotation. Placing a date on the consumer package also gives the erroneous impression that frozen food quality expires suddenly whereas it is more likely to decline very slowly over long periods if held at the required temperature.

References

Bald, W.B. (1991) *Food Freezing Today and Tomorrow*, Springer-Verlag, London.

Bengtsson, N., Liljemark, A., Olsson, P. and Nilsson, B. (1972) An attempt to systemize time–temperature tolerance (T-TT) data as a basis for the development of time–temperature indicators. *Bull. Int. Inst. Refrig.* (Annexe 1972-2) 303–11.

Birdseye, C. and Fitzgerald, G.A. (1932) *Ind. Eng. Chem.*, **24**, 676.

Boegh-Sorensen, L. (1968) *Keeping Times for Frozen Pork Cold Cuts*, Danish Meat Products Laboratory, Copenhagen.

Boeri, R.I., Alamandos, M.E., Ciarlo, A.S., and Gianni, D.H. (1993) Formaldehyde instead of dimethylamine as a measure of total formaldehyde formed in frozen Argentine hake (*Merluccius hubbsi*). *Int. J. Food Sci. Tech.*, **28**, 289–92.

Codex (1982) *International Code of Practice for Processing and Handling of Quick Frozen Foods*, Codex Alimentarius, FAO, Rome.

Connell, J.J. and Howgate, P. (1971) Consumer evaluation of fresh and frozen fish, in *Fish Inspection and Quality* (ed. R. Kreuzer), Fishing News (Books), Surrey, pp. 155–9.

Dalhoff, E. and Jul, M. (1965) Factors affecting the keeping quality of frozen foods, in *Progress in Refrigeration Science and Technology*, vol. 1, Pergamon Press, New York, pp. 57–66.

Earl, W.H., Allen, D.H. and Kindleysides, L. (1985) Simulation modelling of frozen food distribution: retail operations and their effect on quality, in *Refrigeration Science and Technology. Storage Lives of Chilled and Frozen Fish Products*, Proceedings of Meetings of Commissions C2 and D3 of IIR. International Institute of Refrigeration, Paris.

Evans, J. and James, S. (1993) Freezing and meat quality, in *Food Technology International Europe*, Sterling, London.

Fennema, O. (1991) *Instability of Nonequilibrium States of Water in Frozen Foods*, 8th World Congress of Food Science and Technology, Toronto.

Goff, H.D., Caldwell, K.B. and Stanley, D.W. (1993) Influence of polysaccharides on the glass transition in frozen sucrose solutions and ice cream. *J. Dairy Sci.*, **76**(5), 1268–77.

Jose Joseph, P.A., Perigreen, P.A. and Nair, M.R. (1985) Effect of raw material quality on the shelf-life of frozen squid (*Loligo duvaucelli*) mantles, in *Refrigeration Science and Technology. Storage Lives of Chilled and Frozen Fish Products*, Proceedings of meetings of Commission C2 and D3 of IIR, October 1985, International Institute of Refrigeration, Paris.

Jul, Mogens (1984) *The Quality of Frozen Foods*, Academic Press, London.

Kelly, T.R. (1969) Quality in frozen cod and limiting factors on its shelf life. *J. Food Technol.*, **4**, 95–103.

IIR (1986) *Recommendations for the Processing and Handling of Frozen Foods*, International Institute of Refrigeration, Paris.

Labuza, T.P. (1982) *Shelf Life Dating of Foods*, Food and Nutrition Press.

Lane, J.P. (1984) Time–Temperature Tolerance of frozen seafoods. 1. Review of some recent literature on the storage life of frozen fishery products. *Food Technol.*, **18**, 1100–6.

Lindeloev, F. (1978) Freezer storage of salted products. Laboratoriet fur Levnedsmiddel-industri, Danmarks Tekniske Hojskole, Copenhagen.

Love, R.M. (1962) Protein denaturation in frozen food. VI. Cold-storage studies on cod using the cell fragility method. *J. Sci. Food Agric.*, **13**, 269–78.

Mallett, C. (1992) *Frozen Food Technology*, Blackie Academic & Professional, Glasgow.

McGill, A.S., Hardy, R. and Burt, J.R. (1974) Hept-cis-4-enal and its contribution to off-flavour in cold stored cod. *J. Sci. Food Agric.*, **25**, 1477–89.

Magnussen, O.M. (1992) 'Superfreezing' low temperature technology. *Scan. Ref.*, **21**(4), 34–41.

Plank, R., Ehrenbaum, E. and Reuter, K. (1916) *Die Konservierung von Fischen durch das Gefrierberfahrn (Fish Freezing)*, Zentral-Einkaufsgesellschaft, Berlin.

Reid, D.S., Doong, N.F., Foin, A. and Snider, M. (1985) Studies on the frozen storage of fish, in *Refrigeration Science and Technology. Storage Lives of Chilled and Frozen Fish Products*, Proceedings of meeting of Commissions C2 and D3 of IIR, October 1985, International Institute of Refrigeration, Paris.

Rehbein, H. (1971) Does Formaldehyde form cross-links between myofibrillar proteins during frozen storage of fish muscle? In *Fish Inspection and Quality* (ed. R. Kreuzer), Fishing News, Surrey.

Stauffer, C.E. (1992) Frozen bakery products, in *Frozen Food Technology* (ed. C. Mallett), Blackie Academic & Professional, Glasgow.

Steynor, P. (1992) Cold storage reaches lowest temperature. *S. Afr. Refrig. Air Cond., ZA*, Vol. B., (5), 20–22.

Van Arsdel, W.B., Copley, M.J. and Olson, R.L. (1969) *Quality and Stability in Frozen Foods*, Wiley Inter-Science, New York.

Winger, R.J. and Pope, C.G. (1982) The Effect of Processing Variables on the Storage Stability of Frozen Lamb. *Bull. Int. Inst. Refrig.*, **4**(6), 335–9.

Winger, R.J. (1984) Storage life and eating quality of NZ frozen lamb: A compendium of impressive longevity in *Thermal Processing and Quality of Foods* (eds P. Zeuthen, J.C. Cheftel, C. Eriksson, M. Jul, H. Leniger, P. Linko, G. Varela and G. Vos), Elsevier Applied Science, London.

Zeuthen, P., Cheftel, J.C., Eriksson, C., Jul, M., Leniger, H. and Linko, P. (eds) (1984) *Thermal Processing and Quality of Foods*, Elsevier Applied Science, London.

Index